This is the first book to cover not only the economics of the fine arts and performing arts in the United States, but also public policy toward the arts at federal, state, and local levels. The book will interest academic readers seeking a core text on the economics of the arts and arts management or a supplementary text on the sociology of the arts, as well as general readers seeking a systematic analysis of the arts in the United States. Theoretical concepts are developed from scratch so that readers with no background in economics can follow the argument.

The authors look at the arts' historical growth and then examine consumption and production of the live performing arts and the fine arts, the functioning of arts markets, the financial problems of performing arts companies and museums, and the key role of public policy. A final chapter speculates about the future of art and culture in the United States.

THE ECONOMICS OF ART AND CULTURE

The economics of art and culture
AN AMERICAN PERSPECTIVE

JAMES HEILBRUN
Fordham University

CHARLES M. GRAY
University of Saint Thomas

CAMBRIDGE
UNIVERSITY PRESS

Published by the Press Syndicate of the University of Cambridge
The Pitt Building, Trumpington Street, Cambridge CB2 1RP
40 West 20th Street, New York, NY 10011–4211, USA
10 Stamford Road, Oakleigh, Melbourne 3166, Australia

First published 1993

Printed in the United States of America

Library of Congress Cataloging-in-Publication Data
Heilbrun, James.
The economics of art and culture: an American perspective / James
Heilbrun, Charles M. Gray
p. cm.
Includes index.
ISBN 0-521-41991-3 – ISBN 0-521-42212-4 (pbk.)
1. Arts – Economic aspects – United States.   2. United States –
cultural policy.   I. Gray, Charles M.   II. Title.
NX705.5.U6H45   1993
338.4′77′00973 – dc20   92–41895
                                                                              CIP

A catalog record for this book is available from the British Library.

ISBN 0-521-41991-3 hardback
ISBN 0-521-42212-4 paperback

For Carol and Virginia,
and Emily, Margaret, Robert,
and Brian

CONTENTS

FIGURES AND TABLES

Figures

PREFACE

Although U.S. economists have been writing about the economics of art and culture since the mid-1960s, this is the first work to cover not only key segments of the fine arts and the performing arts, but also public policy toward the arts at the federal, state, and local levels. It is thus the first attempt at a comprehensive survey of the subject.

The authors have planned the level and scope of the book to meet the requirements of two groups of readers: first, an academic audience for whom the book can serve as the principal text in a course on the economics of the arts or on arts management, or as a supplementary text in a course dealing with the sociology or politics of the arts; second, those general readers who are ready for a systematic analysis of the economics and the political economy of the arts in the United States.

The book is divided into five parts. Part I, consisting of Chapters 1, 2, and 3, serves as a general introduction, suitable for both the academic and the general reader. Chapter 1 defines the area we propose to study, explains the logic of our definition, and ends with an estimate of the economic size of the arts sector, as so defined, in the United States. Chapter 2 provides an important historical dimension. It describes the growth of the arts in the United States since the 1920s, assesses the claim that we had an "arts boom" in the 1970s and 1980s, and examines the subsequent slowdown in the growth of arts activity. Chapter 3 looks at the size and character of audiences for the arts in the United States, discusses the socioeconomic factors affecting attendance, and compares arts participation rates in the United States with those in other industrialized nations.

Chapters 4 through 8 make up Part II, which deals with the microeconomics of demand and supply and their interaction in markets, and applies those analytic tools to the performing arts industry. In this part all theoretical concepts are developed from scratch, so that students or other readers without previous training in economics will have little difficulty gaining an elementary knowledge of them. However, the general reader who does not want to grapple with the technical apparatus of economic theory can skip Chapters 4 through 7 and pick up the argument of the book at Chapter 8, which looks at the financial problems of firms in the performing arts sector.

Chapters 9 and 10, which analyze the market for paintings and other works of art, and the economics of art museums, make up Part III. Chapter 9 does return to microeconomic analysis to explain how the art market operates and how painters and sculptors earn their living by producing works for the market. The general reader may wish to omit those passages, but will certainly want to read the last section of the chapter, which treats the question of art as an investment.

Public policy toward the arts is taken up in Chapters 11 through 13, which constitute Part IV. Chapter 11 systematically examines a subject that has troubled many observers, namely, the economic justifications of public subsidy for the arts. While the argument favoring subsidy rests on several propositions from microeconomic theory, the bulk of the chapter deals not with the theory but with the question of whether the arts have the characteristics that the theory tells us are necessary to justify public support. The chapter as a whole will therefore be easily intelligible to the general reader.

In Chapters 12 and 13 we put economic theory aside and deal with the political economy of the arts. Chapter 12 introduces the theme of private donational support for the arts, examines the advantages and disadvantages of private versus public support, and compares the level of aid given in the United States and in other industrialized nations when both private and public support are taken into account. The chapter closes with a review of the controversy between Congress and the National Endowment for the Arts over support given for works of art alleged to have been blasphemous or pornographic. Chapter 13 focuses on the history, scale, and mode of public subsidies to the arts in the United States. The chapter analyzes state and local support as well as federal support through the NEA and other agencies, and discusses political as well as economic considerations.

Chapters 14 through 16, covering a miscellany of topics, constitute Part V. Chapter 14 looks at the arts as a profession, invoking microeconomic analysis to explain how the earnings of artists (as workers) are determined in the marketplace. The roles of education, training, and labor unions in the performing arts are examined, and data are presented on artists' incomes by level of education and gender, in order to assess the truth or otherwise of the "starving artist" hypothesis.

The last three chapters of the book will pose no problem for the general reader. Chapter 15 examines the geographic distribution of arts activity, explains why it is highly concentrated in large cities, and analyzes the role of the arts in an urban economy. The substantial economic importance of the arts industry in the New York metropolitan area is compared with its much weaker impact in six typical medium-size metropolitan areas.

In Chapter 16 we analyze the relationship between the mass media, popular culture, and the forms of so-called high art that are the subject matter of this book. The hypothesis is advanced that the mass media have biased public taste away from the high arts, and that public broadcasting is justified as one way of countering the bias. The chapter closes with a discussion of alternative proposals for financing public broadcasting.

Chapter 17 concludes the book with some speculations about the future of art and culture in the United States. We discuss the possible role of an expanded program of arts education in cultivating the taste for high art, thus helping to ensure future growth in the rate at which Americans participate in the arts, but acknowledge that given current attitudes toward public spending, it is unlikely that the necessary funds will be made available.

This book was conceived during a coffee shop conversation at the Third International Conference on Cultural Economics, held in Akron, Ohio, in 1984. Since that date both authors have successfully taught courses on the economics of the arts to undergraduates in their respective liberal arts colleges, using the materials in this book as the principal text. The completed book, we are certain, covers more than enough topics for a one-semester course, although individual instructors may want to supplement it with other readings at selected points.

Both of our courses have been taught within economics departments, but were specifically open to students who were not economics majors and had taken no previous economics courses. Based on that experience, we are confident that the book can also be used as a text for an economics course in arts management programs at the master's level, where students in all likelihood will have no preparation in economics, or for supplementary reading in courses in the sociology or politics of the arts. Finally, we are confident, as well, that the book will be intelligible to the ordinary general reader, just as our courses were to ordinary noneconomists among undergraduates.

Throughout the book we have provided what we hope are ample citations to sources we have found useful. These indicate our intellectual debts to others who have worked on the economics, politics, or sociology of the arts. We hope they will also be helpful to casual readers, students, and scholars who want to pursue at greater length topics we can only touch briefly in a general survey.

In writing this book we have received indispensable help from academic colleagues, artists, arts consultants, and arts administrators in both the private and public spheres. They gave their time and attention generously in providing us with data, information, insights, expertise, and critical commentary. The list is a long one.

We extend our profound thanks to: Diane Aldis, The Breck School; Linda Andrews and Christine Maginnis, Zenon Dance Company; Judy Balfe, City University of New York; Dianne Brace, Dance/USA; Tom Bradshaw and Margaret Jane Wyszomirski, National Endowment for the Arts; Jim Capo, Everett Parker, and Jim Kurtz, Fordham University; Randy Cohen, National Assembly of Local Arts Agencies; Sarah Foote Cohen and Doug Rose, American Council for the Arts; Robert Conrad, Station WCLV; Rebecca Danvers, Institute of Museum Services; Barbara Davis, Arts Resources and Counseling; Paul DiMaggio, Princeton University; Heather Dinwiddie and Mary Brooks, American Symphony Orchestra League; Bill Hendon, *Journal of Cultural Economics* and Association for Cultural Economics; Barbara Janowitz and John Federico, Theatre Communications Group; Ralph Jennings, Station WFUV; David Kamminga and Marcia Peck, Minnesota Orchestra; Young Lee, Corporation for Public Broadcasting; Jeff Love, National Association of State Arts Agencies; Michael Miner, formerly of Actors Theater of St. Paul; Sally Montgomery, Mount Holyoke College; Karen Nelson; Dick Netzer, New York University; Richard J. Orend, arts consultant; Guy Pace, Actors' Equity Association; David Pankratz, arts consultant; Monnie Peters, arts consultant; Pete Peterson, Vanderbilt University; Nancy Roberts, Opera America; Kevin Sauter, University of Saint Thomas; Mark Schuster, Massachusetts Institute of Technology; Charles Shapiro, Austrian Roth Partners; Linda Shapiro, New Dance Ensemble; Cynthia Starkweather-Nelson, artist; Dean Stein, Chamber Music America; Leila Sussmann, Tufts University; Sandra Taylor, artist; George Wachtel, League of American Theaters and Producers; and Joyce Yamamoto, artist. We also thank our students, who read sequential manuscript permutations from the earliest stages and served as proofreaders and commentators extraordinaire.

Many of the illustrations were drawn by Phil Swanson and Barbara Birr.

Both authors are grateful for generous research assistance: Gray's work was supported in part by grants from the Faculty Development Program of the University of Saint Thomas, the Minnesota Private College Research Foundation, and the Blandin Foundation; Heilbrun's by two one-year Faculty Fellowships at Fordham University.

We wish to thank Scott Parris, our editor at Cambridge University Press, for his wise counsel, help, and enthusiasm on behalf of this book. We are grateful as well to Sophia Prybylski, who supervised the book's production, and to Robert Racine for a most attentive job of copyediting.

And finally, the book is dedicated to our wives and children, who provided indispensable encouragement and support while patiently enduring our absorption in a most demanding project.

PART I

The arts sector in the United States: size, growth, and audiences

1

An overview of the arts sector

In the modern era, the making of art has occupied a special position among human activities. Some might rank it as the highest of all callings; many probably think of it as above "mere commerce"; a few might wish that economists would keep their dirty hands off it.

Yet no matter how highly we may value them, art and culture are produced by individuals and institutions working within the general economy, and therefore cannot escape the constraints of that material world. When the Guthrie Theater in Minneapolis hires actors or electricians, it competes in well-defined labor markets and has to pay what the market, or the unions, require. When it sets ticket prices it has to recognize that its sales will be constrained by competition from other forms of recreation and by the tastes and incomes of its potential audience. When federal or state governments, through their arts agencies, make grants to the Guthrie, those agencies have received their funds through a budgetary process in competition with other government programs, and the government itself raises money by making claims on taxpayers that compete with their desire to spend income in the satisfaction of private wants.

In keeping with its title – *The Economics of Art and Culture* – this book will explain how art and culture function within the general economy. In many respects the individuals and firms that consume or produce art behave like consumers and producers of other goods and services; in some significant ways, however, they behave differently. We hope to show that in both cases the insights afforded by traditional economic analysis are interesting and useful.

We will investigate the art and culture industry in much the same way that economists might analyze the steel, food, or health-care industries: we will look first at the historical growth of the industry, then examine

3

consumption, production, the functioning of arts markets, the financial problems of the industry, and the important role of public policy. Individual chapters will also deal with the arts as a profession, the role of the arts in a local economy, and the relation of the mass media to art and culture.

Coverage of this book

First, however, we must explain what part of art and culture we propose to deal with. For the purposes of this book, art and culture comprise the live performing arts of theater, opera, symphony concerts, and dance, plus the fine arts of painting and sculpture and the associated institutions of art museums, galleries, and dealers. It is important to note at the outset that we are here *not* defining art and culture as terms of aesthetic or social scientific discourse, but simply explaining how much of their domain we have chosen to cover in a single volume.

Obviously, the above definition leaves out some important cultural activities. Among the performing arts, we exclude motion pictures (which are *not* live), and rock, pop, and jazz concerts (even though they *are* live). We also exclude writing, publishing, and commercial (but not public) broadcasting.

These exclusions, however, are not arbitrary. First of all, the two included groups are internally coherent. The performing arts categories are all live and share a common production technique: a performance is put on in a venue to which the audience must come; the performance can be repeated in exactly the same way as often as might be desirable to satisfy a larger audience. Thus, if you understand, for example, the economics of theatrical production, you also understand, in principle if not in detail, the economics of opera, ballet, or symphony production. The fine arts category is coherent in a different sense: the subgroups are jointly involved in making, buying and selling, and displaying art objects.

Second, three of the excluded categories – motion pictures, broadcasting, and writing and publishing – are complex industries unto themselves and very unlike the included ones. It would be difficult to generalize about the economics of such unlike activities and impractical to attempt to cover that much diversity in a single volume. Motion picture production and broadcasting do share many traits that would facilitate treating them jointly, but that would require another study.

Third, the included categories – except the Broadway theater, painters and sculptors, and art dealers and galleries – are organized on a not-for-profit basis, while the excluded categories are largely made up of commercial, profit-seeking firms or individuals. The distinction is significant not only because we would expect economic decisions to be made differently in the two sectors, but also because government subsidies are largely confined to the not-for-profit group, and only firms in that sector are eligible to receive tax-deductible private charitable donations. Those forms of support make up an important part of nonprofit sector budgets, again lending coherence to the group and its problems.

Finally, the included categories are old, traditional forms that are sometimes referred to as "high" art, while those that are excluded (except writing and publishing) are new forms that are also called "popular" or "mass" culture.[1] We do not mean to imply that this distinction reflects our own value judgments, but it *is* well established in the literature.

To be sure, there are ambiguities aplenty in this delineation of the field. Writing is a traditional high art but is excluded nonetheless. Motion pictures are potentially a high art, though a new rather than a traditional form. Many movies have a more serious artistic purpose than some Broadway musicals, though the latter are included here while movies are not.

Art and culture as a subject of economic inquiry

With all its defects, our definition does correspond to the one adopted by most economists who have worked in this field. The field itself is relatively new, almost nothing having been written about it before the mid-1960s.[2] Its origin can be dated from 1966, the year in which William J. Baumol and William G. Bowen published *Performing Arts: The Economic Dilemma*.[3] This path-breaking study, which long remained the definitive work in the field, attracted wide notice and quickly drew the attention of economists to an important new concern: the financial condition of the arts in the United States. (The specific questions raised by Baumol and Bowen are dealt with in detail in Chapter 8 of this volume.)

Baumol and Bowen's study was the culmination of a decade of growing interest in the condition of art and culture in the United

---

[1] The notion of high culture as distinguished from what came to be called low or popular culture emerged in the United States in the second half of the nineteenth century. See Lawrence W. Levine, *Highbrow/Lowbrow* (Cambridge, Mass.: Harvard University Press, 1988), esp. chaps. 2 and 3. Levine also argues that we have recently begun to move away from such rigid distinctions (p. 255).

[2] For a detailed account of research activity from 1961 through 1978, see William S. Hendon, *Analyzing an Art Museum* (New York: Praeger, 1979), pp. 4–8.

[3] William J. Baumol and William G. Bowen, *Performing Arts: The Economic Dilemma* (New York: Twentieth Century Fund, 1966).

States. That interest was reflected in the public sector by the establishment of the New York State Council on the Arts in 1961 and the National Endowment for the Arts, at the federal level, in 1965. Evidence of a new awareness appeared even earlier in the private sector. The Ford Foundation initiated a program in the arts in 1957 and by 1965 was offering very substantial support to symphony orchestras and to ballet and opera companies.[4] In the mid-1960s, the Rockefeller Brothers Fund and the Twentieth Century Fund undertook complementary studies of the situation of the performing arts. Baumol and Bowen's massive volume emerged as the contribution of the latter.[5] Since then, interest in the economic problems of the arts has grown steadily. In the 1970s, William S. Hendon and others established the Association for Cultural Economics and began publishing the *Journal of Cultural Economics.*[6] The Twentieth Century Fund returned to the subject when it sponsored Dick Netzer's *The Subsidized Muse,* an important study of the role of government subsidies in support of the arts, published in 1978.[7]

Scholars from many countries have been active in this new field. In England, Mark Blaug and Alan Peacock published numerous papers on the economics of the arts, beginning in the late 1960s.[8] In 1979 the Australian economists C. David Throsby and Glenn A. Withers produced an influential study entitled *The Economics of the Performing Arts.*[9] The Swiss and German economists Bruno S. Frey and Werner W. Pommerehne have written *Muses and Markets: Explorations in the Economics of the Arts,* published in 1989.[10] By now there is a considerable body of useful research not only on the economics but also on

[4] *Sharps and Flats: A Report on Ford Foundation Assistance to American Music,* Ford Foundation, July 1980.

[5] The Rockefeller Panel Report, intended to attract public attention to a wide range of arts policy issues, was entitled *The Performing Arts: Problems and Prospects* (New York: McGraw-Hill, 1965).

[6] The association has also sponsored seven international conferences on cultural economics since 1979 and has published conference proceedings. See notices in the *Journal of Cultural Economics.*

[7] Dick Netzer, *The Subsidized Muse,* a Twentieth Century Fund study (Cambridge University Press, 1978).

[8] See, in part, the papers collected in Mark Blaug, ed., *The Economics of the Arts* (London: Martin Robertson, 1976).

[9] C. D. Throsby and G. A. Withers, *The Economics of the Performing Arts* (New York: St. Martin's, 1979).

[10] Bruno S. Frey and Werner W. Pommerehne, *Muses and Markets: Explorations in the Economics of the Arts* (Oxford: Basil Blackwell, 1989).

the politics and sociology of the arts.[11] (A more detailed account of the origins of public interest in the condition of the arts in the United States is offered at the beginning of Chapter 12.)

Estimating the size of the arts sector

How important is the arts sector in the U.S. economy? Although lack of data is a frequent lament of those studying the economics of the arts, we do have enough information to piece together a rough estimate of the size of the arts industry as it has been defined here. Because there are inconsistencies among the available bits of data, the piecing-together process may seem a little tedious. It is useful to work through its complexities, however, because in doing so we shall also be filling in essential details about the arts institutions that make up the subject matter of this book.

Components of the estimate are shown in Table 1.1. (The table attempts to measure the arts sector as of 1990, but the reader is urged to see the caveats concerning dating set forth in the table note.) Line A shows that in 1990 consumers spent $4.964 billion on admissions to the live performing arts, including both the commercial and the nonprofit theater, as well as nonprofit opera, dance, and symphony concerts. It is for the reader to judge whether that is a large figure or a small one: in the same year consumers spent $3.665 billion on radio and television repairs, $10.257 billion on flowers, seeds, and potted plants, and $10.098 billion on cleaning, storage, and repair of clothing and shoes. Books and maps attracted $17.577 billion of spending.[12]

Since Broadway and road company box office receipts are available separately, we can subtract them from the consumer spending total to obtain an estimate of $4.314 billion for admissions to the *nonprofit* live performing arts. (See the fourth line of Table 1.1.) Gross box office receipts are an excellent measure of the size of commercial theater activity, since the commercial theater has little other income. Consumer expenditure on admissions, however, does not fully measure activity in the nonprofit sector, since nonprofit institutions are legally eligible to

---

[11] Annual conferences on Social Theory, Politics, and the Arts have been held each year since 1974. Selected proceedings have been published in some years. See, e.g., Judith H. Balfe and Margaret Jane Wyszomirski, eds., *Art, Ideology, and Politics* (New York: Praeger, 1985); and David B. Pankratz and Valerie B. Morris, eds., *The Future of the Arts: Public Policy and Arts Research* (New York: Praeger, 1990).

[12] See source cited for consumer spending in Table 1.1.

Table 1.1. *Estimated size of the arts sector, 1990 (millions of dollars)*

A.	Consumer spending on admissions to live performing arts	4,964
	Less Broadway	−283
	Less road companies	−367
	Equals nonprofit sector	4,314
B.	Art museum operating income	1,184
	Less income from government sources	−212
	Less income from private donors	−227
	Plus value of in-kind services	+48
	Equals calculated operating income	793
C.	Direct governmental assistance	904
	Federal	286
	State[a]	278
	Local (estimated)	340
D.	Charitable contributions to the arts	1,469
	Less public broadcasting	−821
	Equals calculated arts contributions	649
Grand total		7,310

Note: Lines A and D refer to calendar year 1990; line B pertains to fiscal year 1988 and line C to fiscal year 1990. Broadway and road company data are for 1989–90 season.
[a]The 50 states plus District of Columbia.
Sources: Line A – Consumer spending: National Income and Product Accounts of the U.S., table 2.4, as revised November 1991; Broadway and road company receipts: League of American Theatres and Producers; Line B – American Association of Museums, *Data Report of the 1989 National Museum Survey*, Table F:73–C for the year 1988. Line C – Federal: See components and sources cited in Table 13.1; state: National Assembly of State Arts Agencies; local: estimated by the authors. Line D – All data are from *Giving USA*, 1991 edition (New York: American Association of Fund-Raising Counsel, 1991), table 28.

receive charitable donations from individuals, corporations, and foundations and may also obtain subsidies from federal, state, and local governments. In the typical case, earned income from admissions and performance fees accounts for only half to two-thirds the total income of a nonprofit performing arts institution. In Table 1.1, governmental assistance and charitable contributions are tabulated separately on Lines C and D. Both categories of contributed income, as it is called, underwrite the expansion of the not-for-profit, live performing arts and of museums, beyond the scope they could achieve if dependent solely on earned income to finance their activities.

Data on aggregate operating income provide a reasonable measure of the economic size of the art museum segment of the arts industry. Line B of Table 1.1 shows that it amounted to $1.184 billion in 1988 (the only recent year for which data are available). Since $212 million of museum income consisted of governmental aid and $227 million came from private contributions, we subtract those amounts from Line B to avoid double counting with Lines C and D. On the other hand, art museums in 1988 received $48 million worth of in-kind services, and that amount must be added to Line B to reach the total of museum operating income, apart from contributions.

"Production" in the fine arts is carried out by painters and sculptors, and distribution of the product is handled by dealers and galleries. Unfortunately, we lack data on the value of these goods and services and so must omit it from Table 1.1.

The value of direct governmental assistance to the arts is estimated to have totalled $904 million in 1990. Since these funds paid for activity over and above the levels reported in Lines A and B, it must be added in separately. The federal and state amounts are firm numbers, but the aid attributed to local governments is necessarily an estimate, since no accurate count is available. (See Chapter 13 for further detail.)

Finally, Line D presents an estimate of the value of private charitable contributions to the arts. When donations to public broadcasting are subtracted, the remaining total is $649 million. Like governmental assistance, this pays for arts activity over and above the amounts shown in Lines A and B.

The grand total of lines A, B, C, and D is $7.310 billion. To put that figure in perspective, consider the fact that in 1990 the gross domestic product (GDP) of the United States – a measure of the value of the output of all goods and services – stood at $5,513.8 billion. The arts sector as measured here amounts to only a little more than one-thousandth of that sum or, to be more precise, .133 percent.[13]

Our estimate may well err on the low side. The performing arts industry includes a lot of very small institutions, and it seems likely that

[13] Given the rapid growth of the arts sector in the 1970s and 1980s, this result appears to be consistent with Netzer's estimate that, in 1975, arts expenditures amounted to .095 percent of GNP. See "How Big is the Arts Industry?" *New York Affairs*, 4, no. 4 (1978): pp. 4–6, cited at table 2. However, using a different methodology, Netzer estimated the income of the *nonprofit* art and culture subsector at $4.71 billion in 1985. Although his 1985 study excludes such commercial activities as the Broadway theater, it includes a wider range of nonprofit activities than we do. Even allowing for expansion between 1985 and 1990, Netzer's 1985 results imply an arts sector *smaller* in dollar magnitude than ours. See Dick Netzer, "Arts and Culture," in Charles Clotfelter, ed., *Who Benefits from the Nonprofit Sector?* (Chicago: University of Chicago Press, 1992), pp. 174–206.

many of the smaller ones are not captured in any statistical net. General museums, history museums, and historical societies often have important collections of art but are not counted here. Art museum income is given for 1988 and would have grown moderately by 1990. The manufacture of classical music recordings and art reproductions is not included. Public broadcasting activity is omitted, although a fraction of it deals with art and culture as defined here. The output of painters and sculptors and the economic contribution of art dealers and galleries are omitted entirely. The value of volunteer labor is not counted except for art museums. The figure for charitable contributions is derived from surveys that do not purport to be a full count. On the other hand, the amounts shown for state and federal support include some to activities such as zoos, botanical gardens, and historic sites that fall outside the boundaries of the arts as defined in this book. (We have tried to avoid that in the estimate of local support, where it is potentially a much greater problem.)

On balance, we believe our total is probably an underestimate. But even a substantial increase in the total would not change the basic message: the art industry is very small in relation to the U.S. economy. Why, then, do we study it? Obviously, we do so not because it is important to the economy but because it is vital to our culture, and therefore to our self-image.

2

Growth of the arts sector

Because the arts industry is crucial to our self-image, we are naturally curious not only about its size, but also about its rate of growth. If it is growing rapidly, we are likely to think better of the state of our society than if it is growing slowly or not at all. In this chapter we trace the growth of the live performing arts in the United States since 1929. For reasons that will become apparent, the principal forms of the live performing arts – theater, symphony, opera, and dance – can readily be analyzed in common. Growth of activity in the fine arts and the growth of art museums will be taken up separately in Chapters 9 and 10.

Although we may all agree that the arts are more than "mere entertainment," they are a form of entertainment, nevertheless, and must compete with its other forms in the budgets of interested consumers. The historical perspective adopted in this chapter allows us not only to measure the arts' long-run growth, but also to see how they have fared in competition with other kinds of recreation, and especially with other forms of spectator entertainment. In addition, it will show us how well the live arts have stood up against the endless flow of technological innovations, from talking pictures through television to the compact disc and the videocassette recorder, that have transformed the *non*live entertainment industry over the same span of years.

Measuring growth

Beginning in the early 1960s, observers of culture in the United States began to speak of a "cultural boom" that had started at the end of World War II.[1] The considerable attention given to the alleged boom

---

[1] See discussion of the "literature of the 'boom' " in William J. Baumol and William G. Bowen, *Performing Arts: The Economic Dilemma* (New York: Twentieth Century Fund, 1966), pp. 36–39.

11

by the media in the 1960s probably indicated that Americans were increasingly self-conscious about the nation's cultural standing and now wanted to be taken seriously as contributors to, or at least appreciators of, high art and culture.

How can we measure the growth rate of the arts or decide when or whether the arts have enjoyed a boom? In economics (and on Wall Street) it is conventional to judge the growth rates of industries by comparing them with the growth rate of the economy as a whole. Such a comparison will be useful in evaluating the position of the arts in U.S. society. If the arts sector is growing faster than the economy, that would be a sign that the arts are becoming more important to the American people as time passes. In that case, we could probably all agree that culture is, indeed, booming in the United States. On the other hand, if the arts sector is growing in an absolute sense, but not as fast as the economy as a whole, we would have to conclude that there is no boom: the American people are not becoming measurably more devoted to the arts with the passage of time. (This approach was first employed by Baumol and Bowen in 1966.)[2]

The U.S. National Income and Product Accounts provide a statistical series for every year since 1929 that is uniquely suitable for making the necessary comparison. These are the accounts in which the Commerce Department calculates the size of the gross domestic product (GDP), a measure of the aggregate value of all final goods and services produced by the United States economy during a single year. GDP is the sum of personal consumption expenditures, gross private domestic investment, net exports, and government purchases of goods and services.[3] The tables on personal consumption expenditure include a total for admissions to "legitimate theaters, opera, and entertainments of nonprofit institutions (except athletics)" that corresponds very closely to the category of the performing arts as defined in this book. A yearly comparison of dollars spent on such admissions with consumers' disposable personal income will show how the movement in arts spending compares with the time trend of aggregate economic activity. (Disposable personal income is consumers' income after deduction of federal, state, and local income taxes and certain other personal payments. It is the income available to consumers for spending or saving.)

It must be borne in mind that consumer spending on the performing arts is not a comprehensive measure of arts activity, which also includes

---

[2] Ibid., pp. 42–50.
[3] For a fuller description of GDP and its components, see any elementary textbook on macroeconomics.

consumer spending on the fine arts and on museums, as well as arts activity paid for by government subsidies, by private contributions, and by the income from arts institutions' endowment funds. These sectors have been omitted in studying growth, because data on their size do not go back as far as the consumer spending figures do and, even now, are not in all cases regularly available. The estimate in the previous chapter (Table 1.1) suggests that in 1990 performing arts admissions accounted for about 68 percent of the more comprehensive total. It seems to be a reasonable proxy for "citizen interest in the arts." Since it is available for every year since 1929 and is consistent through time, it is certainly the best single measure we have with which to investigate the notion of a cultural boom.

Competition among forms of recreation

Attendance at arts performances competes for the consumer's time and money with other recreational activities. The terms of the competition are periodically revolutionized by technological innovations – for example, the invention of the phonograph and motion pictures in the late nineteenth century, the introduction of the motion picture sound track in 1927, the commercial development of television immediately after World War II and then of long-playing records, audio tape systems, home videocassette recorders, compact disc recordings and, most recently, the videodisc. By comparing the trend of consumers' spending on the performing arts with the trend in outlays for other spectator activities and recreation as a whole, we gain insights into both the competitive position of the performing arts and the impact on that position of some of the major technological innovations.

The upper panel of Table 2.1 shows consumer spending on the performing arts and related categories of recreational activity as a percentage of disposable personal income (DPI) from 1929 to 1990. Trends over time for the spectator categories are highlighted in Figure 2.1, in which the percentages of DPI spent on admissions to the performing arts, motion pictures, and spectator sports are plotted in the form of index numbers, with the base year 1929 = 100. For any given year, the index number is calculated as 100 times the ratio of the percentage of DPI spent on admissions in that year to the percentage for the year 1929. For example, Table 2.1 shows the percentages of DPI spent on admissions to the performing arts to be .111 in 1947 and .155 in 1929. Dividing the former by the latter produces a ratio of .716 for 1947, which, multiplied by 100, yields the index of 71.6 for 1947 that is plotted in Figure 2.1. The straightforward meaning of that number is that in 1947 the share of DPI that consumers spent for admission to the per-

Table 2.1. *Consumer spending on admissions to spectator entertainments*

	1929	1939	1947	1970	1975	1980	1985	1990
Consumer spending as percentage of disposable personal income								
Recreation, total	5.301	4.953	5.479	5.966	6.161	6.022	6.384	6.942
Spectator entertainment	1.118	1.178	1.187	0.457	0.375	0.341	0.314	0.331
Performing arts[a]	0.155	0.092	0.111	0.074	0.068	0.092	0.089	0.123
Motion pictures[a]	0.881	0.945	0.944	0.226	0.191	0.132	0.112	0.096
Spectator sports	0.081	0.141	0.132	0.157	0.116	0.117	0.113	0.112
Percent breakdown of consumer spending								
Spectator entertainment as percentage of all recreation	21.1	23.8	21.7	7.65	6.09	5.67	4.91	4.77
Percent distribution of spectator entertainment								
Performing arts[a]	13.9	7.8	9.3	16.1	18.2	26.9	28.4	35.5
Motion pictures[a]	78.9	80.3	79.6	49.4	50.9	38.7	35.6	28.2
Spectator sports	7.2	11.9	11.1	34.5	30.9	34.4	36.0	36.3

[a] In theaters only.
Source: U.S. Department of Commerce, *National Income and Product Accounts of the United States*, statistical tables, various years.

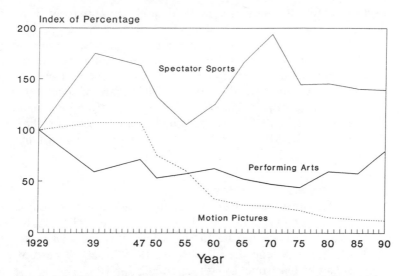

Figure 2.1. Expenditures on admissions as a percentage of disposable personal income (index: 1929 = 100).

forming arts stood at 71.6 percent of its level in 1929. In other words, consumers were spending a smaller proportion of their income on admissions to the performing arts in 1947 than they had done in 1929.

One can place the performing arts sector in perspective by looking at the larger categories of which it is a part. Table 2.1 shows that consumer spending on recreation as a whole has risen gradually from just over 5 percent of DPI in 1929 to almost 7 percent in recent years. Real disposable income per capita nearly tripled over the same period. That the proportion spent on recreation gradually increased tells us that recreation behaves like a "luxury good," something that people want relatively more of as their living standards rise.

Spending on what the Commerce Department identifies as "spectator amusements" makes up only a small part of recreation expenditure as a whole. The lower panel of Table 2.1 shows that in 1929, the earliest year for which we have data, it accounted for 21 percent of the total, and that motion pictures made up almost 79 percent of that share. The movies were then approaching the height of their popularity. Talking pictures had been introduced in 1927 with *The Jazz Singer,* starring Al Jolson. With the advantage of the sound track, movies became more popular than ever during the 1930s. Through the Great Depression and the years of World War II (when travel and recreation opportunities were limited), the movies continued to claim 80 percent of recreation outlays.

The live performing arts did not stand up well under competition with "talking pictures." The decline in real per capita income during the Great Depression may also have hurt the more expensive live performing arts in competition with the movies. Their share of spectator spending fell from 14 percent in 1929 to about 8 percent ten years later. Table 2.1 shows that in 1929 consumers had spent 16 cents on the live performing arts per $100 of DPI. By 1939 such outlays had fallen to just over 9 cents per $100.

The impact of television

The introduction of television broadcasting immediately after World War II had a dramatic effect on consumer behavior. In 1947, as TV broadcasting was just beginning, consumers spent 94 cents of every $100 of DPI to attend the movies. By 1975, when 97 percent of U.S. homes had at least one TV set, spending for admission to the movies had fallen to 19 cents per $100, or one-fifth of its 1947 level, and accounted for just over half of consumer outlays for spectator entertainment.[4] Indeed, consumers were spending as much on radio and television repairs as they were on movie admissions.[5]

While the impact of television on moviegoing was strong and clear, its effect on attendance at the live performing arts was much less dramatic. From 1947 to 1975, spending on the latter group fell from 11 cents to 7 cents per $100 of DPI. Because movie attendance was down so sharply, the share of spectator activity accounted for by the live performing arts actually doubled from 9 to 18 percent.

It is not difficult to see why the live performing arts should prove more resistant than the movies were to the competition of TV. Television and the movies are, in fact, technically similar, an image projected on a flat screen, while the "live" nature of the live performing arts gives them a third dimension and an aesthetic character that cannot be duplicated by the other modes. Ballet provides the most obvious illustration. Television cannot reproduce the three-dimensionality of a live, on-stage performance in which dancers move through real space. Something of aesthetic importance is left out. No one who has developed a taste for live ballet is likely to find ballet on television an adequate substitute

---

[4] Data on television ownership is from *Statistical Abstract of the United States, 1991*, table 919.

[5] U.S. Department of Commerce, Bureau of Economic Analysis, *National Income and Product Accounts of the U.S.*, table 2.4, as revised 1991.

for the real thing. In varying degrees, the same can be said for the other live arts.

Yet the preceding argument overstates the extent to which "liveness" protects the live performing arts against the competition of television, for they must compete not just with broadcast versions of the performing arts, but also with broadcasts of other kinds (not all of them "entertainment"), which make television watching such an attractive occupation. We take a further look at the relationship between the mass media and attendance at the live performing arts in Chapter 3 and again in Chapters 16 and 17, which deal, among other things, with the effect of the mass media on the cultivation of taste for the arts.

Growth of the arts since 1970

Figure 2.1 shows that by 1970 the ratio of consumer spending on the performing arts to DPI was a little less than half as high as it had been in 1929. The argument that the United States is now enjoying a "boom" in art and culture rests on trends some of which began to assert themselves in the 1960s. During the late 1950s and early 1960s, the nation had become self-consciously concerned about the situation of the arts in the United States. Comparisons, most of them unfavorable to the United States, were made with the status of the arts in other advanced industrial nations. An intense new interest in encouraging the arts developed in both the private and public spheres. Private charitable foundations (especially the Ford Foundation) greatly expanded their support for arts companies and artists. With the establishment of the National Endowment for the Arts in 1965, the federal government for the first time began to subsidize artistic activity on a regular and permanent basis. State support along the same lines had begun with the establishment of the New York State Council on the Arts in 1960. (The origins of public support for the arts in the United States are treated in greater detail in Chapter 12.)

This combination of private and public support produced a rapid increase in arts activity during the 1970s. A variety of physical indicators reflecting such growth are displayed in Table 2.2. The top line of the table shows DPI in constant dollars, in other words with the effects of inflation removed. It thus provides a measure of what economists refer to as "real income," the equivalent to a physical measure of income, since its year-to-year movements are not distorted by price changes. The top line is therefore a gauge of "real" aggregate growth with which to compare the growth of "real" arts activity as indicated by the other entries. Many of the indicators of real arts activity showed rates of increase during the 1970s that exceeded the growth of real income.

Table 2.2. *Growth of arts activity in the United States, 1970–90*

	Performance season ending			Percent change	
	1970	1980	1990	1970–80	1980–90
Disposable personal income (billions of 1987 dollars)[a]	2,025	2,734	3,538	35.0	29.4
Broadway playing weeks	1,047	1,541	1,061	47.2	–31.1
Road company playing weeks	1,024	1,351	944	31.9	–30.1
Actors' Equity workweeks					
LORT contract	32,522	42,910	58,550	31.9	26.2
Off-Broadway contract	13,424	9,313	11,840	–30.6	27.1
Chicago-area contract	0	2,093	5,344	—	161.6
Opera, major professional companies					
Performances	—	1,789[b]	2,283	—	27.6[c]
Attendance (millions)	—	2.46[b]	4.14	—	68.3[c]
All opera					
Companies	648	986	1,285[d]	52.2	30.3[e]
Performances	4,779	9,391	15,099[d]	96.5	60.8[e]
Attendance (millions)	4.6	10.7	21.4	132.6	100.0[e]
Symphony orchestras					
Concerts	6,599	22,229	16,725	236.9	–24.8
Attendance (millions)	12.7	22.6	22.2	78.0	–1.8
Major orchestras (number)	28	32	33	14.3	3.1
Metropolitan and regional orchestras (number)	72	144	140	100.0	–2.8
Ballet companies	279	287	283	2.9	–1.4
Modern dance companies	102	289	345	183.3	19.4

[a] For calendar year season ends.

[b] 1983 season.

[c] 1983–90.

[d] 1989 season.

[e] 1980–89.

Sources: "Disposable personal income" data from *Economic Report of the President*, February 1991, table B.27; "Broadway" and "Road company playing weeks" data from League of American Theaters and Producers, and *Statistical Abstract of the U.S.*, various years; "workweeks" are those under Actors' Equity contracts with the League of Resident Theaters (LORT) and with Off-Broadway and Chicago-area producers, reported by Guy Pace in *Equity News*, December issues, 1990 and 1991; "Opera, major professional companies" (refers to members of OPERA America) data from OPERA America, *Profile 1991* and earlier issues; "All opera" data from Central Opera Service, Inc., covering workshop and college productions as well as small and large companies, as reported in *Statistical Abstract of the U.S.*, various years; "Symphony orchestras" data for 1970 and 1980 from American Symphony Orchestra League (ASOL), as reported in *Statistical Abstract of the U.S.*, various years; 1990 data from ASOL memorandum to the authors; "Ballet" and "Modern dance companies," 1970 and 1980, from Leila Sussmann, "Anatomy of the Dance Company Boom," *Dance Research Journal*, 16, no. 2 (Fall 1984), table 3; 1990 compiled by the authors from *Stern's Performing Arts Directory* (successor to *Dance Magazine Annual*, the source used by Sussmann).

Although figures for years before 1970 are not given in Table 2.2, some sectors, including ballet and modern dance, had also shown exceptionally rapid growth during the 1960s. For chamber music, another form that reportedly enjoyed strong growth during the 1960s and 1970s, we entirely lack historical data. (It should be pointed out that changes in the number of Broadway and road company playing weeks shown in Table 2.2 do not necessarily indicate trends, since playing weeks may fluctuate widely from year to year depending on how attractive a particular season's offerings turn out to be, and 1980, the middle date in the table, was one of the strongest seasons in recent decades.)

That the performing arts were growing faster than the economy as a whole during the 1970s and 1980s is confirmed in Table 2.1. After reaching a low of less than 7 cents per $100 of DPI in the mid-1970s, consumer spending on the performing arts rose to 9.2 cents per $100 in 1980 and 12.3 cents in 1990. One should not be misled by the diminutive size of these numbers, for they indicate that between 1975 and 1990 consumer expenditure on the performing arts increased 1.8 times as fast as DPI. That multiple should be enough to persuade even the most skeptical observer that we did, indeed, enjoy a cultural boom in the 1970s and 1980s.

Signs of trouble at the end of the 1980s

Will the boom continue? Signs that it might be losing steam began to accumulate toward the end of the 1980s. Table 2.2 shows that, for the most part, there was a considerable falling off in the growth rate of physical measures of arts activity in the 1980s, as compared with the preceding decade. Although these details are not shown in the table, several such measures actually declined after reaching a high point in the middle or late 1980s. For example, attendance at symphony concerts rose to a peak of 25.4 million in 1986, declined to 22.4 million by 1989, and then leveled off at 22.3 million in 1991. Several orchestras in medium-size cities collapsed financially in the late 1980s but were brought back to life under new auspices; one – the Oakland Symphony – went down for good.[6] Workweeks under the Actors' Equity contract with the League of Resident Theatres (LORT) reached a level of 62,397 in 1989 and then fell to 58,369 in 1991. The number of ballet companies declined from 331 in 1986 to 281 in 1992. Although attendance at main season

---

[6] A report to the American Symphony Orchestra League on the current situation and outlook for symphony orchestras in the United States became available too late to be used in this chapter. See *The Financial Condition of Symphony Orchestras* (Washington, D.C.: American Symphony Orchestra League, 1992).

and festival performances of major opera companies continued to rise through the 1989–90 season (as shown in Table 2.2), the amount of touring activity began to fall off. Thus, there were signs of a downturn in all four of the sectors we are concerned with.[7] At the same time, pessimism among managers and other professionals in these fields was exacerbated by the unexpected decline in public funding for the arts that occurred in 1991 and 1992. (See the discussion in Chapter 13.) Confirming these disparate indicators of decline, the dollar amount of consumer spending for admission to the live performing arts fell 5 percent in 1991, registering its first significant year-to-year decline since 1948. Because DPI rose slightly, spending for admissions fell from 12.3 cents per $100 of DPI in 1990 (as shown in Table 2.1) to 11.2 cents in 1991.

One might well ask how the proportion of consumer income spent on the live performing arts could continue to increase through 1990, if the physical quantity of performing arts activity was level or falling, as shown by numerous indicators for the late 1980s. A plausible explanation would be that ticket prices rose faster than the general price level. Consumer spending on admissions is the arithmetic product of price times number of tickets sold. It is perfectly possible for rising prices to more than offset a decline in the number of tickets sold, resulting in box office revenues that more than keep pace with the rise in DPI. (A necessary condition would be that the demand for tickets be price *in-elastic.* See Chapter 5 for a discussion of price elasticity and its implications for revenue and attendance.) Higher prices, of course, would also be a *cause* of declining ticket sales. Unfortunately, evidence on ticket prices is too sketchy to permit a rigorous analysis of their role in the relative increase of consumer spending on admissions.

Influence of changes on the supply side

It is an important aspect of the economics of the live performing arts that they have to be consumed at the point of production: to see *Hamlet,* one must go to the theater. This contrasts with the case of manufactured goods, which can be produced centrally and then distributed to consumers through a network of retail outlets, and we can gain further understanding of the growth trend in the live performing arts by examining the consequences of this difference.

As the term "consumer sovereignty" suggests, the standard assumption in the economic analysis of a free-enterprise system is that the quantity supplied responds more or less smoothly to changes in demand.

---

[7] For sources of this data, see source notes of Table 2.2.

For example, if the public wants more washing machines, demand for washers will increase (see discussion in Chapter 4); existing factories will expand output at existing locations, and a larger number of washers will be distributed to consumers through existing outlets. Moreover, these outlets do not depend exclusively on washing machine sales for their existence. Supply therefore responds easily and continuously to changes in demand. The situation is very different when, as in the live performing arts, the commodity has to be produced at the point of consumption. In that case, the local market has to be large enough to support a minimum-size producer before local production becomes feasible. Consequently, the adaptation of supply to demand is likely to be intermittent (or discontinuous) rather than smooth. It is well known in the study of regional economics that the local number of retail and service outlets is largely governed by such market-size or "threshold" effects (see discussion in Chapter 15). But no one would argue that the aggregate consumption and production of, say, washing machines, is affected by the fact that small towns do not have distributorships. We know that potential local consumers will go to larger towns to buy them. There is good reason to think the case is otherwise for the live performing arts: few consumers will regularly travel long distances to attend live performances, and the distance is likely to be longer for the performing arts than for a washing machine. Aggregate consumption and production is therefore limited by the number of local places served, and discontinuous increases in the number of such places can cause abrupt surges in aggregate consumption.

With this analysis in mind, it is not unreasonable to suggest that the high growth rate of performing arts activity in the 1970s and 1980s may have resulted not so much from rising consumer demand as from an increase in supply. The availability of government subsidies and of additional private contributions encouraged the formation of new performing arts companies in places that previously had few or none. The same financial support also greatly increased the number and range of performance tours into previously untapped markets. In this process, a latent demand for the arts was satisfied by a sudden burst of new activity, and consumer spending on the arts increased much faster than income. If that is what happened in the 1970s and 1980s, it is a pattern that will be difficult to duplicate in future decades, when the number of unserved markets will have diminished in relative importance.

Like the live performing arts, live spectator sporting events have to be consumed at the point of production, and trends in the spectator sports industry strongly support the argument that discontinuous changes on the supply side have important effects on spending. Figure

2.1 shows that the ratio of spectator sports admission outlays to DPI fell from a relatively high level in 1947 to a low point in the mid-1950s. The decline coincided with a period in which the number of suppliers, as measured by the number of major league teams in baseball, football, basketball, and hockey, was actually declining. Then from 1957 to 1970 the number of teams increased sharply, almost doubling as the leagues expanded into new metropolitan areas in the South and West that had not previously been served. When the latent demand in these new markets was tapped, the ratio of consumer spending on admissions to their DPI soared, reaching an all-time peak in 1969. After 1970 the number of teams continued to increase, but at a much slower rate than before. The spending ratio resumed a steady decline.[8]

Institutional change in the performing arts

To this point, the discussion of growth in the live performing arts has focused on trends in consumer spending and in the physical level of activity. To flesh out the numbers, something must also be said about how these arts are actually produced in the United States: what are the dominant institutional forms and how have they changed in recent decades? Without presuming to offer a history of the arts in the twentieth century, we next outline some major changes in arts institutions that have accompanied their rapid growth.[9]

Theater

The world of theater in the United States has changed shape almost continuously during the twentieth century. From the 1920s through the 1940s "Broadway" was virtually synonymous with "American theater." That had not always been the case, however. In the nineteenth and early twentieth centuries, theater had also thrived outside New York. There were active playhouses in all major cities and in many smaller ones. Typically they either housed a local stock or repertory organization or were visited by touring companies, of which there were reportedly several hundred. The number of active local theaters

---

[8] For supporting data, see James Heilbrun, "Once More With Feeling: The Arts Boom Revisited," in William S. Hendon et al., eds. *The Economics of Cultural Industries* (Akron, Ohio: Association for Cultural Economics, 1984), pp. 34–46, cited at table 4.

[9] In addition to the specific sources cited in this section, useful historical summaries are available in: Baumol and Bowen, *Performing Arts,* chap. 2; *The Finances of the Performing Arts,* vol. 1 (New York: Ford Foundation, 1974), chap. 2; and *The Arts in America,* a report to the president and to the Congress by the National Endowment for the Arts, October 1988, pp. 31–182.

declined precipitously, however, after the second decade of this century. Evidently, the development of motion pictures and radio broadcasting undermined the market for local theater, with the Great Depression contributing the final blow.[10] The Little Theater movement of the 1920s and 1930s, although it had high aspirations as an alternative to what its participants regarded as the excessive commercialism of Broadway, also failed to survive the double blow of the Depression followed by mobilization for war.

In the years since World War II, theater in the United States has been transformed by the development of a solidly based network of nonprofit "resident" or (as they used to be called) "regional" theaters.[11] From a mere handful in the late 1940s, their number has grown to more than 200 in the 1990s. The Theatre Communications Group (TCG), founded in 1961 as a service organization for the nonprofit, professional theater in the United States, had a membership of only 35 in 1966. By 1980 the number had grown to 170 and by 1992, to 226.[12] Equally as significant as the growth in numbers has been the growth of artistic influence. As the number of new productions per season on Broadway gradually diminished during the postwar years, resident theaters became the principal incubators for new playwrights and new productions.[13]

While resident theater was spreading nationwide, New York was undergoing its own theatrical revolution: the development of an Off-Broadway, and later an Off-Off-Broadway theater. Off-Broadway had begun to attract attention as a phenomenon in the early 1950s. To be sure, the Little Theater movement had been a forerunner. The Washington Square Players (later to become the Theatre Guild) began in 1914, and the Provincetown Players, famous for putting on the first productions of Eugene O'Neill, in 1916. But it was not until the early 1950s that small, artistically ambitious theaters became numerous enough to be thought of as a major alternative to Broadway.[14] Thomas Gale Moore tabulated a total of 17 Off-Broadway productions for the 1953–54 season and reports that the number grew to a peak of 134 in

[10] See Thomas Gale Moore, *The Economics of the American Theater* (Durham, N.C.: Duke University Press, 1968), chap. 7.

[11] For a history of resident theater down to the early 1970s, see Joseph Zeigler, *Regional Theatre* (Minneapolis: University of Minnesota Press, 1973).

[12] Memo to the authors from John Federico, Theatre Communications Group, February 14, 1992.

[13] For data showing the decline in the number of new productions on Broadway, see *A Sourcebook of Arts Statistics: 1989,* National Endowment for the Arts, April 1990, tables 4.1 and 4.2.

[14] Stuart W. Little, *Off-Broadway: The Prophetic Theater* (New York: Coward, McCann, & Geoghegan, 1972), chap. 2.

1961–62. Although the number of new productions thereafter declined, the total number of performances continued to increase. By 1963–64, the last year of Moore's data, total Off-Broadway performances actually outnumbered those on Broadway.[15] Workweek data from Actors' Equity (the trade union of the acting profession) indicate that activity in the Off-Broadway theater has fluctuated since the late 1960s, without showing any pronounced trend. (See Table 2.2.)

The Off-Broadway theater is made up primarily of commercial producers but includes some ongoing not-for-profit enterprises, as well. The distinction between Broadway and Off-Broadway theater is formalized in the Equity contract under which Off-Broadway producers operate. The wage scale is lower than Broadway's, but so is house size: it may not exceed 499 seats and, except where special dispensation is given, the venue must lie outside the geographically designated "Broadway" area of midtown Manhattan.

Dance

The explosion of dance as a performance art in the United States is one of the major cultural events of the past forty years. The basic facts are well known. Before World War II there was very little professional ballet on view in the United States. Most Americans probably regarded ballet as a strictly European form, associated with a decadent, moribund aristocracy. European companies, such as the Ballet Russe de Monte Carlo, toured North America, but few U.S. companies had yet been created. The earliest was the Atlanta Ballet, which can trace its origins back to 1929. The San Francisco Ballet began as the San Francisco Opera Ballet in 1933. Ballet Theatre, later to become the renowned American Ballet Theatre, was founded in 1940. No other permanent companies existed before World War II. The choreographer George Balanchine was brought to the United States in 1933 by Lincoln Kirstein to start a school of ballet and a permanent company. He accomplished the first goal in 1934 with the opening of the School of American Ballet in New York City but did not achieve the second until 1946, when he and Kirstein founded Ballet Society. In 1948, with official sponsorship, Ballet Society became the New York City Ballet.

The excitement generated by Balanchine's work and his company and by U.S. tours of the great European ensembles helped to spark the dance boom of the postwar era. In 1963 the Ford Foundation announced a 10-year, $7.8 million grant "to strengthen professional ballet in the United States." By 1984 it had given $42.6 million to dance companies

---

[15] Moore, *Economics*, pp. 16–18 and table I.2.

and related programs.[16] Support from the foundation was critical in helping dance organizations to achieve a modicum of financial stability during their early years of rapid growth.

While ballet was a European art form successfully transplanted, modern dance was essentially invented in the United States by such pioneers as Isadora Duncan, Ruth St. Denis and Ted Shawn, Doris Humphrey, and Martha Graham. Yet despite these now famous few, it cannot be said that modern dance was more than a very small enterprise with a very devoted following before World War II. After the war, however, modern dance also took part in the dance explosion.

Unlike ballet companies, symphony orchestras, opera companies, and theater groups, modern dance companies typically give most of their performances away from their home base. From the late 1960s into the 1970s, the NEA helped fuel the boom in modern dance by joining with local sponsors to finance an extensive dance touring program. This not only gave the companies more weeks of employment, but also helped spread the gospel of modern dance to all parts of the country.

By tabulating the number and character of companies listed in *Dance Magazine Annual* from 1958 to 1980, the sociologist Leila Sussmann has provided the best available measure of the extent of the dance boom. Her study shows that the number of modern dance companies increased from 28 in 1958 to 72 in 1965, 102 in 1970, and 289 in 1980, while the number of ballet companies rose from 18 in 1958 to 161 in 1965, 279 in 1970, and 287 in 1980.[17] Thus, both forms of dance enjoyed extraordinary growth over the period examined, and the overall numbers are strikingly similar. However, the number of ballet companies increased fastest during the 1960s, probably, as Sussmann suggests, the result of aid from the Ford Foundation, while modern dance companies enjoyed their most rapid increase in the 1970s, stimulated by NEA support.

Opera

The Metropolitan Opera in New York City, founded in 1883, is the oldest U.S. opera company. Only a few other companies now in existence date back to before World War II. However, in the late nineteenth and early twentieth centuries the nation was also served by touring European singers who put on operas with the help of a locally

---

[16] Jennifer Dunning, *"But First a School": The First Fifty Years of the School of American Ballet* (New York: Viking, 1985), pp. 107–09.

[17] Leila Sussmann, "Anatomy of the Dance Company Boom, 1958–1980," *Dance Research Journal,* 16, no. 2 (Fall 1984): pp. 23–28, cited at table 3.

Table 2.3. *Founding dates of the ten largest U.S. opera companies*

Opera company	Year founded	Budget ($ millions)	1990–91 main season	
			No. of operas	No. of performances
Metropolitan Opera	1883	106.0	22	208
San Francisco Opera	1923	33.2	11	72
New York City Opera	1944	22.4	15	93
Lyric Opera of Chicago	1954	20.8	8	67
Houston Grand Opera	1955	15.3	13	89
Los Angeles Opera	1986	13.1	8	42
Seattle Opera	1964	9.6	7	41
Washington (D.C.) Opera	1956	8.5	7	56
Santa Fe Opera	1956	6.8	5	37
Dallas Opera	1957	6.4	5	21

Source: Opera America, *Profile 1990*, pp. 26–43.

recruited supporting cast. As a result opera was somewhat better established in the United States than ballet was before the war.

Like ballet and modern dance, opera has enjoyed extraordinary growth during the years of cultural boom. When Opera America, the service organization for major professional opera companies, was formed in 1970, it had only 17 members. By 1990 membership had grown to 117, of which 98 were in the United States. Table 2.3 lists the 10 largest U.S. member companies together with budget size and year of founding. Of the 10, only 3 were started before 1950. As in the case of ballet, but on a somewhat smaller scale, the Ford Foundation contributed important financial support to U.S. opera companies during their years of early growth: between 1957 and 1979 its grants to opera companies totaled $16.9 million.[18]

On a per performance basis, opera is by far the most expensive of the live performing arts to produce, involving as it does elements of all the others, combined typically with a lavish hand. Consequently, it is important economically to play to relatively full houses, so seasons tend to be short. As Table 2.3 suggests, with the exception of the very largest companies, the number of performances per season is usually well below 50.

Table 2.3 reveals the immense size of the Metropolitan Opera: its

---

[18] *Sharps and Flat: A Report on Ford Foundation Assistance to American Music,* Ford Foundation, July 1980, p. 45.

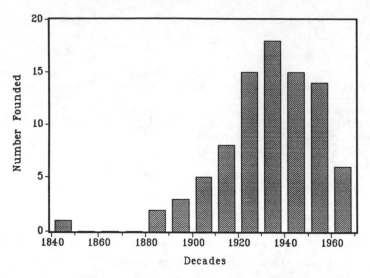

Figure 2.2. Number of symphony orchestras founded by decade.

budget is more than three times the size of the next largest company. It is by far the largest performing arts company in the United States. Indeed, statistical studies of opera companies usually present their results on a with- and without-the-Met basis, in order to avoid its distorting effect on reported averages.

As we shall see in Chapter 3, the popularity of opera and of ballet and modern dance are approximately equal in the United States, as measured by the proportion of the population that attends at least once a year.

Symphony orchestras

Symphony orchestras are by far the oldest of the ongoing institutions in the live performing arts. The New York Philharmonic traces its origins back to 1842. The next oldest surviving orchestras are those of St. Louis (1880), Boston (1881), Chicago (1890), Cincinnati (1894), and Philadelphia (1900). Drawing on data from Philip Hart's massive history of the symphony orchestra in the United States, Figure 2.2 presents the founding dates by decade of 87 U.S. orchestras that in 1971 had budgets in excess of $100,000 per year.[19] It shows that growth in the number of orchestras was greatest between 1920 and 1940, but

[19] Philip Hart, *Orpheus in the New World* (New York: Norton, 1973), app. A.

continued at a respectable pace in the 1940s and 1950s, as well. In Table 2.2 we have already shown that, by 1989, the combined number of major and metropolitan orchestras (categories that correspond approximately to Hart's 1971 group) had increased to 217.

Here, too, the Ford Foundation played a major role. In 1965 Ford announced an $80.2 million grant program to strengthen 61 U.S. orchestras.[20] (It is said to have been the largest single grant program ever mounted in support of the arts.) The foundation was concerned by the low salary level and short playing season faced by musicians in most orchestras in the early 1960s. Its aid was intended to encourage longer seasons, better pay scales, and by increasing the level of professionalism of musicians, a higher quality of performance. Three-quarters of the aid was provided in the form of grants designated to build up endowment funds. The orchestras were required to raise matching amounts within five years. As a result of this program, by 1970–71 the 91 symphony orchestras that took part in the foundation's financial survey had accumulated $120.6 million in endowment funds and were able to use more than $7 million per year of endowment income to support current operations.[21] Twenty years later, U.S. symphony orchestras in the aggregate reported revenue from endowments and investments of $62.5 million, accounting for 8.9 percent of their total income.[22] It should be noted that endowment and investment income is much less important in the budgets of the other branches of the performing arts. In opera it accounted for only 3.1 percent of income in 1989, and for the nonprofit theater, only 2.9 percent in 1990.[23] For ballet and modern dance, its share is virtually nil.

Relative sizes of the four sectors of the performing arts

Symphony orchestras are not only the longest established of the performing arts institutions we will examine, but also, in the aggregate, the largest of the nonprofit group. Their gross income in 1988–89 was $619.4 million.[24] In the same year, the aggregate income of the major U.S. opera companies was reported to be $342.4 million and of the resident nonprofit theaters that were members of TCG, $350.5 million.

---

[20] Ibid., pp. 13–16.

[21] *Finances of the Performing Arts,* vol. 1, app. A, p. 11.

[22] Data was supplied to the authors by the American Symphony Orchestra League.

[23] The opera figure is for a sample of 54 companies (excluding the Metropolitan Opera) reported in Opera America, *Profiles 1990,* p. 23. The theater data is from a sample of 53 theaters reported in Barbara Janowitz, "Theatre Facts 90," *American Theatre,* 8, no. 1 (April 1991): pp. 30–42, cited at 33, 35.

[24] See note 22.

However, Broadway and road company gross receipts in that year totalled $495.7 million, which tells us that in monetary terms theater as a whole is a considerably larger industry than is the making of symphonic music or of opera.[25]

In the absence of reliable ongoing data, Dick Netzer estimated the total income of the dance industry in 1983–84 as approximately $150 million.[26] Even if this figure were adjusted for growth and inflation to bring it up to 1988–89, it would remain well below the total for opera or the nonprofit theater; so it is clear that dance is the smallest of the four sectors on a monetary scale. However, opera outranks dance in monetary terms primarily because of its much greater cost of production. Attendance might tell a different story. Although we lack reliable attendance figures for dance, national studies of the participation rate of the U.S. population in the various art forms, presented in Chapter 3, suggest that if attendance figures were available they would show dance in third place, slightly ahead of opera, but far behind theater and symphony concerts.

Summary

The trend of arts activity described in this chapter is complex and not easily summarized. First came four decades of relative decline: consumer spending on the live performing arts as a percentage of their total disposable income fell substantially from its highest level in 1929 to a low point some 40 years later, as the introduction first of "talking pictures" and later commercial television provided tough competition for the live performing arts. But a turnaround began in the 1960s when a combination of increased public and private support helped to underwrite new companies and new activities, enabling the arts to tap into the demand of previously unserved audiences. By 1990 the proportion of income consumers were spending on the live performing arts, though still very small in absolute terms, had risen almost 80 percent above its 1975 level. Toward the end of the 1980s, however, growth in several arts sectors slowed down or even halted. Soon afterward, the recession of the early 1990s, accompanied by an unexpected decline in public support, put many arts companies under severe fiscal stress.

[25] Opera income is from Opera America, *Profile 1990,* p. 17. Data on commercial and nonprofit theater are from James Heilbrun, "Art and Culture as Central Place Functions," *Urban Studies,* 29, no. 2 (1992): pp. 205–15, cited at tables 2 and 3.

[26] Dick Netzer, "Changing Economic Fortunes of the Dance in the U.S.," Urban Research Center of New York University, May 1986, table 1. See Netzer's accompanying notes and alternative estimates in the same table.

Of course, the growth of the arts has been visible in the expansion of audiences as well as in the multiplication of institutions. In the next chapter we look at the composition and character of audiences for the arts.

APPENDIX: STATISTICS OF ART AND CULTURE IN THE UNITED STATES

There are two general sources of data on the arts. The *Statistical Abstract of the United States,* compiled by the U.S. Department of Commerce, Bureau of the Census, each year presents a table on activity in the live performing arts, with data running back about 20 years. Every two years the National Endowment for the Arts, through an outside contractor, compiles *A Sourcebook of Arts Statistics* (the 1989 edition was about eight hundred pages in length) that is by far the most comprehensive available collection of arts data. It covers all fields that are within the NEA's domain. Hence, it includes statistics on writing and publishing, motion pictures, broadcasting, architecture, design, craft arts, and historic preservation, in addition to the performing arts and fine arts treated in this book. It also contains extensive bibliographies. The *Sourcebook* is made available to the public through the ERIC document system, on microfiche in many libraries. Neither the *Sourcebook* nor the *Statistical Abstract* originates any data; both draw on other sources, which may be either published or unpublished. Some of these are described in the following sections.

Data on activity in individual arts sectors

Most data on the arts activity of nonprofit producers come originally from periodic reports by the service organizations that now exist for every arts subcategory. These are the equivalent of the trade associations that provide data in the commercial sectors of the arts.

Symphony orchestras: The American Symphony Orchestra League, (ASOL), Washington, D.C., is the oldest of the service organizations in the nonprofit performing arts. Each year it tabulates data on number of orchestras by size, number of concerts and attendance (as shown in Table 2.2), and income by source and expenses by type. Some of the statistical series run back into the 1950s. Portions of the data are regularly published in the *Statistical Abstract* and in the *Sourcebook.* Unlike some of the other service organizations, ASOL does not generally release any data on individual member companies.

Opera companies: Opera America, Washington, D.C., is the service organization of the major professional opera companies in the United

States and Canada. Its annual publication, entitled *Profile,* includes for every member company a description of the repertory, and data on house size, staff size, number of performances, attendance, and total expense budget. For the full membership *Profile* also publishes aggregate data on performances and attendance (as used in Table 2.2), and on income by source and expenses by type. In addition, each issue contains aggregate data for a sample of companies for which consistent information is available for five consecutive years. This allows the analyst to examine trends free of the disturbing influence of changes in number of companies and in compliance with reporting requirements that afflicts data for the overall membership.

Data covering *all* opera activity, including university and community groups, were published through 1989 by Central Opera Service (COS), New York City, in its *Central Opera Service Bulletin.* Portions of the data were regularly reproduced in the *Statistical Abstract.* COS, an adjunct of the Metropolitan Opera Association, ceased operation in 1990. Its data archives have been taken over by Opera America, which may continue some of its data gathering functions.

Theater: The League of American Theatres and Producers, New York City, the trade association of Broadway producers and theater owners, publishes data each year (through press releases) on number of productions, playing weeks, tickets sold, and gross receipts for Broadway and Broadway road companies. Similar data are available in *Variety,* the newspaper of the entertainment world. Although there is also a League of Off-Broadway Theatres and Producers, it does not collect or publish data. Existing statistics of Off-Broadway activity have been tabulated by interested scholars from newspaper listings.

Theatre Communications Group (TCG), New York City, is the service organization for U.S. nonprofit resident theaters. TCG publishes *Theatre Profiles* biannually, listing the repertory, house size, expense budget size, and type of labor contract for each member company. In addition, in the April issue of *American Theatre,* its monthly magazine, TCG each year presents "Theatre Facts," comprising a summary of aggregate data for all members and a detailed study of financial results for a consistent sample of theaters over a five-year period.

Actors' Equity Association, New York City, is the trade union for the on-stage acting profession. At the end of each calendar year it publishes in its monthly *Equity News* a tally of workweeks for the preceding season under its various contracts. These figures make up a yearly series on stage activity running back into the 1960s. While the individual series are useful indicators, the aggregate of all contracts is probably not as reliable since the periodic introduction of new contracts reflects changes in the extent of unionization rather than level of activity.

Dance: Dance/USA, Washington, D.C., is the service organization for ballet and modern dance. It conducts an annual data survey of its members, results of which appear in its quarterly publication entitled *Dance/ USA Journal.* Analysis of the survey includes a breakdown by size of company and by ballet versus modern dance. Data on a consistent sample of companies over a five-year period are also expected to be made available. A problem in the dance field is that many companies are too small to afford the staff needed for detailed data reporting. Apparently they are all too busy just dancing.

Chamber music: Chamber Music America, New York City, is the service organization for professional chamber music soloists, ensembles, and presenters. The first statistical survey of its membership, covering the year 1990, was published in 1992 and entitled *Chamber Music in America: Status of the National Chamber Music Field.* Aggregate results are shown separately for ensembles and presenting organizations. Plans call for conducting the survey biannually and also developing data on a consistent sample of members over a five-year period.

Museums: The major organization in this field is the American Association of Museums, Washington, D.C. Art museums make up only a small part of its membership. It does not regularly publish data but occasionally sponsors important surveys. The most recent, covering the entire museum field, and including detailed financial and other data, is entitled *Data Report from the 1989 National Museum Survey* and was published by the association in January 1992. The Association of Art Museum Directors, New York City, represents only the major art museums. It conducts statistical surveys on a range of topics, but they are not regularly made available to the public.

Data on public and private support for the arts

National Endowment for the Arts: In its *Annual Report* the NEA (Washington, D.C.) lists and describes all grants, classified by program category. It has sponsored periodically the Survey of Public Participation in the Arts, as well as an important series entitled *Research Reports,* and a less formal series of research notes, usually dealing with government data on the arts. NEA also arranges for publication of the biannual *Sourcebook of Arts Statistics,* previously described.

Institute of Museum Services: The IMS (Washington, D.C.) lists and describes in its *Annual Report* all its grants to museums, classified by grant category and type of museum.

Budget of the United States: The U.S. Budget lists appropriations made directly to such beneficiaries of federal support as the Smithsonian Institution and the John F. Kennedy Center for the Performing Arts.

National Assembly of State Arts Agencies: The NASAA (Washington, D.C.) represents the arts agencies of the 50 states, Puerto Rico, and the island territories. It publishes a complete annual survey of state arts agency appropriations and of state line item appropriations for the arts, as well as other occasional studies of art agency activity.

National Assembly of Local Arts Agencies: The NALAA (Washington, D.C.) is the counterpart of NASAA at the local level. Its membership, unlike that of NASAA, does not cover the whole field, which is very large and diverse in character. NALAA conducts an annual data survey of its members. Because the number of responses varies from year to year, the results are published in the form of averages rather than aggregates. NAALA also publishes information from its subdivision, the United States Urban Arts Federation, membership in which is made up of the local arts councils of the 50 largest U.S. cities.

American Association of Fund-Raising Counsel: The AAFRC (New York City) publishes data on U.S. philanthropic contributions in its annual report entitled *Giving.* Data go back to 1955 and are classified both by source (corporations, individuals, foundations) and by use (religion, education, art/culture/humanities, etc.).

Other data

Consumer spending: The dollar amount of consumer spending on admissions to the the live performing arts is published annually in table 2.4 (Personal consumption expenditures) in the National Income and Product Accounts of the United States. The NIPA tables for the previous calendar year appear annually in the July issue of *Survey of Current Business,* published by the U.S. Department of Commerce. The data are subject to frequent revisions, which may run back many years.

Participation rates: The extent to which individuals participate in arts activities has been studied in two national surveys: the Survey of Public

Participation in the Arts, 1982 and 1985. A third survey was undertaken in 1992. Paid for by the NEA and carried out by the Census Bureau, the surveys are made available to the public through the ERIC system, available on microfiche at many libraries.

Artists in the labor force: The number of artists in the labor force, by detailed occupational type, is counted by the Census Bureau in each *Decennial Census of Population.* The *Current Population Survey* of the Census Bureau provide updates on artists' employment and unemployment each year. The NEA further processes these data sets and makes them available through its research publications.

Artists' earnings: Figures on artists' earnings are also compiled by the Census Bureau, based on self-reports and self-identification in each *Decennial Census of Population.*

Art prices: The index of art prices used in this book is compiled and copyrighted by Sotheby's, which retains exclusive rights to its use. Between 30 and 40 works in each of several arts sectors, selected from property sold by all the major auction houses around the world, comprise the "market basket" on which the index is calculated. Prices are based on expert opinion and reflect factors underlying both supply and demand. According to Sotheby's standard disclaimer:

> Sotheby's Art Index reflects subjective analyses and opinions of Sotheby's art experts, based on auction sales and other information deemed relevant. Nothing in Sotheby's Index is intended as investment advice or as a prediction or guarantee of future performance or otherwise.

3

Audiences for the arts

In Chapter 2 we measured the growth of the arts by examining trends in consumer spending for admissions. In a free-enterprise economy, consumer spending is the principal source of what economists define as the demand for the arts. It is the source of box office receipts for theaters, concerts, opera, and ballet, the admissions and art shop income of museums, and the royalty income of performing arts companies from the sale of records and tapes. Since these forms of demand originate with the people who attend performances, visit museums, or buy reproductions of art or recordings of music, surveys of arts audiences contribute importantly to an understanding of the economics of the arts. Theater managers, before establishing a range of ticket prices, want to know what kinds of people make up their audience. As we explain in Chapter 4, some people are more price sensitive than others. Museum directors want to know what sort of visitors they are attracting. Business managers of ballet and opera companies want to find out whether they can count on attracting audiences from among those who habitually attend other kinds of performing arts. Officials at all levels of government that provide public subsidies for the arts need to know the extent to which various subgroups in the local or national population participate in arts activities. Donors of private funds want to know what kinds of audiences patronize the companies and institutions they may choose to support. Finally, economists, educators, sociologists, political scientists, and urban planners concerned with the arts are interested in information that will help them to understand the social and economic forces that determine demand for the arts.

Audience surveys versus participation studies

At the outset it is useful to draw a distinction between audience surveys and participation studies. Audience surveys are relatively inexpensive and easy to carry out. Consequently, a great many such studies have been conducted. The basic technique is to pass out a questionnaire to members of a performing arts audience as they assemble or to entrants to a museum or exhibit, and to collect the completed questionnaires before they leave. The questionnaire typically asks for information about the socioeconomic status of the respondent, including age, gender, occupation, educational background, and income level. In addition, it will usually ask about residential location, means of transportation employed, and other circumstances of the particular visit, as well as frequency of attendance at this company's performances or this museum, and at other kinds of events. The results of an audience survey will usually be expressed in percentage terms – for example, by showing the percentage of the audience that falls into each of several age or income classes. Table 3.7 (in a later section of this chapter) provides an illustration of the typical format. Obviously, such surveys can produce a very detailed statistical profile of the audience that attends a particular event or patronizes a particular company or institution. And given the large number of such studies, it is relatively easy to make comparisons of audience characteristics among the categories of the live performing arts – theater, opera, ballet, and so on – and between these and museums, historic sites, and the like.

Audience surveys, however, cannot tell you anything about the behavior of the general population in relation to the arts, since they deal only with the self-selected group that actually attends. It is particularly important in deciding questions of public policy toward the arts to know what proportion of the population at large actually *does* attend and how the socioeconomic character of attenders compares with that of nonattenders. Information of that sort can be obtained only by a survey of the whole population. One need not, of course, ask every citizen about her or his behavior with respect to the arts: a random sample of the population will suffice, but where the behavior is as infrequent as attendance at the arts and the socioeconomic characteristics of interest cover such a wide range, the sample has to be a large one. Consequently, population surveys of arts participation are expensive to carry out and are fairly infrequent.

Participation rates in the United States

The NEA sponsored a Survey of Public Participation in the Arts in 1982. Responses were obtained from 17,254 U.S. adults. A participant was defined as anyone who had attended an activity at least once during the 12 months preceding the survey. Participation *rates* are simply the number of participants divided by the adult population. Results of the

Table 3.1. *Surveys of participation in the arts in the United States*

Art form	Participation rate (percent)	
	NEA survey of United States (1982)	Ford survey of 12 U.S. cities (1973)
Musicals or operettas	19	18
Classical music performances	13	—
Symphony concerts	—	10
Plays (nonmusical)	12	16
Jazz performances	10	—
Jazz, rock, folk performances	—	25
Ballet	4	4
Opera	3	4
Art museums or galleries	22	—
Motion pictures		
Theater	63	69
Televised	—	93

Sources: Col. 1: Survey Research Center, University of Maryland, *Public Participation in the Arts, 1982: Overall Project Report*, ERIC no. ED 256–682 (prepared for the National Endowment for the Arts, 1985), chap. 10, table 1; and National Endowment for the Arts, Research Division, Note no. 8, March 23, 1984. Col. 2: Ford Foundation, *The Finances of the Performing Arts*, vol. 2, 1974, tables 1–7.

NEA survey are given in the first column of Table 3.1. Among the live performing arts, musicals and operettas had the highest participation rate (19 percent), followed by performances of classical music (13 percent), nonmusical plays (12 percent), jazz (10 percent), ballet (4 percent), and opera (3 percent). These figures may strike the reader as remarkably large or surprisingly small, depending on prior expectations. To put them in perspective, however, consider that, according to the same survey, 63 percent of the adult population watched a motion picture outside the home. Visits to art museums or galleries (22 percent) and to historic sites (37 percent) also outranked attendance at the performing arts.

The second column of Table 3.1 summarizes results of a survey of performing arts participation in 12 major cities carried out by the Ford Foundation in 1973. Except for the higher rate of attendance at nonmusical theater, the results are very similar to those in the nationwide NEA study. Although one would expect participation rates to be higher in large cities, with their easy access to resident performance companies, than in the nation as a whole, the Ford data show only slightly higher rates than the nationwide NEA study. Comparisons between surveys, however, must be made with caution because there may be significant differences in definitions or in survey procedures.

Audiences for the several art forms always overlap. Some people may attend only one of the performing arts or may patronize only art museums, but many others participate in several of the listed activities each year. Consequently, the "total audience" for the arts – defined as those who attended at least one arts event in the last year – will always be less than the sum of the number who participated in the individual forms. For example, in the Ford Foundation survey (Table 3.1, Col. 2) the percentages shown to attend nonmusical plays, concerts, opera, and ballet add up to 34 percent. But overlap among the individual audiences was such that the total number of people who attended at least one of those forms was only 23 percent of the population.[1]

As Paul DiMaggio, Michael Useem, and Paula Brown have pointed out, since a participation rate measures the percentage of a certain population that attended productions of a given institution or art form at least once during the year, it can be thought of as recording the *reach* of that institution or art form in the sense of measuring the breadth of its appeal. But total attendance also depends on the *frequency* with which participants attend, or in other words, the strength of their commitment. Thus, growth in attendance could result from increased participation, increased frequency, or both.[2]

Some international comparisons

Table 3.2 allows us to compare participation rates in the United States and eight other countries.[3] We are accustomed in the United States to conceding that Europe's long-established cultures may have a more developed taste than we do for the traditional forms of high art. It may come as something of a shock to most Americans, however, to learn that Australia and Canada, which they probably think of as even more recent converts to high culture, also appear to have higher rates of participation. Differences in the meaning of terms and in survey practices from country to country dictate that we allow a considerable

[1] *The Finances of the Performing Arts* (New York: Ford Foundation, 1974), vol. 2, table 10.

[2] See Paul DiMaggio, Michael Useem, and Paula Brown, *Audience Studies of the Performing Arts and Museums: A Critical Review,* National Endowment for the Arts, Research Division Report no. 9 (New York: Publishing Center for Cultural Resources, 1979), p. 37.

[3] We are grateful to Mark Schuster for his help in providing European and Canadian data.

Table 3.2. *International comparison of participation rates (percent of adult population)*[a]

Country	Classical music	Theater	Ballet	Opera	All museums	Art museums
United States (1982)	13	12	4	3	—	22[b]
Australia (1976)	9	17	10	6	—	—
France (1988–89)	9	14	6[c]	3	30	—
Great Britain (1981)	10	24	4	3	29	19[d]
Italy (1984)	6	10	—	—	—	—
Norway (1983)	16	27[e]	—	—	26	28[d]
Québec, Canada (1989)	16	39	8	—	—	28
Spain (1990)	7	14	—	—	28	—
Sweden (1982–83)	—	33	—	—	—	33

[a] Attended at least once during preceding 12 months.
[b] Art museum or gallery.
[c] Professional dance performance.
[d] Art exhibitions.
[e] Theater and opera combined.
Sources: United States, see Table 3.1; Australia, Throsby and Withers, *Economics of the Performing Arts*, table 7.1; France, Ministère de la Culture et de la Communication, *Les pratiques culturelle des Français: Nouvelle enquête, 1988–1989* (Paris: La Documentation Française, 1990); Great Britain, Market and Opinion Research International, survey conducted for BBC "Panorama," November 26, 1981; Italy, Carla Bodo, "Participation in Cultural Life in Italy," paper presented at the conference "Participation in Cultural Life in Europe," Moscow, April 22–24, 1991, table 1, based on data from Instituto Nazionale di Statistica, 1984; Norway, Statistisk Sentralbyrå, *Statistisk Årbok* (Oslo: Kongsvinger, 1984), table 477; Québec, "Le progrès d'une décennie en matière de participation culturelle, 1979–1989," Direction de la recherche et de la statistique, Ministère des Affaires culturelles du Québec, *Chiffres à l'appui*, 7, no. 2 (June 1992), Figures 3, 4, and 5; Spain, Luis Bonet, *El sector cultural en Espāna ante el proceso de integracion Europea*, 2 (Barcelona: Centre d'estudis de Planificació, 1992), Table 2.3; Sweden, Statistics Sweden, *Cultural Statistics: Activities, Economy, and Cultural Habits, 1980–1984* (Stockholm: 1987), tables 4.7:1, 4.7:2.

margin for uncertainty when making international comparisons. That having been said, the table does seem to show that U.S. participation rates are generally near the low end of the range for industrialized nations. A notable exception is concerts of classical music, where the United States has a substantially higher rate of participation than five of the other countries. The U.S. deficiency is particularly large in the case of theater, where the participation rate is only 12 percent, as compared with figures ranging from 17 percent in Australia to as much as 39 percent in the province of Quebec. In the fine arts, comparisons cannot be precise because the U.S. figure is for "art museums and galleries," while for most other countries it is either for "art exhibitions" or for the category of "all museums." Nevertheless, the United States, with a rate of 22 percent, again appears to be near the low end of the range.

Another perspective on the degree of interest in the arts is provided by the rate of attendance per hundred of population. For any given art form, this rate is the product of the participation rate times the average frequency of attendance of those who participate. For the aggregate of the arts it can be calculated by tabulating total attendance per year and dividing by population size. Throsby and Withers estimated the attendance at performing arts activities in the early 1970s in Australia, Canada, and the United States.[4] Dividing through by population, we obtain rates of attendance per 100 that confirm the pattern shown for participation rates: The United States lagged with attendance of 13 per 100 as compared with 19 in Australia and 31 in Canada.

Tibor Scitovsky carried out a similar comparison between the United States and eight European nations, based on estimates of annual admissions to theaters and concerts per 100 of population in the late 1960s. The United States had by far the lowest number: 22 admissions annually per 100 of population. European countries ranged from a low of 31 in The Netherlands to a high of 88 per 100 in Austria.[5] Of course, the relative U.S. standing may well have changed since the 1960s as a result of the rapid subsequent growth of interest in the arts.

How do participation rates vary in the population?

All studies agree that participation rates in the arts are higher for individuals who have higher incomes, higher occupational status, and greater educational attainment (as measured by level of schooling completed). These findings appear to hold across all art forms.[6] Equally general is the finding that educational attainment, which is also an important determinant of the other two factors, is the single most powerful determinant of arts participation. (We will substantiate this result later.)

---

[4] C. D. Throsby and G. A. Withers, *The Economics of the Performing Arts* (New York: St. Martin's, 1979), table 8.3.

[5] "Arts in the Affluent Society: What's Wrong with the Arts is What's Wrong with Society," reprinted in Tibor Scitovsky, *Human Desire and Economic Satisfaction,* pp. 37–45 (New York: New York University Press, 1986), table 4.1.

[6] See, e.g., *Finances of the Performing Arts,* vol. 2, pp. 12–18, and the study cited in Table 3.3, this volume.

Gender and age are also associated systematically with rate of attendance at the arts. Women are more likely than men to participate in all categories except jazz. Except in the case of jazz, participation tends to increase with age, up to some peak in the middle years, and to fall thereafter. The age of greatest exposure, however, varies with the art form.

Because participation in the live performing arts and at art museums requires a trip to the place of production, we would expect participation rates to be higher in places where arts institutions are more numerous and accessible. Table 3.3 shows that this is, indeed, the case: they are higher in the central cities and suburbs of metropolitan areas than in nonmetropolitan parts of the United States. *Within* metropolitan areas, there is relatively little difference in participation rates between central cities and suburbs. This probably reflects two mutually offsetting effects. On the one hand, the central city offers closer proximity to arts institutions than do the suburbs, which would make for higher participation rates in the city. On the other hand, suburban populations generally rank higher than those of the central city in socioeconomic status, which would make for higher rates in the suburbs.

Table 3.3 shows participation rates for various socioeconomic groups for the three high art forms in which overall participation is greatest: classical music, theater, and art museums. Data are from NEA's 1982 survey. The effect on participation rates of variation in income, education, and occupation is shown in the three top panels of the table. Perhaps the easiest way to demonstrate the importance of these factors is to compare the highest and lowest rates within each socioeconomic classification. For example, the first column shows exposure to live classical music performances. Those with incomes of $50,000 or more reported a participation rate of 30.6 percent, or nearly 4 times the 8.1 percent rate for those with only $5,000 to $10,000 of income. Those with professional occupations reported a 30.0 percent exposure rate, more than 5 times the rate for laborers. Most striking of all, men and women with a graduate school education had a 38.5 percent participation rate, about 20 times the rate for those with only a grade school education.

As we shall show in later chapters, one of the principal objectives of U.S. public policy toward the arts is to increase the rate of arts participation of the citizenry as a whole. Likewise, individual arts institutions are almost always interested in promoting participation in order to increase the size of their audience. From either point of view it is therefore useful to know whether income or education is the more important factor in determining arts participation. For example, if income dominates, the government may wish to support a policy of heavily subsidized

Table 3.3. *Participation rates among different population groups in the United States, 1982 (percent)*

	Classical music	Plays (nonmusical)	Art museums
Average, all groups	13.0	11.9	22.1
Income (dollars)			
5,000– 9,999	8.1	5.5	13.0
10,000–14,999	9.5	8.1	18.2
15,000–24,999	11.1	10.3	20.9
25,000–49,999	18.3	17.9	30.7
50,000 and over	30.6	33.8	47.5
Education			
Grade school	1.9	1.7	2.7
High school graduate	7.6	7.0	16.1
College graduate	29.4	25.9	44.1
Advanced degree	38.5	36.3	55.9
Occupation			
Professional	30.0	27.4	45.1
Managerial	19.3	19.8	36.0
Sales, clerical	14.9	14.8	25.8
Laborers	5.7	5.0	12.7
Service workers	11.3	8.9	20.1
Students	18.3	22.0	35.9
Age			
18–24	11.0	10.7	22.7
25–34	13.0	12.2	26.5
35–44	16.4	15.3	27.1
45–54	14.8	13.4	22.0
55–64	12.8	11.5	18.9
65–74	12.1	9.9	14.6
75–96	7.1	5.2	8.3
Gender			
Male	11.3	10.7	21.0
Female	14.5	12.9	23.1
Location[a]			
Central city of SMSA	14.7	14.1	15.9
SMSA noncentral city	14.3	13.2	24.7
Not in SMSA	10.1	8.5	15.9

[a]SMSA: Standard Metropolitan Statistical Area, an area definition employed by the U.S. Bureau of the Census in measuring the metropolitan population until 1984.
Source: Survey Research Center, University of Maryland, *Public Participation in the Arts, 1982, Overall Project Report,* ERIC no. ED 256–682 (prepared for the National Endowment for the Arts, 1985), table 3.3.

admissions to encourage participation by the relatively poor. On the other hand, if education is the leading factor, then admissions subsidies may be less effective in widening participation than would be a range of other policies centering on education or, more broadly, on promoting familiarity with the arts.

Education versus income

Separating the effects of education from those of income always poses a difficult problem for the social scientist. The difficulty arises because income and educational attainment arc separately correlated with many forms of social behavior, but are also very strongly correlated with each other. For example, from the study of criminal behavior it is known that the well-to-do have a lower propensity for crime than do the poor. But the well-to-do, on average, are also better educated than the poor. Is it their higher income or their higher educational attainment that makes them less prone to crime? Because education and income are so highly correlated with each other, it is statistically very difficult to sort out their separate effects on criminality. (In statistics this is known as the problem of "multicollinearity.") A like problem occurs in trying to separate the effects of income from those of educational attainment in the case of exposure to the arts. However, we have already shown that exposure to the arts varies more widely by level of education than by level of income, which certainly suggests that education is the more important factor.

Further evidence is provided by the Ford Foundation study of exposure to the performing arts. The study sample was divided into four groups: high education with high income, high education with low income, low education with high income, and low education with low income. (High income was defined as a family income of $15,000 or more per year; high education, as a college degree.) Rates of exposure for the four groups were compared in each category of the performing arts. The authors concluded that "the analysis confirms to a startling degree that it is indeed education rather than income that matters most. Within each educational group, the percentage attending is only somewhat higher among the high-income people than among the low-income people. But within each income group, the percentage attending is much larger among the high-education than among the low-education people."[7] This is best illustrated by arranging the results in matrix form, as we do in Table 3.4 for exposure to live ballet performances.

A very clear pattern emerges: the difference in rate of exposure

---

[7] Ibid., vol. 2, p. 16.

Table 3.4. *Income, education, and percentage of exposure to ballet*

	Education		
Income	High	Low	Difference
High	14	4	10
Low	12	2	10
Difference	2	2	—

Source: Ford Foundation, *The Finances of the Performing Arts*, vol. 2, 1974, table 15.

between those with high and low educational attainment was 10 percentage points, regardless of income, while the difference between those with high and low incomes was only 2 points, regardless of educational attainment.

Further evidence that education has a stronger effect than income is provided by the high participation rate of teachers in all modes of art. Table 3.5, based on data from the Ford Foundation study, shows that teachers have substantially higher rates of exposure to theater, symphony concerts, ballet, and opera than do executives or professionals, even though teachers' incomes are certainly lower on average. That education is, in fact, the single most important factor determining arts participation has been verified by statistical analyses that measure the impact of each of the several factors individually while simultaneously controlling for the influence of all the others.

Granted that education has something to do with the development of an individual's taste for art and culture, a fundamental question remains:

Table 3.5. *Participation rate (percent) for teaching compared with other occupations*

	Occupation		
	Teaching	Professional	Managerial
Theater	35	28	24
Symphony	27	18	14
Opera	10	5	6
Ballet	11	9	4

Source: Ford Foundation, *The Finances of the Performing Arts*, vol. 2, 1974, table 13.

Table 3.6. *How participation at live performances, art museums, and galleries relates to media exposure in the United States, 1982*

	Rate of exposure to live performances (percent)			Correlation: hours watching TV and live exposure rate
	Population as a whole	Watched on TV	Listened on radio	Listened to recordings	
Musical plays or operettas	19	41	37	42	−.093
Classical music	13	30	33	35	−.124
Plays	12	25	31	—	−.104
Jazz	10	28	32	32	−.037
Ballet	4	15	—	—	−.077
Opera	3	10	15	14	−.047
Art museums or galleries	22	46	—	—	−.132

Sources: Cols. 1–4: Survey Research Center, University of Maryland, *Public Participation in the Arts, 1982, Overall Project Report*, ERIC no. ED 256–682 (prepared for the National Endowment for the Arts, 1985), chap. 10, table 2; Col. 5: National Endowment for the Arts, Research Division, Note no. 12, June 5, 1985.

what exactly is the basis of the connection? Perhaps such taste is developed directly by arts appreciation courses taken in grade school, high school, or college. Or perhaps it is cultivated by a general liberal arts education without reference to special arts courses. Or more elusive still, perhaps it is developed by growing up in a home where the arts are taken seriously (which is likely to be a home where the average level of education is high). We will look into this question in Chapter 17.

Arts participation and the mass media

Participation surveys reveal a complex relationship between attendance at live arts activities and participation via the mass media. The NEA study found that for every art form, the rate of participation at live performances was much higher among those who also reported watching or listening to arts related material on the mass media. For example, Table 3.6 shows that in the population as a whole (first column), the rate of exposure to live classical music was only 13 percent, but among those who watched or heard it on TV, radio, or recordings (second through fourth columns), the rates of live participation were respectively 30, 33, and 35 percent. Results were similar for all other art forms.

The most straightforward interpretation of these findings is that those who have an already developed taste for the arts participate in both live and nonlive forms. It is also possible, however, that the availability of art via the mass media affects the rate of live participation. Interestingly, the effect could go either way. If arts productions on the mass media stimulate a taste for art, they could *increase* the demand for live attendance. On the other hand, if such productions satisfy demand without stimulating it, they may *reduce* the rate of live attendance. Finally, by competing for the viewer's leisure time the general availability of the mass media, without respect to particular content, probably reduces the demand for live participation. Recall that, in Chapter 2, it was suggested that the rise first of motion pictures and then of TV probably accounted for the decline in the share of income consumers devoted to attending the live performing arts from 1929 to 1975. The NEA survey provides some support for this hypothesis, since it shows a consistently negative (though weak) correlation between hours spent watching TV and participation in live arts events. (See the fifth column of Table 3.6.) We return to the question of competition between the mass media and the high arts in Chapters 16 and 17.

Audience characteristics

Since participation studies can tell us so much about the characteristics of the aggregate audience for particular art forms (see, e.g., Table 3.3), one might well ask why studies of individual audiences are necessary or useful. There are several reasons. The most obvious is that individual arts institutions may have unique characteristics such that they attract an audience different from the industry norm. For example, a drama company that specializes in "experimental theater" is likely to bring in a younger audience than one that emphasizes more familiar works. Second, arts institutions (other than museums, which often attract a high proportion of tourists) draw most of their audience from the city or metropolitan area in which they are located. If the socio-economic character of the population in that area differs somewhat from the national average, one would expect local audience composition to differ in the same direction.

Finally, participation studies focus on the question, Did you attend such and such an arts activity at least once in the last 12 months? and therefore, as we have already pointed out, do *not* reflect the *frequency* of participation of individual respondents. The composition of the audience at a particular event, however, *is* affected by the frequency with which each group attends. Suppose, for example, that the participation rate in a given art form is the same for those aged 25 to 34 and those aged 35 to 44 and that the two population groups are equal in size. Assume, however, that participants in the latter group attend more often per year than those in the former. In that case, the latter group will on average make up a higher proportion of the audience than will the former. In short, audience studies for individual arts institutions may reveal attender characteristics somewhat different than those suggested by nationwide participation studies.

Characteristics of the Broadway theater audience

Table 3.7 presents the results of a study of the Broadway theater audience that adopted the ambitious approach of a participation survey rather than the simpler method of questioning the audience in the hall. Responses were obtained from a representative sample of the population living within 50 miles of Manhattan. This procedure made possible a direct comparison of theatergoers with nontheatergoers. The former were defined as those who had attended a Broadway play or musical at least once in the previous two years. Theatergoers (second column) were found to be younger and better educated and to have higher income and higher occupational status than did nontheatergoers in the adult population of the New York region.

As explained, the composition of actual audiences depends on how often each class of "theatergoer" attends. Since the survey collected data on frequency of attendance, it was possible to weight the characteristics of theatergoers in the second column by those frequencies to yield the results for the "projected audience" in the third column, which can be thought of as the attributes of the aggregate audience for Broadway productions. Since frequency of attendance increases with income, educational attainment, and occupational status, the projected audience ranks even higher on those attributes than do theatergoers as a whole. The difference from nontheatergoers therefore increases. On the other hand, the difference in age composition as compared with nontheatergoers is *reduced* when frequency of attendance is taken into account. Although theatergoers are younger on average than nontheatergoers, frequency of attendance rises (albeit somewhat irregularly) with age, so that the average age of the projected audience is higher than that of theatergoers, although still lower than the average for the remainder of the population.

Audience characteristics over time

The question of audience age has long intrigued arts managers and economists because of its possible implication for future audience growth or decline. If an arts institution finds that its audience is either

Table 3.7. *Composition of the Broadway audience, 1979*

	Percent composition		
	Non theatergoers	Theatergoers	Projected audience
Age			
18–24	18	22	19
25–34	26	35	36
35–49	24	24	22
50 and over	32	19	23
Education			
Not high school graduate	21	5	4
High school graduate	41	29	21
College graduate	10	28	36
Graduate school	4	14	18
Income of household (dollars)			
Under 10,000	23	8	6
10 to 15,000	22	14	14
15 to 25,000	45	37	31
25,000 or above	10	41	49
Occupation			
Professional	16	30	37
Managerial	7	13	14
Technical or sales	11	12	10
Service or clerical	17	16	11
Blue collar	8	3	1
Race			
White	71	83	85
Black	19	11	10
Other nonwhite	10	6	5

Source: The League of New York Theatres and Producers, Inc., *A Study of the New York Audience for the Broadway Theatre*, January 1980.

relatively old or growing older, it may well take that as a warning of future decline in audience size, because the older people, who will eventually drop out of the audience, may not be replaced one for one by younger people newly attracted to it. On the other hand, an institution that now has a relatively young audience may take that as an augur of future growth, on the theory that it can hold onto the young people as they age, while still continuing to draw new young entrants.

Whatever the age profile of their current audience, all arts institutions would now like to attract new young attenders, because they believe that they will thus be building an audience for the future. Marketing strategies may be changing to accommodate that wish. In the 1960s and 1970s, performing arts companies emphasized subscription sales because they were thought to be the most cost-effective way to sell tickets and had the added advantage, so it was hoped, of building audience loyalty. (See discussion in Chapter 7.) But a subscription purchase requires a considerable one-time payment as well as advance planning of recreational choices. These requirements are now seen as a barrier to attracting younger attenders, as well as ethnic minorities, who cannot afford a large cash outlay in advance and may also wish to avoid the rigid commitment entailed by a subscription. For this potential audience, single ticket purchases are the preferred mode. According to Barbara Janowitz of Theatre Communications Group, theater managements in the non-profit sector are now "employing new marketing techniques to attract new and returning single-ticket buyers. . . . Rush tickets for the general public, pay-what-you-can performances, flexible multi-ticket passes . . . are just a few of the single-ticket marketing strategies newly set in place in many theatres across the country."[8]

Public policymakers as well as managers of theaters and other arts institutions have a strong interest in the composition of arts audiences. As we shall see in Chapters 11 and 13, "democratizing the arts" in the sense of increasing the participation of ethnic minorities and those having lower income and occupational status and less education than the traditional arts audience has been a U.S. public policy objective since the 1960s. Although one might hope that if such policies are successful, changes in audience composition would eventually show up in audience and participation studies, definitive evidence of policy impact is unlikely, given the many other social and economic factors that will have changed in the interim.

Indeed, audience composition appears to be ruled by a powerful inertia. In a survey of 270 existing audience studies published by the NEA in 1978, Paul DiMaggio, Michael Useem, and Paula Brown found no consistent evidence of change over time in any of the socioeconomic characteristics on which attention is usually focused, namely, age, gender, educational attainment, occupation, and income.[9] Change does seem to be occuring along one dimension, however: it is clear that audiences for some art forms have aged significantly in recent years. For example, Table 3.7, based on a participation study, showed that in

[8] Barbara Janowitz, "Theatre Facts '89," *American Theatre*, 7, no. 1 (April 1990): pp. 32–43, cited at 36.
[9] DiMaggio, Useem, and Brown, *Audience Studies of the Performing Arts and Museums*, p. 34.

1979 only 23 percent of the projected Broadway audience was aged 50 or more, while a comprehensive audience survey 12 years later found that figure had risen to 33 percent.[10] A similar trend is apparently taking place in the audience at symphonic concerts. It may be that the rapid relative growth of the arts industry since the early 1970s has been accompanied by other changes in audience composition that will only become evident in later audience and participation studies.

[10] League of American Theatres and Producers, Inc., *Profile of the Broadway Audience* (undated, but survey conducted between May 1990 and May 1991), p. 5.

PART II

The microeconomics of demand and supply

4

Consumer demand: an introduction

In Chapter 2 we described the growth of the audience for the arts and in Chapter 3 its size and character. It should be intuitively clear that its size, character, and rate of growth over time depend importantly on consumer behavior in the marketplace. Some consumers enjoy the arts enough to spend time and money on them. They make up the audience. Others, who differ in some way from the first group, do not enjoy them enough to become arts consumers. Are the same factors at work in both cases? What are they? We turn next to a systematic analysis of consumer choice and of what economists call consumer demand.

A number of assumptions underlie the economic analysis of consumer choice. First, because their incomes are limited, consumers cannot afford to satisfy all their material desires. They must therefore choose among the many possible objects of consumption. Second, these choices are made rationally. Consumers try to spend their income in such a way as to get the greatest possible total satisfaction from it. Economists use the term "utility" in place of "satisfaction," so in the jargon of economics, consumers behave as "utility maximizers." Finally, individual commodities are subject to the "law of diminishing marginal utility," to which we now turn.

Measuring the utility of consumption

Propositions about utility are most easily explained if we suppose that the buyer can actually measure the satisfaction obtained from each act of consumption in terms of units of utility. Let us call these units "utils." We thus assume that if you were to ask the potential purchaser of a compact disc how much utility he or she expected to obtain from that recording, the answer would be, let us say, "30 utils." Since the utility obtained from consuming one more unit of any com-

Table 4.1. *Utility of compact discs and concerts to a hypothetical consumer*

Units purchased annually	Compact discs		Concerts	
	Total utility	Marginal utility	Total utility	Marginal utility
0	0	—	0	—
1	50	50	60	60
2	95	45	110	50
3	135	40	150	40
4	170	35	180	30
5	200	30	200	20
6	225	25		
7	245	20		
8	260	15		
9	270	10		
10	275	5		

modity is defined by economists as its "marginal utility," the consumer is telling you, in effect, that the marginal utility of a compact disc is now 30 utils.[1]

We say "now" because the utility to be obtained from buying one more CD depends significantly on how many recordings the consumer already owns. Specifically, the law of diminishing marginal utility tells us that as a person consumes more of any one commodity, holding the consumption of other goods constant, the marginal utility of that commodity diminishes.

It is important to distinguish between the total utility (TU) obtained from any one good and its marginal utility (MU). Marginal utility is the change in total utility that results from a unit increase in consumption. In economics the Greek letter delta (Δ) denotes "change in." Accordingly, if we let Q stand for quantity of a particular good consumed, the marginal utility of that good to a consumer is defined as $\Delta TU/\Delta Q$, where $\Delta Q = 1$. In the usual case we assume that marginal utility remains positive as more units of a good are consumed. Hence, total utility rises. It is only marginal utility that diminishes as units consumed increase. These propositions are illustrated in Table 4.1, which shows a utility

[1] A more advanced treatment of the theory of consumer choice, known as indifference curve analysis, dispenses with the unrealistic assumption that utility can be measured in quantitative units such as utils and assumes only that consumers can rank goods in relation to one another as more desirable, less desirable, or equally desirable (hence "indifferent").

schedule for recordings purchased by a hypothetical consumer. It should be noted that because marginal utility is defined in terms of increments to total utility, the total utility of any quantity consumed necessarily equals the sum of the marginal utilities of the successive units. For example, in Table 4.1, the total utility of four CDs (170 utils) equals the sum of the marginal utilities of the first four purchased (50 + 45 + 40 + 35).

It is difficult to prove scientifically that the law of diminishing marginal utility is correct. Introspection, in fact, provides its strongest support. We are all consumers and will probably all acknowledge that the second pair of shoes adds less utility than the first, the third less than the second, and so on ad infinitum for every object of consumption. There is one other persuasive argument. If diminishing marginal utility were *not* the general case, we would expect some individuals, who find particular pleasure in one kind of good, to spend most of their income on it and consume little else. But we do not observe such behavior, except in cases of addiction, and those we conventionally treat as "pathological." In the normal case, diminishing marginal utility apparently holds.

Consumer budget optimization

If one accepts that consumers can measure the marginal utility of their own consumption, then it is a quite simple matter to explain how they make the choices that give them the greatest possible satisfaction from spending their income. They do so by following the rule for budget optimization, which says allocate income among commodities so that for each good purchased the ratio of marginal utility to price is the same. They thus obtain the same marginal utility for the last dollar spent on each good, which has the effect, as we shall show, of maximizing the total utility of spending.

Employing *MU* for marginal utility and *P* for price, the rule can be written algebraically as follows:

$$\frac{MU_x}{P_x} = \frac{MU_y}{P_y} = \cdots = \frac{MU_n}{P_n} \tag{4.1}$$

where x and y are among the n different goods consumed by an individual. In a competitive market, the single consumer cannot influence the prices at which goods are sold. How then can he or she bring about the stated equality? The answer is that the consumer can vary the quantity purchased of each good and thus bring the ratios into equality by causing the marginal utilities to change. We can demonstrate that the rule does, indeed, maximize the consumer's utility by showing that if he or she starts from a position where the ratios are *not* equal across all goods purchased, moving toward equality will produce a utility gain. Suppose that the consumer whose utility schedules are given in Table 4.1 currently purchases five CDs per year at a price of $10 each and attends four concerts at a cost of $20 per ticket. The table shows that the marginal utilities of the fifth CD and of the fourth concert both equal 30 utils. However, their prices are not equal, so we know that the consumer's budget is not optimized. The inequality of the ratios *MU/P* is shown in Equation 4.2:

$$\frac{MU}{P} : \overset{\text{CDs}}{\frac{30 \text{ utils}}{\$10}} \neq \overset{\text{Concerts}}{\frac{30 \text{ utils}}{\$20}} \neq \overset{\text{Other}}{\frac{2 \text{ utils}}{\$1}} \tag{4.2}$$

Let us assume that for all other goods purchased by this consumer, the ratio of marginal utility to price is 2 utils per dollar. This is shown by the right-hand term in Equation 4.2. To bring the ratios for CDs and concerts into line with all other goods, the consumer can attend one less concert and buy two more CDs per year. Table 4.1 shows that the marginal utility of a concert thus rises to 40 utils, while that of a CD falls to 20 utils. Prices remain the same, so the consumer saves $20 on concert tickets, which is just enough to pay for two more CDs. Total spending is therefore unchanged, but the consumer has gained utility: giving up the fourth concert reduced welfare by 30 utils, but buying a sixth and seventh CD added 45 utils, producing a net gain of 15. The consumer's final position, which satisfies the rule for budget optimization, is as follows:

$$\frac{MU}{P} : \overset{\text{CDs}}{\frac{20 \text{ utils}}{\$10}} = \overset{\text{Concerts}}{\frac{40 \text{ utils}}{\$20}} = \overset{\text{Other}}{\frac{2 \text{ utils}}{\$1}} \tag{4.3}$$

The commonsense meaning of the optimization rule should now be clear. If the ratios of marginal utility to price are not equal for all goods purchased, take dollars away from goods where marginal utility per dollar is lower and spend them on goods where marginal utility per dollar is higher. Obviously, such rearrangements will always produce a net gain.

Deriving demand curves

The hypothetical consumer whose optimum budget is given by Equation 4.3 obtains two utils per dollar for the marginal unit purchased in every line of actual consumption. Keeping that ratio in mind, we can

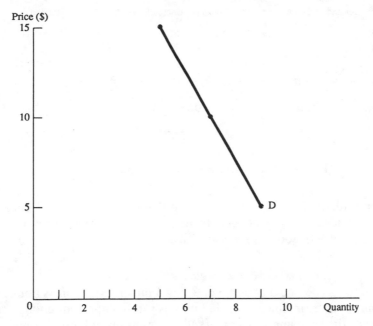

Figure 4.1. Demand curve for an individual consumer.

use Table 4.1 to show the effect of changes in price on the quantity of CDs purchased. Taking Equation 4.3 as the starting point, we find that at a price of $10 per unit, the consumer obtains two utils per dollar by buying seven CDs. Suppose the price now falls to $5. CDs have become a better buy. We know that the consumer will want to purchase more of them. Table 4.1 tells us how many more: in order to maintain a ratio of two utils per dollar at the margin, the consumer will now buy nine CDs per year. Reversing direction, if the price of CDs rose to $15 the consumer (in order still to obtain two utils per dollar at the margin) would choose to cut purchases to five CDs per year.

Obviously, given our hypothetical consumer's utility schedule and the desired number of utils per dollar to be obtained at the margin, we can predict the number of CDs that he or she will purchase at any given price.[2] When these prices and quantities are plotted on a diagram such as Figure 4.1, they show what economists call the demand curve of one

---

[2] The analysis has been simplified by ignoring the fact that when money income is held constant, a change in the price of any good purchased by the consumer will alter the level of the consumer's *real* income, thus producing effects on consumption in addition to those caused by the price change.

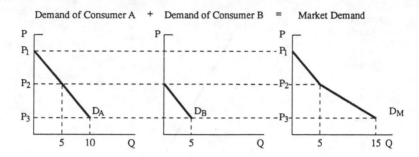

Figure 4.2. Deriving a market demand curve.

individual for compact discs (here denoted *D*). Demand curves characteristically slope downward to the right, since consumers purchase
more of any good as its price falls.

The market demand curve

The demand curve of a single buyer, however, is not usually of
much interest, since a single buyer is rarely important enough to influence the outcome in any market. Far more useful in economic analysis
is the aggregate demand curve of all consumers of a particular product.
That curve is often referred to as the market demand curve, in the sense
that it sums up the demand brought to bear in the market by all consumers of the product in question. The market demand curve is literally
the sum of the relevant individual curves. In Figure 4.2 we present the
demand curves for compact discs of two individuals, A and B, and show
how they (and, by extension, any number of individual curves) are added
up to obtain the market curve. The latter shows the aggregate quantity
of compact discs consumers will buy at any given price. To obtain it we
must add up the quantities that all individuals will buy at each price. In
Figure 4.2 we do that graphically by adding horizontally the quantities
demanded by A and B at selected prices and plotting the sum as the
market demand in the right-hand panel.

Demand, supply, and the determination of price

While developing the theory of consumer choice, we treated
price as a "given." That was appropriate since the individual buyer does
have to accept whatever prices are established in the marketplace. Now,
however, we wish to explain *how* competitive markets establish prices.
The answer will turn out to be that prices are determined by the inter-

action of supply and demand, and in order to explain that process we require a supply curve as well as a demand curve.

Just as a market demand curve shows the aggregate quantity that consumers will purchase at any given price, the market supply curve indicates the aggregate quantity that producers will offer for sale at each of those prices. Demand curves slope downward to the right because consumers will buy more as the price falls. Supply curves, especially in the short run, slope upward to the right because producers will increase output and offer more for sale as the price rises. A general explanation for the upward slope is that at higher prices it becomes profitable to extend output by using productive resources in combinations that would not pay their way at lower prices. For example, a manufacturer might hire overtime labor at premium prices to increase output when prices are high enough to cover the added cost.

It must be pointed out that, in the long run, market supply curves may well be flat rather than upward sloping. Given sufficient time to adjust, producers will be able to expand output by replicating the most efficient production methods rather than by resorting to such expensive expedients as overtime labor. Indeed, the long-run supply curve of an industry is likely to be upward sloping only if the industry's expansion pushes up the prices of its inputs, as might occur, for example, if the supply of some inputs is constrained by natural scarcity. At this point, however, we are concerned only with the short run and can therefore plausibly assume that supply curves are upward-sloping. Because both demand and supply curves show a relationship between quantity and price, they can be plotted on a single diagram, with price on the vertical axis and quantity on the horizontal. Figure 4.3 shows hypothetical market demand and supply curves for compact discs and provides a simple graphic solution to the problem of price determination. If the market is freely competitive, the price will tend to settle at the level where quantity supplied equals quantity demanded. Those quantities are equal at the point on the diagram where the supply and demand curves intersect. The corresponding market price is P_e, and quantity sold, Q_e.

P_e is also referred to as the "equilibrium price" in the sense that if the price of CDs is for some reason displaced from that level, market forces are automatically set in motion that tend to bring it back to P_e. The process is illustrated in Figure 4.3. If the price were at P_1 (higher than P_e), producers would offer Q_{S1} CDs for sale (corresponding to the point of intersection of P_1 with the supply curve), but buyers would purchase only Q_{D1} (as shown by the intersection of P_1 with the demand curve). Quantity supplied would exceed quantity demanded by an amount labeled "excess supply" on the diagram. In order to move this

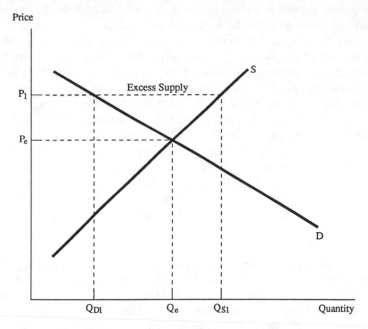

Figure 4.3. Supply, demand, and market equilibrium.

unwanted excess off their shelves, suppliers would begin to lower their prices in a competitive process that would end only when equilibrium was restored at price P_e. By a perfectly analogous argument, if the price were for some reason at a level *below* P_e (not shown in the diagram) quantity demanded would exceed quantity supplied, giving rise to "excess demand" in the market. Suppliers would find that they could not fill all their orders for CDs at the lower price and would take advantage of the opportunity to raise prices in a process that would continue until the level rose to P_e. We will show in Chapter 11 that if all markets were perfectly competitive, price–quantity solutions such as P_e, Q_e in Figure 4.3 would be socially optimal in the sense that resources are thereby allocated among alternative uses in the proportions that best satisfy consumer wants. It is precisely that optimizing feature of perfect competition that makes it so attractive in the eyes of many economists.

Ticket pricing on Broadway

Given the rough edges of the real world, markets do not always operate with the frictionless freedom assumed in economic models. Ticket pricing on Broadway provides an instructive example of the inefficiencies that develop when market price is not allowed to move freely to its equilibrium level. In order to analyze the problem, however, it is necessary to adjust the supply and demand model to reflect the special circumstances of the performing arts. It is an obvious characteristic of any single production in the performing arts that in the short run the supply of tickets that can be offered exactly equals the number of seats in the house where the performance takes place (assuming that no standing room tickets are made available). Unlike the standard case in which the quantity supplied increases as price rises, so that the supply curve slopes upward to the right, the supply curve of seats for a single performing arts production is a vertical straight line, at a quantity equal to the capacity of the house.

It is a peculiar feature of ticket pricing in the Broadway theater that prices are established before opening night and are not altered thereafter, even though the producers do not know in advance of the opening what the demand for tickets will be. The resulting difficulties can be demonstrated with supply and demand analysis. We must emphasize that the following analysis does *not* purport to show how theatrical producers choose the profit-maximizing ticket price for a new offering. That analysis will be presented in Chapter 7. At this point we look only at the short-run effects of rigid ticket-pricing decisions without explaining how the prices were arrived at.

The problem of inflexible ticket prices

Figure 4.4 illustrates the case in which producers have underestimated the demand for a play that turns out to be a smash hit. The play opens in a relatively small theater where the number of seats is Q_{S1}, and the supply curve is therefore S_1. In advance of opening night, the producers set the price at P_1. When the play opens they discover that the daily demand for tickets is represented by demand curve D_A. Consequently, at a price of P_1 there is an excess demand for seats, equal to $Q_{D1} - Q_{S1}$. Given the high level of demand, they could have charged a price of P_2 and still filled the house (see point e). By holding the price down to P_1, they are sacrificing potential revenue. The lost revenue is equal to the price difference $(P_2 - P_1)$ multiplied by the number of tickets that can be sold (Q_{S1}). But the product $Q_{S1} \times (P_2 - P_1)$ is also the area of the shaded rectangle P_2efP_1; hence, that rectangle measures the lost revenue. (It is a useful property of supply–demand diagrams that revenues, i.e., sales proceeds, can be precisely measured by areas.)

One solution to the problem illustrated in Figure 4.4 would be to move the play into a larger theater. For example, in a house with capacity S_2, the producers could satisfy all the excess daily demand that existed

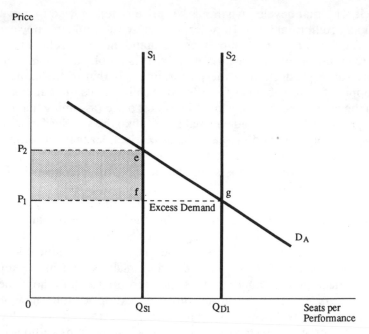

Figure 4.4. Excess demand for tickets: a Broadway hit.

at price P_1 in the smaller house and take in the additional revenue measured by the rectangle $Q_{S1}fgQ_{D1}$, while incurring very little additional production cost.

But perhaps a theater with capacity greater than S_1 is not available. In that case, why don't the producers of this smash hit raise prices to P_2 after the play has opened? Economists have often asked that question, since they like to see the price system operating efficiently and do not expect business people, who are profit maximizers, to stand in the way. The answer, apparently, is that tradition runs against altering prices (either up or down) after a play has opened. The result, in the case of smash hits, however, has occasionally been to create a black market in tickets to the underpriced show. In Figure 4.4, the unsatisfied customers $(Q_{D1} - Q_{S1})$ are willing to pay prices well above P_1 to obtain seats. A customer able to buy a ticket at the box office for P_1 could resell it on the black market (in violation of New York state law) at a substantial profit. In fact, for hit shows, especially musicals, a well-organized underground ticket market developed, the profits on which came to be

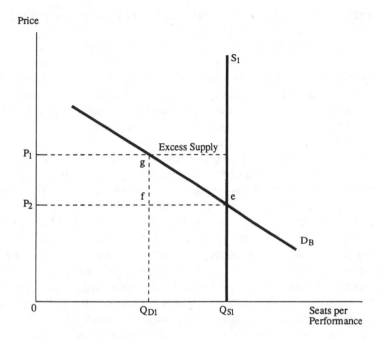

Figure 4.5. Excess supply of tickets: a Broadway flop.

known as "ice."[3] One of the irrational results of this arrangement was that substantial revenues that might have accrued through the box office to the producers, authors, composers, and others with an ownership interest in the production instead went to speculators and "scalpers" who had no such connection.

Less formal black markets often develop for rock concert tickets, if prices are set below the level (such as P_2 in Figure 4.4) at which quantity demanded would just equal the number of seats available. If, as frequently happens, the concert is sold out in advance, ticket holders can dispose of seats outside the gate at a substantial profit to those who made up the "excess demand" for seats at the lower price.

Next consider the case, illustrated in Figure 4.5, of a play that is *not* a smash hit. Ticket price P_1 is established before the play opens. After the run begins the producers realize they cannot sell all the available tickets at that price, given the demand curve D_B. There is an excess

---

[3] See the discussion in Thomas Gale Moore, *The Economics of the American Theater* (Durham, N.C.: Duke University Press, 1968), pp. 84–88, 134–38.

supply equal to $Q_{S1} - Q_{D1}$. Why don't they lower the price to P_2 at which level all seats could be filled?

Again, traditional practice dictates not changing prices after the show has opened. In the case of a price reduction, there are two supporting arguments. First, those who bought tickets in advance at the higher price might be angered to find themselves sitting next to people who paid less for similar seats to the same performance. Second, lowering the price in order to sell more tickets involves both gains and losses in revenue. The additional tickets sold at price P_2 would bring in revenue equal to the area of rectangle $Q_{D1}feQ_{S1}$. However, reducing the price from P_1 to P_2 would entail a loss of revenue equal to the area of rectangle P_1gfP_2 on the seats that could have been sold at the higher price. Whether total revenue rises or falls therefore depends on which rectangle is larger, and *that* in turn depends on how responsive quantity sold is to the fall in price. If, as we assume in Figure 4.5, it is fairly responsive, a price reduction would produce a net gain in total revenue. (The responsiveness of quantity demanded to a change in price is measured by the price elasticity of demand, a highly useful gauge that will be described in the next chapter. As the attentive reader will discover, we have here assumed that the demand for theater tickets is "price elastic.")

In recent years Broadway theater producers have agreed to a two-price system that goes a long way toward solving the problem of price reductions. At noon each day, all theaters put their unsold tickets for the day's performances on sale at half price at a booth in Times Square and at two other locations in the city. From the producer's point of view this is probably better than an across-the-board price reduction. Referring back to Figure 4.5, what they accomplish, in effect, is to maintain price P_1 for advance sales and charge something less than P_1 for the remaining unsold tickets. This is a form of "price discrimination" – that is, selling the same product at different prices to different customers.[4] But it may benefit customers as well as producers. Those who want assured seating, planned for in advance, can obtain it by paying the full price. Those who want to save money and are willing to take their chances at the last minute, may be able to attend at half price.

The determinants of demand

The analysis up to this point has emphasized the effect of prices on consumer choice. But there are several other factors that importantly influence demand for a particular good, including the level of consumer

---

[4] A full analysis of the possibilities of price discrimination can be found in any textbook of microeconomic theory.

income, consumers' tastes, and the prices of related goods. We shall examine these in turn.

Income

In most cases (with exceptions to be noted later), consumers' demand for a particular commodity or service will increase as their incomes rise. We showed in Chapter 3 that the average middle-class family attends the live performing arts more frequently than does a poor family, and the average wealthy family more frequently still. Such a statement looks at the matter "cross-sectionally," that is, by comparing families with different incomes at a *moment* in time. But a similar relationship was found in Chapter 2 when we looked at consumption *through* time, that is, longitudinally: as the average level of family income rises in a society that is enjoying economic growth, the demand for attendance at the live performing arts increases. Since income is an obviously important determinant of consumer behavior, we shall pay a good deal of attention to its influence on the demand for art and culture.

Taste

Economists use the term "taste" as a shorthand way of referring to the system of preferences that so clearly affects the pattern of every consumer's demand. To take a simple example, some consumers prefer white bread to whole wheat or rye, while some prefer rolls to bread. Obviously, the aggregate of these preferences influences the demand for white bread as compared with the other types, or of bread compared with rolls. Analogously, in the realm of culture some consumers prefer the visual to the performing arts, some enjoy the theater but have no taste for music, and some watch television in preference to attending any sort of arts activity. We all recognize that in the aggregate these preferences must strongly affect the dimensions of our cultural life.

The tradition in economics has been to assume that consumer taste cannot be explained and that it is just as well not to try. This attitude is consistent with the philosophy of liberal capitalism, which most U.S. economists probably endorse, namely, that it is an important function of an economy to respond efficiently to consumer preferences. If consumers want to wear hats, it is desirable that business produce hats. If tastes change and fewer hats are wanted, fewer will be produced, and that's all right, too. There is no need to agonize about the virtue of changes in taste. Whatever consumers want (provided it does them no serious harm), they should get. Thus, economists do not usually investigate taste. They simply treat it as a "given," that is, as an ultimate datum for the economy.[5]

The case of the arts is somewhat different. A good many people, including a respectable number of economists, think it would be desirable to stimulate the consumption of art. (We examine their reasons in Chapter 11.) Art is said to be an "acquired taste," in the sense that you have to be exposed to it in order to develop the taste, and perhaps exposed under the right circumstances and for rather a long time. Therefore, to stimulate consumption, so the argument goes, we must help people to acquire the taste both by making the arts accessible and by directly stimulating exposure. The cultivation of taste is such an interesting and important question in the economics of art and culture that we devote considerable attention to it in the last two chapters of this book.

Prices of related goods

Every consumer good has substitutes. Demand for the good itself is affected not only by its own price but also by the prices of the substitutes. The quantity of tea consumers will buy depends in part on the price of coffee, the quantity of pork on the price of beef. Likewise, in the realm of art and culture the demand for symphony tickets is affected by the price of such substitutes as compact discs or the price of admission to other entertainments. When two goods are substitutes in consumption, the relation between the price of one and demand for the other is always positive: the higher the price of admission to theatrical productions, the greater the demand for symphony tickets. Indeed, we could logically reverse that statement: we know that two goods are substitutes if empirical studies show that the price of one is positively correlated with demand for the other.

In many instances one consumer good is necessarily (or often) used in combination with a particular other good. In such cases, the relationship is said to be complementary. For example, the demand for automobiles depends in part on the price of the complementary good gasoline. In the field of musical recordings, the demand for compact discs is significantly affected by the price of the compact disc player that is its essential complement. In the case of the performing arts, there is an important complementary relationship between the demand for tickets and the *non*ticket costs of attending a performance, such as the costs

---

[5] A notable exception is John Kenneth Galbraith, who emphasizes the role of producers in generating "tastes" for the goods they wish to sell. See his *The Affluent Society* (Boston: Houghton Mifflin, 1958), chap. 11.

of transportation, parking, and restaurant meals. Thomas Gale Moore, in his well-known study of the Broadway theater, found that, on average, complementary expenditures accounted for about half the cost of an evening at a Broadway play or musical.[6] The demand for a given good always moves in the opposite direction to the price of its complement: if the nonticket costs of an evening at the theater rise, the demand for theater tickets falls.

A hypothetical demand function

The connection between demand for a good or service and the factors determining it can be seen most clearly if the relationship is written out in the form of a demand equation or, as it is often called, a "demand function." In this section we construct a hypothetical demand equation for theater tickets.

The equation is written in the following general form:

$$Q_t = a + bP_t + cY + dP_s + eP_c \tag{4.4}$$

The variable on the left-hand side is the "dependent variable," in this case the quantity of theater tickets demanded per time period. The premise underlying the analysis is that the value of this dependent variable is explained by the factors written on the right-hand side. These are the "independent" or "explanatory" variables. The variables have the following definitions:

Q_t = quantity of theater tickets demanded per time period
P_t = the price of theater tickets
Y = average annual per capita income
P_s = weighted average price of substitutes (movies, concerts, spectator sports, etc.)
P_c = composite price of complementary goods (transportation to theater, dinner out, etc.)
a = constant term

$\left.\begin{array}{l} b \\ c \\ d \\ e \end{array}\right\}$ = coefficients measuring change in value of the dependent variable per unit change in the respective independent variables

Note that there is no variable to measure taste, even though we have argued that taste is a fundamental determinant of demand. That is because taste is not truly quantifiable. Instead of trying to represent

[6] Moore, *Economics of the American Theater*, table V.9, p. 87.

Table 4.2. *Hypothetical values of variables for Equation 4.4*

	Case 1	Case 2
Independent Variables		
P_t	15	15
Y	3,000	4,000
P_s	16	16
P_c	12	12
Parameters		
a (constant)	65,000	65,000
b	−5,000	−5,000
c	40	40
d	1,000	1,000
e	−1,600	−1,600
Value of Q_t		
calculated from Equation 4.4 (See Table 4.3)	106,800	146,800

taste indirectly by the use of some proxy such as educational attainment, the analysis proceeds on the assumption that *given* the state of consumers' preferences, that is, the tastes that underlie their choices in the marketplace, the quantity of theater tickets demanded will be determined by this equation. If tastes were to change for any reason, the value of the constant term and/or of the coefficients in the equation would change, too.

To put Equation 4.4 to work, we must supply hypothetical values for all the independent variables and their coefficients and calculate the resulting value of the dependent variable, Q_t. Alternative sets of hypothetical values are shown in Table 4.2. In Case 1 we assume the price of a theater ticket is $15, average annual per capita income is $3,000, the average price of substitute entertainments is $16, and nonticket costs of attending the theater average $12 per person. The coefficient b has an assumed value of −5,000, indicating that for every $1 increase in ticket prices, 5,000 fewer theater tickets will be sold. Coefficient c has a hypothetical value of 40, which means that for every $1 increase in per capita income, ticket sales will rise by 40 (or for every $100 increase, by 4,000.) Note that the sign on coefficent d is positive, while that on coefficient e is negative, showing that sales of theater tickets rise when the price of substitute entertainments goes up but fall with a rise in the price of complementary goods. When Equation 4.4 is evaluated employing the hypothetical numbers assumed in Case 1, the quantity of theater tickets demanded is 106,800. (See Table 4.3 for calculations.)

We are now in a position to explain more fully the meaning of demand

Table 4.3. *Calculating quantity demanded from a demand function*

	Value of terms assumed in Case 1	Contribution to value of dependent variable
Components of Equation 4.4		
a	65,000	65,000
$b \times P_t$	$-5,000 \times 15$	$-75,000$
$c \times Y$	$40 \times 3,000$	120,000
$d \times P_s$	$1,000 \times 16$	16,000
$e \times P_c$	$-1,600 \times 12$	$-19,200$
Dependent variable		
Q_t (sum of the above contributions)		106,800

curves in economics. A demand curve shows the relationship between price and quantity demanded under the assumption of ceteris paribus, that is to say, when all other variables that might affect demand are held constant. In general, the important other variables are precisely those included in Equation 4.4, namely, income and the prices of sub-stitutes and complements, plus taste, which, as already explained, is not included in the equation because it is not directly measurable.

A particular demand curve for theater tickets is implied by the re-lationships expressed in Equation 4.4 in combination with the values of the coefficients and independent variables assumed in Case 1. In Table 4.3 we have already calculated one point on that curve: when $P_t = 15$, $Q_t = 106,800$. To sketch out the rest of the curve, one could reevaluate Equation 4.4 at various values of P_t, while holding all other variables constant at their Case 1 levels. For example, if P_t falls to $10, Q_t rises to 131,800. However, it would be tedious to plot the entire curve one point at a time. Accordingly, we proceed as follows. An equation for the demand curve in question can be calculated from the information in Table 4.3. The values of all the terms in that table, excluding Q_t and bP_t, add up to 181,800. We can therefore write the following demand equation:

$$Q_t = 181,800 - 5,000P_t \tag{4.5}$$

We know that this demand curve is linear (i.e., a straight line), because each time price falls by $1, Q_t rises by the constant increment of 5,000 indicated by the value of coefficient b. Furthermore, the intercepts of this curve on a price–quantity diagram (see Figure 4.6) can be obtained by analyzing Equation 4.5: if P_t falls to zero, quantity demanded rises

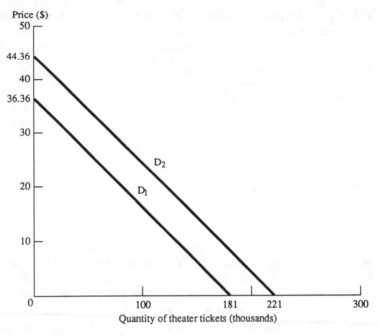

Figure 4.6. Demand curves derived from a demand function.

to 181,800. That is the intercept on the horizontal axis. On the other hand, if P_t rises to $36.36, quantity demanded falls to zero (since 181,800 − 5,000 × 36.36 = 0). That is the intercept on the vertical axis. Since the demand function is known to be linear, we can connect the two intercepts with a straight line, yielding demand curve D_1 in Figure 4.6. To summarize, we have now plotted a demand curve that shows how many theater tickets can be sold at any given price, assuming that all other relevant variables remain at the levels specified in Case 1. The next step is to ask, What happens if the value of one of those variables now changes?

Shifting of demand curves

The answer is straightforward. If one of the variables previously impounded under the restraint of ceteris paribus now changes its value, the demand *function* (Equation 4.4) necessarily yields a different demand *curve*. Economists usually refer to this as a "shift of the demand curve." The curve is said to "shift up" if demand increases, "shift down" if demand decreases. By observing the signs on the independent variables in Equation 4.4, one can see at once which way it will shift for a given change in any of the variables. The sign on income (Y) is positive, meaning that quantity demanded rises with income. Hence, if average per capita income increases, the demand curve will shift up. An increase in the price of substitutes (P_s) will also cause an upward shift, while a rise in the price of complementary goods (P_c) will cause the demand curve to go down.

In Table 4.2 the values listed for the independent variables in Case 2 are identical in all respects with those in Case 1 except that income per capita has increased from $3,000 to $4,000 per year. This $1,000 increase, when multiplied by 40 (the value of the income coefficient, c) adds 40,000 to the number of theater tickets demanded at the still unchanged values of the other variables. Q_t consequently rises from 106,800 to 146,800.

The new demand curve, D_2, is also plotted in Figure 4.6. As predicted, it lies above D_1. Because, on the average, their incomes have increased, consumers are now willing to buy more tickets than previously at any given price. The equation of the new curve is

$$Q_t = 221,800 - 5,000P_t \qquad (4.6)$$

Supply and demand with shifting demand curves

What effect will shifting demand curves have on market price and quantity sold? The answer clearly depends on the shape of the relevant supply curve. Figure 4.3 incorporated a hypothetical supply curve for compact discs drawn sloping upward to the right, to reflect the fact that in the short run increased output usually entails higher unit costs for suppliers. In Figure 4.7 we again assume an upward-sloping supply curve for CDs. At a given level of income as well as prices of substitutes and complements, and with a given set of consumer preferences (or taste), the demand for CDs is shown by demand curve D_1. The market is in equilibrium at price P_1 and quantity Q_1. If, now, the average level of income should rise, consumer demand would increase, as shown by an upward shift of the demand curve to D_2. Out of their larger incomes, consumers would be willing to pay higher prices than previously for any given quantity of recordings. Equilibrium price and quantity sold would rise to P_2 and Q_2 as producers increased output to meet the greater demand. It might seem puzzling that quantity demanded would now be greater than before $(Q_2 > Q_1)$ even though price has increased $(P_2 > P_1)$. This does *not*, however, contradict the earlier finding that quantity demanded *falls* when price *rises*. That conclusion was qualified by the assumption of "all other things being the same"

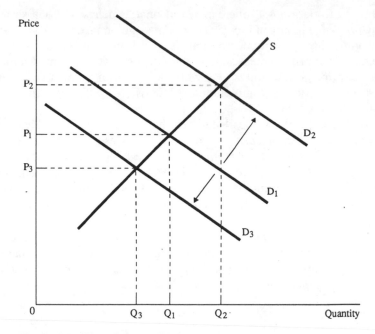

Figure 4.7. Changing equilibria with a shifting demand curve.

and referred to a movement *along a given demand curve,* in fact, along the specific curve that was consistent with the assumed underlying conditions. In the present case, we specifically assume a *change* in one of the underlying conditions. Consequently, the demand curve shifts. Instead of seeing movement along a given demand curve, we observe a series of equilibrium points generated by the movement of a demand curve along a given *supply curve.* Consumers willingly pay a higher price for a larger quantity because their incomes have increased.

By analogous arguments, supply and demand analysis can also show the expected effects of demand curve shifts caused by changes in the levels of other independent variables such as prices of substitutes and complements. For example, suppose that an increase in government subsidies to musical organizations causes the number of concerts to rise and the price of concert tickets to fall. Attendance at live concerts is a substitute for buying recorded music. At the lower ticket price, some consumers will attend more concerts and buy fewer CDs. The demand curve for CDs will shift down along the supply curve, for example, to D_3 in Figure 4.7. When the market reaches a new equilibrium, the price of CDs will have fallen to P_3 and the quantity demanded to Q_3.

Although consumer taste is not directly measurable, supply and demand analysis can also show, at least in terms of direction of movement, how a change in taste will affect market price and quantity sold. For example, suppose that as a result of the cultivation of taste, consumers began to substitute time spent listening to music for time devoted to watching television. The demand for compact discs would shift upward, perhaps from D_1 to D_2. At any given level of CD prices (and of other variables, including income and the prices of substitutes and complements), consumers would now buy more CDs than before, and their price would tend to rise.

Figure 4.7, however, depicts only the short-run outcome. In the long run, as suggested earlier, the supply curve of the recording industry might be horizontal rather than upward-sloping. In that case, as the taste for music increased and the demand curve for CDs shifted to the right, the quantity supplied would increase while the price remained more or less constant.

What if many variables change simultaneously?

In the real world, economic change never occurs in only one variable at a time. Discussion of actual events is usually made difficult by the fact that so many relevant forces are changing simultaneously. It is a great virtue of supply and demand analysis that it allows us to focus on one change at a time and indicates clearly the expected effects of each.

The foregoing discussion was limited to changes occuring on the demand side of the market. The demand curve was allowed to shift, while the supply curve remained fixed. To analyze other questions, it would be appropriate to hold demand conditions constant, while shifting the supply curve. One such application will be developed in Chapter 14 when we analyze the effect of a change in labor supply on the output of a theater company. (See Figure 14.3 and the accompanying discussion.)

Summary

In this chapter we have explained the elementary theory of consumer demand, discussed the principal determinants of demand, including prices, consumer income, and taste, and shown how supply and demand interact in the market to establish prices and determine the quantity of output for all commercially traded goods. The relevance of supply and demand analysis to the arts was illustrated with some problems in theater ticket pricing. However, the full analysis of factors affecting supply in the arts is reserved for later chapters: for the performing arts, Chapters 6 and 7; for the fine arts, Chapter 9; and for performing artists in the labor market, Chapter 14.

Because the supply and demand model is so flexible, it can be used to investigate a remarkably wide range of questions in economics. Many of these, drawn from the world of art and culture, will be examined later in this volume.

5

The characteristics of arts demand and their policy implications

The nature of demand equations and the demand curves that can be derived from them was explained in the preceding chapter. We now wish to take a closer look, to see what that economic apparatus can tell us about the response of consumer demand to changes in the forces on which it depends. We begin by defining a highly useful property called elasticity. Derivable from a demand equation, this measure can be employed to gauge the response of the dependent variable – quantity demanded – to changes in any of the independent variables, such as price or income, that influence it. The price elasticity of demand, for example, tells us how sensitive the consumption of a good or service is to changes in its price. Thus, the manager of a symphony orchestra who knew the size of the price elasticity of demand for its tickets could predict whether raising ticket prices would increase the orchestra's income or, to the contrary, would so discourage attendance that income would actually drop.

The price elasticity of demand

The price elasticity of demand (ϵ_p) is defined as the percent change in quantity demanded that results from a given percent change in price, all other things remaining the same. Using the Greek letter delta (Δ) to signify "change in," the formula can be written algebraically as

$$\epsilon_p = \frac{\Delta Q/Q}{\Delta P/P} \tag{5.1}$$

For some purposes, it is convenient to rearrange Equation 5.1 to read

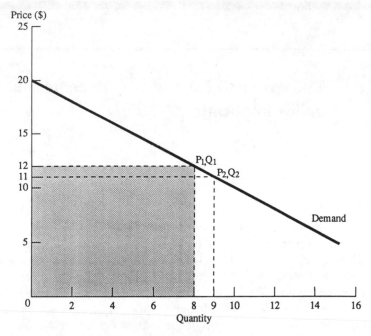

Figure 5.1. Demand curve and total revenue.

$$\epsilon_p = \frac{\Delta Q}{\Delta P} \times \frac{P}{Q} \tag{5.2}$$

If price changes from P_1 to P_2 and, as a result, quantity demanded moves from Q_1 to Q_2, the formula can also be written as

$$\epsilon_p = \frac{(Q_2 - Q_1)/Q_1}{(P_2 - P_1)/P_1} \tag{5.3}$$

since, in that case, $P_2 - P_1 = \Delta P$, and $Q_2 - Q_1 = \Delta Q$.

Using Equation 5.3 we can illustrate the calculation of price elasticity when the values of P and Q at two points on a demand curve are known. Consider the hypothetical case illustrated in Figure 5.1. At a price of \$12, quantity sold is 8; when price falls to \$11, quantity sold rises to 9. Thus, $P_1 = 12$ and $P_2 - P_1 = -1$; $Q_1 = 8$ and $Q_2 - Q_1 = 1$. Putting these numbers into Equation 5.1, we obtain

$$\epsilon_p = \frac{1/8}{-1/12} = -1.5$$

Price and quantity always change in opposite directions along a demand curve. As a result, ΔP and ΔQ always have opposite signs, and the value of the price elasticity of demand, using any of the previous formulas, is always negative. However, since it is confusing to compare negative numbers in terms of "more" or "less," as will have to be done in discussing elasticity, we will hereafter follow the convention of dropping the negative sign.

It is a great virtue of all elasticities that as the ratio of one percentage of change to another, they are "dimensionless numbers." Consequently, one can, for example, compare the price elasticity of demand for gasoline with that for electric power without worrying about the fact that gasoline is measured in gallons and electricity in kilowatt hours.

As we have already indicated, the price elasticity of demand tells you how sensitive the demand for a commodity is to changes in its price. In the hypothetical case being described, quantity demanded turns out to be quite sensitive to price changes since an 8⅓ percent price decline induces a 12½ percent increase in units purchased. The range of possible values of price elasticity is divided by economists into three classes, as follows:

$\epsilon > 1$ is called "elastic demand"
$\epsilon = 1$ is called "unitary elasticity"
$\epsilon < 1$ is called "inelastic demand"

When demand is elastic ($\epsilon > 1$), the percent change in quantity *exceeds* the percent change in price, indicating that quantity purchased is quite sensitive to price.

When demand is *inelastic* ($\epsilon < 1$), quantity purchased changes by a *smaller* percentage than price does, indicating that demand is relatively *in*sensitive to price.

When demand has unitary elasticity, the percent change in quantity purchased exactly equals the percent change in price but is, of course, in the opposite direction.

Explaining differences in price elasticity

What lies behind these differences? Why is the demand for one good price elastic, for another inelastic? One significant explanation is that elasticity rises with the availability of substitutes. The more, or the closer, the available substitutes for a given good or service, the more readily consumers will switch to something else when the price of that good or service rises relative to other prices. Thus, price elasticity is always higher for a subcategory like pork, for which there are good substitutes within the larger class of meat, than it is for meat as a whole. Likewise, the price elasticity of demand is higher for meat than for food, for there are many substitutes for meat within the category of food, but none for food itself. For the same reasons we would expect the price elasticity of demand to be higher for the tickets of a single live performing arts company than for the live performing arts industry as a whole, and higher for that industry as a whole than for the entertainment sector, broadly defined to include movies and spectator sports, as well as live performance. This point will become relevant later in the chapter.

Price elasticity and total revenue

It is important to note the connection between price elasticity and the total revenue (or gross receipts) generated by sale of the commodity in question. Total revenue is simply price × quantity. In the hypothetical case of elastic demand shown in Figure 5.1, total revenue was \$96 at the higher price of \$12 (\$12 × 8 = \$96) but rose to \$99 when price was reduced to \$11 (\$11 × 9 = \$99.) This illustrates the rule that when demand is price elastic, total revenue rises if price falls. (Reading the illustration in the opposite direction, one can also see that total revenue falls if price rises.) There is a commonsense explanation for this result. A price fall, in and of itself, would have the effect of reducing revenue. But there is an offsetting gain because quantity rises. However, the value of ϵ_p is greater than one precisely because the percentage rise in quantity is *greater* than the percentage decline in price. Therefore, the gain on quantity outweighs the loss on price, and total revenue increases as price falls.

If demand is price inelastic, on the other hand, total revenue falls when price falls and rises when price rises. Again, the explanation is straightforward. The value of ϵ_p is less than one because the percent change in quantity is smaller than the percent change in price. Hence, if price declines, the loss on price exceeds the gain on quantity, and total revenue falls.

Between elastic demand and inelastic demand lies the case of unitary elasticity. This has the interesting property that total revenue is unchanged when price changes, because the percent changes in quantity and price are exactly offsetting.

It is a useful feature of a supply–demand diagram that because its dimensions are price and quantity, rectangular areas in the quadrant measure dollar revenues. In Figure 5.1 the dimensions of the shaded rectangle are $P = 12$, $Q = 8$, making the rectangle's area 96, which also equals the total revenue when price = \$12.

Although elastic demand curves are usually depicted as fairly flat and inelastic curves as steep, it would be a mistake to equate the slope of a demand curve with its elasticity. The former is measured by the ratio $\Delta P/\Delta Q$. The latter contains the inverse of that ratio and in addition the ratio P/Q. (See Equation 5.2.) A straight-line demand curve, such as the hypothetical examples drawn in this and the preceding chapter, has the same slope throughout. Its elasticity, however, varies from point to point, as one can deduce from the fact that the P/Q term necessarily changes value as one moves along the curve. Indeed, below a price of \$10, the demand curve drawn in Figure 5.1 becomes inelastic.[1]

Price, total revenue, and marginal revenue

In order to analyze the behavior of producing firms (whether in the arts or elsewhere), as we shall do in Chapter 7, it is essential to understand the precise connection between changes in price, the elasticity of demand, and change in total revenue. The term "marginal revenue" is used to describe the change in total revenue that occurs when price is reduced sufficiently to sell one more unit of output. If we denote total revenue as *TR,* and marginal revenue as *MR,* and take ΔQ to be a one-unit change in quantity sold, then in algebraic terms, $MR = \Delta TR/\Delta Q$. In the case illustrated in Figure 5.1, reducing the price from \$12 to \$11 increased the quantity sold by one unit and raised total revenue from \$96 to \$99. Hence, the marginal revenue obtained by selling the last unit was \$3.

The derivation of marginal revenue is illustrated in Table 5.1, which contains data for the hypothetical demand curve shown in Figure 5.1. Multiplying the price, in Column 1, times the quantity that can be sold at each price, in Column 2, gives total revenue for each price–quantity combination in Column 3. Marginal revenue, in Column 4, is found by taking the successive differences in total revenue.

Given that demand curves slope downward to the right, marginal revenue will always be less than price. This can be explained as follows. When price is reduced in order to sell one more unit, revenue is increased by the amount for which the marginal unit is sold. But there is an offset to this: we assume that sellers charge the same price to all customers. Therefore, revenue is reduced by the lower price charged for the units

---

[1] For a more detailed explanation of how price elasticity changes along a linear demand curve, see Mark Hirschey and James L. Pappas, *Fundamentals of Managerial Economics,* 4th ed. (Orlando, Fla.: Dryden, 1992), pp. 178–82.

Table 5.1. *Hypothetical demand and revenue data*

(1) (2) Demand data		(3) Total revenue (Col. 1 × Col. 2)	(4) Marginal revenue ($\Delta TR/\Delta Q$)	(5) Price elasticity of demand
Price	Quantity			
20	0	0	—	
19	1	19	19	
18	2	36	17	
17	3	51	15	
16	4	64	13	
15	5	75	11	Elastic
14	6	84	9	
13	7	91	7	
12	8	96	5	
11	9	99	3	
10	10	100	1	
9	11	99	− 1	
8	12	96	− 3	
7	13	91	− 5	
6	14	84	− 7	
5	15	75	− 9	Inelastic
4	16	64	−11	
3	17	51	−13	
2	18	36	−15	
1	19	19	−17	
0	20	0	−19	

that could have been sold at the higher price. Hence, marginal revenue is necessarily less than price. Consider the preceding example. To sell the ninth unit, price was reduced from $12 to $11. The ninth unit added $11 to revenue. But the eight units that could have gone for $12 each now bring in only $11. Hence, revenue from them is reduced by $1 × 8 = $8, and marginal revenue turns out to be $11 − $8 = $3.

The general relationship between elasticity, price changes, and changes in total revenue was explained in nonmathematical terms earlier in this chapter. Making use of the concept of marginal revenue, we can now state that relationship more precisely as follows:[2]

$$MR = P\left(1 - \frac{1}{\epsilon_p}\right) \tag{5.4}$$

For example, if the price is $20 and the elasticity of demand at that price is known to be 2.0, then we have

[2] For a rigorous derivation, see ibid., p. 182, n. 2.

$$MR = 20\left(1 - \frac{1}{2.0}\right) = 20(.5) = 10$$

Since marginal revenue is positive, this confirms the earlier statement that if demand is elastic (i.e., greater than 1.0), a price reduction will raise total revenue.

On the other hand, if at a price of $20 the elasticity of demand is only 0.8, the formula shows that marginal revenue will be negative, confirming the earlier conclusion that when demand is inelastic, total revenue is reduced if price falls:

$$MR = 20\left(1 - \frac{1}{0.8}\right) = 20(-.25) = -5$$

By testing the formula with other values of ϵ_p, the reader can confirm the following general results:

$$
\begin{aligned}
&\text{If } \epsilon_p = \infty, \quad MR = P \\
&\quad\, \epsilon_p > 1.0, \; MR > 0 \\
&\quad\, \epsilon_p = 1.0, \; MR = 0 \\
&\quad\, \epsilon_p < 1.0, \; MR < 0
\end{aligned}
$$

Figure 5.2 plots demand and marginal revenue curves from the data in Table 5.1. Marginal revenue turns negative when price falls below $10. The price elasticity of demand drops below 1.0 at the same point.

Deriving elasticity values from a demand equation
In Chapter 4 a hypothetical demand equation for theater tickets (Equation 4.4) was written in the following form:

$$Q_t = a + bP_t + cY + dP_s + eP_c \qquad (5.5)$$

The coefficients b, c, d, and e in such an equation contain information from which one can calculate elasticity values. For example, the ticket price coefficient, b, tells us how much the quantity of tickets demanded (Q_t) varies when the price of a ticket (P_t) changes by $1. In algebraic terms we can therefore say $b = \Delta Q_t / \Delta P_t$. In other words, the coefficient b provides a value for the $\Delta Q / \Delta P$ term that appears in the formula for price elasticity given by Equation 5.2. Also needed to calculate price elasticity are a consistent pair of values for P and Q. These can be obtained by supplying a set of hypothetical values for the coefficients and variables in Equation 5.5 (which is the same as Equation 4.4) and then solving it for the value of Q_t. For example, in Table 4.2, Case 1, we assumed a ticket price (P_t) of $15 and a value of $-5,000$ for coefficient

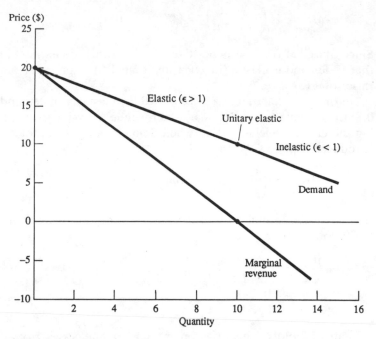

Figure 5.2. Demand, marginal revenue, and price elasticity.

b. When Equation 4.4 was solved using those numbers, we obtained a value of 106,800 for Q_t.

With this information we can calculate the price elasticity of demand for theater tickets when their price is $15 as follows:

$$\epsilon_p = \frac{\Delta Q_t}{\Delta P_t} \times \frac{P_t}{Q_t} = \frac{-5,000}{1} \times \frac{15}{106,800} = \frac{-75,000}{106,800} = -.70 \qquad (5.6)$$

Since demand curve D_1 in Figure 4.6 was derived from the same data used in this calculation, Equation 5.6 also gives the price elasticity of demand along that curve at the point where $P = 15$ and $Q = 106,800$.

In the real world, of course, one would not proceed on the basis of hypothetical values. To obtain a reliable figure for the price elasticity of demand, it would be necessary to employ econometric techniques to estimate the parameters of a demand equation (e.g., the constant a and coefficients b, c, d, and e) and then calculate the price elasticity from that equation.[3]

---

[3] See ibid., pp. 194–98, for an elementary introduction to methods of estimating actual demand functions.

The income elasticity of demand

Just as price elasticity measures the responsiveness of demand to changes in price while income and other variables are unchanged, so income elasticity measures its responsiveness to changes in income, when price and other variables are held constant. It is defined as the percent change in quantity demanded that results from a given percent change in income. Letting Y stand for income, it can be written algebraically as

$$\epsilon_y = \frac{\Delta Q/Q}{\Delta Y/Y} \tag{5.7}$$

or alternatively as

$$\epsilon_y = \frac{\Delta Q}{\Delta Y} \times \frac{Y}{Q} \tag{5.8}$$

or as

$$\epsilon_y = \frac{(Q_2 - Q_1)/Q_1}{(Y_2 - Y_1)/Y_1} \tag{5.9}$$

Although the preceding equations define income elasticity as a relationship between income and *quantity* purchased, it may be convenient, when suitable quantity measures are not available, to think of it as a relationship between income and consumer *expenditure* on a particular good. This is defensible because in theory the price of the good being studied is held constant over the range of observations used in calculating income elasticity, and if price is held constant, the percent change in expenditure will be the same as the percent change in the unobservable quantity. The expenditure approach is certainly convenient in studying the performing arts in the United States, where as already explained in Chapter 2, consumer spending data from the National Income Accounts are by far the best available historical data series.

To estimate income elasticity, the analyst obviously requires statistical observations in which the level of income displays some variation. There are two possibilities. First, one can measure variation "longitudinally," using historical time series such as the National Income Accounts data. In that case one might observe, for example, the year-to-year variation in consumer spending on admissions to the performing arts as compared with year-to-year variation in disposable personal income (DPI) per capita. With economic progress, DPI per capita rises through time. Thus, when income elasticity is measured longitudinally, its value suggests how consumer spending on the arts will be affected by economic growth.

Alternatively, one can measure variation in income and quantity demanded (or spending) among households at a moment in time. The data usually come from a sample survey of household income and consumption. This is described as the "cross-sectional approach," since observations are "across" households at a single date. The resulting elasticity measure answers such questions as, How do differences in income among consumers affect the consumption of art?

The range of possible values of income elasticity extends from negative through zero to positive, as follows:

$$\epsilon_y \;>\; 1 \qquad \text{is called income elastic}$$
$$\epsilon_y \;=\; 1 \qquad \text{is called unitary elasticity} \qquad \left.\right\} \;\;\text{"normal}$$
$$0 \;<\; \epsilon_y < 1 \;\text{is called income inelastic} \qquad\qquad \text{goods"}$$
$$\epsilon_y \;<\; 0 \qquad \text{is called an "inferior good"}$$

Income elasticity, consumer budgets, and industry growth

It is important to understand the connection between these four categories and the composition of the typical consumer's budget. If a good has an income elasticity *greater* than one, consumers' spending on it rises *faster* than their income does. As a result the proportion of income spent on the item increases as income increases. Such things are often described as luxuries, that is, goods that are consumed rarely or never when income is low, entering the typical consumer's budget only when income reaches the middle or upper range. Examples might be foreign travel, Cadillac cars, or tickets to the Metropolitan Opera.

The reader should be able to see intuitively that there is also a connection between the income elasticity of demand for a product and the rate of growth of the industry that produces it. If the income elasticity is greater than one, aggregate consumer spending on the good (at constant relative prices) rises faster than aggregate consumer income. This implies that output by the industry in question must be growing faster than output of the economy as a whole. Table 5.2 summarizes the connections between income elasticity, the composition of the consumer's budget, and industry growth.

If demand for a good displays unitary income elasticity, spending on it rises exactly in proportion to income, and the proportion of income spent on it remains constant as income rises. That, in turn, implies that the industry in question will grow at the same pace as the economy does.

Many consumer goods fall in the inelastic range, with income elasticities greater than zero but less than one. Consumer spending on them rises as income increases but less rapidly than income does. Conse-

Table 5.2. *Income elasticity of demand, composition of the consumer's budget, and industry growth*

Type of elasticity	Value	Effect on consumer's budget: as consumer's income rises	Effect on industry: as GDP rises, this industry
Income elastic	$\epsilon > 1.0$	proportion spent on this good rises	grows faster than GDP
Unitary elasticity	$\epsilon = 1.0$	proportion spent on this good remains constant	grows at the same rate
Income inelastic	$0 < \epsilon < 1.0$	proportion spent on this good falls	grows less rapidly than GDP
Inferior good	$\epsilon < 0$	absolute amount spent on this good falls	decreases in size

quently, the proportion of income spent on such goods *decreases* as income goes up. Food, with an income elasticity of demand around 0.5, is a good example. Such goods are important in the consumer's budget when income is low (they are sometimes classed as necessities), but spending on them does not increase rapidly when income rises. Consequently, the industries producing such goods grow less rapidly than the economy as a whole.

Finally, there are some objects of consumption for which income elasticity *falls* as income rises. These are known technically as "inferior goods," a fitting name, since their odd behavior is accounted for by the fact that they are for the most part the lowest quality and therefore the cheapest members of some larger class of goods. For example, the income elasticity of demand for frankfurters is probably negative – as income rises, consumers give them up in favor of higher-quality meats. Anything with an income elasticity of demand above zero is classified as a "normal good."

Deriving income elasticity from a demand equation

Using the hypothetical values of Case 1 in Table 4.2, we have already shown how the value of the price elasticity of demand can be derived from a known demand equation. The value of the income elasticity can be calculated in the same way. In Equation 5.5 the coefficient c shows how much the quantity of theater tickets demanded (Q_t) varies when the average per capita income (Y) of consumers changes by \$1. Thus, in algebraic notation $c = \Delta Q/\Delta Y$, which is one of the terms in the formula for income elasticity presented in Equation 5.8. The other values we require to calculate income elasticity are Y and Q. In Case 1, Y was assumed to have a value of $3,000. When Equation 5.5 was solved using the values of Case 1, Q_t was found to be 106,800. Consistent with the values of coefficients and variables assumed in that case, the income elasticity of demand turns out to be as follows:

$$\epsilon_y = \frac{\Delta Q_t}{\Delta Y} \times \frac{Y}{Q_t} = \frac{40}{1} \times \frac{3,000}{106,800} = \frac{120,000}{106,800} = 1.12 \qquad (5.10)$$

This result tells us that at the defined point, the demand for theater tickets is moderately income elastic. Specifically, it says that if income should rise 1 percent above $3,000 per capita while all other relevant variables remained constant, quantity of theater tickets demanded would increase 1.12 percent.

Cross-price elasticity of demand

The theory of consumer behavior tells us that the quantity demanded of a given good or service depends not only on its own price but also on the prices of substitutes and complements. Just as the price elasticity of demand measures the responsiveness of quantity purchased to changes in "own" price, so we can also define a cross-price elasticity (or "cross-elasticity," for short) that measures responsiveness to changes in the prices of substitutes or complements.

In order to define cross-elasticity in terms sufficiently general to cover both substitutes and complements, let us consider two hypothetical goods, J and K. The cross-elasticity of demand for J with respect to the price of K is defined as the percent change in the quantity demanded of J that results from a given percent change in the price of K. This can be written algebraically as:

$$\epsilon_{jk} = \frac{\Delta Q_j / Q_j}{\Delta P_k / P_k} \qquad (5.11)$$

or, alternatively, as

$$\epsilon_{jk} = \frac{\Delta Q_j}{\Delta P_k} \times \frac{P_k}{Q_j} \qquad (5.12)$$

Note that as in the case of price elasticity, this is a relationship between change in *quantity* and change in price, *not* a relationship between two *prices*. The sign of the cross-elasticity indicates whether the two goods are substitutes or complements: it will be positive for substitutes, negative for complements. Algebraically

$\epsilon_{jk} > 0$ indicates J and K are substitutes

$\epsilon_{jk} < 0$ indicates J and K are complements

The economic explanation of these statements is straightforward. If J and K are substitutes, an increase in the price of K will cause the quantity demanded of J to rise as consumers abandon the now more costly K in favor of its substitute, J. Thus ΔP_k and ΔQ_j will both be positive, and elasticity will have a positive sign. By the same argument, if the price of K *falls,* the quantity demanded of J will also fall. In that case ΔP_k and ΔQ_j will both be negative, but since one negative number divided by another yields a positive number, the elasticity will still have a positive sign.

To illustrate with an actual example, we know that butter and margarine are substitutes in consumption. Presumably, if the price of margarine rises while the price of butter remains constant, some consumers will switch from margarine to butter, so that the quantity demanded of the latter will increase. In fact, an empirical study of U.S. consumption found that to be the case: the cross-elasticity of demand for butter with respect to the price of margarine was estimated to be $+0.67$.[4]

For patrons of the live performing arts, a large city obviously offers many possibilities of substitution in consumption. For example, in the Twin Cities of Minneapolis/St. Paul, the concertgoer might give up the Minnesota Orchestra in favor of the St. Paul Chamber Orchestra if the price of tickets to the former rose too high relative to the latter. Table 5.3 presents estimated cross-elasticities of demand between various sectors of the live performing arts and their substitutes. As expected, all are positive.

If the two goods are complementary in consumption, an *increase* in the price of one will lead to a *decrease* in the quantity demanded of the other. Faced by a higher price for the complementary good K, which is used in combination with J, consumers will cut back their purchases of the latter. Thus, ΔP_k and ΔQ_j will have opposite signs, one positive, the other negative, which necessarily gives the cross-elasticity a negative sign. Alternatively, if the price of K *falls,* the quantity demanded of J will *rise.* Again ΔP_k and ΔQ_j will have opposite signs, rendering the cross-elasticity negative.

An actual example of complementarity in consumption is provided by sugar and fruit, two foods that tend to be eaten together. If the price of fruit rises, consumers will buy less fruit and will presumably need less sugar to go with it. Consequently, the demand for sugar will decrease.

[4] See Dominick Salvatore, *Microeconomics: Theory and Applications* (New York: Macmillan, 1986), table 5.5, p. 143.

Table 5.3. *Estimates of the elasticity of demand for attendance at the performing arts*

Investigator	Industry and place	Time period	Type of study	Elasticity estimate		
				Own price	Price of substitutes	Income
Moore	Broadway theater, New York City	1928–63	Time series	−.48 to −.64	—	.35 to .37
Moore	Broadway theater, New York City	1962	Cross section	—	—	1.03
Houthakker and Taylor	Theater, opera, and nonprofit performing arts, United States	1929–64[a]	Short-run time series	−.18	—	.74
Lange and Luksetich	Symphony orchestras, United States	1970	Long-run time series	−.31	—	1.26
			Cross section	−.49	—	—
Throsby and Withers	Theater, opera, and nonprofit performing arts, United States	1929–73	Time series	−.90	.68	1.08
Gapinski	Theater, London	1972–83	Pooled time series	−.05 to −.10	.09 to .18	—
Gapinski	Opera, London	1972–83	Pooled time series	−.12 to −.25	.13 to .15	—
Gapinski	Symphony, London	1972–83	Pooled time series	−.19 to −.35	.44 to .65	—
Gapinski	Dance, London	1972–83	Pooled time series	−.18 to −.81	.21 to 2.28	—
Goudriaan and de Kam	Theater, The Netherlands	1948–75	Time series	−.50	—[b]	—
Goudriaan and de Kam	Concerts, The Netherlands	1948–75	Time series	−.58	1.50	—
Goudriaan and de Kam	Theater, The Netherlands	1979	Cross section	—	—	.104
Goudriaan and de Kam	Concerts, The Netherlands	1979	Cross section	—	—	.482

[a]Excluding 1942–45.

[b]Not statistically significant.

Sources: Thomas Gale Moore, *The Economics of the American Theater* (Durham, N.C.: Duke University Press, 1968), app. D; H. S. Houthakker and Lester D. Taylor, *Consumer Demand in the United States* (Cambridge, Mass.: Harvard University Press, 1970), p. 131; Mark D. Lange and William A. Luksetich, "Demand Elasticities for Symphony Orchestras," *Journal of Cultural Economics* 8, no. 1 (June 1984), table 3; C. D. Throsby and G. A. Withers, *The Economics of the Performing Arts* (New York: St. Martin's, 1979), table 7.7; James H. Gapinski, "The Lively Arts as Substitutes for the Lively Arts," *American Economic Review*, 76, no. 2 (May 1986), table 1; R. Goudriaan and C. A. de Kam, "Demand in the Performing Arts and the Effects of Subsidy," in William S. Hendon *et al.*, eds. *Economic Research in the Performing Arts* (Akron, Ohio: Association for Cultural Economics, 1983), table 4.

This result has been verified in a study of consumption in the United Kingdom that found the cross-elasticity of demand for sugar with respect to the price of fruit to be -0.28.[5]

There are complementarities in the arts field, as well. Since the customer has to travel to the point of production to enjoy the live performing arts, transportation and parking are important complementary goods. We would expect the demand for tickets to fall if the cost of these complements rose significantly.

In connection with cross-elasticity of demand, the concepts of elasticity and inelasticity, with their precise dividing line, are not useful. However, the size of the elasticity coefficient may be of interest in indicating the strength of the indicated relationship. The closer it is to zero, the weaker the relationship. Indeed, in the polar cases of two goods that are completely unrelated in consumption, we would expect the cross-elasticity to be zero.

Deriving cross-price elasticities from a demand equation

Repeating the analysis carried out for the price and income elasticities of demand, we can now calculate the values of two cross-elasticities from the hypothetical demand function data in Table 4.2. In Equation 5.5 the coefficient d measures the response of theater ticket demand to a unit change in the average price (P_s) of such substitutes as movies, concerts, and spectator sports. Using algebraic notation, $d = \Delta Q_t / \Delta P_s$, which is the equivalent of the term $\Delta Q_j / \Delta P_k$ in the formula for the cross-elasticity given in Equation 5.12. In order to measure that elasticity we also need values for Q_t and P_s. Taking these from Case 1 in Table 4.2, we calculate the value of the cross-elasticity of demand for theater tickets with respect to the average price of substitutes as follows:

$$\epsilon_{ts} = \frac{\Delta Q_t}{\Delta P_s} \times \frac{P_s}{Q_t} = \frac{1,000}{1} \times \frac{16}{106,800} = \frac{16,000}{106,800} = .15 \qquad (5.13)$$

Using hypothetical data from the same source, we can also calculate the cross-elasticity of demand for theater tickets with respect to the composite price of complementary goods such as transportation to the theater and restaurant meals:

$$\epsilon_{tc} = \frac{\Delta Q_t}{\Delta P_c} \times \frac{P_c}{Q_t} = \frac{-1,600}{1} \times \frac{12}{106,800} = \frac{-19,200}{106,800} = -.18 \qquad (5.14)$$

Because the coefficient d, relating quantity of theater tickets demanded to the price of substitutes, carries a positive sign, the cross-elasticity

[5] Ibid.

with respect to the price of substitutes in Equation 5.13 is appropriately positive. On the other hand, the coefficient *e* relating quantity of theater tickets to the price of complementary goods is negative. Hence, in Equation 5.14 the cross-elasticity with respect to the price of complements is appropriately negative.

Expected values of the price elasticity of demand in the performing arts

Using econometric techniques, analysts have estimated the actual values of the price and income elasticities of demand for the live performing arts in several countries and over a number of different time periods. This book is not the appropriate place to explain either the complexities of such techniques or their limitations. In Table 5.3 we simply present a selection of results.[6] However, before discussing them it is useful to work out what elasticity values we would expect for the performing arts on the basis of prior knowledge.

It was pointed out in Chapter 4 that the price elasticity of demand for any consumer good depends primarily on the availability and quality of substitutes. If we think of the live performing arts as forms of entertainment or, even more generally, of recreation, then they have a good many substitutes, including books, newspapers and magazines, motion pictures, television and radio broadcasts, tapes and recordings of music, videotapes of many kinds, attendance at cabarets and nightclubs, eating out, spectator sports, and even participatory recreational activities. Indeed, the list could be extended to include anything else that people might do in their leisure hours. The availability of such a large number of substitutes, of so many opportunities competing for the consumer's leisure time and spending power, suggests that we should expect a fairly high price elasticity of demand for the live performing arts.

There is an important contrary force, however. The live performing arts are almost certainly an acquired taste, meaning one that grows stronger with exposure, and the effect of that is surely to make substitutes less acceptable. Those who acquire a taste for ballet, opera, or the theater become "hooked" on the live performances. Versions on film, tape, or television may be pleasant, but they are no substitute for the real thing. As the passion of such devotees grows stronger, they become less concerned about the price of admission. In short, their demand becomes relatively price inelastic.

---

[6] The interested reader may consult any of a number of econometrics texts. See, e.g., A. H. Studenmund and H. J. Cassidy, *Using Econometrics: A Practical Guide* (Boston: Little, Brown, 1987), esp. chaps. 1–3.

The same argument works in reverse for those who are outside the established audience. The arts are an acquired taste that they have not acquired. Few experiences can be more boring than an evening spent at a symphony concert, opera, or ballet by someone who has no understanding or appreciation of these art forms. Such people will not be easily drawn into the audience simply by lower ticket prices. Again, the acquired taste effect is to hold down the price elasticity of demand.

Empirical results and their implications: price elasticity

Most studies have shown the demand for attendance at the live performing arts to be price inelastic. Table 5.3 shows the findings of six investigations. Estimates of price elasticity are presented in the fifth column. Only Throsby and Withers found price elasticity to be as high as .90. The other five produced estimates ranging from a low of .05 to a high of .64.

If these price elasticities seem surprisingly low, one reason may be that most performing arts institutions are in the not-for-profit sector of the economy. As we shall argue in Chapter 7, they are strongly motivated toward holding ticket prices down in order to increase attendance. But at low prices demand is very likely to become inelastic, as illustrated in Table 5.1

The implication that some analysts have drawn from these findings is that if performing arts institutions in the nonprofit sector are finding it difficult to balance their budgets, they may be setting ticket prices too low; for if demand is price inelastic, attendance will not fall very much if ticket prices are raised, and total revenue will increase substantially. In the hypothetical case illustrated in Table 5.1, for example, if the firm were selling tickets at a price of $5, its total revenue would be $75, but if it raised its price to $6, revenue would increase to $84.

Several cautions are in order, however. The first is suggested by the importance of private donations in helping to support nonprofit arts institutions. It has been argued that performing arts firms in the nonprofit sector are not seeking to extract maximum revenue from ticket sales alone. Instead, they look at revenues from the combination of ticket sales and private donations, and they may well believe (perhaps correctly) that the additional revenue obtainable by charging higher ticket prices across the board would be more than offset by a reduction in donations from the segment of the audience (perhaps as high as 40 percent) who now willingly offer donational support.[7]

---

[7] See Henry Hansmann, "Nonprofit Enterprise in the Performing Arts," in Paul J. DiMaggio, ed., *Nonprofit Enterprise in the Arts* (New York: Oxford University Press, 1986), pp. 17–40.

A second point to keep in mind is the distinction between the demand for the output of a single firm and that for an entire industry. With the exception of Gapinski's study, the works cited here estimate the elasticity of the demand curve faced by the performing arts industry (or some major sector of it), not the demand curve faced by an individual firm. We would normally expect the firm's demand curve to be more elastic than that of the industry since elasticity rises with the availability of substitutes, and unless the single firm enjoys a local monopoly, the outputs of other local performing arts institutions are available to consumers as substitutes. Thus, the individual firm may face a price-elastic demand curve, even though the industry does not. In that case, a single firm, by raising its prices while its competitors did *not* do so, would diminish rather than increase its own revenue. Only if all firms in each market raised their prices simultaneously would each be able to enjoy higher revenues.

Table 5.3 also presents several estimates of the cross-elasticity of demand between the performing arts and their substitutes. As expected, these cross-elasticities are all positive, indicating that when the price of a substitute good rises, the demand for attendance at the performing arts increases. Surprisingly, the cross-elasticity turns out to be stronger than the own-price elasticity in most of these studies.

Expected value of the income elasticity of demand in the performing arts

On the basis of a priori reasoning alone, most economists would probably expect the demand for admission to the performing arts to be income elastic, that is, to have an income elasticity greater than 1.0. They would argue that life's essentials – food, clothing, shelter, medical care – enter the budget first, and that goods such as tickets to the theater or opera, like trips to the Riviera or the Bahamas, cannot be considered until income reaches a fairly comfortable level. The statistical consequences of such a consumption pattern will be that as we go up the income scale from poor to rich, we will find spending on the live performing arts increasing faster than income. Therefore, a study comparing consumption patterns across income classes at a given moment in time would show the income elasticity of demand for the arts to be greater than 1.0.

The same result would be expected if consumption patterns were studied *through* time instead of cross-sectionally. As living standards rise, more consumers pass over the threshold at which they can begin to spend on the arts. Consequently, spending on arts will increase faster than income, resulting in an income elasticity greater than 1.0.

Empirical results: income elasticity

Three of the studies presented in Table 5.3 found the income elasticity of demand for admission to the performing arts to be slightly above 1.0. Several others found it to be well below that level. But even if we take 1.0 to be the "consensus result," it is a good deal lower than many observers would have expected, given their belief that the arts behave as a luxury good in the consumer's budget.[8]

One explanation for this outcome is suggested by consideration of the way the need to allocate time influences consumer behavior. In Chapter 4 we assumed (implicitly) that consumption requires the expenditure only of money. In fact, it also requires time, and the amount of time available to each consumer is strictly limited by the clock. Hence, as income rises the amount of income available *per hour of consumption time* increases, as does the value that consumers place on an hour of that time. Consequently, as their incomes rise consumers, as Thomas Gale Moore puts it, "will substitute in consumption those goods which use relatively little time for those that use a great deal."[9] Attendance at the live performing arts is a fairly time-intensive activity, especially when round-trip travel is added to performance time. Hence, there is an adverse effect of time cost on attendance as income rises that tends to offset the positive "pure income effect" of greater buying power. The measured income elasticities shown in Table 5.3 are the net result of a positive pure income effect, offset in part by a negative time cost effect.[10]

If this sounds too abstract, consider the choice between listening to a recording at home and attending a live performance in the concert hall. No doubt listening at home has gained in popularity for a number of reasons, including revolutionary improvements in audio technology and the low price and high durability of recordings as compared with concert tickets. But the time factor is important, too: Mahler's Third Symphony can be heard at home in an hour and 43 minutes. To enjoy it in the concert hall requires that plus an hour or two of time spent getting there and back.

Earlier in this chapter we reviewed the connection between income elasticity and economic growth and pointed out that if the income elasticity of demand for a product is around 1.0, then, at constant relative prices, the industry producing the good could be expected to grow at

---

[8] See, e.g., Thomas Gale Moore, *The Economics of the American Theater* (Durham, N.C.: Duke University Press, 1968), p. 175.

[9] Ibid.

[10] See the discussion in C. D. Throsby and G. A. Withers, *The Economics of the Performing Arts* (New York: St. Martin's, 1979), p. 114, and results reported in their table 7.7, p. 113.

about the same annual rate as the economy as a whole. If the estimates by Moore, Houthakker and Taylor, and Throsby and Withers presented in Table 5.3 are accurate, that would appear to be the long-run prospect for the performing arts industry in the United States. That's not quite an "arts boom" according to the definition offered in Chapter 2, but most arts advocates would probably settle for it as good enough.

Summary

This and the previous chapter have dealt with the demand for the arts. We have suggested that the arts share most attributes of ordinary consumer goods, and that the standard tools of demand analysis can usefully be brought to bear on them. In this chapter we developed the concept of elasticity of demand and showed how knowledge of elasticity values can help arts administrators in the conduct of their business. Price elasticity in particular – because it affects revenue from ticket sales and therefore potentially influences budget deficits and fiscal health – is relevant not only to individual arts companies and institutions, but also to those concerned with public policy toward the arts.

In the next two chapters the focus shifts to the supply side: we will examine production, supply, and the behavior of producing firms in the live performing arts. On the supply side, we will find some interesting divergences between the arts and the more usual sorts of goods and services, but the tools of economic analysis will prove no less applicable, for all that.

6

Production in the performing arts

Chapters 3, 4, and 5 dealt with audiences for the arts and with the measurement and analysis of the economic demand those audiences generate in their role as arts consumers. The concept of supply was introduced in summary fashion in Chapter 4 to show how supply and demand interact in the market to yield the prices paid by consumers. We now take a closer look at the supply side. The technical process of production in the performing arts is examined in this chapter. In Chapter 7 we will analyze the way in which the performing arts firm finds the optimum price–output combination by bringing together information on market demand and on its own production costs. Production and supply are organized very differently in the visual arts than in the performing arts and so will be treated later in Chapter 9.

The measurement of output

In analyzing the economics of production, economists have conventionally chosen their examples from agriculture or manufacturing, probably because the measurement of output in those industries is relatively straightforward. A farm produces bushels of wheat or gallons of milk. A factory turns out yards of cloth, tons of steel, or cases of beer. In the service industries, including the arts, the measurement of output is typically much harder. First of all, it may be difficult even to *define* satisfactory quantitative units. How do you measure the output of a bank or a police department or an art museum? Second, in the service industries a quality dimension may be important, and yet even harder to identify than quantity. For many kinds of agricultural or manufactured products, it is possible to define standard qualities. That is rarely the case in the arts. No one would argue that a symphonic performance by an amateur group is equal in quality to that of the finest professional orchestras. Yet *how much* different is it? Even though we know that quality is of the very essence in the arts, we are generally at a loss to measure it directly and must fall back instead on indirect measures, or "proxies."

Output in the performing arts

Throsby and Withers discuss four possible measures of output for a performing arts firm:[1]

1. Number of performances. From the point of view of cost, or supply, this is undoubtedly a good measure, since a substantial part of production cost is cost incurred per performance in the form of wages, salaries, rent, electricity, and the like.

2. Number of separate productions. From the artistic point of view, this may be an important measure of output. A company that puts on 30 performances each of *Hamlet, The Three Sisters,* and *A Streetcar Named Desire* is, in some sense, producing more artistic experience than one that concentrates on producing 90 performances of *Hamlet* alone.[2] And costs, too, vary directly with the number of productions as well as the number of performances.

While the number of performances or the number of separate productions are useful output measures with reference to cost or supply, they are deficient in two respects. First, they are not units in terms of which the demand for output can be brought into the analysis, since patrons commonly buy single seats rather than the entire house. Second, they do not measure the number of "artistic experiences" that occurs in connection with a performance, which depends on the number of people who actually attend it. We therefore consider two more possibilities.

3. Number of tickets available for sale. This is the product of (number of performances) × (capacity of house). Since this measure is denominated in terms of seats, it does allow us to deal with demand in the same analysis as production and cost. Thus, it overcomes the first deficiency cited. However, it does not overcome the second, since available tickets will not necessarily all be sold.

4. Number of tickets sold. This is also referred to as paid admissions and equals (number of performances) × (capacity of house) × (percent utilization of capacity). This concept measures the actual number of artistic experiences provided by a given performance, thus overcoming

---

[1] C. D. Throsby and G. A. Withers, *The Economics of the Performing Arts* (New York: St. Martin's, 1979), p. 11.

[2] Ibid., p. 12.

both of the deficiencies just cited. However, when used to measure output and cost it introduces other difficulties, which will be discussed in Chapter 7. Therefore, in that chapter, when setting up a model of the economics of a performing arts firm we shall employ number of tickets available for sale, rather than number actually sold, as the measure with which to calibrate both demand and supply.

Some basic cost concepts

To construct a model of the economics of the performing arts firm we need not only a usable measure of output, but also an appropriate set of cost concepts. Let us begin with the fundamental economic definition of cost. The true (or "real") cost of any endeavor, according to economists, is measured by the value of the resources that are used up to carry it out. The value of those resources, in turn, is measured by the utility of the other products that were forgone when resources were used in this endeavor, rather than in the next best alternative. Since cost is thus based on the value of forgone opportunities, this has come to be known as the doctrine of "opportunity cost."

Consider the following illustration. Many localities have a community orchestra staffed entirely by volunteers, and these organizations frequently offer "free" concerts to the public. Most of us would agree that the availability of these cultural events is a boon to the local citizenry, and we would particularly appreciate the fact that they are offered at no charge. But are they really free? Economists would have to say no. Although musicians, administrators, and others contribute their time "free of charge" to such enterprises, we have to recognize that time and creative energy are scarce resources. To the extent they are used in producing a community performance, they are not available for other potentially valuable pursuits. The lawyer who volunteers her time to draw up the articles of incorporation for the community orchestra is forgoing the use of her time and talents in serving other clients. Hence, while we may regard a community concert as "free," in fact it is not. Many resources are used up in its production, even though there may be no explicit cost or direct money outlay for some of them.

The concept of opportunity cost is particularly important when one is making judgments about the welfare effects of economic policies. We will make use of it in Chapter 11 when we take up the question, Should the government subsidize the arts?

Production costs

The standard notions of production cost that economists have used in developing the abstract "theory of the firm" are perfectly applicable in the performing arts and will be defined in this chapter. An important initial distinction must be drawn between fixed and variable costs of production. *Fixed costs* are those that do not vary with the level of output in the short run. Included are such things as the cost of plant and equipment, long-term salary contracts, debt service, insurance, and rent (if production premisses are not owned). They vary with the scale of the undertaking, but once the firm sets up in business at a given scale, they are fixed and do not vary with short-run fluctuations in the level of output.

Variable costs, on the other hand, are those that *do* change as the level of output within the given-size establishment fluctuates in the short run. A list would include such costs as wages, raw materials and supplies, and telephone and electric power charges.

Total fixed costs (*TFC*) and total variable costs (*TVC*) are measured per unit of time (say a month or a year). Dividing by the quantity of output in the same time period (*Q*), we obtain the following measures of average unit cost:

Average fixed cost (AFC) = TFC/Q
Average variable cost (AVC) = TVC/Q
Average total cost (ATC) = $AFC + AVC$

Finally, the concept of *marginal cost* (*MC*) is indispensable in analyzing the behavior of producing firms. Marginal cost is the additional cost incurred in producing one more unit of output. Since *fixed* costs do not rise when output increases in the short run, marginal cost necessarily equals the rise in total *variable* costs, when output increases by one unit. Algebraically, we can write

$$MC = \frac{\Delta \, TVC}{\Delta Q}$$

Production costs for a theatrical enterprise

In this and the following chapter we use a hypothetical theatrical enterprise as the prototype for production in the performing arts. Assume to begin with that the enterprise in question is a commercial venture of the sort typical in the Broadway theater. (It will be shown in Chapter 7 that the same production model is applicable as well to the noncommercial theater and such other nonprofit enterprises as opera and ballet companies.)

The distinction between fixed and variable costs is very clear in a theatrical enterprise. Fixed costs are the expenses of mounting a pro-

Table 6.1. *Average production and operating costs on Broadway, 1960–61*[a]

	Production costs (Preopening) (dollars)	Weekly operating costs (dollars)
Scenery, props and costumes, including designers	45,135	—
Advertising and publicity	14,906	3,050
Actors' salaries	6,661	7,297
Crew and stagehands	5,865	1,268
Electrical and sound	5,661	—
Directors' fees	5,172	573
Stage and company managers	4,587	974
Legal and audit	3,481	NA
Office	1,844	NA
Theater rent or share	2,205	7,639[b]
Authors' royalties	—	2,334[b]
Total	111,422[c]	27,309[c]

[a]Sample of 15 plays and musicals.
[b]Based on a percentage of box office gross receipts.
[c]Includes costs not itemized.
Source: *The Economics of the American Theater*, Thomas Gale Moore, © 1968 Duke University Press. Reprinted with permission of the publisher.

duction, what Throsby and Withers refer to as the "setting up costs."[3] These are incurred before a play opens and are in no way affected by the length of its subsequent run. Included among those fixed costs are items such as the cost of scenery, costumes and props, rehearsal wages to the cast, the director's basic fee, stagehands' wages, pre–opening night advertising and publicity, theater rental, and office, legal and audit expenses. Table 6.1, using data from Moore's study of the economics of the theater, shows that production costs averaged $111,422 for a sample of 15 shows that opened on Broadway during the season of 1960–61. Such costs are paid in advance of opening night by the producer, investing his or her own capital as well as funds obtained from other "backers" who become partners in the venture.

In a theatrical enterprise variable costs are the operating expenses of the show, which begin on opening night and continue at more or less the same rate for each performance. As Table 6.1 shows, the most important of these costs are salaries of actors and stage and company managers, wages of stagehands and technical crew, and expenses for

[3] Ibid., p. 13.

advertising and publicity. On Broadway the share going to the owner of the theater and the royalties paid the author are calculated as percentages of gross box office receipts. This places them on a somewhat different footing from the previously listed variable costs, which do not depend on receipts, but for practical purposes they can also be regarded as operating expenses. In Moore's 1960–61 sample, Broadway operating costs, including the shares going to the author and the theater, averaged $27,309 per week, or $3,414 for each of eight performances. The hope of theatrical investors is that box office receipts will be more than sufficient to cover these operating costs as the play runs, providing a surplus sufficient not only to pay back their investment but also to yield a profit.

How unit cost varies with output

In order to analyze the output and pricing decisions of performing arts firms (as we shall do in Chapter 7), it is necessary to show how their unit costs vary with the level of output. Following the conventional approach of microeconomic theory, we do this by plotting "cost curves" on a diagram that shows unit costs on the vertical axis and quantity of output on the horizontal, as in Figure 6.1. Number of performances (which is equivalent to "length of run") has been chosen as the measure of output quantity since, as already argued, that is the unit of quantity to which the important category of variable costs is most directly related. It is important to note that in this analysis input prices are assumed constant. The variation of unit cost with output arises from forces inherent to the production process rather than from changes in wage rates or materials prices.

Curves showing average fixed cost, average variable cost and average total cost are displayed in Figure 6.1. The AFC curve falls sharply over an initial range of outputs but appears almost to level off as number of performances (i.e., length of run) reaches a high level. The character of this curve is mathematically determined by the fact that $AFC = TFC/Q$, and the numerator, TFC, is a constant. Therefore, when Q first increases beyond zero, the value of the quotient TFC/Q declines very rapidly. For example, suppose $TFC = 60$. Then as Q increases from 1 to 2 to 3, AFC falls from 60 to 30 to 20. But when Q is already large, further increases reduce the value of the quotient only a little. For example, as Q goes from 40 to 41 to 42, AFC declines only from 1.50 to 1.46 to 1.43. In fact, the AFC curve necessarily takes the form of a rectangular hyperbola, a geometric figure for which the product of the values on the two axes equals a constant. In this instance, since by definition $AFC = TFC/Q$, it is also the case that $AFC \times Q = TFC$. What are the economic implications of all this? Forsaking mathemat-

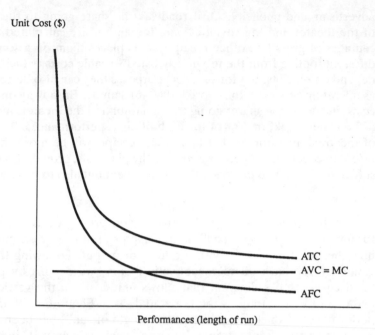

Figure 6.1. Performing arts costs and output.

ics in favor of plain common sense, the declining *AFC* curve simply shows the process that business people refer to as "spreading your overhead."

The *AVC* curve in Figure 6.1 is drawn as a horizontal straight line. Its height above the quantity axis represents the average variable cost of putting on a single performance of the given production. *AVC* is constant as output (i.e., number of performances) increases because the inputs of labor and materials required are identical for every performance, no matter how long the show runs.

Marginal cost, it should be recalled, equals the additional variable cost required to produce one more unit of output. But if average variable cost is constant as output rises, then the additional variable cost entailed by one more unit is always equal to the average that has been required up to that point. Thus, when *AVC* is constant, *MC* necessarily equals *AVC* and is also constant. Therefore, in Figure 6.1 the *AVC* curve also represents *MC* and is so labeled.

Average total cost equals the sum of average variable cost and average fixed cost. In Figure 6.1 the *ATC* curve is therefore drawn as the sum, in the vertical direction, of *AVC* plus *AFC*. Since *AVC* is parallel to the quantity axis, the *ATC* curve lies at a constant distance above *AFC*. Like the latter, it falls sharply at first, but appears almost to level off as quantity increases.

The arts as a special case

It is a singular feature of production in the performing arts that average variable cost and marginal cost are constant for all outputs. Readers familiar with the elementary principles of economics may recall that in the usual cases of manufacturing or farm production analyzed in microeconomics, the short-run *AVC* and *MC* curves are always U-shaped, and the outcome of every application turns out to be determined by their upward-sloping right-hand branches. Why are the conditions of production so fundamentally different in the live performing arts? In the usual cases production is carried on under conditions such that the law of diminishing returns applies when the firm increases output in the short run. The law of diminishing returns says that when variable inputs (such as labor and materials) are applied in uniformly increasing doses to a fixed input (such as a factory or a farm), the increments of output obtained per added dose of inputs will eventually begin to diminish. But if the increments to output per added unit of input *diminish,* then the unit cost of additional output, which we have defined as marginal cost, must be rising, and if marginal cost is increasing then average variable cost must be also. Hence, the *MC* and *AVC* curves eventually turn upward because of diminishing returns in production.

In the performing arts, however, production is organized in such a way that the law of diminishing returns does not come into play. Each performance is a repetition of the same "production process" as the previous one. Output of the firm increases because we measure output by performances, but inputs are used over and over again in the same proportions as before. Thus, the conditions under which diminishing returns would occur are simply not present.

Summary

This chapter has extended the economic analysis of production and cost to the performing arts. Despite measurement difficulties, the arts seem to lend themselves well to this adaptation. In the next chapter we shall examine the economic behavior of firms in the live performing arts. A distinction will be drawn between profit-maximizing firms, such as producers for the Broadway theater, and firms organized on a not-for-profit basis, such as the typical resident theater company outside of New York City. We will show that for both types of arts producers, the cost concepts and cost curves developed in this chapter play a crucial role in the explanation of behavior.

7

Firms and markets in the performing arts

In this chapter we investigate the economic choices – especially the price–output choices – made by performing arts firms. These choices are largely determined by the following factors:

1. The level and character of consumer demand for the firm's output.
2. The method and cost of producing that output.
3. The type of market in which the firm operates.
4. The firm's artistic and financial objectives.
5. The availability of government subsidies or of private donational support.

Consumer demand was analyzed in Chapters 4 and 5 and production and cost in Chapter 6. We begin this chapter with a discussion of market types and how they influence the behavior of performing arts firms.

Types of markets

Conventional economic analysis recognizes four types of market structure, distinguished from one another by the size and number of suppliers and by whether the goods sold are homogeneous or differentiated. Homogeneous goods are such products as wheat, steel, or potatoes, which are graded and standardized so effectively that buyers do not care which supplier they deal with for any given grade. Products are said to be differentiated if the unique features of style, quality, design, or brand name are sufficient to convince buyers that sellers are *not* offering virtually identical goods. Examples of differentiated products are automobiles, magazines, toothpastes, and theatrical productions.

Perfect competition

Perfect competition exists when there is a large number of sellers of a homogeneous product, and no one seller is large enough in relation to the size of the market to influence the market price. When these conditions exist, suppliers treat market prices as given and concentrate on deciding how much to produce at those prices. Agriculture, which has both homogeneous products and large numbers of sellers, would come closer to being perfectly competitive than any other industry, were it not for the pervasive influence of government farm policy in setting prices and regulating output.

The analysis of perfectly competitive markets occupies an important place in economics because even though few, if any, such markets exist, the price–quantity outcome under perfect competition is theoretically clear. It is also optimal in the sense that, as a result of competitive pressures, goods will be produced to satisfy consumer preferences at the least possible economic cost. Hence, perfect competition provides a very useful theoretical benchmark with which to compare outcomes in other types of markets. (See further discussion in Chapter 11.) No market in the performing arts, however, comes close to being perfectly competitive. First of all, the number of sellers is never large enough. Second, the goods sold are differentiated, rather than homogeneous, even when the same work of art is being produced. Lovers of classical music will not agree that one performance of a Beethoven symphony is just like another, much less that a Beethoven symphony is interchangeable with one by Shostakovich.

Pure monopoly

At the opposite pole from perfect competition is pure monopoly, where there is only one seller of the good in question. If public regulation does not interfere (as it sometimes does), the firm is free to choose the price–quantity combination along the demand curve for its product that best satisfies its objectives. It should be noted, however, that a monopolist cannot *force* anyone to buy at high prices. Whatever *price* the firm chooses, the demand curve dictates the *quantity* that can be sold.

Performing arts firms are sometimes monopolists within a predominantly local market. The price–output choices they make, however, will depend on whether they are in the commercial sector, in which case they will be seeking to maximize profit, or in the not-for-profit sector, in which case their motivation will be more complex. We shall examine both cases in this chapter.

Monopolistic competition

Just as its name suggests, monopolistic competition is a type of market structure that blends elements of monopoly with elements of competition. Typically, the industry contains a moderate to large number of sellers, whose products are differentiated rather than homogeneous. Book publishing, shoe and apparel manufacturing, and automotive repair are examples. In each of these industries there is competition because a large number of firms are selling goods or services that are close substitutes for one another. But there is an element of monopoly, as well, insofar as each firm has a monopoly over its own brand, type, quality, or design. However, it is a crucial characteristic of monopolistic competition that there are enough sellers so that each assumes its pricing decisions will not provoke a reaction from the others. Firms are, in others words, "price independent."

Among individual sectors of the performing arts industry, the Broadway theater can be accurately described as monopolistically competitive. Thirty or more plays and musicals open during a single season and certainly compete with each other for an audience. Yet each company clearly has a monopoly over its own show and sets prices on the assumption that its own policies will not provoke a response from competitors. If we adopt a broader definition, under which all the live performing arts make up a single industry, then the industry itself, in most large cities, is monopolistically competitive: the opera company, the symphony orchestra, the dance groups, and the resident theater companies compete with each other by offering products that are unique, and yet closely substitutable as forms of artistic entertainment.

Oligopoly

The final major type of market structure is oligopoly. Its basic characteristic is that a few very large firms, anywhere from, say, 2 to 10 or 15, dominate the market. A larger number of very small firms may be present, as well. The product of an oligopolistic industry may be either homogeneous – as, for example, with steel, cement, and petroleum products – or heterogeneous – as in the case of automobiles, airplanes, and household appliances. It is an essential feature of oligopoly that the number of major firms is small enough so that each assumes that the others *will* respond in some way to its own pricing decisions and, therefore, makes its decisions taking the probable responses to them into account. For example, if one of the big three U.S. automakers – GM, Ford, or Chrysler – decides to reduce prices in order to boost sales, it certainly anticipates that the others will somehow respond, and its decision allows for that response. In other words, these firms, unlike monopolistic competitors, are "price interdependent."

The performing arts market in some cities may appear to have the characteristics of oligopoly since a few large institutions, say a symphony orchestra, an opera company, and one or two resident theaters may dominate the scene. Nevertheless, the oligopoly analysis does not apply because performing arts firms other than the Broadway theater are usually operated as nonprofit enterprises and therefore do not become involved in the competitive pricing strategies typical of oligopolies operating in large national markets.

Artistic and financial objectives

The objectives or goals of performing arts firms depend on whether they are in the commercial or the not-for-profit sector of the economy. If the former, it can be assumed that like other commercial enterprises, their objective is to maximize profits. The price and production policies that this implies will be described later in this chapter.

The motivation of firms in the not-for-profit sector, as Throsby and Withers suggest, is best understood by separating the dimensions of quality and quantity.[1] Each performing arts institution chooses for itself some portion of the universe of art and some mixture of tradition and innovation. Within that realm it tries to offer performances that satisfy its own standards of excellence. Thus, its quality objectives can be thought of as embodied in its choice of repertoire and standard of performance.

We argued in Chapter 6 that because of the way production is organized in the live performing arts, the firm does not run into diminishing returns in *production*. It does seem likely, however, that a form of diminishing returns is encountered when the firm seeks to attain the desired standard of *quality* in its productions. For example, choosing inputs so as to produce a desired level of quality as economically as possible is analogous to the problem the conventional manufacturing firm faces in trying to produce a given level of output at the lowest possible cost. The solution for the manufacturer is to use inputs in such proportions that at the margin each contributes the same quantity of output per dollar of expenditure on it. (See any textbook of microeconomic theory for a full explanation.) In the case of a performing arts firm establishing a level of quality, the solution is to choose inputs in such proportions that each contributes at the margin the same boost to

[1] C. D. Throsby and G. A. Withers, *The Economics of the Performing Arts* (New York: St. Martin's, 1979), p. 14.

quality per dollar of expenditure. For example, a theatrical firm would try to arrange its budget so that an additional hundred dollars spent on scenery would yield the same increment to quality as an additional hundred spent on costumes or on hiring better actors. Diminishing returns plays a part in this process because using more of any *one* input (scenery, costumes, actors), while holding the others constant, does seem likely to yield diminishing increments to quality.

Of course, quality is usually a subjective matter, and we are not suggesting that it can be measured in quantitative units. What we *are* suggesting is that rational decision making about quality requires that the firm's directors, using their best judgment, behave *as if* they could so measure it.

As for the quantitative goal, Throsby and Withers point out that performing arts firms in the nonprofit sector try "to make their product available to as large an audience as possible. Practitioners . . . tend to have a crusading spirit about their profession, and the larger the audience that can be attracted the happier they are." This attitude is easy to explain. The performer would obviously rather play to "full houses than to empty ones." In addition, the members of the organization typically share a belief that art "is intrinsically good and socially necessary" and should therefore be displayed before the widest possible audience.[2]

Even the most crusading entrepreneurs for the arts, however, cannot ignore economic realities. Their qualitative and quantitative goals are therefore pursued subject to the constraint that if the enterprise is to survive, its revenues must, in the long run, cover its costs. Combining the quantitative and qualitative objectives and the constraint of a balanced budget, Throsby and Withers conclude that the motivation of a performing arts enterprise in the nonprofit sector can be described as follows: over an appropriate period of time, the firm tries to maximize attendance, while presenting a repertoire that meets its own quality standards, subject to the constraint that revenues from the box office plus other sources must be sufficient to cover costs.[3] The possible other sources of revenue are primarily government subsidies and (especially in the United States) private charitable donations. As we shall see, this formulation leads to clear predictions about pricing policies of arts enterprises both with and without outside support.[4]

---

[2] Ibid., pp. 14–15.
[3] Ibid., p. 15.
[4] The analysis that follows is based, with some modifications, on the model developed in ibid., pp. 15–25.

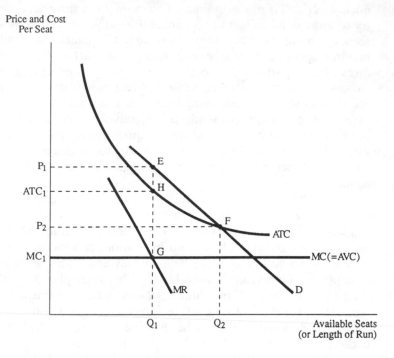

Figure 7.1. Price and output determination for a theatrical enterprise.

A model of the firm in the live performance arts

Figure 7.1 depicts the demand and cost situation facing a firm in the live performing arts. The diagram reproduces the average total cost and marginal cost curves already explained in Chapter 6. Average fixed cost is not shown separately. Because $AFC = ATC - AVC,$ it can be read from the diagram as the vertical distance between those two curves. In Figure 6.1 the cost curves were drawn with number of performances as the measure of quantity on the horizontal axis. In Figure 7.1 the number of performances is multiplied by the capacity of the house. Thus, the horizontal axis now measures quantity as the number of seats available for sale, increasing in the rightward direction as the number of performances increases. For example, if the house contains 1,000 seats, one performance = 1,000 seats, five performances = 5,000 seats, and so on. Costs, therefore, are now measured per available seat rather than per performance. This does not affect the shapes of the curves, only their height, as measured in dollars, on the vertical axis.

The advantage of calibrating quantity this way is that since consumer demand is expressed in price per seat, it allows us to plot the demand and marginal revenue curves on the same diagram as the cost curves. These are shown as *D* and *MR* in Figure 7.1. (The concept of marginal revenue was explained in Chapter 5.)

A demand curve for tickets, it should be noted, shows number of seats sold at any given price. In order to argue that the number of seats sold equals seats available for sale and can be converted into number of performances at a fixed ratio, we require the additional assumption that the house is sold out for every performance (at any rate, up to the last one). That assumption may seem unrealistic, but without it the length of the run would be indeterminate in the model depicted in Figure 7.1. With it the quantity scale can be thought of as measuring number of performances, length of run, or total attendance.

Throsby and Withers adopted a different strategy. They elected to use as a quantity measure the actual number of seats sold over the life of a given production. That has the advantage of dispensing with the assumption of a constantly sold-out house. In fact, Throsby and Withers assume, not implausibly, that attendance per performance will fall off toward the end of the run, so that if cost per performance is constant, cost per seat sold will rise. That gives them a marginal cost curve that rises toward its right end as marginal cost curves do in the cases of manufacturing or agricultural firms, instead of remaining horizontal, as in Figures 6.1 and 7.1.[5] But that upward slope, it should be noted, results not from diminishing returns in production, as in the conventional case, but from production conditions modified by factors arising on the demand side. Thus, their model makes unit cost depend on the conditions of demand as well as supply, which violates the usual practice in microeconomic analysis of formulating independent explanations for supply and demand. We have chosen available seats, rather than seats sold, as the unit of output to avoid the melding of supply and demand factors and to maintain simplicity and clarity in the analysis.[6]

---

[5] See ibid., p. 17; and C. D. Throsby, "Production and Cost Relationships in the Supply of Performing Arts Services," in K. A. Tucker, ed., *Economics of the Australian Service Sector* (London: Croom Helm, 1977), pp. 414–32, cited at 418, 425.

[6] See objections to Throsby and Withers's procedure in Mark Lange, James Bullard, William Luksetich, and Philip Jacobs, "Cost Functions for Symphony Orchestras," *Journal of Cultural Economics*, 9, no. 2 (December 1985): 71–85, cited at 73–74.

Price, output, and profit in the commercial theater

Let us assume to begin with that the firm in question is producing a play for the Broadway theater. The firm's objective is to maximize profits by finding the best price–output combination for this production, where "output" equals number of seats sold but also length of run. The possible combinations are those that lie along the demand curve for the firm's play. Which will be the most profitable? The answer is that the firm should choose the price at which the last unit sold just adds as much to revenue as it costs to produce. In technical terms, that means output should be carried to the point where the marginal revenue obtained from selling one more seat just equals the marginal cost of providing a performance for one more attendee. In Figure 7.1, MR intersects MC at point G when Q_1 seats are sold. We can see that this is the profit-maximizing output by reasoning as follows: to the left of G, MR lies above MC, indicating that additional sales would add more to revenue than to cost, thus boosting profits; to the right of G, MC lies above MR, so that additional sales would add more to cost than to revenue, thereby reducing profits. Profits are therefore greatest at point G. Moving vertically up to the demand curve from G, we see that Q_1 seats can be sold at a price of P_1, as indicated by point E. The profit-maximizing price and quantity for this production are therefore P_1 and Q_1.

At output Q_1, the average total cost per seat is ATC_1, as indicated at point H. Profit per seat is therefore $P_1 - ATC_1$, and aggregate profit $= (P_1 - ATC_1) Q_1$, or the area of the rectangle P_1EHATC_1. We can describe the play depicted in Figure 7.1 as "a hit." The public's desire for tickets is strong enough that the demand curve lies considerably above the ATC curve for a range of possible outputs, and the play is able to earn back its costs plus a profit. If interest in the play had been so weak that the demand curve lay below the ATC curve at all price–output combinations, we would have to call the play "a flop," for there would be no price at which the producer could sell enough seats to break even, let alone earn a profit.

The performing arts are an example of what economists call a decreasing cost industry. Cost per seat falls continuously as output is extended through time because the fixed costs of mounting a production are spread over a larger and larger number of performances. Consequently, in the commercial sector the longer the run, the greater the financial success. (As we shall see in the next section, an analogous version of success applies in the not-for-profit sector.)

Our analysis of a Broadway production using Figure 7.1 has implied that the play would close after the number of performances is equivalent to Q_1 available seats. That conclusion, however, is based on the assumption that a single price (or more realistically, a single range of prices) must be charged throughout the play's run. In fact, it may be profitable for the producer to extend the run beyond Q_1 by lowering prices. By the time Q_1 is reached with ticket prices at P_1, the production has recovered its fixed costs plus a profit. The additional cost of further output is only MC_1. If the producer can sell additional seats by reducing the price below P_1, while keeping it still above MC_1, it will pay to do so. The run can be profitably extended by the sale of "twofers" or by other off-price arrangements. This is a form of price discrimination through time. Like other forms of price discrimination (e.g., charging different fares for first-class and economy-class seats on airlines), it is a way of increasing the firm's profits by charging different prices to customers whose demands differ.

Price and output in the nonprofit sector

Figure 7.1 can also be used to analyze the price–output decisions in the nonprofit sector. Assume initially that the production previously described as a commercial enterprise is now mounted instead by a not-for-profit theater company. The company's objective, as already argued, is to maximize attendance, at productions of suitable quality, subject to the constraint of balancing its budget. If no subsidies or private donations are available, it will try to produce the quantity of output at which price just covers average total cost. The demand and average total cost curves intersect at point F, indicating that the optimum price and quantity are P_2 and Q_2. Comparing this outcome with the result when the same play is produced commercially, we see that ticket price is lower and total attendance (or length of run) greater under a not-for-profit organization.[7]

It is unrealistic, however, when analyzing the nonprofit sector, to frame the analysis in terms of single productions. Most nonprofit performing arts companies put together a repertory of events each season. A resident theater group may mount four plays, an opera company two or three operas, a classical dance company half a dozen short- to medium-length ballets, combined into several evening-length performances. The model depicted in Figure 7.1 can handle this complication quite realistically. The quantity scale, total seats sold, now measures "length of season" rather than length of run, since the productions do not have

---

[7] However, see objections to this conclusion in Edwin G. West, "Nonprofit Versus Profit Firms in the Performing Arts," *Journal of Cultural Economics*, 11, no. 2 (December 1987): 37–47, and the response by James Heilbrun, "Nonprofit Versus Profit-Making Firms: A Comment," *Journal of Cultural Economics*, 12, no. 2 (December 1988): 87–92.

individual "runs." Instead of applying to individual productions, the cost curves now refer to aggregates for the chosen repertory. Thus, total fixed costs are the aggregate production costs (i.e., setting-up costs) for the season. *AFC* declines because *TFC/Q* decreases as the season (*Q*) grows longer. *AVC* and *MC* now refer to the operating cost per production averaged over the season's repertory and are constant, as before.

Subscription sales now account for an important fraction of all admissions to nonprofit performing arts programs. Thus, it also makes good sense to draw a single demand curve (as we have done in Figure 7.1) that applies to the aggregate repertory rather than to think in terms of separate demands for individual productions.

Increased popularity for the offerings of a company over successive seasons would show up as a shift of the demand curve to the right. Assuming that the cost curves do not shift, the intersection of *D* and *ATC* would also occur further to the right. The increased quantity of tickets sold would indicate a longer season for the company.

For performing arts groups trying to establish themselves as permanent institutions, longer seasons are taken as an important sign of success. Imagine how difficult a professional career is for a musician or ballet dancer whose company guarantees only 15 or 20 weeks' work over a whole year. Longer seasons strengthen a company immeasurably, both by augmenting performers' incomes and by giving them a greater opportunity to develop their skills. Undoubtedly, longer seasons also make it easier to retain top-notch performers and to design high-quality productions.

Production costs in the long run

In analyzing production costs, economists draw a useful distinction between the long run and the short run. Up to this point our analysis of production and cost has dealt only with the latter, which is defined as a period short enough so that one or more factors of production are effectively fixed in quantity. In the case of manufacturing – the conventional example dealt with in microeconomics – the fixed factor is plant and equipment. The short run is the period in which the manufacturer has to decide how much output to produce, and at what prices, *from the firm's existing plant*. The long run is defined as a period long enough so that *all* factors of production become variable. In the manufacturing case, that means a period long enough so that the firm could plan to build one or more new plants, discard old ones, or even go into a new line of business.

What are the analogous definitions in the live performing arts? In the case of plays offered in the commercial theater, the short run is the life of a single production. Over that period the play's production costs, comprising all expenses that were committed before opening night, are a fixed cost. The producer's decisions are limited to deciding how long the play should run and at what ticket prices. The long run in the commercial theater is a period over which the producer can contemplate mounting additional plays or musicals, different in type, larger or smaller in scale, in the same or other venues.

We argued that it is unrealistic to think in terms of single productions in the not-for-profit sector, since most companies put on a season or repertory of productions each year. This logic applies equally well to theater, opera, ballet and modern dance, and symphony concerts. Accordingly, the short run for the nonprofit performing arts organization is best defined not as the run of a single production, but as the length of one season. The season is the planning unit. The individual productions are conceived not singly but as a package, complementary with one another. While it may sometimes be possible to change course in midseason, that is rarely done. Thus, the production costs for a given season are essentially fixed once the season begins, which gives "the season" its economic character of being "the short run." The long run is then a period longer than a single season. In the long run, management can contemplate putting on more or less elaborate productions, a longer or shorter season, a season comprising a larger or smaller number of individual productions, or it can move to a different venue or even go out of business.

One of the most interesting questions that can be asked about any production process is, How do costs per unit of output behave when the scale of production increases? By scale, economists mean the size of the producing enterprise, with size measured by physical output when plant and equipment are operated at designed capacity. If we plot scale on the horizontal axis and average unit cost on the vertical, we generate the firm's long-run average cost curve. So another way of putting the preceding question would be, What is the shape of the firm's long-run average cost curve?

The question is interesting in part because there is no a priori answer; each industry has to be investigated empirically. Three possible long-run cost patterns are denoted as follows: economies of scale, if unit cost falls as the scale of output increases; constant returns to scale, if unit cost is unchanged; diseconomies of scale, if unit cost rises. In most cases the outcome will be some combination of these tendencies. In manufacturing, for example, firms in most industries enjoy economies of scale up to some minimum efficient size, after which there is a broad range of output marked by constant returns to scale. At very large scales, diseconomies may set in. Evidence on this last point, however, is hard to come by. Indeed, in a competitive world we would not expect to find many firms that had expanded into a range where unit costs were increasing, since such behavior would be self-destructive.

Economies of scale in the live performing arts

Since the season is the planning unit for most nonprofit performing arts enterprises, *length* of season, as measured by number of performances – or, for symphony orchestras, the number of concerts – is the appropriate indicator of scale for studying the behavior of costs in the long run. (This is analogous to the use of plant size as the measure of scale in the manufacturing case.)

The existence of economies of scale in the live performing arts has been confirmed empirically a number of times. Baumol and Bowen, probably the earliest to do an empirical study, found that for most of the 11 symphony orchestras in their sample, cost per concert fell significantly as the number of concerts per year increased. In the typical case, unit cost did not decline over the entire range of outputs. Rather, it reached a minimum at a point that varied across orchestras at somewhere from 90 to 150 concerts per year and then leveled off.[8]

The authors speculated that the observed economies of scale probably arose from two sources. Most important would be the fact that up to some point an orchestra can play more concerts without investing in more rehearsal time. For example, if it sells subscriptions in three series (say, Thursday evenings, Friday evenings, and Sunday afternoons), it can perform the same music three times a week. If demand picks up to the point where a fourth series is justified, it can play the same music a fourth time without additional rehearsal expense. A second source of economies of scale (probably less important) is the fact that the administrative expense of running the orchestra need not increase with each increase in the number of concerts performed. Thus, "overhead" can be spread over more output, reducing the level of average fixed cost per concert as the season lengthens.

Savings analogous to both economies of scale should be available to producers of theatrical repertory, opera, ballet, or other kinds of dance. Hence, we would expect to find economies of scale operating in all kinds of live performance art. Steven Globerman and Sam H. Book, using a somewhat different methodology than Baumol and Bowen, studied a sample of Canadian symphony orchestras and theater companies. They

---

[8] William J. Baumol and William G. Bowen, *Performing Arts: The Economic Dilemma* (New York: Twentieth Century Fund, 1966), pp. 201–7, 479–81.

confirmed the existence of economies of scale in orchestra performance up to a level of about 115 performances per year. For theater companies they found that economies of scale extended much farther: "minimum cost per performance . . . was obtained at approximately 210 performances."[9] They surmised that the greater economies of scale available to theater groups reflected higher fixed costs per production in theatrical activity, as compared with symphony concerts.

Finally, in 1985 Mark Lange and his coauthors, using a much larger data set than Baumol and Bowen and a different econometric technique, also confirmed the existence of economies of scale for symphony orchestras.[10] They found that average cost per concert declined as output rose from 1 to 65 concerts per year, was constant over the wide range between 67 and 177 concerts, and rose sharply at higher outputs. The authors speculated that greater commitments to touring or special events, or other differences in the type or quality of output, might explain the higher unit costs encountered by orchestras giving the most concerts per year, but they were unable to confirm that statistically.

The effects of donations and grants

Firms in the commercial sector of the live performing arts do not receive government grants and are not eligible to accept tax-deductible charitable donations. Consequently, they rise or fall on their ability to sell tickets at the box office or (very rarely) to sell movie or other ancillary rights to their artistic properties. Nonprofit firms, on the other hand, do sometimes receive public funds and are also eligible to accept tax-deductible private donations. In fact, the principal reason they are organized on a not-for-profit basis is to become eligible for such tax-deductible private support. A survey of the finances of 166 nonprofit performing arts institutions by the Ford Foundation revealed that charitable contributions by individuals, business firms, and foundations accounted for 35 to 38 percent of total operating income in the years from 1965 to 1971.[11] Indeed, such support is so important in the United States that we devote most of Chapter 12 to it.

Grants-in-aid from the federal government, through the National Endowment for the Arts, and from state and local governments, through their arts councils, are also significant in the budgets of nonprofit firms.

---

[9] Steven Globerman and Sam H. Book, "Statistical Cost Functions for Performing Arts Organizations," *Southern Economic Journal*, 40, no. 4 (April 1974): 668–71, cited at 671.

[10] Lange et al., "Cost Functions for Symphony Orchestras," pp. 71–85.

[11] *The Finances of the Performing Arts*, vol. 1 (New York: Ford Foundation, 1974), app. C, table 4.

The arguments for and against public subsidies will be carefully weighed in Chapter 11. This is the appropriate point, however, at which to examine the probable effects of both private donations and government grants on the price–output decisions of nonprofit performing arts producers.

Donations and grants may be given either with conditions attached that specify how they must be spent or as unrestricted contributions that can be used in whatever way the recipient chooses. Since aid to nonprofit performing arts institutions usually takes the unrestricted form, we assume it in the following analysis.[12]

Once the objective of nonprofit firms in the performing arts is understood, the probable effect of grants and donations on their price–output choices becomes clear. We have argued that their objective is to maximize attendance, while presenting a repertoire that meets self-imposed quality standards and is subject to the requirement of a balanced budget. Assume initially that the quality of the chosen repertoire is not affected by the availability of donations or grants. In that case, the effect of such contributions will be to allow the firm to reduce ticket prices and thus expand attendance. This result is illustrated in Figure 7.2, in which the demand and average total cost curves are carried over from Figure 7.1. (The marginal revenue and marginal cost curves have been omitted, since they are irrelevant when profit maximization is not the objective.) In the absence of donations or subsidies, the firm operates at point F. Q_2 tickets are sold at a price of P_2, which just covers average total cost. When contributed income becomes available, prices can be set *below* the level of cost, by an amount that reflects the available subsidy. In this instance they are reduced to P_3 (at point K) and attendance rises to Q_3. The average total cost per seat at output Q_3 is ATC_3 (as indicated by point J). There is now a deficit per seat of $ATC_3 - P_3$. The aggregate deficit of $Q_3 \times (ATC_3 - P_3)$ is indicated by the shaded rectangle and, if the firm's financial forecasts are accurate, just equals the amount of contributed income that is available. The diagram has been drawn so that contributed income covers 40 percent of total expense, approximately the proportion that obtained in the performing arts during the 1980s.[13]

It may be too restrictive, however, to assume that the quality of output established by a nonprofit performing arts firm is unaffected by the

---

[12] Throsby and Withers, *The Economics of the Performing Arts,* analyze the effects of additional types of subsidy at pp. 22–25.

[13] See, e.g., the data on 32 major U.S. dance companies in 1984 in Dick Netzer, "Dance in New York: Market and Subsidy Changes," *American Economic Review,* 76, no. 2 (May 1986): 15–19, cited at table 1, p. 17.

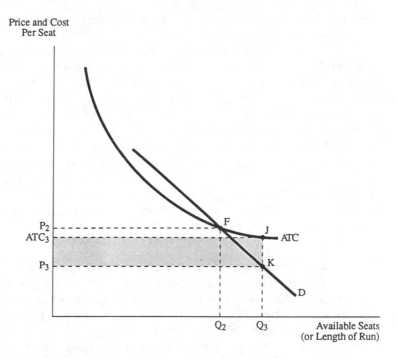

Figure 7.2. Effect of a subsidy on price and output: a nonprofit performing arts firm.

availability of contributed income. Although dollars can be wasted in the arts as elsewhere, it is nevertheless true that higher quality performances and productions generally cost more to put on. Consequently, it is likely that some firms will try to improve the quality of their productions or will choose a higher quality repertoire when financial aid is available to help cover the higher cost.[14] Indeed, donations and grants are sometimes given expressly for the purpose of improving performance or production quality. If the beneficiary responds to that stimulus by raising quality, the average total cost curve shown in Figure 7.2 would shift upward when donations or grants become available. Assuming demand to be unaffected by the change in quality, the decline in ticket prices and the rise in attendance would then be less than depicted in Figure 7.2. If, however, the demand curve were to shift upward in response to higher quality, there would be an additional impetus both to greater attendance and to higher prices. In either case, at the end of the process in which quality was adjusted, we would expect prices to be

[14] Throsby and Withers, *The Economics of the Performing Arts,* pp. 23–24.

lower and quality and attendance higher than they would have been in the absence of contributed income.

It has already been pointed out that donations are nowadays an important source of income to nonprofit performing arts groups. Henry Hansmann notes that a large fraction of the donations received from individuals appears to come "from people who actually attend the groups' performances." The willingness of these donors to contribute is likely to be inversely related to ticket prices. Consequently, he argues for (and develops) a theory of behavior in which the nonprofit firm explicitly takes into account the effect of its ticket prices on donations.[15] He considers various possible objectives for the firm, among which the goal of maximizing aggregate revenue from ticket sales and donations is only one. Needless to say, his theory is far more complex than the one that has been presented in this chapter.

Institutional size, market structure, and innovation

Although donations and grants are sometimes given for the purpose of underwriting new productions or raising the general level of quality attained by performing arts companies, they may indirectly exert an opposite influence as well. Paul J. DiMaggio points out that contributed income, especially when it is given in the form of "challenge grants," is usually associated with institutional growth.[16] The receiving organization is encouraged not only to seek "matching" funds, but also to add administrative staff assigned to development, marketing, and financial administration. Sometimes contributions are earmarked for acquisition of a larger hall in which to perform. The inevitable result of such growth is a large increase in overhead costs, and that may, in subtle ways, affect artistic policy.

It has often been noticed that as institutions grow they become more conservative. The very phrase "the establishment" connotes conformity, inflexibility, an unwillingness to take risks. In a study of the repertories of U.S. nonprofit theaters, Paul DiMaggio and Kristen Stenberg tested the hypothesis that institutional size is positively related to conformity or, to put it the other way, negatively associated with innovation and

---

[15] Henry Hansmann, "Nonprofit Enterprise in the Performing Arts," in Paul J. DiMaggio, ed., *Nonprofit Enterprise in the Arts* (New York: Oxford University Press, 1986), pp. 17–40.

[16] Paul J. DiMaggio, "The Nonprofit Instrument and the Influence of the Marketplace on Policies in the Arts," in W. McNeil Lowry, ed., *The Arts and Public Policy in the United States* (Englewood Cliffs, N.J.: Prentice-Hall, for the American Assembly of Columbia University, 1984), pp. 57–99, cited at 70.

risk taking.[17] They obtained data on the more than 150 nonprofit drama companies that were members of the Theatre Communications Group in the 1977–78 and 1978–79 seasons. Included were almost all of the large resident (or "regional") U.S. theaters. DiMaggio and Stenberg measured conformity–nonconformity by means of an index equal to the average number of times that each play in a given theater's repertory was produced by *all* theaters in the study group over the two seasons. If a given theater had a score of 1, that meant no other company produced any of the same plays. On the other hand, a score of 4 meant that, on average, three other theaters in the group also produced each play in the given company's repertory. The higher the index the more conformist (i.e., the less innovative) was the given company's repertory.

DiMaggio and Stenberg's results show clearly that, outside of New York City, conformity of repertory increases both with institutional size, as measured by the operating budget, and with size of the company's house.[18] In other words, holding other variables constant, the larger its budget and the more seats it has to fill by appeal to the market, the less innovative a company is likely to be. It is hard to avoid the conclusion that theatrical groups (and probably other performing arts institutions, as well) grow less creative as they become more successful, at least as success is measured in the marketplace. Thus, grants and donations, to the extent that they contribute to "success," may indirectly create burdens that limit creativity.

Competition encourages artistic innovation

But there is a second part to this story, leading to a more optimistic conclusion. For nonprofit theaters in New York City, Di-Maggio and Stenberg obtained very different results. First, the average index of conformity was much lower in New York than elsewhere. Second, size of house has no effect on conformity in New York, and the effect of budget size on conformity is much weaker than elsewhere. The authors conclude that the much higher level of innovation found on the New York stage is attributable in part to the intense competition between nonprofit companies and the Broadway theater, so different from the situation in smaller, less developed markets. As they put it:

> In most American cities, a single major theatre holds a virtual monopoly of regular programming. In New York, competition encourages

---

[17] Paul DiMaggio and Kristen Stenberg, "Why Do Some Theatres Innovate More than Others? An Empirical Analysis," *Poetics,* 14 (1985): 107–22.
[18] Ibid., pp. 115–18.

differentiation and different theatres occupy different niches. Because the commercial Broadway stage entertains the casual theatregoer more lavishly than resident theatres can, the latter are pressed towards innovation as a competitive strategy.[19]

In that situation, as DiMaggio has written elsewhere, "innovation is not a poor market strategy." Even though larger companies may be more conformist, larger markets apparently lead, by way of greater competition, to increased innovation.

These findings are encouraging because they suggest that as the audience for the arts grows larger in any locality and the number of local companies increases, competition will bring greater diversity, more risk taking, and increased creativity. Thus, in the longer run "more" may also mean "better."

Summary

In this chapter we have presented a model of the performing arts firm – applicable alike in the fields of theater, ballet, opera, and symphony – that predicts how firms will set ticket prices and determine the length of run or, in the case of repertory production, length of season. It was shown that ticket prices will tend to be lower and, therefore, length of run longer in the nonprofit as compared with the commercial sector. The model also suggests that economies of scale exist in the live performing arts: as length of run or season increases, cost per seat declines.

The chapter opened with a description of the four kinds of market structure – perfect competition, oligopoly, pure monopoly, and monopolistic competition – that according to standard economic analysis, differentially affect firms' price and output decisions. It was pointed out, however, that only the last two are relevant for analysis of the arts. The chapter closed with a summary of DiMaggio and Stenberg's research on the repertory of nonprofit theater companies, which showed that market structure also has a strong effect on *qualitative* aspects of performing arts output: where the market is larger and therefore more competitive, as in New York City, theater companies are more innovative or, in artistic terms, more creative than are otherwise similar companies in smaller markets. The interesting implication of this finding is that as local audiences grow larger, local performing arts producers will probably become less risk-averse and hence more creative.

[19] Ibid., p. 116.

8

Productivity lag and the financial problem of the arts

Both economists and laypersons understand "economic growth" to mean growth in output per capita, in other words, the happy situation in which a society's total production grows faster than its population, so that more goods and services become available per person. Only when a nation's economy consistently produces such growth can its citizens enjoy a steadily rising standard of living. But what can bring this about? The answer is a rise in productivity. Assuming for simplicity that the length of the workweek and the proportion of the population that is working remain constant as the economy grows, a given rise in productivity, which is the name economists give to output per work-hour, will bring about an equivalent increase in output per capita and therefore in living standards.

Until the 1970s, productivity in the U.S. economy had increased by an average of 2 to 3 percent per year.[1] During that decade, the average growth declined to 0.5 percent per year before recovering somewhat in the 1980s.[2] However, the long-run growth pattern has not been uniform across industries. In particular, output per worker has risen much faster in manufacturing than in certain kinds of service industries like education, nursing home care, barbershops, appliance repair, gourmet food preparation, and – relevant for the purposes of this chapter – the live performing arts. Such industries are said to suffer from "productivity lag." Diverse as their outputs may sound, these industries have in common a single characteristic that inhibits increases in output per work-hour: in each of them it is difficult, perhaps impossible, to substitute

---

[1] See William J. Baumol and William G. Bowen, *Performing Arts: The Economic Dilemma* (New York: Twentieth Century Fund, 1966), p. 162.
[2] Edward F. Denison, *Accounting for Slower Economic Growth: The United States in the 1970s* (Washington, D.C.: Brookings Institution, 1979), esp. chaps. 1–3.

machinery for labor, and more machinery per worker is an important source of increased productivity.

As we shall show in this chapter, interindustry differences in the trend of productivity have one very important consequence: they cause related but opposite differences in the trend of unit costs. The cost of services in which output per work-hour increases slowly rises relative to the cost of goods for which gains in output per work-hour are more rapid, and the cost of services like education or the live performing arts, in which output per work-hour is almost unchangeable, rises most of all. The connection between lagging productivity and rising cost in the live performing arts was first explored by Baumol and Bowen in their classic 1966 study, *Performing Arts: The Economic Dilemma,* and the dilemma referred to in the title is the problem of financing the live performing arts in the face of ineluctably rising unit costs.[3]

The productivity lag argument

The argument we shall be making in this chapter, based on Baumol and Bowen's analysis, can be summarized as follows: costs in the live performing arts will rise relative to costs in the economy as a whole because wage increases in the arts have to keep up with those in the general economy even though productivity improvements in the arts lag behind. It is not suggested that artists must be paid the same hourly wage as workers in other jobs, since working conditions and the non-monetary satisfaction obtained from employment differ across occupations. Rather, the argument is that all industries, including the arts, compete to hire workers in a nationally integrated labor market and that artists' wages must therefore rise over time by the same proportion as wages in the general economy to enable the arts industry to hire the workers it needs to carry on.

In any economy there are five possible sources of growth in physical output per work-hour:

1. Increased capital per worker. If workers are provided with more machinery, output per work-hour rises: ten workers with two front-loaders and two trucks can move more earth in an hour than ten workers with one front-loader and one truck.
2. Improved technology. Technology can be defined as the state of knowledge about methods of production. The introduction of bulldozers and front-loaders to replace pickaxes and shovels, for example, was an improvement in technology that vastly increased output per work-hour in the earth-moving trades.

---

[3] Baumol and Bowen, *Performing Arts,* esp. chap. 7.

3. Increased labor skill. Obviously, if workers are more skillful they can produce more output per hour. Skills may be improved either by education or by on-the-job training.
4. Better management. If managers develop more efficient ways of organizing the production process, output per workhour will rise.
5. Economies of scale. In some production processes (there is no rule about this) output per unit of input rises when the *scale* of production increases. Automobile manufacturing is a prominent example. Such industries are said to enjoy economies of scale and, among other things, display increased output per work-hour as the scale of output rises. (Economies and diseconomies of scale were discussed in Chapter 7.)

As one might guess from this list of causes, productivity increases are achieved most readily in industries that make use of a lot of productive equipment. Output per worker can then be increased either by using more machinery or by investing in new equipment that embodies improved technology. As a result, in the typical manufacturing industry the amount of labor time needed to produce a physical unit of output declines dramatically decade after decade. The live performing arts are at the other end of the spectrum. Machinery, equipment, and technology play only a small role and, in any case, change very little over time. That is not to say that technological improvements are entirely absent. For example, stage lighting has been revolutionized by the development of electronic controls and audience comfort greatly enhanced by air-conditioning, which also facilitates longer seasons and more flexible scheduling. But these improvements are not central to the business at hand. As Baumol and Bowen point out, the conditions of production themselves preclude any substantial change in productivity because "the work of the performer is an end in itself, not a means for the production of some good."[4] Since the performer's labor *is* the output – the singer singing, the dancer dancing, the pianist playing – there is really no way to increase output per hour. It takes four musicians as much playing time to perform a Beethoven string quartet today as it did when it was first published in 1800.

Of the five sources of increased productivity cited, only economies of scale, in this case the result of longer seasons, is really effective in the live performing arts. With only that factor to rely on, the live performing arts, as Baumol and Bowen emphasize, "cannot hope to match the remarkable record of productivity growth achieved by the economy as

[4] Ibid., p. 164.

a whole."[5] As a result, cost per unit of output in the live performing arts is fated to rise continuously relative to costs in the economy as a whole. That, in brief, is the unavoidable consequence of productivity lag.

On the other hand, industries in the "progressive" sector, in which productivity rises at a substantial rate, find themselves in a very favorable position. They can raise wages each year at the same rate at which productivity improves without increasing their unit labor costs at all. Hence, their prices need not rise even though their wages do.

Algebraic explanation of the effects of productivity lag

These propositions can be supported by formal analysis. Let us define the following terms:

w = wage per hour
opw = physical output per work-hour (productivity)
ulc = unit labor cost = w/opw
k = annual rate of increase in output per work-hour in the general economy

Subscripts 0 and 1 will be used to indicate values in successive years, beginning with year 0.

We make the following assumptions:

1. There is no *general* inflation. When we speak of cost increases in the live performing arts we mean increases relative to a stable general price level.
2. Productivity, measured by physical output per work-hour, rises by k percent per year in the general economy.
3. Productivity does not rise at all in the live performing arts. Therefore, productivity lag in the arts sector is k percent per year.
4. Wages in the general economy rise at the same rate as opw does, namely, k percent per year.
5. Wages in the arts also rise by k percent per year so that the arts can remain competitive with other industries in the labor market.

Given these assumptions, we can show:

a. Unit labor costs remain constant in the general economy, allowing prices to remain constant even though wages are rising.
b. Unit labor costs rise in the arts sector at a rate equal to the rate of productivity lag.

[5] Ibid., p. 165.

c. It follows from statements a and b that costs rise in the arts relative to those in the general economy at the same rate at which arts sector productivity lags.

The algebraic argument is as follows:

In the general economy in year 0, we have

$$ulc_0 = \frac{w_0}{opw_0}$$

In year 1,

$$ulc_1 = \frac{w_1}{opw_1} = \frac{(1 + k) \, w_0}{(1 + k) \, opw_0}$$

But since the $(1 + k)$ terms cancel out,

$$ulc_1 = \frac{w_0}{opw_0} = ulc_0$$

Thus, wages in the general economy can rise at the same rate as productivity without causing unit labor costs to increase.

In the live performing arts in year 0,

$$ulc_0 = \frac{w_0}{opw_0}$$

In year 1, recalling that wages increase while productivity does not, we have

$$ulc_1 = \frac{w_1}{opw_1} = \frac{(1 + k) \, w_0}{opw_0}$$

Substituting ulc_0 for w_0/opw_0, we find that

$$ulc_1 = (1 + k) \, ulc_0$$

Thus, unit labor costs in the arts sector rise by k percent per year, which is the annual rate by which the growth of arts productivity "lags." Since unit labor costs are constant in the general economy, it also follows that costs in the arts rise k percent per year relative to those in the general economy.

A numerical example

If this demonstration is disturbingly abstract, it can easily be illustrated numerically. In Table 8.1 the upper panel shows the situation in a hypothetical manufacturing industry where productivity is increasing. Assume that widgets are the product. Output per work-hour is

Table 8.1. *Hypothetical illustration of productivity lag*

	1980	1990	Percent change, 1980–90
Widget industry			
Output in widgets per workhour (*opw*)	20	24	+20
Wage per hour (*w*), dollars	10	12	+20
Unit labor cost (*ulc*) per widget = *w*/*opw*, dollars	.50	.50	0
Symphony orchestra			
Output, measured by admissions per workhour (*opw*)[a]	2	2	0
Wage per hour (*w*), dollars	20	24	+20
Unit labor cost (*ulc*) per admission = *w*/*opw*, dollars	10	12	+20

[a]Explanation: Size of concert hall = 1,600; concerts per week = 5; potential admissions per week = 8,000; number of musicians = 100; musician workhours per week = 40; orchestra hours per week = 4,000; output per workhour: admissions per week ÷ orchestra hours per week = 8,000 ÷ 4,000 = 2.

therefore measured by widgets produced per worker per hour. The first row shows that *opw* rises from 20 widgets in 1980 to 24 in 1990, an increase of 20 percent. Wages, shown in the second row, rise at the same rate as productivity, increasing from $10 per hour in 1980 to $12 an hour in 1990. Unit labor cost, equal to wages per work-hour divided by output per work-hour, is shown in the third row. In 1980, *ulc* = $10/20 widgets, or 50 cents per widget. In 1990 unit labor cost is unchanged. Though wages have risen 20 percent, so has output per work-hour, leaving *ulc* still at 50 cents per widget. Thus, wages in a progressive industry can rise as fast as productivity without causing any increase in costs.

The lower panel of the table shows the situation in a hypothetical symphony orchestra, a live performing arts institution in which productivity is stagnant. We assume the following production conditions. The orchestra consists of 100 musicians. It plays five concerts per week in a hall that seats 1,600. Potential admissions (the "output" of the orchestra in productivity terms) is therefore 8,000 per week. The musicians work a 40-hour week. Output per work-hour of the orchestra is therefore 8,000/40 or 200 admissions. Since there are 100 musicians, output per work-hour per musician is 2 admissions. This is shown as *opw* in the first row of the lower panel and is unchanged from 1980 to 1990.

The second row of the lower panel shows that wages per hour for players in the orchestra rose from $20 in 1980 to $24 in 1990, an increase of 20 percent that matches the upward movement of wages in the general economy. Unit labor costs for the orchestra are shown in the third row. In 1980 hourly wages were $20 and output per work-hour was 2 admissions, yielding ulc = $10 per admission. By 1990 wages had increased to $24 an hour, while opw remained at 2, so that unit labor cost increased to $12 per admission. These hypothetical numbers show that in the live performing arts, unit labor costs rise over time by the same rate at which productivity gains in the arts lag behind those in the general economy.

Historical evidence on costs

The historical record strongly supports the hypothesis that because of productivity lag, unit costs in the live performing arts increase substantially faster than the general price level does. A great deal of such evidence was unearthed by Baumol and Bowen.[6] Their earliest cost data are for productions at the Drury Lane Theatre in London in the eighteenth century. They compared average cost per performance at the Drury Lane in the seasons 1771–72 through 1775–76 with costs per performance of the Royal Shakespeare Theatre in 1963–64. In that period of almost two centuries, cost per performance multiplied 13.6 times. Over the same period a historical index of overall British prices shows them to have increased only 6.2 times.[7] These increases can also be expressed as compound annual rates of growth, that is, as the annual growth rate that, if applied to the starting figure and compounded over the period in question, would result in the indicated final magnitude. On that measure, theatrical costs increased 1.4 percent per year while the annual rate of increase for the general price level was only 0.9 percent.

In the United States, Baumol and Bowen put together a nearly continuous cost history for the New York Philharmonic Orchestra beginning in 1843. Between that date and 1964, cost per concert rose at a compound annual rate of 2.5 percent, while the U.S. index of wholesale prices rose an average of 1.0 percent per year. As Baumol and Bowen point out, the apparently small difference between these numbers leads to a startling divergence in costs when compounded decade after decade: the orchestra's cost per concert multiplied 20 times over in 121 years, while the general price level only quadrupled.[8]

For the years after World War II, Baumol and Bowen analyzed data

---

[6] Ibid., chap. 8.
[7] Ibid., pp. 182–83.
[8] Ibid., p. 187.

on 23 major U.S. orchestras, three opera companies, one dance company, and a sample of Broadway, regional, and summer theaters. In every group, the same results showed up: cost per performance increased far more rapidly than the general price level. Moreover, they found a pattern in the postwar experience of Britain's Royal Shakespeare Theatre and London's Covent Garden (venue for the Royal Opera and Royal Ballet) so strikingly similar to U.S. experience that they were encouraged to speculate that the structural problem of production in the live performing arts is one "that knows no national boundaries."[9]

The consequences of productivity lag, or why worry about it?

The facts of productivity lag are not in doubt. Everyone agrees that it causes costs, and presumably prices, in the live performing arts to rise relative to costs in the general economy, and that in the long run an extraordinary divergence in prices can occur. But one may well ask, So what? Why should we worry about it? After all, many service activities besides the arts are afflicted with productivity lag. It takes a barber just as long to cut hair, or a fine restaurant just as long to prepare and serve a gourmet meal, now as it did 50 years ago. Consequently, the prices of those services (and many others in which technological improvements are absent or unimportant) have risen far more rapidly than the general price level. Yet we hear no outcry about a haircutting crisis or an impending financial collapse of the gourmet restaurant industry. Why should we worry about productivity lag in the live performing arts? Why not let the arts suffer whatever consequences the uneven progress of technological change metes out for them?

The answer must be that the arts are a matter of special social concern and that we are therefore unwilling to leave their fate to the dictates of the market as we do haircuts and gourmet meals. This, however, is not the place to discuss how or why the arts may be different: those questions are taken up in detail in Chapter 11. At this stage we simply explain the two principal points made by those who are concerned about the effects of productivity lag.

First, as we have already seen, productivity lag leads to steadily rising ticket prices for the live performing arts. This, in turn, makes it increasingly difficult to attract people of low or moderate income to the audience. The availability at relatively *low* prices of *non*live entertainment via the mass media – TV, motion pictures, records, tapes, and compact discs (precisely the modes in which technological progress *has* been

[9] Ibid., p. 201.

important) – makes it even more difficult to attract the relatively poor. We have already documented (in Chapter 3) the fact that in U.S. arts audiences, those with low or even moderate incomes are grossly underrepresented. Anyone who believes that this virtually automatic exclusion of the poor is socially undesirable is likely to be alarmed at the inexorable rise in ticket prices dictated by productivity lag.

The second unfortunate effect of productivity lag is that it puts the nonprofit institutions responsible for most of our live performing arts under unremitting financial pressure. Because relative costs are continuously increasing, they are under great pressure to raise ticket prices faster than the general rate of inflation, a strategy that is not easy to carry out and that they probably find philosophically repugnant. While it is difficult to demonstrate rigorously, it seems reasonable to believe that a nonprofit firm would find it easier to balance its budget in a technologically progressive industry, where unit costs are stable or falling year by year, than in a lagging one, where real costs are constantly moving upward and prices charged to customers must do likewise.

The financial problems facing performing arts groups as a result of productivity lag were emphasized by Baumol and Bowen.[10] For them and for later writers, a company's "earnings gap," defined as the difference between its expenditures and its earned income, has appeared to be the most useful (though a far from unambiguous) measure of the financial strain it faces. In general the gap is covered by some combination of private donations and government subsidy. Later in this chapter we will discuss the size of the gap in some typical arts organizations, whether it has been growing relative to expenditures, and what, if any, trends are discernible in the kinds of financing used to cover it. First, however, we must look at some possible countervailing forces to the effects of productivity lag.

Offsets to the effects of productivity lag

By countervailing forces to productivity lag, we mean not policy responses initiated by the arts institutions themselves, but rather economic effects that can be expected to operate on their own to ease indirectly the pressures generated by productivity lag. The first of these is rising living standards.

The effect of rising living standards

The problem of productivity lag exists only because there is persistent technological progress in the general economy, which causes

[10] Ibid., esp. chaps. 6 and 12.

a rise in output per work-hour and in real wages, in other words, a rise in per capita income. Income per capita, as we have seen, is one of the determinants of demand for the arts. Regardless of what the exact value of the income elasticity of demand for art turns out to be, we can be certain that it is well above zero. Therefore, as income rises, other things remaining the same, the demand for art will increase. In the case of the live performing arts, the demand curve for tickets will shift to the right: at any given price level, the public will be willing to buy more tickets than it did previously. Thus, while productivity lag causes ticket prices to rise, which would lead to a *decline* in quantity demanded, rising income to some extent offsets that effect by *stimulating* ticket purchases. This does not mean that productivity lag causes no problems, but only that rising living standards will work to mitigate them. Perhaps an analogy is in order. Because of productivity lag in the business of high-quality food preparation, the price of a meal in a gourmet restaurant has risen sharply in recent years. That probably causes a good deal of anguish both to customers and to owners, but it has not prevented the gourmet restaurant business from growing. A similar effect is likely in the live performing arts. Baumol and Bowen have been criticized for giving it insufficient emphasis.[11]

The effect of economies of scale

It was shown in Chapter 7 that the live performing arts display systematic economies of scale in production. When length of run or season is taken as the measure of scale, the unit cost of output falls as output rises because the fixed costs of any one production or any given repertory can be spread over more performances as their number increases. This effect works in tandem with rising living standards. As per capita income increases, demand curves for admission shift to the right, more tickets are sold, and performance seasons grow longer. The resulting decline in unit costs can help to offset the cost-increasing effect of productivity lag.

Income from the mass media

Although technological progress has had little direct effect on the live performing arts, its indirect impact via the mass media is potentially large. In the past hundred years, technological change has given us (in rapid sequence) the phonograph record, motion pictures, radio broadcasting, television, long-playing records, tape recording, satellite

---

[11] See, e.g., C. D. Throsby and G. A. Withers, *The Economics of the Performing Arts* (New York: St. Martin's, 1979), pp. 51–52, 170–71, and esp. 291.

and cable systems, videocassette recorders, and, most recently, compact discs and videodiscs. With the possible exception of motion pictures, each of these innovations provided a market for *non*live performance art that could yield significant income to groups producing the *live* version. Such income could help to offset the adverse budgetary impact of productivity lag. Symphony orchestras, to pick the most obvious example, might now earn royalties from the sale of prerecorded tapes or compact discs or, some years back, from phonograph records. Theater, ballet, and opera companies, in addition to earning royalties from the sale of prerecorded tapes or videodiscs, could be paid for performances on broadcast or cable TV. Indeed, in the analogous case of professional sports, earnings from television far outweigh income from ticket sales.

Unhappily, this potential revenue has not materialized. Royalties from recordings are trivial for most U.S. symphony orchestras, and the trend has been down. Two important reasons are the flight of the classical music recording industry to Europe, where performance costs are far lower, and the impact of technological progress itself – tape recordings made at home, either from broadcast music or from borrowed records devastated the commercial sale of recorded music in the 1970s. New innovations, for example, the compact disc and the videodisc, raise hopes that sales and royalties may revive. But in the long run it seems likely that homemade copies of some sort will limit the market for new recordings. And it must be remembered that even at its highest just after the introduction of long-playing records in the 1950s, the income that most symphony orchestras earned from recordings was insignificant.

Income from television performances has been equally disappointing, A retail grocer, standing in front of his shop, was asked how business had been that day. He replied: "It was kind of quiet in the morning. Then in the afternoon it slowed down." That is also the story of culture on commercial television. In the early days of commercial TV, the networks made a modest effort to present high culture on the tube. Even then, however, the number of performances contracted for was so low, when measured against the size of the arts industry nationwide, that the income earned from broadcasting could only be described as negligible. The Ford Foundation study of finances in the performing arts found that in 1965–66 earnings of symphony orchestras from the combined categories of recordings, films, radio, and TV amounted to only 1.2 percent of total operating income. By 1970–71, the last year covered in the study, the figure had fallen to 0.8 percent.[12]

---

[12] *The Finances of the Performing Arts* (New York: Ford Foundation, 1974), vol. 1, app. C, p. 31.

As time went by and public television became increasingly important, the commercial networks virtually abandoned cultural programming to the public stations. Arts companies' performance income from broadcasting remained trivial. A new wave of hope gathered strength in the early years of cable TV. Enthusiasts for culture believed that the increasing number of homes served by cable would make it commercially feasible to cater to specialized audiences such as those who might want to hear and watch opera, dance, and serious dramatic productions at home. The new strategy was described as "narrowcasting." Unhappily, as a way of distributing culture, it has not worked out. If managers of opera, ballet, or theater companies thought that cable TV would open up the important new source of performance income that broadcast television had been unable to deliver, they were again seriously disappointed. (For additional detail see Chapter 16.)

In assessing the prospect that the mass media might at some future date become heavy purchasers of performing arts entertainment, there is further bad news to keep in mind: Hilda Baumol and William J. Baumol have pointed out that program production costs on TV are subject to inflation on account of productivity lag for exactly the same reason as costs in the live sector are. They found that TV production costs per program hour for material technically similar to live performance entertainment rose 143 percent between 1964 and 1976.[13] The Producer Price Index over the same interval rose only 81 percent. Productivity lag probably accounts for the difference. Thus, the same cost problem that bedevils live productions of the performing arts reappears to limit the prospect of substantial sales to the mass media.

Competition with the mass media for inputs

Not only have the mass media failed to yield significant income for the live performing arts, they have actually made matters worse in that sector by bidding up prices of the professional inputs that both the mass media and the live performing arts employ. Of course, the performers whose incomes have increased as a result of this labor market competition will not regard it as a bad thing. But the institutions that employ them to produce live performances will find their personnel costs rising at a very uncomfortable rate.

Since the wage effect referred to here is transmitted from one sector (the mass media) to another (the live performing arts) through com-

---

[13] Hilda Baumol and William J. Baumol, "The Mass Media and the Cost Disease," in William S. Hendon et al., eds., *The Economics of Cultural Industries*, pp. 109–23 (Akron, Ohio: Association for Cultural Economics, 1984), table 2, p. 113.

petition to hire in the labor market, it bears a strong formal resemblance to the productivity lag effect. The point is that performers of "star" quality like Meryl Streep, Liza Minelli, or Luciano Pavarotti can command enormous salaries when they work in motion pictures or on TV. They earn such salaries because the mass media now have a vast audience in an international market, and the presence of a star performer can make a big difference at the movie box office or (for TV) in the ratings war.[14] Inevitably, wage inflation at the upper end exerts an upward pull on the wages paid to actors and singers who play "supporting" roles, and so eventually the whole spectrum of performance wages is drawn upward, not only in the mass media, but also in the live arts, which must compete with the mass media for talent. A like effect probably operates for other artistic personnel such as stage, music, and dance directors whose services are required by both the mass media and the live performing arts. In Chapter 14 we will reexamine this matter from a labor market perspective.

The process just described might be called "the mass media wage effect." Whatever we call it, however, it is not a new story. In his study of the economics of U.S. theater, Thomas Gale Moore found that during the 1930s, a decade of nationwide deflation brought on by the Great Depression, operating costs on Broadway actually *rose*. He attributed this increase to the arrival of sound in Hollywood. The first "talking picture" was *The Jazz Singer,* which opened in 1927. Thereafter, Hollywood developed a ravenous appetite for singers, dancers, and composers, for writers who could compose dialogue, actors who could project it, and directors who could put it all together. The longtime home of these talents was the Broadway stage. Hollywood began to hire them away in the 1930s and in the process drove up wages and costs on Broadway, despite the fact that in the nation as a whole, prices and costs had gone down.[15]

In assessing the problem of costs in the live performing arts, the mass media wage effect must be thought of as additive with the effect of productivity lag: it is evil tidings piled on top of bad news.

Costs and revenues in the performing arts

Table 8.2 provides an account of costs, revenues, and the earnings gap of a hypothetical nonprofit firm in the performing arts. The

---

[14] See Sherwin Rosen, "The Economics of Superstars," *American Economic Review,* 71, no. 5 (December 1981): 845–58.

[15] Thomas Gale Moore, *The Economics of the American Theater* (Durham, N.C.: Duke University Press, 1968), pp. 14–15.

Table 8.2. *Expenditures and income for a typical ballet company, 1970–71*

	Dollar amount	Percentage of total	Percentage of subtotal
Expenditures	1,500,000	100	
Personnel	860,000	57	
Artistic	620,000	41	
Performing	470,000	31	
Nonperforming	150,000	10	
Stagehands, crew, shop	95,000	6	
Admin., clerical, maint.	145,000	10	
Fringe benefits	70,000	5	
Nonsalary costs	570,000	38	
Income	1,500,000	100	
Earned	930,000	62	100
Performance	840,000		90
Ticketed	650,000		70
Fee-based	190,000		20
Nonperformance	90,000		10
Contributed	570,000	38	100
Private	440,000		77
Individuals	130,000		23
Foundations	115,000		20
Corporations	85,000		15
Other	110,000		19
Governmental	130,000		23
Federal	63,000		11
State and local	67,000		12
Earnings gap (Expenditures − earned income)	570,000	38	

Sources: Total income and expenditure of the average ballet company are for 1970–71, as given in the Ford Foundation, *The Finances of the Performing Arts* (1974), vol. 1, app. B, pp. 14–15. (The data have been rounded off.) Distribution of expenditures is from the same volume, app. C, p. 45. Distribution of income is based on the percent breakdown in Dick Netzer, "Changing Economic Fortunes of Dance in the U.S.," Urban Research Center, New York University (May 1986), table 3. Netzer's figures are for 1984 and therefore reflect the rise in contributed income from corporations and from all levels of government that occurred after the date of the Ford Foundation study from which the total income and expenditure data come.

firm is a ballet company equal in size to the average ballet company in the Ford Foundation's 1974 survey *The Finances of the Performing Arts.* The table is useful for several reasons. First, by listing the major components of cost and revenue, it tells us a good deal about how performing arts firms actually carry out their functions. Second, it allows us to look systematically at the relative magnitudes of the principal financial categories. Finally, it gives us a precise definition of the earnings gap.

The table reveals that personnel costs make up 57 percent of total expenditure in this typical ballet company. Artistic personnel, the workers among whom productivity lag is bound to be a problem, account for nearly three-quarters of that, or 41 percent of total expenses. Nonsalary costs, however, are clearly not negligible, amounting to 38 percent of the total. The three largest nonsalary categories (not shown separately in the table) are scenery, costumes, and lighting (7.1 percent of all outlays), transportation and per diem costs incurred while on tour (7.8 percent), and nonsalary subscription and promotion costs (6.2 percent).

The earnings gap is generally defined as the difference between operating expenditures and earned income. Earned income in the performing arts, as illustrated in Table 8.2, comprises both performance and nonperformance income. The former, it is important to understand, can be further divided into two distinct types. Ticketed income is revenue from the sale of tickets to performances for which the company itself is the financially responsible producer. Such performances are usually limited to those at the company's home base. When the company is on tour, that is, performing away from home, it usually does so in return for "fees for service." These are paid under contracts between the company and a "presenting organization" at each stop on the tour.

The role of presenting organizations

If a ballet company based in Philadelphia tours through Indiana, its performance in South Bend might be sponsored by a local presenting organization calling itself, say, "South Bend Arts." That organization would guarantee a fixed payment to the ballet company, would advertise and sell tickets to the performance, rent a hall, and take financial responsibility for the whole enterprise. In the unlikely event that ticket sales more than cover expenses, the local presenter is entitled to keep the net proceeds. Likewise, it is responsible for covering any deficit.

Because local presenting organizations play a crucial role in the distribution of performance art in a nation as large as the United States, it is appropriate to add a few words about the often complex economics of their operations. During the course of a season they will typically present a variety of touring attractions, for example, a symphony orchestra, a ballet company, a modern dance group, and a chamber music ensemble. They may also sponsor a number of vocal or instrumental soloists. Subscriptions can then be solicited for one or more groups of these offerings. Single ticket sales will, of course, also be promoted.

Since very few arts performances break even, presenting organizations, too, are likely to require unearned income to cover a financial gap. For that purpose they can tap the same sources available to the performing institutions themselves: individual and business contributors, who can make tax-deductible donations, and government organizations that can provide subsidies. In the case of local presenters, subsidies are more likely to come from a state or local council on the arts than from the National Endowment for the Arts. (The economics of private donations is discussed in Chapter 12, public support in Chapter 13.)

Fee-based income will be most important for companies that do a great deal of touring. Our hypothetical ballet company earns less than a quarter of its performance income from fees. The proportion would be somewhat higher for the average symphony orchestra and would be close to 100 percent for the typical modern dance company, which tours widely and rarely performs except on the basis of a contracted fee.

Nonperformance earned income in the performing arts may sound like a contradiction in terms. It is not. Companies that own their own hall can earn income by renting it to others during the off-season. More generally, many companies have discovered that they can earn worthwhile income by selling souvenir programs, books, posters, and T-shirts at their own performances.

Earned versus unearned income

The share of total revenue accounted for by earned as compared with unearned income – or, as the latter is often called, "contributed income" – varies widely among firms and across art forms. Symphony orchestras have the lowest earned income ratio among the five major categories. They are in general the oldest institutions in the nonprofit performing arts industry, many of them having been established in the nineteenth century. Consequently, they have long-standing ties with well-to-do patrons, especially with what is sometimes referred to as "old money." Private contributions accounted for almost 35 percent of their total revenue in 1970–71, and income from endowments (funds that are the result of generous past benefactions) made up an additional 6 percent. As a result, earned income amounted to only 47 percent of total revenue for the average symphony orchestra.[16] At the other end of the

---

[16] *Finances of the Performing Arts,* vol. 1, app. C, p. 31.

scale, modern dance companies in 1970–71 relied on earned income for almost 69 percent of their revenue. Ticket income accounted for less than 1 percent of revenue. As already pointed out, these companies generally do not have a home base at which to sell tickets. Most of their earned income therefore consists of fees received for performances on tour.

Since modern dance companies tend to be relatively small and relatively new, they do not attract private contributions as readily as larger and older institutions do. In 1970–71 almost two-thirds of their unearned income came from government grants and only one-sixth from private sources (other than national foundations).[17]

The earnings gap

Since total income approximately equals expenditures and the earnings gap equals the difference between expenditures and *earned* income, it follows that the earnings gap also approximately equals *un*-earned income. The relative size of the gap is usually measured by taking the gap as a percentage of expenditures. Changes in the gap can be measured as changes in either its absolute or relative size over time.

The ballet company depicted in Table 8.2 has a total expenditure budget of $1.5 million a year. Total income equals expenditures, but earned income amounts to only $930,000, leaving an earnings gap of $570,000. In relative terms the gap equals 38 percent of expenditures. More than three-quarters of that is covered by private contributions: 23 percent from individuals, 20 percent from foundations and 15 percent from corporations. These proportions have changed substantially in recent years. Twenty years ago foundations would have been the leading source of private donations to dance companies, with individuals a close second and corporations a very distant third. The sharp rise in the relative share of corporate contributions testifies to the fact that ballet (and modern dance), once regarded suspiciously in the United States, are now considered "mainstream."

Is the earnings gap growing?

If expenditures and earned income grow at the same rate, the earnings gap will grow in absolute size, but its relative size will be unchanged. On the other hand, if expenditures grow faster than earned income, not only the absolute but also the relative size of the gap will increase. Writing in the mid-1960s, Baumol and Bowen found that for a number of institutions, the relative size of the gap had increased during

[17] Ibid., p. 48.

Table 8.3. *Relative size of the earnings gap*

	Ford Foundation			Schwarz and Peters		
	Sample size	Percent		Sample size	Percent	
		1965–66	1970–71		1969–70	1978–79
Theater companies	27	28.4	33.8	18	39.6	30.8
Opera companies						
Including Met Opera	31	35.5	32.1	21	38.6	41.6
Excluding Met Opera	30	41.8	42.8	20	40.8	48.9
Symphony orchestras	91	37.4	49.4	31	52.4	51.4
Ballet companies	9	42.6	38.7	8	44.9	35.8
Modern dance companies	8	35.4	29.3	13	42.3	36.8
Aggregate, all companies						
Including Met Opera	166	35.4	42.0	91	46.4	45.5
Excluding Met Opera	165	37.3	44.9	—	—	—

Note: Relative earnings gap = (expenditures) − (earned income) ÷ expenditures.
Sources: For Ford Foundation data, see Chapter 8, note 19; for Schwarz and Peters, see Chapter 8, note 20.

the postwar period. On the basis of that experience, they estimated that in the next 10 years expenditures would grow at between 5 and 7 percent per year while earned income would rise only 3.5 to 5.5 percent yearly, resulting in continued relative growth of the gap.[18]

Table 8.3 summarizes the best available data on the actual behavior of the gap since the date of Baumol and Bowen's initial study. The left-hand panel, using data from the Ford Foundation's study of finances in the performing arts, shows how the relative size of the earnings gap behaved from 1965–66 through 1970–71.[19] In relative size it increased for theater companies and symphony orchestras, declined slightly for opera companies (if the Metropolitan Opera is included), and fell substantially for ballet and modern dance companies. For the aggregate of all companies in the Ford sample, it rose substantially between 1965–66 and 1970–71. But the aggregate figure can be misleading if it is taken to represent the financial situation of the performing arts as a whole, because the aggregate is dominated by the category of symphony orchestras. Although the numbers are not shown in Table 8.3, this group accounted for more than half the dollar amount of the gap at both dates

[18] Baumol and Bowen, *Performing Arts*, pp. 388–93.
[19] *The Finances of the Performing Arts*, vol. 1. Calculated from data in app. B.

and also for its relative increase over the interval. For the aggregate of all other groups, the relative size of the gap actually fell during the same period.

The right-hand panel of Table 8.3 summarizes the results of a study by Samuel Schwarz and Mary G. Peters covering a sample of 91 companies over the nine years from 1969–70 through 1978–79.[20] Like the Ford Foundation study, theirs shows that trends differed among arts categories. The relative size of the gap increased slightly for opera companies, was approximately unchanged for orchestras, and fell substantially for theater, ballet, and modern dance companies. For the aggregate of all companies in the sample (a figure the authors did not emphasize), the gap was down very slightly. It is interesting to note that only ballet and modern dance companies showed a trend in the gap (in this case downward) that was maintained over the time periods of both studies.

On the whole, then, dire predictions that productivity lag would lead to a relentlessly increasing earnings gap proved to be incorrect. What happened? As we indicated earlier in this chapter, a number of factors can work to offset the effects of productivity lag. In this instance expenses of performing arts companies did increase more or less as predicted, but earned income increased at an equal or slightly higher rate, so the relative size of the gap, on average, was approximately unchanged. But what explains the rise in earned income? Evidently, ticket prices rose much faster than the general price level without causing a drop in attendance. Hence, box office revenues, adjusted for inflation, rose substantially.[21] Thus, productivity lag is alive and well, but so are some of its potential offsets.

Interpreting the earnings gap

Something more must be said by way of interpretation. Schwarz and Peters point out that since performing arts firms in the nonprofit sector cannot normally operate with a cash deficit, an earnings gap cannot exist unless *unearned* income is available to cover it.[22] As we

---

[20] Samuel Schwarz and Mary G. Peters, *Growth of Arts and Cultural Organizations in the Decade of the 1970s,* a study prepared for the Research Division, National Endowment for the Arts (Rockville, Md.: Informatics General Corporation, 1983).

[21] See Dick Netzer, *The Subsidized Muse,* a Twentieth Century Fund study (Cambridge University Press, 1978), p. 41; and James Heilbrun, "Once More with Feeling: The Arts Boom Revisited," in Hendon et al., eds., *The Economics of Cultural Industries* (Akron, Ohio: Association for Cultural Economics, 1984), pp. 34–46, cited at 39–41, and esp. table 3.

[22] Schwarz and Peters, *Growth of Arts,* pp. 217–19.

have seen, such income flows from both private donations and public grants. Emphasis on the earnings gap as the starting point in a financial analysis leads one to think of unearned income as a passive factor that responds after the fact to the financial needs of the company. But we could just as well look at it the other way around and argue that the existence of unearned income makes it *possible* for a performing arts firm to finance expenditures in excess of earned income. A very large earnings gap for a given firm might indicate not that the firm is in serious financial trouble, but rather that it has succeeded in finding generous outside support, probably in response to its very high quality of operation.

Still, there is a sense in which firms operating with a large earnings gap may seem to have given hostages to fortune: suppose that government grants are cut back because of a fiscal squeeze or that private donations decline because of a change in tax law or a serious economic recession? Is it not safer to depend on ticket income a little more and public or private charity a little less?

Is there an "artistic deficit"?

Faced with the continual upward pressure on costs generated by productivity lag, firms in the live performing arts might be expected to seek ways of economizing by gradually altering their choice of repertory or their production process. For example, theatrical producers might look for plays with smaller casts or plays that could be mounted with a single rather than multiple stage sets. Or they might try to compensate for higher costs by shunning artistically innovative plays that do not draw well at the box office and so have to be "carried" by revenues from more conventional offerings. Consistent with the Chapter 7 analysis of the effect of market structure on innovation versus conformity in the theater, we would expect this to occur most often in smaller cities where a single company might have a virtual monopoly on professional production. Orchestras and opera companies, too, might be driven away from innovative or "difficult" material by box office considerations. Or operating on the cost side, they might select programs with an eye to reducing rehearsal time or hire fewer outside soloists or other high-priced guest artists. Ballet companies could cut down on the use of specially commissioned music or choreography and could eschew new productions that require elaborate sets or costumes. (This topic is revisited in Chapter 14.)

Although economics clearly teaches us that firms will respond to rising input costs by economizing in their use of the offending inputs, economists interested in the arts are likely to be disturbed when they find firms in the performing arts doing just that. They are offended at the notion that *Hamlet* is no longer viable because its cast is too large, or that piano concertos will be less frequently heard because soloists (or at any rate the well-known ones) have become too expensive. Hilda Baumol and William Baumol express their dismay at the notion that rising costs should narrow "the economically feasible range of artistic options."[23] When that occurs it has been said that performing arts firms are reducing their fiscal deficit by incurring an "artistic deficit."

It is worth noting that this problem is peculiar to the performing arts. In the fine arts – for example, in architecture – we fully expect practitioners to adapt their "products" to changes over time in the relative prices of alternative inputs. We are not surprised to find that modern buildings are devoid of the elaborate hand-carved stonework that decorated important buildings in earlier times. Indeed, the aesthetic rationale of the modern movement in architecture was precisely to design buildings that could use machine-finished materials in place of the increasingly costly hand-finished ones. In this instance it is not too strong to say that the necessity of adapting was the challenge that gave rise to a whole new school of design.

What makes the performing arts different is the fact that the past provides much of the substance that we wish to see performed. We do not want *Hamlet* with half the characters omitted because of the high cost of labor. Nor do we wish to give up symphony concerts in favor of chamber music recitals simply because symphonies employ too many musicians. We want the "range of artistic options" to include the option of hearing or seeing performances of great works that were invented under very different economic circumstances than our own. There would indeed be an artistic deficit if today's companies became financially unable to present for us the great works of the past.

But there remains an unsettled question: is it demonstrable that our performing arts institutions have already begun cutting back along some dimensions of quality? Are we even now the victims of an artistic deficit? There is some evidence that says we are, but it is mostly of the sort that social scientists call "anecdotal." For example, Schwarz and Peters quote the following passage from Ruth Mayleas, who is describing how the cost squeeze has affected the well-known Arena Stage in Washington, D.C. (Zelda Fichandler was its producing director until 1991):

---

[23] Hilda Baumol and W. J. Baumol, "The Future of the Theater and the Cost Disease of the Arts," in Mary Ann Hendon et al., eds., *Bach and the Box: The Impact of Television on the Performing Arts* (Akron, Ohio: Association for Cultural Economics, 1985), pp. 7–31, cited at 17.

> Next season, for the first time, Arena will not be able to do as many large plays. . . . Fichandler has never before let financial pressures influence repertoire, but now she finds no other choice. If one looks back, the economic effect on production has *already* been felt: In 1967 Arena's "The Great White Hope" was done with 62 actors and 237 costumes. That production would be impossible today, says Fichandler.[24]

However, one would like to have more systematic evidence. As this quotation suggests, changes in cast size over time would be one way of testing empirically for the existence of an artistic deficit in theatrical productions. Evidence on that score is, as yet, sketchy.[25] Other dimensions of quality that might provide an empirical test, such as hours of rehearsal time or number of stage sets per production, are even more difficult to measure. A cautious observer would have to conclude that the existence of an artistic deficit is an interesting hypothesis that has not yet been fully tested.

Conclusion

This chapter introduced the problems associated with productivity lag in the performing arts. Rising costs and higher ticket prices threaten to reduce the audience for the arts, but these difficulties may be at least partially offset in a growing economy by rising consumer incomes, an increasing taste for the arts, and falling unit costs attributable to economies of scale. One can thus remain guardedly optimistic about the continued financial viability of the performing arts. However, the troubling question of whether growth of the earnings gap has been forestalled in part by an increasing artistic deficit awaits further research.

[24] Schwarz and Peters, *Growth of Arts,* p. 217.
[25] See, e.g., the paper by Baumol and Baumol cited in note 23, and National Endowment for the Arts, Research Division Report no. 11, *Conditions and Needs of the Professional American Theatre,* May 1981, table 10.

PART III

The fine arts and museums

PART VI

9

The market in works of art

It is said that Van Gogh sold but a single painting during his lifetime. Yet in 1987 one of his paintings, *Irises,* sold at auction for nearly $54 million and garnered headlines around the world. In 1990 one of his portraits brought $82.5 million, and more than a few knowledgeable dealers in art works expect prices of selected works to exceed $100 million in the near future.

Recent trends in the prices of some categories of paintings are depicted in Figure 9.1. The basis for these charts is Sotheby's Index of art prices, where the value for 1975 is 100.[1] From 1975 through the early 1980s, art prices increased steadily but unspectacularly. Beginning in 1985 the prices of impressionist paintings began to grow more rapidly, and soon thereafter the other price rises accelerated. This period was known as the "boom" in art, and the boom ended with the "correction" of 1990.[2]

What causes a boom? Why are some works of art so expensive while others are so cheap? Why do some paintings increase in value while others decline? What are the implications for creators and purchasers of art? Are some museums being priced out of the market, and will the larger public experience diminished access to great art?

---

[1] Sotheby's Art Index reflects the subjective analyses and the opinions of Sotheby's art experts. In its standard disclaimer, Sotheby's cautions that "nothing in . . . [the] Index is intended or should be relied upon as investment advice or as a prediction or guarantee of future performance or otherwise."

[2] These trends attracted writers from the financial press. Among the more interesting of a wide variety of treatments are the following: Meg Cox, "Boom in Art Market Lifts Prices Sharply, Stirs Fears of a Bust," *Wall Street Journal* (November 24, 1986); Susan Lee, "Greed Is Not Just for Profit," *Forbes* (April 18, 1988), pp. 65–70; Dana Wechsler, "A Treacherous Market," *Forbes* (November 27, 1989), pp. 292–4; and Peter Passell, "Vincent Van Gogh, Meet Adam Smith," *New York Times* (February 4, 1990).

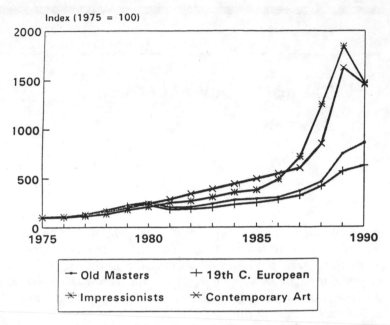

Index (1975 = 100)

Figure 9.1. Sotheby's Index of art prices: selected categories, 1975–90.

In this chapter we turn our attention to the market in what is known as the visual arts or the plastic arts. We will examine the process by which artists make their creations available to purchasers, including the role of dealers, auction houses, and other modes of sale. We will also inquire into why and how individuals, firms, and others decide to acquire art. These decisions create the supply of and demand for art, and the interaction of supply and demand help to explain both the levels of art prices and changes in those levels.

Some preliminary considerations

The concepts of supply and demand, as developed earlier, must be refined so that they more nearly fit the face-to-face nature of markets in art. Following some preliminary definitions, an overview of market structures and processes in the arts sets the stage. Then our focus will be the supply side of the market, particularly the behavior of the artist. The demand for the arts is approached through a description of the theory of asset demand and an application of that theory to arts markets. As the reader is now well aware, full understanding of the market – the price of art and the amount sold – requires exploration of both supply and demand.

The discerning reader may by this point feel some need to address the matter of defining art. So do we, but that is not so easily done. Edward Banfield, a noted political scientist and art collector, issued a caveat before defining art for his purposes:

> Highly civilized people can define art in profoundly various ways. Here [in his book] art will be defined as that which has the capacity to engender in a receptive viewer an aesthetic experience.[3]

While we cannot disagree with this definition, it only substitutes one question for another: what is an aesthetic experience? Leslie Singer has evaded such metaphysical entrapments by noting that works of art have two attributes: decorativeness (size, weight, medium, physical condition, subject matter, etc.) and intellectual appeal (art-historical significance, quality of work, artist reputation, etc.).[4] These attributes apply to paintings, drawings, sculptures, and related collectibles. We will consistently use paintings as a convenient example in illustrating the nature of the markets in question. Principles that apply to the market in paintings can easily be extended to markets in other media.

We must also define two concepts – transactions costs and information costs – that will help us to understand the functioning of the markets and the roles played by some of the participants. Transactions costs refer to the costs, over and above the payment for goods sold, incurred by all parties in bringing about a transaction. Examples from the buyer's perspective would include time spent looking for and examining merchandise, waiting in lines, and discussing alternatives. For example, it is to reduce the sum of transactions costs that shoppers seeking only a few grocery items are willing to pay a price premium at a convenience store rather than spend time searching through a supermarket and standing in a checkout line.

Imperfect information in a particular market means that participants in a transaction may not be well informed about such things as product quality, resale value, and the price and availability of substitutes. However, obtaining accurate information may be costly in terms of time, effort, and even money. The higher is the cost of being wrong, the more likely is a potential buyer to expend resources in obtaining better in-

---

[3] Edward C. Banfield, *The Democratic Muse: Visual Arts and the Public Interest* (New York: Basic, 1984), p. 21.

[4] Leslie Singer, "Microeconomics of the Art Market," *Journal of Cultural Economics*, 2 (1978): 21–39.

formation. Otherwise the buyer lacks assurance of obtaining what he or she really wants or needs.[5]

Arts markets

Readers of such popular business periodicals as *Business Week, Forbes,* and the *Wall Street Journal* surely have noticed the increasingly frequent coverage of transactions in art objects. According to a writer in *Forbes:*

> Almost unnoticed, art has turned from an obscure, chaotic and esoteric market to an organized and highly sophisticated market. Works of art have become ... quasifinancial instruments, because the art market itself has become more of a financial market.[6]

The market in paintings really consists of at least two components: a primary market and a secondary market. A similar distinction applies to trading in securities. We will explore the nature of each of these markets in turn.

The primary market

The primary market is one in which original works are sold for the first time. As is the case in any other market, the resulting price reflects the operation of the forces of supply and demand. This market includes artists' studios, art fairs and festivals, galleries, and similar outlets.[7] As might be expected, participants in the primary market are hampered by imperfect information and encounter considerable transactions costs. The works of new artists – the "unknowns" – and the new works of more established painters are traded in this market. Purchases of art via primary market participation may entail a fair amount of risk, largely because the intellectual appeal is uncertain for many people (I may not know art, but ...), even though the decorativeness attributes may be more widely recognized and understood (I know what I like).

---

[5] This topic and such related matters as informational asymmetry are treated in greater detail in Paul Milgrom and John Roberts, *Economics, Organization, and Management* (Englewood Cliffs, N.J.: Prentice-Hall, 1992), pp. 140–43, 467–75.

[6] Lee, "Greed is Not Just for Profit," pp. 65–66.

[7] Singer further divides the art market into a tertiary component. This seems to us unnecessarily complicated, as the first two will describe the market quite nicely. But any such classification scheme abstracts from the usual blurring between categories. For example, dealers participate in the secondary as well as the primary market, while auction houses are extending their reach into the primary market.

Neophyte buyers may not know what works are being offered for sale, whether they are of high quality, or where the works are available without considerable expenditure of time and effort.

The process by which the primary market in paintings operates is much like other markets. The prospective buyer goes to the point of sale, perhaps a studio or gallery where works are displayed, often – but not always – with prices attached.[8] In a not atypical scenario, an artist may have established an exclusive relationship with a dealer who arranges an exhibition of the artist's work. Under such an arrangement, the artist provides the creative work, and the dealer contributes market knowledge and experience. The prices that they attach to the works reflect the "reserve price" of the artist plus a best guess of what the work can command over the reserve price. The reserve price is the minimum the artist is willing to accept in bringing a work to the market. Setting the price is tricky; it should exceed the reserve price without being too high for buyers.

To the extent that the artist and her representative may be uncertain of the price that a given work can command, they may rely on a "feel for the market" or use such rule-of-thumb practices as "markup pricing." The feel for the market is based on experience in selling the artist's work in the past, the prices of similar works at the present, and knowledge of trends in buyer preferences. For new, unestablished artists, a dealer may keep prices low in the first show. A sellout encourages slightly higher prices for a subsequent show. Markup pricing in most markets is a standard percentage of increase – say, 50 percent – above the costs of production. Usage in this market is necessarily less precise, since a very large component of the production costs consists of the opportunity cost of the artist's time, and this itself may be unclear.

Figure 9.2 depicts a hypothetical market for a given work of art. As developed in Chapter 4, the market demand curve is the horizontal sum of the individual demand curves in the market. The supply curve is vertical at a quantity of one, there being, after all, only one of a unique work. Conceptually, the "market clearing" or equilibrium price is P_1. Actual sale at this price depends on attracting the individual who is willing to pay this price. Since the new artist cannot rely on this fortuitous circumstance, she will likely choose instead to set a price, P_2, above her reserve price, P_r, but below P_1. Any of a number of potential buyers who deem the acquisition worthwhile at this price may make the purchase on a first-come, first-served basis. The buyer is very likely to preserve a substantial amount of "consumer surplus," which is the dif-

---

[8] Prices may in fact be in a price list posted or available at the front desk.

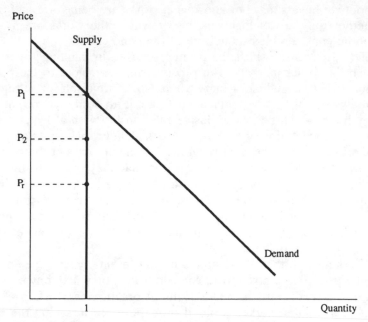

Figure 9.2. Supply and demand: single work of art.

ference between what he actually paid and what he would have been willing to pay.

New works of well-known artists may also be sold through dealers who have represented them historically. However, auction houses, which will be described more fully in the next section, are increasingly active in the sale of these works. Some of the reasons for this evolution are presented later.

The secondary market

The exchange of existing works of art constitutes the secondary market, and in contrast with the primary market, participants are likely to have very good information about artists and their "seasoned" works. Acquisition of recognized work in this market is not so risky as the purchase of unknowns. "News about the art world can be had at the corner newsstand. More than 100 magazines are dedicated to reporting on and explaining art, and most big-city dailies have a section devoted to art happenings."[9] In this instance, attributes of both decorativeness and intellectual appeal are likely to be well known.

[9] Lee, "Greed is Not Just for Profit," p. 67.

Transactions costs in secondary art markets have fallen in recent years. Not too long ago, dealer markups were routinely two to four times the wholesale price. Auction house commissions, by contrast, may total no more than 20 percent of the sale price.

Another innovation is that galleries more frequently post prices of exhibited works. Newcomers to these markets may be surprised to learn that prices have not always been posted. By keeping prices private, dealers could size up potential buyers and quote a price in keeping with a subjective estimate of willingness to pay.[10] Posted prices protect potential buyers from possible "gouging."

Auctions: "An auction is a market institution with an explicit set of rules determining resource allocation and prices on the basis of bids from the market participants."[11] Auctions are used when markets have neither breadth (numerous buyers and sellers) nor depth (a number of closely related products that can be considered substitutes, even if imperfectly). Under such circumstances, market interaction does not produce a standard valuation reflected in a market price. As we will show, sale at auction may gain the maximum price for the seller.

Works of art typically are sold via what is known as an "English auction," where the price is raised until only a single bidder remains. One feature of such a process is that all bidders know the current high bid for a work. The most famous auction houses are the British firms of Christie's and Sotheby's, each of which has offices and auction rooms in the United States. Figure 9.2 can also be used to illustrate the operation of such a process. If the top price that anyone is likely to offer is P_1, a large number of potential buyers – represented by the smooth demand curve – can be expected to drive the price up to P_1, providing maximum revenue for the seller and eliminating any consumer surplus.

The more likely case might be represented by Figure 9.3, where the demand curve is discontinuous, or a stair step line, indicating a limited number of potential buyers with varying preferences. The most eager purchaser, Bidder A, who might be willing to pay as much as P_a, need only offer P_a' to top the bid of Bidder B, at P_b. The price received by the seller still exceeds the reserve price, P_r, by a substantial amount, while the successful bidder preserves some consumer surplus. For

[10] See Meg Cox, "What Effrontery! Art Dealers are Told to Price Their Stuff," *Wall Street Journal* (March 17, 1988), and Dwight V. Gast, "Pricing New York Galleries," *Art in America*, 76, no. 7 (July 1988): 86–7.

[11] R. P. McAfee and John McMillan, "Auctions and Bidding," *Journal of Economic Literature*, 25, no. 2 (June 1987): 699–738, cited at 701.

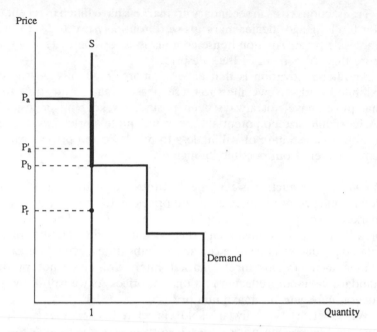

Figure 9.3. Supply and demand: limited number of buyers.

example, if Bidder A would have been willing to pay as much as $100,000 for a painting, but needs to offer only $91,000 to top Bidder B's top offer of $90,000, then A receives $9,000 in enjoyment from the painting above what she actually paid.

In the event that the highest bid fails to exceed the reserve price, as illustrated by Figure 9.4, the painting will be "hammered down" at the reserve price and "bought in." The seller rejects the bid of P_1 and, in effect, buys it from herself, but the appearance of an actual sale is maintained. If she were not willing to accept less than $1 million, but bidding ceased at, say, $800,000, then her representative might offer a bid of $1 million. Although the casual observer may think that a sale has occurred, in fact the current owner simply keeps the work.

The supply of art

Not too long ago, James Rosenquist wrote, "Art isn't really done for any reason other than a means of the artist's self-expression."[12]

---

[12] James Rosenquist, "Artists and Planning," in Lee Evan Caplin, ed., *The Business of Art* (Englewood Cliffs, N.J.: Prentice-Hall, 1982), pp. 21–28, cited at 25.

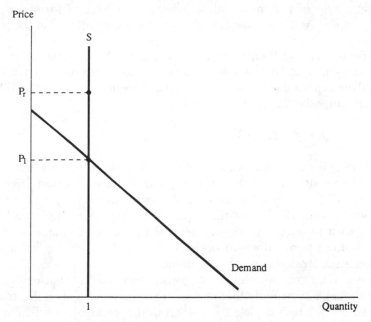

Figure 9.4. Art auction bid below reserve price.

While this may be consistent with many artists' professed self-images, it certainly is not consistent with sustained material well-being. Some of the motivations of artists are developed more fully in Chapter 14, where we seek to understand how and why artists choose their professions. Suffice to say at this point that most economists (and most artists as well) recognize the commercial motivation for producing art.

Artistic products can be regarded as either commissioned or speculative. Commissioned works are those that are specifically requested by a client who is familiar with the artist's technique, such familiarity having been gained from previous exposure. Portraits typically are commissioned, and established artists are more likely to secure commissions. William Grampp recounts numerous examples even of old masters acquiescing to specific expressions of consumer preference. More often than the lay public realizes, paintings have in the past been made to order, altered, and updated, adding a new child to a family portrait or more luxuriant growth to a landscape.[13]

Speculative works are those produced by the artist with no guarantee of sale. The artist invests time, talent, and materials in producing art

---

[13] William Grampp, *Pricing the Priceless: Art, Artists, and Economics* (New York: Basic, 1989), pp. 46–51.

that may – or may not – subsequently be purchased for a reasonably high price. As already described, these works are offered in the primary market.

Schneider and Pommerehne view the supply of works of art in the primary market as dependent on two factors, the costs of production and the expected selling price.[14] This can be summarized by the following equation, adapted from their work,

$$Q = f(MC, p^e) \tag{9.1}$$

where Q is the quantity of art supplied by a painter, MC is the marginal or incremental cost of the painting, and p^e is the expected price.

The higher the production cost, the less willing is the artist to produce a work, while the higher the expected selling price, the more likely is the artist to bring a work to market. In the case of unique works, this boils down to an either–or decision. Either the market conditions support a supply decision, or they do not.

A painter may offer his or her works to the market sparingly, seeking to avoid an oversupply that may depress the price. This is illustrated by Figure 9.5, which depicts the market in the works of a particular artist. An increase in supply, with a shift in the supply curve from S to S', causes a decline in the market price from P to P'. Works produced at a rapid pace may also be retained in the artist's own inventory as a hedge against unexpected price increases. This is one means by which an artist can take advantage of being "discovered." Another means is through a resale right, or *droit de suite,* which is a legal entitlement in many European countries and in the state of California. This right entitles an artist to a fixed percentage of the sale price of a work whenever it changes hands. The California law provides for payment to the artist or heirs of 5 percent of the sale price.[15]

---

[14] Freiderich Schneider and Werner Pommerehne, "Analyzing the Market of Works of Contemporary Fine Arts: An Exploratory Study," *Journal of Cultural Economics,* 7, no. 2 (December 1983): 41–67, cited at 42.

[15] For discussions and analyses of the *droit de suite,* see Carl Colonna and Carol Colonna, "An Economic and Legal Assessment of Recent Visual Artists' Reversion Rights Agreements in the United States," *Journal of Cultural Economics,* 6, no. 2 (December 1982): 77–85; Randall Filer, "A Theoretical Analysis of the Economic Impact of Artists' Resale Royalties Legislation," *Journal of Cultural Economics,* 8, no. 1 (June 1984): 1–28; and Roger McCain, "Artists' Resale Dividends: Some Economic-Theoretic Considerations," *Journal of Cultural Economics,* 13, no. 1 (June 1989): 35–51.

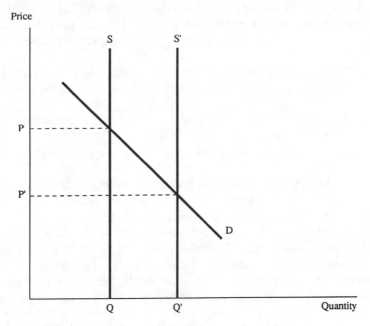

Figure 9.5. Price impact of supply increase by artist.

The demand for art

The demand side of the market includes a number of participants, including collectors, dealers, museums, corporations, and anyone
else with a desire to possess a work of art. Museums are the subject of
Chapter 10, and we will postpone further discussion of their participation
until then. Although the other market participants may differ in size,
awareness, and taste, they share enough characteristics for us to lump
them together and simplify the discussion a bit. We will refer to buyers
of paintings as "households," but our analysis can easily be extended
to all of the other purchasers.

Households must make a number of decisions regarding the dispo-
sition of their income. The first decision is how much to spend and how
much to save. The amount spent must then be allocated among a very
large number of consumer goods and services. The amount saved will
be divided among a number of assets, both real and financial. Although
the U.S. Department of Commerce classifies acquisitions of works of
art as consumption expenditure, they might more properly be regarded
as additions to a household's asset portfolio. In that regard, they are
akin to saving.

When households are considering the acquisition of assets, they weigh, at least implicitly, a number of attributes of those assets. According to the theory of asset demand, the decision to acquire art depends on the following:

1. Wealth, or the total resources available to the household.
2. Expected return on the asset relative to the return on all potential substitutes.
3. Expected risk, or the degree of uncertainty associated with the return on the asset relative to that of other assets.
4. Liquidity, or how quickly and easily the asset can be converted to cash.
5. Tastes and preferences. Although usually taken as given, here we mention them explicitly because of their importance in arts markets. (See the discussion in Chapter 4.)

A change in any of these elements can cause the demand curve for paintings to shift, and a favorable shift will result in a price increase and an increase in earnings for those currently offering the paintings for sale (as well as a potential increase in earnings for other current owners). Each of the demand factors is discussed more fully in upcoming sections.

Wealth

Households that are wealthy can buy more assets, including art, than those that are not wealthy. Accordingly, we would expect purchases of most types of art to increase as household wealth increases. Among the exceptions to this general rule are so-called inferior goods, purchases of which may actually decline as wealth rises. Examples from the art world might include reproductions or art posters, which in many households are relegated to the basement or storage closets in response to growing affluence. The degree to which asset demand responds to wealth changes is known as the wealth elasticity of demand, similar in concept to the price and income elasticities of demand. It is written as

$$\epsilon_w = \frac{\%\Delta Q}{\%\Delta W} \tag{9.2}$$

where Q is quantity demanded, and W is wealth. If ϵ_w is greater than 1, that means that the quantity demanded is very responsive to wealth changes, and such assets are regarded as luxuries. If ϵ_w is less than 1, the asset is more likely to be a necessity. If ϵ_w is less than 0, the asset may be one of those reproductions. In an approximation of this measure, Michael Bryan found the value of the "real economic growth elasticity" for paintings to be about 1.35.[16] This supports the contention that paintings, in general, can be considered luxury goods.

This may help to explain the recent and substantial Japanese entry into the art market. As Japanese wealth has grown, one would expect increased purchases of luxury goods and acquisition of assets.

To summarize, an increase in wealth increases the quantity demanded for most assets, and the increase is likely to be greater for luxuries than for necessities.

Expected return

The return on an asset measures how much we expect to gain from holding that asset. The return can be written as

$$r = \frac{C + P_{t+1} - P_t + S}{P_t} \tag{9.3}$$

where r is return, C is a dividend or coupon payment received, P_{t+1} is the expected price in the next time period, P_t is the actual purchase price, and S is the nonpecuniary benefit derived from ownership. For a work of art, we would expect that C would equal zero, but it might in fact be negative, when such things as insurance premiums, maintenance, and other outlays are taken into account. Normally, S would have some positive value. For a typical financial asset, on the other hand, S would likely be zero and C would have some positive value.

An example may help to illustrate the role of expected return. Suppose a dealer quotes the price of a painting at $5,000 and the collector has reason to believe that this particular artist will soon gain popularity, leading to a substantial increase in the prices of his paintings. If the collector feels that she will be able to sell the painting in a year for $6,000 and that while it is in her possession, she will derive aesthetic pleasure worth another $1,000, then the return from holding the painting for a year would be calculated as

$$r = \frac{6,000 - 5,000 + 1,000}{5,000} = .40 \tag{9.4}$$

or 40 percent. If this exceeds the return on other assets and seems not to entail a great deal of risk, the collector will acquire the painting.

The pure speculator, someone who is not likely to derive aesthetic benefits, will require a higher expected monetary return to be persuaded

---

[16] Michael F. Bryan, "Beauty and the Bulls: The Investment Characteristics of Paintings," *Economic Review*, Federal Reserve Bank of Cleveland (First Quarter 1985): 2–10, cited at 4.

to purchase the work. For this person, $S = 0$, and the expected return reduces to

$$r = \frac{6{,}000 - 5{,}000}{5{,}000} = .20 \tag{9.5}$$

If everything else is the same, the speculator is less likely to acquire the painting than is the collector since the expected return has fallen by half.

Equation 9.3 can be rewritten to identify the highest price that a collector and a speculator are likely to offer for a painting. We can solve for P_t as follows:

$$P_t = \frac{C + P_{t-1} + S}{1 + r} \tag{9.6}$$

Suppose both the collector and the speculator expect that a painting will sell next year for $6,000, and that the best return either could expect on an alternative financial asset is 15 percent. The only difference is that the collector still derives $1,000 worth of aesthetic pleasure from holding the painting for a year, hanging it on a wall, impressing her friends. The speculator will be willing to pay a price of

$$P_t = \frac{6{,}000}{1 + .15} = 5{,}217 \tag{9.7}$$

The collector, on the other hand, would be willing to offer

$$P_t = \frac{6{,}000 + 1{,}000}{1 + .15} = 6{,}087 \tag{9.8}$$

If the collector and the speculator are bidding at auction for the painting, the collector will outbid the speculator. The role played by aesthetic pleasure in setting art prices causes some analysts to regard speculators as unlikely to remain in the art market for long. Uninformed speculators may also regard the market as too risky, and now we turn our attention to that attribute of art.

Risk

The amount of risk associated with an asset affects the quantity demanded. In our presentation and use of Equation 9.3, we presumed that various parties could predict the selling price of a painting in a year. Both the collector and speculator acted as if the painting would sell for $6,000 a year hence. In fact, they may be very uncertain of what the selling price will be. A simple example may help to illustrate the role of risk.

Suppose two paintings, one by an established artist and one by a new discovery, happen to be priced at $5,000 each. The painting by the established artist is expected to sell in a year for $6,000, while the work of the unknown may sell for as much as $10,000 – or as little as $2,000. If each of these outcomes is equally likely, we would say that the expected value of the price in a year is the average of the two possible outcomes, or also $6,000. However, buying the latter painting entails the possibility of a substantial loss. The buyer who prefers a sure $6,000 (a gain of $1,000) to a range of $2,000 to $10,000 (with a possible loss of as much as $3,000) would buy the established work. Such a person would be described as "risk averse," and most of us seem to be risk averse most of the time.

To summarize, if we are confident that a work of art – say, a Picasso – will increase in value, we are more likely to acquire it. If we are far less certain about the future course of the asset's price, we are less likely to be interested in purchasing it. Most contemporary paintings actually depreciate in value. According to one knowledgeable gallery owner, "The percentage of contemporary paintings that are resold at a profit is minuscule."[17]

Liquidity

An asset that can be readily converted to cash – sold in a secondary market – is likely to be more attractive, and hence command a higher price, than one that is not so liquid. The work of a master can be resold; that of a novice may or may not be resold. The former is more liquid than the latter.

In general, the development of arts markets has made many works more liquid. Less than 20 years ago, Robert Anderson was able to say:

> The vast majority of collectors and most domestic museums give little or no thought to resale possibilities when buying art works. Even in private collections holding periods typically span generations; paintings are usually sold only to settle estates.[18]

As Lee points out, works of art may, in the past, have been owned for 40 years and more; now they more typically reappear on the market

---

[17] Robin Graham, owner of Graham Gallery, quoted in Lee, "Greed is Not Just for Profit," p. 67.

[18] Robert Anderson, "Paintings as an Investment," *Economic Inquiry,* 12, no. 1 (March 1974): 13–26, cited at 15.

within 5 to 7 years.[19] A collector can quickly sell a painting through the major auction houses.

Tastes and preferences

In considering most markets, economists take tastes and preferences as given. We choose to vary from that practice because of the unique nature of arts markets. Most consumers are able to recognize the quality of, say, tomatoes, and we can be fairly certain of the quality and usefulness of items that are widely advertised. We have a lot of information and/or experience in consumption.

To the extent that the arts are a luxury good, however, many possible buyers by definition do not enter the market until they are sufficiently wealthy. Hence, they are less likely to have experience in purchasing and face the prospect of investing a great deal of their time and energy in learning about the market. But the fact that they have become wealthier may also indicate that the value of their time has increased. This creates a potential conflict that may be resolved in different ways. Some collectors may rely on "experts," the art critics, gallery owners, and others who may be in a position to divine (shape?) current public taste. Others can economize on information costs by purchasing, and then reselling, only recognized works, thereby reinforcing the superstar phenomenon in the art world, where works of the most recognized creators, whether living (Wyeth, Lichtenstein) or dead (any of the masters), often command extraordinary sums, while new talent encounters ever higher hurdles.

Summary

The demand for art, as developed here, depends on several factors. These include wealth of the purchaser, expected return on art as an asset relative to that of other assets, the risk associated with art relative to other assets, the liquidity of art relative to other assets, and consumer tastes and preferences. In the next section we consider in greater depth the question of art as investment.

Art as Investment

Now that we have developed the underpinnings of both supply and demand in the art market, we may inquire whether art is a good investment. Several studies have sought to ascertain precisely that, and we will review some of the findings.

Table 9.1 lists both the average return and the risk for a variety of

[19] Lee, "Greed is Not Just for Profit," p. 67.

Table 9.1. *Pretax returns and standard deviations of alternative household investments, 1975–90 (annual rates)*

	Rate of return[a]	Standard deviation
Rate of inflation	5.7	2.1
Asset		
Paintings, average[b]	19.0	18.3
AAA corporate bonds	10.4	1.9
Gold	10.1	32.6
Three-year Treasury notes	9.4	2.3
Dow-Jones industrials	8.4	19.4
Paintings		
Modern	21.6	18.1
Impressionist	21.5	21.5
Contemporary	21.1	21.3
American	19.0	16.3
Old master	16.8	17.6
Nineteenth-century European	14.1	15.0

[a]Based on price or index increases or market interest rates.
[b]Unweighted averages.
Sources: Paintings: Sotheby's Index; gold: *Commodity Yearbook* (New York: Commodity Research Bureau, various issues); all other: *Economic Report of the President, 1991* (Washington, D.C.: Superintendent of Documents).

"household investments" for the period 1975–90. In this case, return is the capital gain plus any additional monetary payment (e.g., the coupon or interest payment received on AAA corporate bonds) on a variety of assets, and risk is measured by the standard deviation of annual rates of return.[20] Among assets other than art, gold offered one of the highest returns (an annual average of 10.1 percent) but was also very risky, with a standard deviation of 32.6. This means that investors who prefer high returns and are not particularly worried by risk (we would call them risk-neutral or, in the extreme, risk-seeking individuals) would exhibit

---

[20] Standard deviation measures how much the observed values of a work of art vary from their average values. The standard deviation is calculated as

$$\sigma = \sqrt{\frac{\Sigma(X - \mu)^2}{N}}$$

where X is the value of a work of art at some time, μ is its average value over the period covered, and N is the number of different values observed over the time period covered.

a preference for gold compared with most of the other assets. At the other extreme, those who have a strong distaste for uncertainty might opt for the least risky asset that offers at least a reasonable return. In this case, the AAA corporate bonds not only offered a very attractive average return over the period covered, but they also entailed the least risk.

Of special note is the comparison between the paintings index and stocks, as measured by growth in the Dow-Jones Industrials Index. Taken as a group, paintings would appear to be superior on both counts. For the period considered, they offered a higher return *and* less risk. Although average returns for *all* the paintings categories exceeded returns on the other assets, we do observe a bit of variety among the paintings. The modern, impressionist, and contemporary paintings all offered similar returns (between 21 and 22 percent), although the modern category was somewhat less risky. The American and old master paintings were in the middle on both return and risk, and the nineteenth-century European paintings offered both the lowest return and least risk.

It is important to note, however, that the high rates of return on art investments in the 1980s were historically exceptional. They should not be taken to indicate that it is easy to make money in art. On the contrary, investing in most art, in most periods, might well lead to losses rather than profits, for it is only after the fact that we find out what the profitable choices would have been in any given era. "The history of art connoisseurship . . . tells us that the main lesson imparted by the test of time is the fickleness of taste whose meanderings defy prediction."[21] William Baumol's skepticism is grounded in his study of 640 arts transactions during the period from 1652 to 1961, as listed in Gerald Reitlinger's *The Economics of Taste.*[22] Baumol calculated the *real,* or inflation-adjusted, rates of return associated with specific works of art and concluded that the average annual compounded rate of return was .55 percent in real terms, about one-third as high as the real return on a government security. Returns varied from a high of 27 percent to a low of − 19 percent per year. Based on this evidence, art seems indeed to be a risky investment, and the risk seems not to be compensated by a persuasive return.[23]

[21] William J. Baumol, "Unnatural Value or Art Investment as Floating Crap Game," in D. V. Shaw et al., eds., *Artists and Cultural Consumers* (Akron, Ohio: Association for Cultural Economics and University of Akron), pp. 1–14, cited at 1.

[22] Gerald Reitlinger, *The Economics of Taste: The Rise and Fall of the Picture Market, 1760–1960* (New York: Holt, Rinehart & Winston, 1961).

[23] Baumol, "Unnatural Value," pp. 7–9.

Ownership of art works . . . may well represent a very rational choice for those who derive a high rate of return in the form of aesthetic pleasure. They should not, however, let themselves be lured into the purchase of art by the illusion that they can beat the game financially and select with any degree of reliability the combination of purchase dates and art works that will produce a rate of return exceeding the opportunity cost of their investment.[24]

Another study, that by Frey and Pommerehne, extended Reitlinger's data up to 1987 and included more recent auction data from France, Germany, and The Netherlands.[25] Taking into account inflation, commission fees, and other pertinent factors, they calculated the average rate of return to paintings over the entire period to be about 1.5 percent per year. Under the assumption that art has come into its own as a financial investment only in the years since World War II, they also calculated the real rate of return for the period 1950–87 and determined it to be only 1.6 percent annually. Furthermore, like Baumol, they found a great variability in return, leading to their conclusion that "it is no easier to make speculative financial profits in art than anywhere else."[26]

Michael Bryan applied what is known as the "capital asset pricing model" to the Sotheby's Index for the period 1970–84.[27] For this shorter period, Bryan concluded that "the returns in the art market were lucrative for the pure art speculator."[28] Bryan's generally optimistic assessment is tempered somewhat by disagreement over the reliability of the Sotheby's Index.[29]

The fickle nature of the market is further illustrated by a recent account in the *New York Times:*

> The price of paintings by Sandro Chia . . . rose from $10,000 to $60,000 after the influential collector Charles Saatchi bought seven. But when

[24] Ibid., p. 13.
[25] Bruno S. Frey and Werner W. Pommerehne, "Is Art Such a Good Investment?" *Public Interest,* 91 (Spring 1988): 79–86.
[26] Ibid., p. 86. This cautious approach to investing in art is supported by at least two additional studies. See Robert C. Anderson, "Paintings as an Investment," *Economic Inquiry,* 12, no. 1 (March 1974): 13–26; and John P. Stein, "The Monetary Appreciation of Paintings," *Journal of Political Economy,* 85, no. 5 (1977): 1021–35.
[27] See Bryan, "Beauty and the Bulls." For an introduction to the capital asset pricing model, see Michael C. Jensen, "Capital Markets: Theory and Evidence," *Bell Journal of Economics and Management Science,* 3, no. 4 (Autumn 1972): 357–98.
[28] Ibid., p. 7.
[29] See Alexandra Peers, "Art Index of Sotheby's is Really More Art than Index, Some Say," *Wall Street Journal* (March 23, 1989).

Mr. Saatchi sold them all without explanation, the Chia star fell as fast as it had risen.[30]

It should not be particularly surprising, then, that studies of different time periods and varying data sources reach conflicting conclusions on the investment value of art. One conclusion that all observers would agree on, however, is that investing in art for financial gain is an unusually risky business that is best left to well-informed professionals.

The extraordinary rise in art prices during the 1980s undoubtedly helped some artists and pleased some investors. It has had seriously adverse consequences, however, for art museums and their audiences, since museums have been virtually priced out of the market for great works of art. They simply cannot afford to pay tens of millions of dollars for a single work. (A rare exception is the well-financed Getty Museum in California, which in 1989 paid $35.2 million at auction for a painting by the sixteenth-century Florentine master Jacopo Pontormo.)[31] It is the world's wealthy private collectors who have bid art prices up to their recent highs. Unhappily, the works they purchase will not be available for viewing by the art-loving public, unless they lend, donate, or bequeath them to museums. It is to the economics of art museums that we turn in the next chapter. (See Chapter 12 for a discussion of the effects of the income tax on donations of art.)

[30] Passell, "Vincent Van Gogh, Meet Adam Smith."
[31] *New York Times* (Rita Reif), June 1, 1989.

10

The economics of art museums

By all accounts, the fine arts in the United States, like the performing arts, have flourished in recent decades. Looking at the industry from the supply side, we saw in Chapter 9 that the number of professional painters and sculptors rose from 86.8 thousand in 1970 to 153.2 thousand in 1980.[1] Those numbers indicate a rate of growth more than twice that of the aggregate U.S. labor force. On the demand side we have no data on aggregate consumer spending for works produced by artists and sculptors that would be comparable to the National Income Accounts data on consumer spending for admission to the performing arts. We did show, however, in Chapter 9, that the prices paid for fine art have increased enormously in the past 20 years. While strong international demand played an important role in driving art prices up, it can scarcely be doubted that greater spending on art by U.S. consumers has also been a factor.

Attendance at art museums

Attendance at art museums is a good indicator of the public's interest in the fine arts. Table 10.1, which summarizes the available data, shows that attendance has increased very rapidly in the past 40 years, rising from 11 million in 1952 to almost 50 million in 1979, and 75.9 million in 1988.[2] Since population did not increase nearly as fast, the number of attendances per hundred of population rose from 7.0 in 1952 to 22.1 in 1979 and 30.8 in 1988. But because some people attend

[1] *A Sourcebook of Arts Statistics: 1989* (Washington, D.C.: National Endowment for the Arts, 1990), table 2.2.

[2] Since the reported data come from several studies, they do not make up a consistent historical series. Caution should therefore be used in interpreting the apparent "trend."

169

Table 10.1. *Attendance at U.S. art museums*

Date	Attendance (millions)	U.S. population (millions)	Attendance per 100
1952	11.1	157.6	7.0
1957	13.5	172.0	7.8
1962	22.0	186.5	11.8
1975	42.1	216.0	19.5
1979	49.8	225.1	22.1
1986	70.3	241.6	29.1
1988	75.9	246.3	30.8

Sources: Attendance: *A Sourcebook of Arts Statistics: 1989* (Washington, D.C.: National Endowment for the Arts, 1990), tables 7.27 and 7.28, and American Association of Museums, *Data Report of the 1989 National Museum Survey*, Table E:47.A; population as of July 1: *Statistical Abstract of the United States, 1990*, table 2.

museums more than once a year, those figures do not mean that 30.8 percent of Americans were museum attenders in 1988.

What proportion of the public *does* attend? The Survey of Public Participation in the Arts commissioned by the National Endowment for the Arts, allows us to answer that question. In the 1985 survey, 22 percent of all adults reported having visited an art museum or gallery in the previous 12 months.[3] Because the surveys were taken only in 1982 and 1985, we have no reliable data on the long-term trend in participation rates, but the strong growth in attendance per hundred suggests that participation rates must also have risen sharply.

The surveys allow us to compare the public's rate of attendance at museums of art with its propensity to engage in other recreational activities. The participation rate at art museums is slightly below that reported for science or history museums. It is higher than that for any of the individual live performing arts, among which the highest rate is 17 percent for musical plays and operettas. On the other hand, it is far below the rate for such other entertainments as movies away from home (59 percent), sports events (50 percent), and amusement parks and carnivals (45 percent).[4]

It was pointed out in Chapter 3 that participation rates in the arts rise dramatically with increases in individual income, occupational status,

[3] Ibid., table 9.1.
[4] Ibid., table 9.2.

and educational attainment. Table 3.2 showed that these generalizations hold for art museums as well as for the performing arts. Using Ford Foundation survey data, it was also shown in Chapter 3 that for the performing arts, education is a more important determinant of participation than is income. Mark Schuster reaches a similar conclusion for museum attendance. Employing data from the Survey of Public Participation in the Arts, he shows that the art museum participation rate increases from 4 percent for adults in the lowest education group to 55 percent for those in the highest group, a difference of 51 percentage points. By comparison, the participation rate increases only 29 percentage points from the lowest to the highest income group. Thus, differences in education are associated with far greater changes in museum attendance than are differences in income, which tells us that education is the more powerful explanatory variable.[5]

A profile of museum visitors

Because the rate of museum attendance rises strongly with education, income, and occupational status, it follows that art museum audiences will rank higher on those socioeconomic measures than does the U.S. population as a whole. Table 10.2, drawn from DiMaggio, Useem, and Brown's survey of 270 audience studies, allows us to compare the socioeconomic character of art museum visitors, visitors to other kinds of museums, and audiences for the live performing arts. What it shows us is that museum visitors as a whole do not rank as high on socioeconomic measures as do performing arts attenders. In other words, they are somewhat closer to the U.S. average (although still well above it). But the table also shows that *art* museum visitors rank much higher than museum visitors as a whole and are quite similar in character to those who attend the performing arts; it is the visitors to *other* museums (which are mainly in science, history, and natural history) who pull down the ranking for museum audiences as a whole. Educational attainment is an exception: on that measure, art museum audiences remain well below those in the performing arts, but part of the gap is explained by the fact that some of the museum studies included school children in their survey sample, and that would obviously reduce the measured level of educational attainment.

---

[5] J. Mark Davidson Schuster, *Perspectives on the American Audience for Art Museums*, a research monograph based on the 1985 Survey of Public Participation in the Arts, Cambridge, Mass., July 1987 (mimeo), cited at 18.

Table 10.2. *Socioeconomic character of museum and performing arts audiences*

Type of audience	Median income (1976 dollars)[a]	Occupation: professional (median percent)[b]	Education: college graduate or above (median percent)[b]
All museums	17,158	42.2	41.1
Art museums	18,148	59.2	48.0
Other museums	16,757[c]	41.9	34.4
All performing arts	18,903	59.1	61.8

[a]Income is the median of the median incomes reported in the studies reviewed.
[b]Entries are the median of the percentages reported in studies reviewed.
[c]History museums only.
Source: Paul DiMaggio, Michael Useem, and Paula Brown, *Audience Studies of the Performing Arts and Museums: A Critical Review*, Research Division Report no. 9 (Washington, D.C.: National Endowment for the Arts, 1978), tables 3, 5, 6. The authors caution that because of the methodology employed in their study, the results should be interpreted only as estimates (see, e.g., pp. 12 and 21).

What do museums do?

A survey conducted by the American Association of Museums estimated that in 1989 there were 8,179 not-for-profit museums in the United States. Of these, only 1,214 were classified as art museums.[6] History museums made up the largest group, with 2,401. The science category, including science and natural history museums, zoos, aquariums, and the like, numbered 1,243, about the same as the arts group.

Museums are essentially collections of objects that have been systematically gathered to provide information and stimulation to the attending public. Alma S. Wittlin points out that they are characteristically flexible because "they allow a wide gamut of differences in the use people make

[6] American Association of Museums, *Data Report of the 1989 National Museum Survey* (Washington, D.C.: American Association of Museums, January 1992), table A:A. In 1992, after this chapter was written, an important work entitled *The Economics of Art Museums* (Martin Feldstein, ed.) was published by the University of Chicago Press for the National Bureau of Economic Research. The NBER study, completed before the already cited *National Museum Survey* was available, therefore made use of unpublished data collected by the Association of Art Museum Directors, covering about 150 of the largest art museums, rather than the 1,214 included in the *National Museum Survey*.

Table 10.3. *Operating expenditures of art museums, 1979*

	Percent
Curatorial	13.6
Exhibits	12.8
Conservation	2.8
Education	9.8
Development	2.3
Membership	2.6
Public information	2.7
Paid advertising	0.5
Security	9.2
General administration	22.9
Building and maintenance	15.1
Other	5.7
Total	100.0

Source: Lewis C. Price, Lisa DiRocco, and Janice D. Lewis, *Museum Program Survey, 1979* (Washington, D.C.: National Center for Educational Statistics, 1981), table 25.

of them," and that "many, if not most, visitors to a museum hardly distinguish between learning and recreation."[7]

The variety of functions performed by art museums reflects the breadth of the demands the public makes on them. Their principal business may be to collect and display art, but they perform several other functions as well, notably conservation, research, and education.[8] Table 10.3, drawn from a 1979 survey, presents a breakdown of the expenditures of nonprofit art museums among categories, some of which can be roughly assigned to these functions. Collection and display would appear to account for most of the expenditures under the headings of curatorial (14 percent), exhibits (13 percent), and security (9 percent), and for a major fraction of those included in general administration (23 percent), building and maintenance (15 percent), and public information (3 percent). Adding up those categories makes it clear that collection and display account for well over half of art museum operating costs.

[7] Alma S. Wittlin, *Museums: In Search of a Usable Future* (Cambridge, Mass.: MIT Press, 1970), p. 2.

[8] For an influential discussion of this topic, see Joseph Veach Noble, "Museum Manifesto," *Museum News,* 48, no. 8 (April 1970): 17–20. Noble describes five "basic responsibilities": acquisition, exhibition, conservation, study, and interpretation.

(And keep in mind that the capital costs of *buying* art to build the collection are not counted here.)

Conservation accounts for only 3 percent of art museum operating budgets. To carry out conservation "in house" would require hiring a trained conservator and maintaining an up-to-date laboratory. A recent estimate put the minimum setup costs for such a facility in the range of $18,000 to $25,000.[9] When the annual cost of materials and supplies and a conservator's salary are added on, the minimum expense becomes considerable. Consequently, only one-third of art museums (presumably the largest) do it themselves. The rest, if they do not neglect the problem (and some do), contract for the service with outside specialists in conservation or with other museums that have the requisite facilities. In 1979, 20 percent of art museums reported doing conservation work for others.[10]

Educational programs are the next most expensive after collection and display. According to Table 10.3, they account directly for 10 percent of art museum operating budgets. To that should be added some part of general overhead costs. Educational programs comprise such activities as public lectures, art appreciation courses, programs in cooperation with local public schools and colleges, teacher training programs, and courses for academic credit. (Of course, if we were to adopt a broader definition of learning consistent with Wittlin's previously quoted statement, much of the expense of collection and display could also be labeled educational.) Clearly, museum directors and their boards of trustees believe that providing an education program is one of their civic responsibilities. Moreover, it is an important one to carry out if they wish to retain or expand subsidy support from their local government. But an education program also serves a museum's self-interest by building an appreciative audience among which the institution's future financial supporters may be found. (We pursue this topic later in the chapter as well as in Chapter 12.)

Research in an art museum consists in trying to determine as precisely as possible the origin, authorship, and character of each object in the collection. Since that is the responsibility of the curator, we can assume that some fraction of expenditure listed in Table 10.3 as curatorial is allocable to research. Also assignable to research would be the cost of maintaining a library, which is not shown separately in the available

---

[9] Paul S. Storch, "How to Equip Your Conservation Laboratory for Success." *Museum News,* 69, no. 3 (May–June 1990): 92–94.

[10] Lewis C. Price, Lisa DiRocco, and Janice D. Lewis, *Museum Program Survey, 1979* (Washington, D.C.: National Center for Educational Statistics, 1981), table 11.

data. We do know, however, that, in 1979, 66 percent of art museums reported having a library.[11] In addition, a part of the outlay for exhibitions might be classified as research, since important research is often carried out when new exhibitions are mounted.

Finally, Table 10.3 shows that in 1979 membership accounted for 3 percent and development 2 percent of operating outlays. These are the costs of obtaining outside financial support for a not-for-profit organization. Membership programs seek to enroll ordinary citizens who are willing to pay $20, $30, or $50 a year to become a "friend" of the museum. As we shall see, in 1988 membership dues produced a substantial share of the earned income of nonprofit art museums. "Development" is the polite word for large-scale fund-raising. If membership is fund-raising at the retail level, development is fund-raising at the wholesale level. The development staff try to obtain large charitable donations from wealthy and/or generous persons or foundations, as well as grants from state or federal agencies. They, as well as the senior curatorial staff and the members of the board of trustees, also work at persuading wealthy private collectors to donate or bequeath works of art directly to the museum. Rooms or even entire wings of museums may be named in honor of patrons who donate a large collection or pay for the construction of an addition to the galleries.

Museums as a decreasing cost industry

We look now at the cost conditions under which museums operate. This will provide the background needed for discussion of the contentious question of museum entrance fees. The analysis focuses especially on the display function, since that is by far the most costly, and of course, it is to see the museum's displays that the public would be asked to pay an admission fee.

The question we wish to answer is, How does the cost of making the museum's displays available to the public vary with the level of public admissions? In this formulation, admissions serve as the measure of output for the display function. The analysis deals only with short-run variation, hence the museum's galleries (its "plant") are assumed to be fixed in size. What we are really asking, therefore, is, How does cost vary with output in the short run, or in other words, what is the shape of the short-run cost curves for the display function? The answer, we shall argue, is that the display function operates under conditions of short-run decreasing unit cost.

Figure 10.1 shows the relationship between daily display function cost

[11] *Sourcebook 1989*, table 7.16.

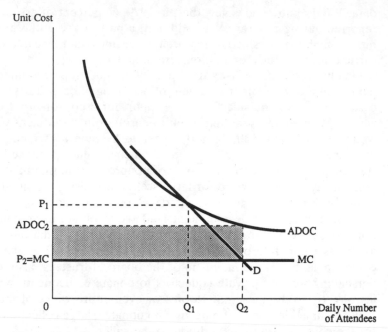

Figure 10.1. Economies of the museum display function.

per visitor and the number of visitors per day. Since there have been no empirical studies of the short-run cost curves of art museums, the shapes of the curves shown in Figure 10.1 are deduced from what we know about the way museums operate. It is useful to divide the cost of operating the display function into two parts. (1) *Basic operating cost* for the galleries includes heating, lighting, maintenance, insurance, office staff, and basic security service. These can be thought of as the minimum costs that must be incurred if the galleries are to open each morning. They are a fixed sum that does not vary with the number of visitors per day. The cost per visitor of this component therefore falls as the number of visitors increases. (2) The museum also incurs a *marginal cost* (*MC*) for each person/visit to cover the cost of additional security, information, and cleaning personnel imposed by attendees.

In drawing Figure 10.1 we assume, for the sake of simplicity, that marginal cost per visitor is constant. It is therefore shown as a horizontal line in the diagram. (In fact, once basic operating costs have been incurred to open the museum for the day, the marginal cost of a visitor might well be zero over some relatively low range of visits.) Basic operating cost per attendee is not shown separately, but we know how it behaves: since it consists of a fixed component divided by an increasing quantity, it would have the shape of a rectangular hyperbola, sloping downward exactly like average fixed cost in Figure 6.1. By adding this component vertically onto marginal cost, we generate the downward-sloping average daily operating cost curve ($ADOC$) in the diagram. (Basic operating cost per visitor can be read as the vertical distance between MC and $ADOC$.) Thus, the museum display function operates under conditions of decreasing unit cost because, as more visitors enter, the basic cost of opening the galleries to the public can be spread over more visits.

Full cost versus marginal cost pricing

In order to analyze the effect of charging for admission, we need information about the public's willingness to pay for visits. In Figure 10.1, curve D shows the demand for visits as a function of the price charged. If the museum wished to set a price just high enough to cover the full cost of the display function, it would charge the price indicated by the intersection of the demand curve and the average daily operating cost curve: at a price of P_1, Q_1 visitors would enter per day and the average daily operating cost would exactly equal the price charged. The display function would break even. Some analysts who oppose government subsidies for museums have argued strenuously in favor of that.[12] However, at output Q_1, marginal cost is well *below* price. Charging price P_1 therefore violates the welfare rule, which says that price should be set *equal* to marginal cost. There is a measurable welfare loss to society in charging price P_1, indicated by the fact that potential visitors between Q_1 and Q_2, who are willing to pay more than the full marginal cost of their visit, but not a price as high as P_1, are nevertheless denied attendance. (This welfare argument will be developed more fully at the beginning of Chapter 11.) On the other hand, if the museum followed the welfare rule, it would set price at the level indicated by the intersection of D and MC: at price P_2 there would be Q_2 visits per day. The welfare rule would be satisfied, but because price would be below cost, the display function would incur a daily operating deficit of Q_2 ($ADOC_2 - P_2$), equal to the area of the shaded rectangle in Figure 10.1.

Because the size of the potential deficit is large, the issue raised here is not a trivial one. Operating expenditures of art museums totaled in excess of $1.113 billion in 1988. We estimate that the display function (including its share of administrative and maintenance costs) accounts

[12] See, e.g., Ernest van den Haag, "Should the Government Subsidize the Arts?" *Policy Review,* 10 (Fall 1979): 63–73.

for about 64 percent of that, or $712 million for the year. Dividing by the 1988 attendance of 75.9 million, reported in Table 10.1, yields an average cost per visit (or $ADOC$) of $9.38. That is far above the probable marginal cost per visitor, which may in fact be close to zero. It also greatly exceeds the $3.00 median entrance fee (or "contribution") that museums were then charging (if they charged anything at all).[13]

The certainty that charging a price equal to marginal cost would result in operating deficits for museums is a powerful argument for providing them with government subsidies. The question of subsidies and/or alternative ways of covering museum deficits is discussed further in Chapter 11, as well as in the section of this chapter dealing with museum finances.

The analysis to this point has overlooked the phenomenon of congestion that may occur at very popular special exhibitions or, as they have come to be known, "blockbusters." (See the discussion of this topic later in the chapter.) Crowding at an exhibition reduces the pleasure obtained by viewers. This reduction in pleasure can be thought of as a cost that visitors who enter a congested exhibition impose on other simultaneous visitors and can be treated as an increase in marginal and average cost, starting at the point when visitors begin to get in each other's way. If the museum were setting fees equal to marginal cost, such an increase in marginal cost would justify higher charges for blockbusters than for ordinary exhibitions. The higher fees, if set correctly, would reduce congestion to the optimal level and make some contribution toward covering the deficit incurred during uncongested periods.[14]

Entrance fees and equity considerations

To this point the discussion of admission charges to museums has dealt only with what economists call the "efficiency" issue: it was argued that charging a price in excess of the presumably very low marginal cost would be inefficient in the sense of violating the $P = MC$ welfare rule. But charging for admission also raises issues of "equity" or "redistribution." Historically, most art museums in the United States have charged visitors little or nothing not because they understood the economist's arcane welfare rule, but rather because they believed it was

---

[13] Total operating costs and median admissions fees are from *1989 Museum Survey*, tables F:74.A and E:50.A.

[14] See the discussion of optimum highway congestion tolls in any urban economics text, e.g., James Heilbrun, *Urban Economics and Public Policy*, 3d ed. (New York: St. Martin's, 1987), pp. 191–96.

their mission to make great art available to the masses, and they feared that substantial entrance fees would prevent the relatively poor from partaking. It is therefore worthwhile to ask whether entrance fees, even those as low as the marginal cost of an admission, would in fact tend to filter out low-income visitors.

There is not much empirical evidence on this question. However, Rene Goudriaan and Gerrit Jan van't Eind did carry out a "before-and-after" study in Rotterdam, at the time when that Netherlands municipality imposed fees of about $1.35 for adults in four museums that had previously been open free of charge. Their results were somewhat surprising.[15] The proportion of low-income families in the audience *rose* significantly instead of falling! The authors could suggest no explanation for this counterintuitive outcome. Policymakers interested in encouraging the cultivation of a taste for art might have feared that imposing a fee would create a barrier to first-time attendance, but such was not the case: the relative frequency of first visits was not affected significantly. In the aggregate, attendance fell 30 percent, but the smaller number of visits was offset by an increase in average duration. Apparently, the fee tended to filter out short visits. Attendance at the maritime museum (regarded by the authors as "recreational") fell the most – 40 percent – while visits to the art museum were off by only 18 percent, indicating a lower price elasticity for the latter type. Whether that is good news or bad depends on where the comparison starts. It is encouraging to know that *imposing* charges does not greatly *reduce* attendance, but it is discouraging to reflect that for the same reason, holding the price *down* does not greatly *increase* it.

Acquisition policies of art museums

Art museums reported spending $120.5 million acquiring works for their collections in 1988. In addition, they reported donations of art works valued at $92 million.[16] The latter figure may err on the low side because some museums were unable to estimate the value of the works they received as gifts. Since museums are not required to calculate the aggregate value of their collections (it would be a superhuman task), it

[15] Rene Goudriaan and Gerrit Jan van't Eind, "To Fee or Not to Fee: Some Effects of Introducing Admission Fees in Four Museums in Rotterdam," in Virginia Lee Owen and William S. Hendon, eds., *Managerial Economics for the Arts* (Akron, Ohio: Association for Cultural Economics, 1985), pp. 103–09. The fee imposed was 2.50 Dutch guilders, here converted at the rate of 1.85 per dollar.

[16] Based on unpublished tabulations from *1989 Museum Survey*.

is impossible to say what these numbers imply about the rate at which collections are currently growing.

Donations of works of art that appreciated in value after the donor purchased them are strongly affected by provisions of the federal tax code. This important question will be examined in detail in Chapter 12.

Acquisition policies have always been a sensitive topic in the museum world. Directors and boards of trustees are reluctant to tip their hands for fear of adversely affecting the art market. In their annual reports, they do show aggregate cash expenditures for acquisitions, and they are happy to list the works acquired, but they do not have to report the prices they paid or the estimated value of donated works. They are eager to avoid controversy, and as we shall see in the next section, in the museum world nothing more easily leads to controversy than decisions affecting a museum's holdings.

Managing a museum's collection

When economists look at an art museum, they see an institution that has a large stock of capital held in the form of works of art and of buildings in which the art is either displayed or stored. But why "stored"? If display is their principal function, why not show the entire collection? The answer is that few museums have the gallery space to display all their holdings simultaneously. As a result, some pieces are consigned to the basement. These are likely to be either works in a style that is no longer considered interesting or else less important pieces in a category of which they have better examples on display. Works in storage are known as "the reserve." In some cases, they exceed by many times over the number of pieces actually on display.

To an economist, the problem of managing a museum's collection, which is its capital, appears to raise some of the same questions that occur in managing the assets of a business firm. Unlike a commercial enterprise, the museum is not trying to maximize profits. But it is presumably trying to attain some set of definable objectives, for which purpose it ought to deploy its assets efficiently. With this in mind, an economist might ask whether the right balance has been struck between the quantity of art owned and the amount of building space available to display it. For example, a museum with a large number of high-quality pieces in its reserve might be better advised to build more gallery space rather than spend funds purchasing more works of art that it lacks space to display. In economic terms, it is a matter of comparing at the margin the benefits to be obtained by investing an additional dollar in building gallery space as compared with the benefit of investing that dollar in additional works of art and then spending the money where the benefit per dollar is greatest.

The problem of "deaccessioning"

The "trade-off" between investing in art or in structures is a relatively simple matter to discuss. Much stickier is the question of how to manage the museum's art holdings themselves. It might seem reasonable for a museum that owns a relatively large number of paintings by Vincent Van Gogh, the nineteenth-century Flemish postimpressionist, and several by Henri Rousseau, the turn-of-the-century French primitive, but none by Annibale Carracci, an important sixteenth-century Bolognese mannerist, to sell a Van Gogh and a Rousseau and use the proceeds to buy a Carracci. An economist might say, "They're just trying to deploy their assets rationally." But when the Metropolitan Museum of Art did just that in 1972, it ran into a storm of protest. "Deaccessioning" of major works – the term refers to selling an object out of the museum's permanent collection – almost always leads to controversy.

The justification usually given for deaccessioning is that it allows the museum to better meet its chosen objectives. The criticism often comes from those who disagree with the objectives. A museum as large as the Metropolitan may wish to cover the field of art very broadly and has the resources to do so successfully. In that case, selling a Van Gogh and a Rousseau to buy a picture that will help to fill a gap in the collection would seem to make sense. Such, at any rate, was the conclusion of J. Michael Montias, an economist who carefully analyzed the Carracci affair at the Metropolitan.[17]

Small or medium-size museums, on the other hand, may decide to specialize in the art of one period or country and will therefore deaccession objects that fall outside their chosen field and use the proceeds to buy additional works within that specialty. A case in point, reported by Evan Roth, is the Walker Art Center in Minneapolis, which some years ago decided to concentrate on contemporary, especially twentieth-century U.S. art. In May 1989 at Sotheby's in New York, it auctioned 22 very fine nineteenth-century U.S. paintings and announced that the proceeds, amounting to $10.5 million, would be used to buy works that "better reflect the artistic mission of the museum." But Roth reports that "the sale was not universally well received" and quotes Jonathan Yardley of the *Washington Post* as complaining that "thanks to selling off giants of the

---

[17] J. Michael Montias, "Are Museums Betraying the Public Trust?" *Museum News* 51, no. 9 (May 1973): 25–31, reprinted in Mark Blaug, ed., *The Economics of the Arts* (London: Martin Robertson, 1976), pp. 205–17.

19th century, the museum has the money to buy up more pygmies of the 20th."[18] Evidently, Yardley disagrees with the Walker's objectives.

Sarah Montgomery has suggested that fear of being proved wrong may be one reason museum professionals resist deaccessioning: because critical judgment about art does change with time, what they sell off today may be viewed tomorrow as having "special aesthetic value." Far safer, they think, to keep currently uninteresting works in storage.[19]

Deaccessioning does raise difficult questions. Some argue that it will shake the confidence of potential donors, who do not like to think that the works of art they reluctantly part with may later be sold by the museum on the open market, perhaps passing back into private hands. But deaccessioning would probably have to be carried much further than now seems likely before it would seriously undermine the willingness of potential donors to give works of art to museums. Donors often try to ensure the permanence of their gifts by stipulating that they cannot be resold. Museum directors who would like to make some changes (and their legal counsel) have to decide how far they are bound by such arrangements, especially if they were made in the very distant past. Finally, there are those who would argue that museums violate a public trust if they dispose of *any* object that has been given into their safekeeping. That view, as Montias puts it, "would confine all sales and barters to works of art purchased by museums from unrestricted funds."[20]

Some questions of distribution

The previous section, which dealt with the problem of rationally managing a *single* museum's collection, leads us to the important question of the distribution of art *among* museums. It is a puzzling fact that our larger museums have extensive reserves holding many objects, which, though rarely displayed, may be of a higher quality than works currently on display in smaller museums. Would not the less well endowed places be delighted to have a few of the rejects in the basement of the Metropolitan? Montias points out that this sort of misallocation of social resources is made worse by the fact that museum directors

---

[18] Evan Roth, "Deaccession Debate," *Museum News,* 69, no. 2 (March–April 1990): 42–46, cited at 42 and 44.

[19] Communication to the authors, January 22, 1992.

[20] Montias, "Are Museums Betraying the Public Trust," in Blaug, p. 212. Also see the many references to deaccessioning in Feldstein, ed., *Economics of the Arts.*

have virtually no incentive to refuse a bequest. The result, he thinks, is that works of art "often end up in places that have no need for them."[21]

When a misallocation of resources exists, social gains (theoretically measurable in dollars) can be made by overcoming it. If an appropriate way can be found to divide those gains between the affected parties, it's possible that all of them can be made better off in the process of overcoming the misallocation. In the case of museum holdings discussed here, economic intuition suggests that there must be a conceivable arrangement by which less well endowed institutions could rent under-utilized objects (long term) from museums that are, in effect, over-stocked. Economists point out that when voluntary trades are made in the marketplace, both parties benefit – otherwise they would not have agreed to the trade. Hence, if the arrangements suggested here were carried out voluntarily, we could assume that both lender and borrower gained from the transaction. Perhaps the problem is that museum directors and boards of trustees would prefer to spend their available funds (however meager) buying art to add to the museum's collection rather than renting it. "Renting" sounds decidedly second rate when compared with the accomplishment implied by "new acquisition." But with art prices in the marketplace rising to levels that are referred to on all sides as astronomical, the time may be near when novel arrangements for sharing existing museum resources will become acceptable.

Stephen E. Weil, deputy director of the Hirschhorn Museum of the Smithsonian Institution, reaches a similar conclusion, but without using explicitly economic arguments. He sees no reason why large and small museums need pursue identical policies. Instead, he calls for a division of labor "with each size of institution specializing in what it did best." He suggests that large museums could

> serve as the principal repositories and caretakers of our material heritage . . . and . . . the primary source of loans. Small museums . . . would concentrate on presenting special exhibitions and other programs that drew on the collection resources of the larger museums and addressed the aesthetic historic, political and scientific issues relevant to their communities.[22]

Small museums could thus give up trying to do what they cannot do very well, that is, collect art, while concentrating on what they are

---

[21] Montias, "Are Museums Betraying the Public Trust," p. 214.
[22] Stephen E. Weil, *Rethinking the Museum* (Washington, D.C.: Smithsonian Institution Press, 1990), p. 38.

uniquely well suited to do, that is, mount exhibits relevant to their own communities. In this way, Weil argues, the museum field as a whole could best serve the public interest. He admits, however, that the scheme leaves medium-size museums out of account. They would probably have to go on pretty much as they have done, both collecting and exhibiting.

Weil has also pointed out that joint acquisition by several museums is another constructive response to the nearly prohibitive current cost of adding to a museum's collection. He cites several cases in which U.S. museums have jointly purchased works of art under an agreement that provides for the regular circulation of the objects among the partners. For example, in 1975 a group of museums in the state of Washington formed the Washington Art Consortium for the purpose of purchasing a collection of U.S. drawings and other works on paper. Each participant, Weil writes, "is guaranteed the right to show the entire collection for at least four months during any two-calendar-year period." The NEA supported this cooperative effort with a $100,000 grant in 1975.[23]

Collection sharing and franchising on a large scale

Two major U.S. museums now see collection sharing on an international scale as a way to serve wider audiences while simultaneously augmenting their own income. In October 1991 the Museum of Fine Arts in Boston announced an agreement with a Japanese group to supply art from the Boston museum's extensive collections to a new museum planned for the city of Nagoya. According to the announcement, the Boston museum will "develop both long term and temporary exhibitions" from its own holdings for the Nagoya museum. It will "also make its expertise available in all areas of the new museum's operations, and will be appropriately compensated for its services."[24]

An even more elaborate scheme for collection sharing is under consideration at the Solomon R. Guggenheim Museum in New York City.[25] The Guggenheim specializes in twentieth-century European painting, of which it has one of the world's greatest collections, reportedly num-

---

[23] Stephen E. Weil, "Custody Without Title," in a collection of his papers entitled *Beauty and the Beasts: On Museums, Art, the Law, and the Market* (Washington, D.C.: Smithsonian Institution Press, 1983), pp. 151–59, cited at 153.

[24] *MNEWS,* a press release from the Museum of Fine Arts, Boston, October 24, 1991, p. 1.

[25] Michael Kimmelman, "What on Earth is the Guggenheim Up To?" *New York Times,* October 14, 1990; and idem, "At the Guggenheim, Bigger May Be Better," *New York Times* (June 21, 1992). Also see references to the Guggenheim in Feldstein, ed., *Economics of the Arts.*

bering around six thousand pieces. Its building, a deservedly famous structure designed by Frank Lloyd Wright, can display only a few hundred objects at a time. A small annex has been added, but further expansion at the existing site is impossible. The proposed solution, in addition to a branch recently opened in the SoHo district of lower Manhattan, is a "franchising" system, under which additional "Guggenheims" would be established at selected locations in Europe or Asia. The cost of constructing them would be borne by foreign governments or localities eager for the prestige and tourism such a facility would undoubtedly confer. Art to fill these branches would be on loan from the Guggenheim in New York, which would also provide curatorial services and would presumably receive substantial fees in return. If this revolutionary scheme works as planned, the additional income would enable the Guggenheim to round out its collection by purchasing late-twentieth-century works.

Theoretically, the franchise plan does help to overcome the misallocation of resources, which, as we indicated earlier, is implied by large, undisplayed reserves of art. Nevertheless, many observers worry about its risks: first, that the Guggenheim may become financially overextended in playing the game of international expansion and thus risk losing control of the collection it exists to protect; second, that by emphasizing autonomy, the scheme tends to undermine the alternative of cooperation between museums; third, that the art itself will be at risk when shipped back and forth across the globe to rotate the stock at the new Guggenheim satellites. We take up the risks of transporting art to international exhibitions at the end of the next section.

Special exhibitions, tours, blockbusters!

Special exhibitions and tours have a major impact on the geographic distribution of art display. In effect these events substitute the transportation of art for the transportation of people. In the last 30 years, they have grown enormously in frequency and importance. Many formats are possible. A museum of almost any size may decide to put on a special exhibition of the work of some artist, school, or period in which they own a nucleus of a few or more objects. The bulk of the exhibition will consist of works borrowed from other museums or from private collectors. Since the expense of organizing such a "loan exhibit" (including curatorial staff time, packing and transportation charges, and insurance) is considerable, the organizers will usually try to spread the costs by sharing the exhibition with other museums, in effect, putting the show on tour. The NEA estimates that U.S. art museums organize at least twelve hundred such exhibits per year.[26] Since the typical exhibit travels to several museums and is usually a "featured attraction" wherever it goes, the total impact of these endeavors is surely impressive.

These events increase the availability of art to the viewing public along two dimensions. First, there is a "concentration effect": they bring together far more works on a given subject than the viewer could otherwise hope to see in any one place. The impact is powerful and the museumgoer is far more likely to come away with lasting aesthetic impressions than would be the case if only a few works of any given type were on view during a single visit. Second, there is a "distribution effect": special exhibitions and tours carry this concentration of works, with its powerful aesthetic impact, to places that may be remote from major collections. (Incidentally, it should be pointed out that traveling exhibitions are shown not only at museums but also at local "arts centers" that have exhibition space, but no collection of their own.)

Special exhibitions of sufficiently grand size, or blockbusters, are usually loan exhibitions dealing with the work of a major (and very popular) painter, such as Van Gogh, Degas, or Matisse, or that bring to the public works not readily accessible, such as the King Tut exhibit of Egyptian art or the exhibition of masterpieces from the Hermitage in St. Petersburg. Museums may sometimes charge a special admission fee for a blockbuster, and so may come out ahead financially on a particularly well attended exhibit. In addition, when an exhibition goes on tour, the institution that organized it is entitled to collect participation fees from the museums it visits. The Whitney Museum of American Art in New York City reports that revenue from traveling exhibitions totaled $681,658 in 1989 and $232,893 in 1990. Related direct costs to the museum in the two years were $410,272 and $97,754. Although the Whitney does not make a point of it, the figures indicate that the museum earned a considerable net return on traveling exhibitions in both years.[27] That may not be typical since, according to the NEA, most special exhibitions do not make money. However, they do attract visitors, and "for most museums, attendance translates ultimately into income."[28] It is worth noting that the Whitney's traveling exhibitions include a special set, not shown at the home base in New York, that are made up of works from the museum's permanent collection. In that way the Whitney is able to

---

[26] *The Arts in America: A Report to the President and to the Congress* (Washington, D.C.: National Endowment for the Arts, October 1988), pp. 170–71.

[27] *Bulletin of the Whitney Museum of American Art, 1988–89,* p. 104; and *1989–90,* p. 104.

[28] *The Arts in America,* p. 172.

share objects drawn from its valuable reserves with other, usually much smaller museums in the United States.

To be sure, the recent vogue for special exhibitions has its detractors. Blockbusters usually attract major support from corporate sponsors. Some observers object that in their eagerness for corporate support, museums are permitting themselves to be commercialized and losing sight of their artistic objectives. Others argue that emphasis on special exhibitions has undermined the public's willingness to attend just for the sake of studying the regular collection. There are staffing problems, as well. The larger museums, having attractive collections, must process an enormous number of loan requests, which puts a heavy and, from their point of view, unproductive burden on their professional staff. Finally, some art lovers worry about the potential for catastrophic loss should an airplane crash while carrying irreplaceable masterpieces to an internationally organized blockbuster. One critic who raised that objection (as well as some others) did, however, admit that international exhibitions have not yet been responsible for serious damage to works of art, although some appalling acts of vandalism and burglary have occurred in major museums during the ordinary course of business.[29]

Museum revenues

The analysis of performing arts company finances in Chapter 8 focused on the problem of the "earnings gap," which was defined as the difference between total expenditures and *earned* income. The revenue shortfall was covered by *unearned* income, consisting of government grants and income contributed by private supporters. Following Baumol and Bowen's lead, it was pointed out that productivity lag in the performing arts intensified their financial problem. The term "earnings gap" implies its opposite, the notion that performing arts companies could conceivably balance their budgets out of earned income. After all, the commercial theater does it. So do promoters of rock concerts and other profit-making live popular entertainments, and it is taken for granted that not-for-profit performing arts companies will also charge a price for admission. In that context, one of the tasks of economic analysis is to explain why ticket revenue might fall short of expenses, leaving an earnings gap.

We adopt a different perspective in dealing with art museums. Many of them were founded with the intention that they be open to the public free of charge. There were and are commercially operated museums,

---

[29] Francis Haskell, "Titian and the Perils of International Exhibition," *New York Review* (August 16, 1990), p. 9.

Table 10.4. *Operating income of art museums*

	1979	1988
Total operating income ($ millions)	294	1,184
	Percentage by type or source	
Earned income, total	26.3	28.3
Admission fees	5.4	4.6
Tuition fees	4.4	3.1
Membership dues	7.3	8.1
Museum shop, food, and aux. serv.	5.3	7.7
Other earned income	3.9	4.8
Unearned income, total	73.5	71.7
Investment and endowment income	22.0	19.6
Federal government support	8.4	6.3
State government support	4.8	8.5
Local government support	14.3	10.8
Individual contributions	6.3	12.9
Corporate and foundation support	10.0	10.0
Other unearned income	7.7	3.6

Sources: 1979 – *Museum Program Survey 1979*, tables 23 and 24. Investment and endowment income have been reassigned from the earned to the unearned category. 1988 – *1989 Museum Survey*, tables F:73.A, F:73.C, F:73.E, and unpublished tabulations.

but not in the field of art. Since the earned income of art museums was traditionally close to zero and, in any event, was never expected to cover expenses, the term "earnings gap" seems inappropriate. Let us look at their finances without emphasizing that term.

Table 10.4 shows the sources of art museum operating income, according to the two most recent surveys. Earned income accounted for only 26 percent of the total in 1979 and 28 percent in 1988. At both dates membership dues were the largest category of earned income. Admission fees ranked second in 1979 but by 1988 were overtaken by net income from museum shops, food, and auxiliary services, which increased sharply. We have already seen that there are strong economic arguments *against* using high admission fees to increase museum income, so their relatively modest role in generating revenues is not necessarily to be regretted. On the other hand, policymakers have encouraged museums to raise as much net income as they can by operating a restaurant, bookstore, or gift shop for visitors in order to reduce their dependence on outside financial assistance. The Metropolitan Museum of Art, which does everything on a large scale, has gone as far as to open "satellite" shops in Connecticut and New Jersey. But the nation-wide growth of museum shops has led to a counterattack by commercial interests, who point out that various tax exemptions give stores operated by not-for-profit institutions an unfair advantage. Accordingly, they have brought pressure on Congress to amend the tax law.

Clearly, museums are heavily dependent on *unearned* income to balance their budgets. It should be noted, however, that as a result of generous past support from wealthy donors, many museums have large endowment funds. Table 10.4 shows that investment and endowment income made up 22 percent of total income in 1979. That share fell to slightly below 20 percent by 1988. Although the value of endowments increased substantially, their yield apparently did not grow as fast as museum budgets did. Even so, in 1988 the yield covered 27 percent of the difference between earned and total income. To that extent, museums do not have to scratch and scramble to meet their expenses. (In the performing arts, only symphony orchestras have significant endowment funds, but they are relatively smaller and accounted for only 6 percent of orchestra income in 1970–71.)[30] Nevertheless, museums are heavily dependent on contributed funds. As revealed in Table 10.4, government grants and donations by individuals, corporations, and foundations accounted for 43.8 percent of total income in 1979 and 48.5 percent in 1988.

Contributed private support

Private support contributed by individuals, foundations, and corporations amounted to 16.3 percent of total museum revenue in 1979. It rose sharply to 22.9 percent by 1988. The share donated by foundations and corporations was steady at 10 percent, but individual contributions soared from 6.3 to 12.9 percent of total revenue. Membership dues accounted for an additional 8.1 percent of total revenue in 1988, bringing the share of total private support to 31 percent. Yet membership and fund-raising programs in 1988 made up only 6.7 percent of museum expenditures.[31] On the face of it, spending 7 percent to take in 31 percent seems like a pretty good thing.

Indeed, the substantial effort that art museums put into fund-raising pays off quite handsomely. William S. Hendon, in his comprehensive economic study of the Akron Art Institute, shows that in 1971–72 the museum's development activities produced measurable benefits of

---

[30] *The Finances of the Performing Arts,* vol. 1 (New York: Ford Foundation, 1974), table 4, p. 42, and app. C, p. 31.
[31] Unpublished tabulations are from *1989 Museum Survey.*

$128,533 at a cost of only $57,812.[32] Using data from the 1979 *Museum Program Survey,* William Luksetich, Mark Lange, and Philip Jacobs found that for art museums as a whole, the marginal return from an additional dollar spent on fund-raising was $7.44 in added revenue from private and public sources combined.[33] This is a provocative result, for as long as the return from a dollar spent is more than a dollar gained, logic suggests that museums should spend even more than they do to raise money. The authors also found that the largest art museums were more successful than smaller ones at raising money, which may point to economies of scale in fund-raising. However, the smallest museums were more successful in obtaining support from the federal government. That result probably indicates an intentional bias in federal policy, which favors grants to small museums as a way of encouraging the spread of art to underserved areas or cultural groups. (See the discussion in the following section.)

The economics of private contributions to arts organizations, including museums, is discussed in detail in Chapter 12. Special attention is paid there to the controversial role of corporate support.

Federal assistance to museums

The largest single federal expenditure on behalf of museums is its annual appropriation for the Smithsonian Institution. Created by Congress in 1846, the Smithsonian is now by far the largest museum in the United States, if not in the world. In 1990 Congress appropriated $225 million to support its operating costs. An additional $21 million of federal funds was spent on repair and restoration of its buildings.[34] The Smithsonian operates 11 museums. Only 5 are primarily museums of art, and they are not among the Smithsonian's largest components. Collectively in 1990, they absorbed $21.9 million of federal funds, out of $86.5 million allocated to museum programs. We estimate that their

---

[32] William S. Hendon, *Analyzing an Art Museum* (New York: Praeger, 1979), table 9.2. In the same volume Hendon also applied benefit–cost analysis to the Akron museum's education and exhibition functions. For a more general explanation of the benefit–cost analysis of cultural activities, see his "Evaluating Cultural Policy Through Benefit/Cost Analysis," in Anthony J. Radich and Sharon Schwoch, eds., *Economic Impact of the Arts: A Sourcebook* (Denver, Colo.: National Conference of State Legislatures, May 1987), pp. 159–83.

[33] William Luksetich, Mark Lange, and Philip Jacobs, "The Effectiveness of Museum Fund-Raising Efforts," in Harry Hillman-Chartrand et al., eds., *Paying for the Arts* (Akron, Ohio: Association for Cultural Economics, 1987), pp. 187–97.

[34] *Budget of the United States Government,* Fiscal year 1992, pt. 4, pp. 192, 1183.

proportionate share of overhead and public service costs paid for out of federal funds would amount to another $13.9 million.[35]

In the arts, the federal government also assumes responsibility for the operating costs of the National Gallery of Art in Washington, D.C. Congress appropriated $40 million for that purpose in 1990. Building maintenance and renovation cost an additional $1.3 million in federal funds.[36] Art museums not directly owned or operated by the national government may receive federal support through a number of channels, including the Institute of Museum Services, the NEA, and the National Endowment for the Humanities (NEH).

The Institute of Museum Services: Created by Congress in 1976, the IMS went into operation the following year. Its principal purpose, mandated by Congress, was "to ease the financial burden borne by museums as a result of their increasing use by the public."[37] This was to be accomplished by providing museums with direct operating support to help cover their general expenses. At the federal level, grants for general operating support were a new idea and a radical departure from the already established practice of the NEA and NEH. The two endowments give grants only for well-defined purposes – usually a "project" or "program" of some sort, for which the applicant submits a detailed proposal – and specifically avoid general operating support. (It is different at the state level: state arts councils frequently give general operating support to well-regarded institutions within their own states.)

If a federal agency is going to offer general operating support to museums, the logic of the situation might suggest that every qualified museum should receive its pro rata share as a virtual entitlement. The National Museum Services Board, which determines policy for the IMS, thought otherwise. It was decided from the beginning that museums should compete for the available funds through an application procedure. To ensure that the large museums would not soak up most of the available funds, a maximum allowable amount per grant was established at a level that would allow the IMS to fund approximately 30 to 40 percent of all applicants. Currently, a museum may receive an operating support grant amounting to up to 10 percent of its operating income, but not to exceed $75,000.[38] This means, in effect, that museums

[35] *Smithsonian Year, 1990,* annual report of the Smithsonian Institution for the year ended September 30, 1990, table 2.
[36] *Budget,* pt. 4, p. 1183.
[37] Institute of Museum Services (IMS), *The Collaborative Spirit: Partners in America, Tenth Anniversary, 1977–1987* (Washington, D.C., n.d.), p. 5.
[38] Ibid., pp. 6–7.

whose operating budgets exceed $750,000 per year (not a large sum these days) receive proportionately less aid than do very small institutions. Within the universe of museums, IMS programs are therefore highly redistributive. That may be perfectly consistent with the general tendency of U.S arts policy to favor programs that will carry art to underserved areas or constituencies. Undoubtedly, it also serves the political purpose of garnering votes for the agency by spreading benefits to as many congressional districts as possible.

It must be pointed out that the IMS assists all types of museums, not just museums of art. They define the term "museum" broadly enough to include aquariums and botanical and zoological parks, as well as museums of history, natural history, science, ethnography, and such specialized interests as medical history, horticulture, and even antique steam engines. In the face of that competition, art museums receive slightly less than one quarter of IMS grant funds.

In fiscal year 1990, funds obligated by the IMS totaled $22.7 million. Grants for general operating support accounted for $17.7 million, a bit more than three-quarters of the whole. Art museums awards for general operating support amounted to $4.3 million.[39] Conservation of museum collections is the only other large IMS program. The institute adopted conservation as a major concern in the mid-1980s.[40] In 1990 conservation projects were awarded a total of $2.65 million, of which only $356,495 went to art museums.[41] We shall see in Chapter 11 that the desire to pass a nation's artistic heritage on to future generations is one of the strongest justifications for government subsidy to the arts. Hence, it is entirely appropriate that the IMS should use its funds to encourage conservation.

As was also the case for the two endowments, appropriations for the IMS became a matter of controversy during the 1980s. President Reagan twice tried to eliminate the agency. Congress, however, insisted on maintaining it. Appropriations reached $20 million in 1984 and then rose very slowly to $22.7 million in 1990. Given the rate of inflation since 1984, the real value of the agency's appropriation has fallen considerably since then.

The National Endowment for the Arts: In 1990 the NEA committed $12.1 million in program funds to museums (not counting challenge

---

[39] IMS, *1990 Annual Report*, pp. 8–9, 26.
[40] IMS, *The Collaborative Spirit*, pp. 6–7.
[41] IMS, *1990 Annual Report*, pp. 13–14.

grants).[42] That made museums the NEA's third largest program category, exceeded only by music ($15.3 million) and media arts ($13.9 million). Until the mid-1980s, museums had ranked second after music. Although grants under the museum program have not diminished since that time, support for media arts has substantially increased, pushing the museum program into third place. Following are the four largest NEA museum programs, together with the amounts committed to them in 1990:

> Catalogue: A program to finance the systematic documentation of, or the publication of a catalogue on, some part of a museum's holdings ($949,200)
>
> Presentation: A program to support the reinstallation or exhibition of important parts of ·a museum's collection ($1,577,500)
>
> Conservation: A program to enable museums to plan and implement conservation programs ($1,169,800)
>
> Special exhibitions: A program to help museums organize special exhibitions or pay the cost of borrowing exhibitions organized elsewhere ($4,920,000). The large size of this category relative to the program as a whole testifies to the importance special exhibitions have now assumed in the museum world.

The NEA makes no grants to finance construction, maintenance, or remodeling of buildings or, with one exception, the acquisition of works of art. The single exception is the Museum Purchase Plan, which supports the purchase of works of art in all media by living U.S. artists ($698,500). This program is intended both to expand public interest in contemporary U.S. art and to assist artists. The sum committed was divided among 61 recipients, so the average grant was not much more than $10,000, a modest price for art in today's market.

The National Endowment for the Humanities: The NEH also provides a degree of support to art museums. Since the study of art falls within the "humanities," the fields covered by the two endowments naturally overlap. Support to museums is offered by both. Museums are eligible for NEH aid from its Division of General Programs, in a category entitled Humanities Projects in Museums and Historical Organizations.

---

[42] Data on funding are from National Endowment for the Arts, *1990 Annual Report,* pp. 155–84 and 334.

In 1990 this program included a total of $8.8 million in grants.[43] However, since these funds go to museums of every type as well as to historical societies, art museums receive only a fraction of the total. In the field of art, the NEA is obviously the more important source of funding. In the typical case, an NEH grant would be given in support of a special exhibition (often a traveling exhibition) and an accompanying catalogue and public education program. Emphasis on the last two elements is, of course, consistent with the endowment's mission to support education and scholarship in the humanities.

State and local government support

Direct state and local government support for art museums is even more important than federal support. Table 10.4 shows that while the federal share in art museum budgets fell from 8.4 percent in 1979 to 6.3 percent in 1988, the state and local share held steady at a little over 19 percent. In fact, the state share increased sharply between those dates, reflecting the fact that state support for the arts as a whole tripled during that period. (See Chapter 13 for details.) In a study based on 1987 data, Paul DiMaggio estimated that state arts agencies allocate 12 percent of their funds to art museums and exhibition spaces, approximately the same proportion as the NEA does.[44]

The relatively high level of local government support for art museums is particularly noteworthy. As indicated in Table 10.4, it accounted for 14.3 percent of their operating income in 1979 and 10.8 percent in 1988. By contrast, performing arts organizations as a whole (in 1971–72) derived only 2 percent of operating income from local government grants.[45] Not counted here is the considerable value of the indirect subsidy museums receive from local government because their land and buildings, like those of other nonprofit institutions, are exempt from the local property tax.

In some cases a museum's connection with local government goes back to the legal arrangements under which the museum was founded. New York City, for example, gives extensive operating and capital construction support to museums that have been built on public land, even though the museums themselves are private philanthropic corporations,

---

[43] National Endowment for the Humanities, *Twenty-Fifth Anniversary Annual Report, 1990,* pp. 94–100 and 190.

[44] Paul J. DiMaggio, "Decentralization of Arts Funding from the Federal Government to the States," in Stephen Benedict, ed., *Public Money and the Muse* (New York: Norton, for the American Assembly, 1991), pp. 216–52, cited at 236.

[45] *Finances of the Performing Arts,* vol. 1, app. C, p. 4.

rather than entities of the local government. In this way the Metropolitan Museum of Art received $15.6 million in operating support from the city in fiscal 1989–90. That amounted to 20.7 percent of the museum's $75.2 million operating income.[46] Under similar arrangements in the same year, the city of Buffalo and Erie County contributed $539,096 of support to Buffalo's Albright-Knox Art Gallery, providing 19.0 percent of that museum's $2.8 million operating revenue.[47]

Museums do seem to occupy a special place in the local public consciousness. We can only speculate as to the reasons. Perhaps the high visibility of the grandiose buildings they inhabit makes them particularly potent symbols of civic pride. Or it may be that their role in conveying culture to the people is especially attractive to taxpayers in a society that has always insisted on its devotion to popular education. (The question of government subsidies for art and culture is further analyzed in Chapters 11, 12, and 13.)

[46] The Metropolitan Museum of Art, *Annual Report for the Year 1989–90*, p. 70.
[47] The Buffalo Fine Arts Academy and Albright-Knox Art Gallery, *Annual Report, 1989–90*, p. 33.

Part IV

Public policy toward the arts

11

Should the government subsidize the arts?

Although history tells us that the arts have been subsidized by Medici princes, Austrian emperors, Russian czars, English parliaments, and French republics, the question, Should the government subsidize the arts? still strikes economists as eminently worthy of debate. How can this be so? The answer is quite plain. The dominant tradition among Western economists holds that given the existing distribution of income, competitive markets in most circumstances can be relied on to satisfy consumer preferences optimally. According to this view there are two principal grounds for justifying government subsidies or other forms of intervention.

The first would be that markets are *not* competitive or display other imperfections. These are the efficiency arguments, so-called because some form of "market failure" has led to an inefficient allocation of resources, which it is the task of intervention to correct. Moreover, economists are in substantial agreement about which imperfections justify what sorts of government intervention. Debate therefore focuses not on the theoretical arguments for intervention, but on whether the art and culture industries, in fact, operate under the justifying conditions.

The second justification for intervention would be a belief that the existing distribution of income is unsatisfactory. We say "belief" to emphasize the fact that judgments about the distribution of income cannot be scientific, but are necessarily based on ethical conviction. This is the so-called equity argument: subsidies are called for not because markets are working inefficiently, but because it is alleged that some participants lack the income to buy a minimum fair share.

Optimization in perfectly competitive markets
That perfectly competitive markets produce an optimum allocation of resources can be demonstrated by means of demand and supply

199

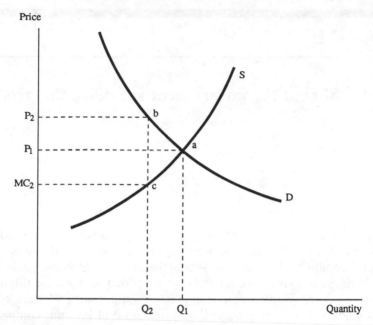

Figure 11.1. Optimization in a perfectly competitive market.

analysis, provided we recall the factors that lie behind demand and supply. It was explained in Chapter 4 that demand for a given commodity is based on the utility consumers expect to obtain by using it. The prices recorded along any given demand curve show the amount that consumers would willingly pay for the corresponding quantities. Since they are willingly paid, these prices must measure the marginal utility (in dollars) of the successive units purchased. Figure 11.1 shows hypothetical demand and supply curves for shoes sold under conditions of perfect competition. When Q_1 pairs are purchased, the price is P_1, indicating that the marginal pair has a utility of P_1 to the consumer who buys it. More shoes could be sold only if the price fell below P_1 because the marginal utility of shoes to consumers falls as more are purchased.

Marginal cost operates on the supply side in a way analogous to marginal utility on the demand side. As explained at the end of Chapter 6, short-run supply curves in competitive manufacturing industries slope upward because as firms increase production, the law of diminishing returns causes the marginal cost of output to rise. Thus, in Figure 11.1 the prices recorded along the supply curve S show the marginal cost of supplying the successive quantities of shoes measured along the horizontal axis. At a price of P_1, Q_1 pairs are supplied, indicating that the marginal cost of the last pair sold is P_1. Furthermore, since factor markets are also assumed to be perfectly competitive, shoe manufacturers, in order to hire inputs, must pay them an amount equal to what they could earn in their next best employment. Therefore, the marginal cost of the last unit measures the opportunity cost to society of the resources employed in its production, that is to say, it measures the value of the other products that were forgone when resources were used up to make this pair of shoes.

We are now in a position to see how competitive markets optimize the allocation of resources. When the shoe market is in equilibrium, Q_1 pairs are sold per time period at a price of P_1. The marginal unit provides P_1 of utility to its buyer, which exactly equals the value to society of the resources used up in producing it. If additional units were sold, their marginal utility to consumers would be less than P_1 (because the demand curve D slopes down to the right) while the cost to society of producing them would be more than P_1 (because the supply curve slopes up to the right). Since the utility of the additional units would be less than their cost, producing them would clearly reduce aggregate social welfare.

By analogous reasoning we can see that social welfare would also fall if shoe output were reduced below Q_1. At quantities below that level, the demand curve, which measures marginal utility, rises above the supply curve, which measures marginal cost. Thus, if we failed to produce units to the left of Q_1, the loss in utility to consumers would exceed the reduction in cost to society. Again, aggregate social welfare would be reduced.

Another way of putting this is that welfare is maximized if the equilibrium level of output is such that price equals marginal cost. The argument can be further clarified with the help of Figure 11.1. If output were reduced from Q_1 to Q_2, price would rise to P_2, while the marginal cost of production would fall to MC_2. Consumers would lose utility equal to the area under the demand curve between Q_1 and Q_2, which equals Q_1abQ_2. Costs, on the other hand, would be reduced by an amount indicated by the equivalent area under the supply curve, or Q_1acQ_2. The net loss to society, equal to the positive difference between the reductions in utility and cost, would be the area of the triangle abc.

Thus, Q_1, the equilibrium level of shoe production under perfect competition, is clearly the optimum, since social welfare would be reduced if output were either greater or less than that amount. By extension of this argument one can see that if all markets were perfectly competitive, so that price everywhere equalled marginal cost, the allocation of resources would be optimal throughout the economy.

The problem of market failure

When markets work efficiently, we rightly let them operate on their own. We do not find it necessary for the government to intervene in the markets for running shoes, TV sets, or tennis rackets. We do not have a national shoe policy or a national tennis racket policy or policies to influence the output of countless other consumer goods. Instead, we accept the market outcome. Why should the arts be an exception? Why not leave arts output to be settled in the marketplace alongside the output of TV sets, tennis rackets, and running shoes? A possible answer, which we now look into, is that markets do not always operate efficiently, and market failure, as it has come to be called, provides an argument for public intervention. The principal causes of market failure are monopoly, externalities, public goods, declining cost industries, and lack of information. We will examine them in that order and ask in each case whether they seem to operate in the fields of art and culture. If they do, that argues strongly in favor of corrective public policy.

Monopoly

Monopoly is a cause of market failure because the monopolist is in a position to restrict output and earn extra profits by raising prices above the marginal cost level that would prevail under competition. Because output stops short of the level at which marginal cost equals price, some consumers are denied goods for which they would pay more than the incremental cost of production. Such an outcome is economically inefficient. It would occur, for example, if output were restricted to Q_2 in Figure 11.1, instead of expanding to the competitive level of Q_1, since over the range from Q_2 to Q_1, the price consumers are willing to pay always exceeds marginal cost.

As explained in Chapter 7, arts institutions frequently operate as monopolists within their local market. Rarely is there more than one art museum, professional symphony orchestra, opera, or ballet company in a U.S. city. This is not usually treated as a source of market failure, however, because most arts institutions are organized on a not-for-profit basis. If they charge prices above marginal cost, it is not because they are trying to maximize profits, but because they operate under conditions of decreasing cost, so that marginal cost is always below the average total cost of production. The problem of decreasing cost industries will be discussed later.

Externalities or collective benefits

Externalities exist when the activities of one firm or individual affect other firms or individuals in ways for which no compensation is paid. For example, if an electric generating plant produces air pollution, it imposes damage costs on nearby firms and residents for which they are paid no compensation. Pollution is the classic case of an external cost. But externalities can also be beneficial. When a suburban home-owner maintains a highly visible flower garden, neighbors and passersby obtain an external benefit for which they cannot be charged. Because externalities, whether positive or negative, are not mediated through markets, the resources used in their production are not subject to the rationalizing influence of the price system. They are an important cause of market failure.

Since the arts are often alleged to be a source of external benefits, but rarely of external costs, only the benefit case will be examined here. In order to avoid prejudging its applicability to the arts, however, we will illustrate it by reference to education. Education produces both a private benefit to the person receiving it and an external benefit to society at large. The private benefit consists of higher earning power and greater ability to take part in and enjoy the nation's material and immaterial culture. The external benefit is the advantage conferred on the rest of society by the education of each individual member. In a democratic community, each citizen is affected by the way others vote and carry out their civic responsibilities. Each of us gains if our fellow citizens are literate and well informed rather than ignorant. Consequently, your education confers a benefit on the rest of us, over and above what you personally gain from it. Since this kind of external benefit is conferred broadly on the members of society, who consume it collectively, it can also be called a "collective benefit."

Figure 11.2 shows both the private and the external (collective) benefits attributable to the education of a hypothetical individual. Years of schooling are measured along the horizontal axis and cost and benefit per year along the vertical. The curve D_p measures the marginal private benefit that the individual obtains from successive years of schooling. We assume that the marginal benefit declines as years of schooling increase. D_p is also the individual's demand curve for education, since it measures what he or she would be willing to pay for each additional year of schooling. The marginal cost of schooling, indicated by the curve *MC*, is here assumed constant per incremental year at level C_1. If the individual were required to pay the market price for schooling, he or she would purchase it up to Q_1, the level at which price just equals marginal private benefit.

While this outcome is optimal for the individual, it is suboptimal from the viewpoint of society as a whole, because it fails to take account of collective benefits. Each year of schooling acquired by the individual student

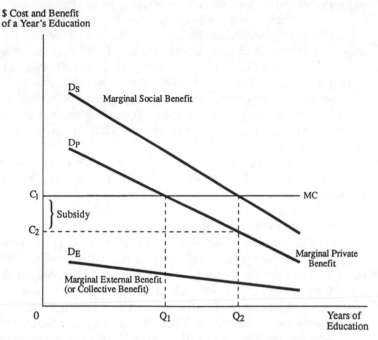

Figure 11.2. Private, external, and social benefits of education.

confers a collective benefit on the rest of society, the value of which is measured by curve D_E. (How this value could be determined will be discussed ahead.) Accordingly, society as a whole would be willing to pay up to the amounts measured along D_E to encourage the individual to buy successive years of schooling. In short, D_E is society's demand curve for the collective benefits of a single individual's education.

Adding together the private and collective benefits of each year's schooling, we obtain curve D_s, which measures the marginal *social* benefit of education. Graphically, D_s is the vertical sum of D_E and D_p and represents the social demand for education. From society's point of view, the optimal amount of schooling for the individual is Q_2 years, the level at which the marginal social benefit of an additional year just equals its cost. We can now see that Q_1, the free-market solution, is not optimal. The market, left on its own, will ignore external benefits and therefore produce too little output. Externalities thus cause market failure.[1]

---

[1] In his classic article "The Problem of Social Cost" (*Journal of Law and Economics,* 3 [October 1960]: 1–44), R. H. Coase showed that if the number of affected parties is small enough so that transactions costs are low, we would

How can society prevent market failure in the face of externalities? The answer is it can encourage production by paying a subsidy equal to the marginal value of the externality. In the hypothetical case illustrated, if a subsidy lowered the cost from C_1 to C_2 per year, the individual would freely choose to pay for Q_2 years. The amount $C_1 - C_2$ equals the value of the marginal external benefit of year Q_2. Thus, public policy can, in theory, solve the efficiency problem posed by the existence of collective benefits.

Do the arts produce collective benefits?

Does the analysis developed to describe the benefits of education apply equally well to art and culture? It is clear that the arts, like education, confer private benefits on those who consume them. These benefits consist of the joy, stimulation, and enlightenment that individuals gain when they attend the live performing arts, visit museums and galleries, or are otherwise engaged with works of art. But after such individual pleasures are accounted for, however rich and exciting they may be, is there anything additional that should be classified as an external or collective benefit? The question is controversial; no aspect of the economics of art has been debated at greater length, which in itself suggests that the answer is not unambiguous. Perhaps that is inevitable, for it is in the nature of the case that the external benefits of art and culture are likely to be diffuse and unobservable. Each of the alleged external benefits in the list that follows has been endorsed by at least one economist studying the arts. We have added doubts and qualifications where that seemed appropriate.

1. Legacy to future generations. A number of eminent economists suggest that preserving art and culture as a legacy to future generations qualifies as a collective benefit.[2] The argument is that both those who enjoy the arts and those who do not would be willing to pay something today to ensure that art and culture are preserved for the benefit of future generations who are not here to register their preferences. None of us would wish to risk handing on to our descendants a culture less rich than the

---

expect them to arrive at a bargaining solution in which the effects of externalities are fully and optimally taken into account. In the case of education, however, the number of parties is clearly too large for such a solution.

[2] See William J. Baumol and William G. Bowen, *Performing Arts: The Economic Dilemma* (New York: Twentieth Century Fund, 1966), pp. 384–85; Alan Peacock, "Welfare Economics and Public Subsidies to the Arts," *Manchester School,* 37, no. 4 (1969): 323–35, cited at 330–31; Dick Netzer, *The Subsidized Muse* (Cambridge University Press, 1978), p. 23.

one we inherited from the past. This argument applies not only to the preservation of books and musical scores, architectural monuments, and works of art in museums, but also to the maintenance of the skills, tastes, and traditions required for ongoing excellence in the performing arts.

The legacy argument is a powerful one but does require qualification: suppose that the private sector on its own takes such a strong interest in art and culture that preservation is amply ensured *without* government subsidy? In other words, one may agree that handing on the cultural tradition is a genuine external benefit, and yet believe that the marginal value of still more "legacy" is so low that it does not warrant subsidy.

2. National identity and prestige. Some people take pride in the international recognition received by the artists and performers of their own country. Not long ago many people in the United States were apologetic about the fact that the country had produced few painters, singers, dancers, choreographers, conductors, or musicians of "international stature." That deficit no longer exists. There is a degree of collective benefit that at least some Americans feel at the great reputations and legacies of artists such as Isaac Stern, Leonard Bernstein, Jackson Pollock, Jessye Norman, Suzanne Farrell, or Martha Graham.

Although these feelings of national pride are real enough, some observers may believe them unworthy of support. Perhaps national pride is among the sins of this age that ought *not* to be subsidized.[3] Or if national prestige *is* worthy of support, how are we to know, as Alan Peacock asks, whether it is more effectively promoted by subsidizing the arts or by sending talented sports teams on subsidized foreign tours?[4] Peacock is here making a more general point: ideally, before calling for arts subsidies one should verify not only that they are a possible way of reaching a valid objective, but also that they are the most cost-effective way.

3. Benefits to the local economy. Arts activity may provide spillover benefits to other producers in the local economy. This can occur in either of two ways. First, the arts may attract out-of-town consumers, who in addition to buying tickets to a local performance or visiting a museum, also spend money in local shops, restaurants, and hotels. This spending stimulates the local economy exactly as merchandise exports

---

[3] See, e.g., C. D. Throsby and G. A. Withers, *The Economics of the Performing Arts* (New York: St. Martin's, 1979), p. 179.

[4] Peacock, "Welfare Economics," p. 330.

would. Second, the presence of cultural amenities may help a city to induce new firms to locate there instead of somewhere else.

These propositions are both true, but strictly *local* economic benefits would not seem to justify payments by a *national* government, for there is no reason why a national government should wish to subsidize arts activity in order to attract tourists or firms to one city rather than another. From the point of view of the nation as a whole, the arts can provide an economic stimulus only to the extent that they attract tourists or firms from abroad. Even from a locality's point of view, we must bear in mind the caveat that there may be more effective ways of stimulating the local economy than by subsidizing the arts.[5] (These matters will be taken up in greater detail in Chapter 15.)

4. Contribution to a liberal education. As Baumol and Bowen put it, if it is generally conceded that "a liberal education confers indirect . . . benefits upon the community, the same must be true of the arts" because they are an indispensable part of a liberal education.[6] Since the importance of the collective benefits from education is widely acknowledged, this would appear to be a powerful argument. Yet it is not often mentioned, perhaps because it seems to imply that only art education, rather than its production and distribution outside any specific educational setting, deserves subsidy. In fact, such a narrow reading of policy implications is unwarranted. Consumers can learn about art in any institutional setting they find congenial. We return to the important question of art education in the final chapter of the book.

5. Social improvement of arts participants. It has sometimes been alleged that participation in the arts makes us better human beings by exercising our sensibilities or by exposing us to the highest and best achievements of our fellows. If this was so, it would be an external benefit because the individual in general seeks only his or her own personal satisfaction through participation in the arts. If that individual's behavior is somehow improved in the process, that is a satisfaction to others, hence external to the participant. Thomas Gale Moore, citing A. C. Pigou's belief in the "elevating influence" of arts consumption, agrees that "a good play

---

[5] See Netzer, *The Subsidized Muse,* pp. 24–25; and Bruce A. Seaman, "Economic Impact Studies: A Fashionable Excess," in Anthony J. Radich and Sharon Schwoch, eds., *Economic Impact of the Arts: A Sourcebook* (Denver, Colo.: National Conference of State Legislatures, May 1987).

[6] Baumol and Bowen, *Performing Arts,* p. 385.

or good opera may, in fact, improve the quality of citizens."[7] Throsby and Withers, only partly in jest, respond by asking, "What happens to citizens who see bad plays and bad opera?" They add that there is no scientific evidence to support the alleged beneficial effect of art on individual personality or behavior.[8] Perhaps listening to Beethoven's string quartets or studying the paintings of El Greco, however delightful the experience may be, does not, in fact, have much "elevating influence." Moreover, the claim that art improves the citizen or elevates the soul smacks so much of snobbism that it is likely to be counterproductive in building public support for the arts, and it risks seeming to diminish art's principal function for the individual, which is to provide aesthetic pleasure.

Now these strictures may seem to contradict the view that the arts provide a collective benefit by contributing to a liberal education. Perhaps the contradiction is avoided if we explain that, yes, we would like our fellow citizens to have a liberal education so that they understand the collective traditions of our art and culture, but that there is no scientific evidence that understanding art and culture makes them better individuals in the sense of being less prone to violence, envy, greed, or other unpleasant psychological disorders.

6. Encouraging artistic innovation. It is commonly recognized that invention – or more broadly, scientific, technological, and managerial innovation – is a major source of economic progress. It is also understood that innovation would be inhibited if its initiators were unable to claim adequate rewards for their risks and efforts. That is why we allow technical inventions to be protected by patents. In the field of the arts, however, innovation cannot be patented. Specific works of art, such as a painting, musical composition, or piece of choreography, are protected by copyright. But copyright does not afford any protection to the innovative *principle* – for example, a new *technique* in painting, or a new dance *style* – that is embodied in the specific work, and failure to provide such protection may be socially inefficient. Artistic experiment is costly and subject to failure. When it fails, the artist or not-for-profit organization who made the attempt must bear the full cost (and without the tax offsets available in business situations). But when it succeeds, the innovators cannot prevent others from using the new technique free of charge. Consequently, the scales are loaded against artistic innovators,

---

[7] Thomas Gale Moore, *The Economics of the American Theater* (Durham, N.C.: Duke University Press, 1968) p. 117.
[8] Throsby and Withers, *Economics of the Performing Arts,* pp. 176–77.

and they probably undertake less experiment than would be socially desirable. Both Moore and Netzer regard this as a form of market failure that justifies subsidies to the arts.[9] Netzer points out that the same problem occurs in the physical and social sciences, and that "the federal government has a long tradition of subsidizing experimentation . . . on just these grounds."[10]

A word of caution is in order, however: as a practical matter one cannot assume that much of the available public subsidy would be used to encourage innovation and experiment. Grant-giving bodies have a strong inclination to play it safe by shunning experimentation, perhaps for sound political reasons. They know that opponents of public support (as we shall see in Chapters 12 and 13) like to reinforce their case by citing what seem to them to be objectionable experimental arts projects that received public support.

External benefits as public goods

We must now take up the important question of how the actual value of external benefits from the arts might be determined. These external or collective benefits, if they exist, have the character of what economists call a "public good," which is a good that displays one or both of the following characteristics. First, it is subject to joint consumption, meaning that one person can consume it without diminishing the amount that remains for others to enjoy. Examples include such diverse programs as national defense, air pollution control, or public health. Joint consumption is certainly *not* a characteristic of ordinary "private" goods: two people cannot wear the same pair of shoes at the same time. Second, a public good is generally *not* subject to exclusion, meaning that once the good exists, there is no way of preventing someone's benefiting from it, even if that person refuses to pay for the privilege. And since no one can be compelled to make a specific payment for the privilege of consuming it, a public good cannot be financed, as ordinary goods are, by prices charged in the marketplace by a private producer. Instead, they must be paid for (though not necessarily produced) by the public sector, whence the term "public goods."

Upon reflection, it should be clear that the external benefits allegedly produced by the arts have the characteristics of a pure public good: they are subject to joint consumption, but not to exclusion. The benefit that one person's daughter will enjoy 30 years hence because the arts have

---

[9] Moore, *Economics of the American Theater*, pp. 121–22; Netzer, *The Subsidized Muse*, p. 24.
[10] Netzer, *The Subsidized Muse*, p. 24, n. 12.

been preserved for posterity will not diminish the benefit that someone else's son can obtain from the same source, nor can parents be compelled to pay for that prospective benefit by threatening to exclude their off-spring from consuming it, for such exclusion is impossible.

In the case of ordinary goods we know that competitive markets will automatically guide production in accordance with consumer prefer-ences. If public goods cannot be sold in the marketplace, however, how can society assure that they, too, are produced in the right quantities to satisfy consumers? The correct answer, in theory, is that the govern-ment should poll its citizens to find out how much they are willing to pay for alternative levels of the public good and then provide it up to the quantity at which the public's willingness to pay for one more unit just covers its marginal cost.[11]

Police service, for example, is a locally provided public good. If a town was trying to decide how large a police force to provide, the authorities would ask each citizen how much he or she would be willing to provide for a first police officer, a second, a third, and so on. The aggregate amount indicated for each quantity would be a point on the public's demand curve for the collective good called police service. The optimum quantity to provide would be found as the point of in-tersection between this demand curve and the labor market supply curve for police officers.

In the case of the externalities of art and culture, there are no physical units (such as number of police officers) in which to calculate the op-timum quantity to produce. What we can try to find out, however, is whether the public (who, after all, should be the final judges in this matter) believe there *are* any external benefits from art and culture and, if so, how much they would be willing to pay for them. Aggregate willingness to pay can then be compared with the current level of gov-ernment subsidies to see whether actual subsidies fall short of, equal, or exceed the value the public puts on arts externalities.

Throsby and Withers carried out a sample survey of residents of Sydney, Australia, in order to study consumer attitudes toward the externalities of art and culture.[12] The first step was to ask questions

---

[11] On the theory of public goods, see Paul A. Samuelson, "The Pure Theory of Public Expenditure," *Review of Economics and Statistics,* 36, no. 4 (November 1954): 386–89; and idem, "Diagrammatic Exposition of a Theory of Public Expenditure," ibid., 37, no. 4 (November 1955): 350–56; and R. A. Musgrave, *The Theory of Public Finance* (New York: McGraw-Hill, 1959), chaps. 1, 4.

[12] C. D. Throsby and G. A. Withers, "Measuring the Demand for the Arts as a Public Good: Theory and Empirical Results," in James L. Shanahan et al., eds., *Economic Support for the Arts* (Akron, Ohio: Association for Cultural Economics, 1983), pp. 37–52.

Table 11.1. *External benefits of art and culture: an Australian survey*

	Percentage		
	Agree or strongly agree	Disagree or strongly disagree	No opinion or don't know
The success of Australian . . . [artists] etc. gives people a sense of pride in Australian achievement	94.8	4.4	0.8
The arts help us to understand our own country better	84.6	13.8	1.6
The arts only benefit those people who attend . . .	34.9	64.1	1.0
The arts . . . [are important] in making us look at our way of life	80.6	17.3	2.1
The arts should not be allowed to die out	96.9	2.3	0.7
It is important for school children to learn . . . [arts] as part of their education	96.5	3.2	0.4
The arts often harm our society by being too critical	14.8	81.2	4.0
All . . . [arts institutions] should be made to survive on their ticket sales alone	20.7	78.1	1.2

Source: See note 12, this chapter.

designed to reveal whether respondents believed the arts to have properties that could be identified as external benefits. For example, one question, intended to test the idea that national prestige is an external benefit of the arts, asked whether respondents agreed with the statement that "the success of Australian painters, singers, actors, etc. gives people a sense of pride in Australian achievement." Ninety-five percent either agreed or strongly agreed with the statement. Table 11.1 shows the responses to all of the questions (some of which have been abridged to save space). Throsby and Withers concluded that the results "indicate that there is an overall acceptance of public benefit accruing from the arts."[13]

Eliciting willingness to pay for external benefits: Throsby and Withers's next step was to estimate the public's willingness to pay for the external benefits of the arts. Respondents were asked, What is the maximum

[13] Ibid., p. 42.

Table 11.2. *Willingness to pay for the arts out of taxes (Australian dollars per year)*

	Mean	Median
With full tax liability	96.7	18.2
With no tax liability	154.8	20.2

Source: See note 12, this chapter.

you would want paid out of your taxes each year to support the arts at their current level . . . ? "Current level" was specified so that the answers could be interpreted as measuring the demand for the collective benefits of the arts that accrue at a specific level of arts output, rather than as indicating a desire for more arts activity.

Economists have long recognized that in a voter survey it would be difficult to elicit answers indicating true willingness to pay for public goods. Two kinds of strategic bias could occur. On the one hand, if voters understood that they would be *required* to contribute whatever amount they said they were *willing* to pay, they would have an incentive to understate their true willingness in the belief that other people's contributions would pay for a sufficient supply. This is the well-known "free-rider" problem. On the other hand, if voters were told they would not have to make *any* payment to back up their stated willingness, they would have an incentive to overstate their preference for the public good in the hope of encouraging a greater supply at no personal cost.

Throsby and Withers handled the strategic bias problem by posing the question both ways to each respondent. One answer (full payment required) could then be regarded as indicating the lower boundary of willingness to pay, while the other (no payment required) would indicate the upper boundary. Presumably, the true value would fall somewhere between those limits.

Results of the willingness-to-pay questions are summarized in Table 11.2. When no tax liability was suggested, mean willingness to pay turned out to be $155 (Australian) per person. With full tax liability, the mean was reduced to $97. Both results far exceeded the actual level of expenditure of tax receipts on the arts in Australia, which at the time amounted to only about $6 per capita. It must be recognized, however, that mean values can be pulled upward by a small number of extremely high responses. Median values are not subject to that effect. The medians in this case were $20 and $18, still greatly in excess of actual tax outlays at the time. Thus, whether or not economists believe that the arts produce significant external benefits, Throsby and Withers's study demonstrates the Australian public's conviction that they do, and furthermore that those benefits justify subsidies considerably in excess of current levels, even when it is understood that taxpayer liability would rise accordingly.

A quite similar survey by William G. Morrison and Edwin G. West of willingness to pay by voters in the Province of Ontario, Canada, confirmed that Canadians, too, recognize the existence of significant external benefits from the arts. In the Canadian survey, however, the median voter appeared to find the current (1981) level of tax support to be "just right." The authors argued that that level – $128 (Canadian) per adult, per year, for art and culture broadly defined – could therefore be taken as an approximate measure of the value of the purported externalities. Or as they put it, "The relevant external benefits appear to have been already captured (internalized) via current public expenditures."[14]

Declining cost industries

A declining cost industry is one in which the average unit cost of production falls continuously over the range of output demanded in the market. In Chapter 10 it was shown that museums commonly operate under those conditions. Figure 10.1 illustrated the resulting dilemma. As long as average cost is declining, marginal cost must lie below it. In order to break even, the museum has to charge a price equal to average cost, but that price will necessarily be higher than marginal cost. The result is a form of market failure in the sense that the norm of setting price equal to marginal cost is violated. In the case illustrated in Figure 10.1, if the museum charges a price P_1, potential visitors between Q_1 and Q_2, who are willing to pay more than the full marginal cost of their visit, but not a price as high as P_1, are denied attendance.

Public subsidies are one way of trying to correct this problem: the museum charges marginal cost prices for admission (e.g., P_2 in Figure 10.1) and therefore runs a deficit, but the deficit is covered by a yearly public subsidy. However, there is a drawback to this arrangement from the social welfare point of view: taxes levied to cover the deficit may have harmful effects – for example, by driving a wedge between marginal

[14] William G. Morrison and Edwin G. West, "Subsidies for the Performing Arts: Evidence on Voter Preference," *Journal of Behavioral Economics,* 15 (Fall 1986): 57–72, cited at 70. For a full analysis of the survey method for evaluating willingness to pay for public goods, see Robert Cameron Mitchell and Richard T. Carson, *Using Surveys to Value Public Goods: The Contingent Valuation Method* (Washington, D.C.: Resources for the Future, Inc., 1989).

cost and price elsewhere in the economy – that offset the welfare gain from using marginal cost pricing at the museum.

Private charitable donations and membership fees offer a solution that avoids the harmful effects of tax finance. The museum could employ marginal cost pricing for admission to its exhibits and then cover the difference between total costs and total admission revenues by soliciting charitable donations and selling annual memberships to interested members of the public. This approach is a version of the "two-part tariff" scheme that many economists regard as the best available solution for declining cost industries. A two-part tariff describes any scheme under which units of output are sold at marginal cost, thus satisfying the marginal cost-equal-to-price rule, while the producing organization's deficit is covered by a periodic, lump-sum fee required of all potential users. It is an advantage of this arrangement when employed by a museum that those who are directly interested in the institution and presumably benefit from it also cover its deficit, instead of laying off the burden in the form of taxes on distant third parties. However, a distinction can be made between local and national tax finance. Since museums provide a largely local service, using general local tax revenues to cover their deficits is consistent with the intent of the two-part tariff: those paying the taxes are at least potential users of the subsidized service.[15]

As these comments suggest, the museum case is particularly complicated. Museums typically perform several functions, and subsidies may therefore be justified on several grounds. The declining cost problem as discussed is entirely independent of the question of external benefits. Thus, even if it is decided that deficits resulting from marginal cost pricing should be covered by donations and membership fees rather than out of tax funds, we may still wish to subsidize museums because they preserve art for future generations, perform an educational function, or are the source of other external benefits.

Lack of information

Markets cannot operate with complete efficiency unless all participants have full information about the goods and services being sold. Consumers, for example, have to be aware of all the available options if they are to make optimal choices. Ignorance on the part of consumers is therefore a source of market failure. The arts are rightly said to be an "acquired" taste, meaning that the consumer has to be familiar with

---

[15] See the discussion in Richard A. Musgrave and Peggy B. Musgrave, *Public Finance in Theory and Practice,* 4th ed. (New York: McGraw-Hill, 1984), pp. 736–37.

them to enjoy them and that once consumers do become knowledgeable, their demand is likely to increase markedly. But consumers are not in a position to acquire the taste if they lack information about the arts. ("Information" is here understood broadly as including not only "facts" but also the opportunity to experience the thing itself.)

In the field of art and culture, two ill effects might result from lack of information. First, a number of consumers will be deprived of potential utility because they are ignorant of the arts and therefore do not partake. Because art is an acquired taste, we are entitled to believe that the loss is potentially substantial. Second, because demand is held back, many arts enterprises will be prevented not just from growing (we have already counted that loss under the category of lost utility to consumers), but also from achieving the economies of scale of which we know they are capable. In other words, the unit cost of production will tend to be higher if demand is lower.

Many ordinary commercial activities face the same problem and are able to deal with it by advertising and promotion. (Indeed, its alleged promotion of economies of scale is one of the standard defenses of advertising made against critics who call it wasteful.) Netzer points out, however, that this solution is not available to arts enterprises because "the markets for most art forms are segmented, specialized, and too modest in size to make mass advertising campaigns profitable." He concludes that government subsidies to encourage widespread production of the arts are justified as a way of overcoming ignorance by giving "consumers . . . firsthand experience of them."[16]

Productivity lag and subsidies for the arts

The hypothesis that productivity lag is bound to cause a long-run increase in the real cost of the performing arts, first proposed by Baumol and Bowen, has often been cited by arts advocates as a justification for government subsidies. Without subsidies, it was asserted, either ticket prices would have to rise continuously, which would end all hope of reaching new audiences, or else performing arts companies would face increasingly large deficits that would ultimately force many of them out of business. The productivity lag hypothesis was analyzed in Chapter 8, and it was shown that there are some alternatives to these gloomy predictions. Leaving those qualifications to one side, it must now be emphasized that productivity lag per se does not provide justification for government subsidy.

Productivity lag is a market process that would cause unit cost to rise

---

[16] Netzer, *The Subsidized Muse*, p. 26.

in any technologically unprogressive industry. But there is no reason to subsidize an industry simply because it is technologically unprogressive. Given that its real costs are rising relative to those in more progressive industries, it is best to let its prices increase to reflect the rise in real costs. As long as markets are operating efficiently, those higher costs will be absorbed optimally by the economy. We would all be better off if there were no technologically unprogressive industries, but since there are, matters are made worse, not better, if we use subsidies to prevent market prices from reflecting their true costs. Lag or no lag, subsidies can be justified only by some form of market failure or else by the distributional or merit good considerations to which we turn next.

Up to this point we have been concerned with the "efficiency" arguments for public support of the arts. Market failures of many kinds were shown to interfere with the optimal satisfaction of consumer preferences. It was demonstrated that in those circumstances public subsidies may actually improve the efficiency with which the economy fulfills consumers' wants.

We turn now to arguments for public support that involve considerations other than efficiency in the allocation of resources. The principal justifications to be taken up are those concerned with equity in the distribution of income and those alleging that the arts belong to a special class of "merit goods" for the production of which consumer preferences are a deficient guide.

Equity and the distribution of income; merit goods

Concern with the distribution of income can enter the discussion of public support for the arts in two ways. First, how does the existing distribution of income affect access to the arts? Does inequality of income make art and culture so inaccessible to the poor as to constitute a justification for public subsidy? A second question is almost the reverse of the first: not how does the distribution of income affect access to the arts, but how do subsidies to the arts affect the existing distribution of income? Are subsidies likely to help the poor at the expense of the rich or vice versa? In either case, are the distributional consequences a problem? We take up first the question of how the existing inequality of income affects participation in the arts.

Egalitarian arguments

It was shown in Chapter 3 that audiences at the performing arts and visitors to museums include very few people with low incomes. According to Baumol and Bowen's surveys, those with incomes below $5,000 made up only 8.5 percent of arts audiences in the early 1960s, although they accounted for 35.2 percent of the U.S. urban population. The median income of arts audiences was a little more than double the urban median.[17] Clearly, the poor were greatly underrepresented in the audiences for art and culture. Subsequent surveys show very little change in these patterns.

Although education is a more important determinant of arts participation than is income, it is nonetheless true that at market prices the relatively poor (including a large number of youths and students) simply cannot afford much live art and culture as we define those goods. Thus, the desire to ensure as nearly as possible universal access to our civilization's cultural tradition provides one of the most powerful arguments for subsidizing the arts. As Netzer puts it:

> There is something intrinsically abhorrent about a policy of making the cultural and artistic heritage of our civilization available to only, say, the richest 20 or 30 percent of our population, the group to which enjoyment of the arts would be limited in the absence of all support outside the marketplace.[18]

This is essentially a moral argument. It reflects the fundamental U.S. belief that every individual should have equal opportunity for self-development. Moreover, the problem is not only that access is limited by high prices and low income. There is also a regional dimension. As Baumol and Bowen point out, many communities simply lack the facilities and institutions to present the performing arts or the fine arts with any regularity at a professional level.[19] Subsidies are therefore needed to help distribute art and culture geographically as well as to increase its accessibility to the relatively poor.

Most analysts who favor public subsidies for the arts place a very high value on the objective of improving access for all the people. Because it is rooted in the U.S. egalitarian ethic, that position also enjoys wide political support: the first of the stated objectives of the National Endowment for the Arts is "to make the arts more widely available to millions of Americans."[20]

Arts subsidies and the distribution of income

If the unequal distribution of income provides a strong argument for subsidizing the arts, it may seem paradoxical to suggest that current

---

[17] Baumol and Bowen, *Performing Arts*, table IV.1, p. 76.
[18] Netzer, *The Subsidized Muse*, p. 19.
[19] Baumol and Bowen, *Performing Arts*, p. 379.
[20] Quoted in Netzer, *The Subsidized Muse*, p. 19.

arts subsidy programs might actually increase the existing inequality. Whether arts subsidies help the poor at the expense of the rich or the other way around depends on how the distribution of subsidy benefits compares with the distribution of tax costs across income classes. Because the well-to-do participate in arts activity so much more frequently than do those with lower incomes, it should not be surprising if they also reap a large share of any subsidy benefits. Indeed, estimates by Throsby and Withers for Australia in 1974–75 indicate that benefits from subsidies to the arts exceeded the taxes paid to support them among upper-income groups while falling short of taxes paid by those of lower income.[21] If these estimates are correct, the impact of the combined package of arts subsidies and taxes in Australia at that date was to make the distribution of income *more* unequal. On the other hand, a study by Netzer suggests the opposite outcome in the United States.[22] He estimated that in 1985 the impact of the combination of arts subsidies and the taxes to pay for them in the United States was mildly pro-poor. Those with incomes of $50,000 and above apparently paid more in taxes than they received in arts benefits; those in a middle range with incomes between $25,000 and $50,000 approximately broke even, while those with incomes below $25,000 were net gainers. Again, a word of caution is in order, however: the results obtained in all studies of distributional impact depend heavily on the assumptions used to estimate both benefits and taxes by income class. In fact, Netzer shows the reader some of the variation in outcome that occurs under alternative assumptions.

We must recognize that art subsidies can have distributionally perverse results in any country unless either the tax system is fairly progressive or assistance to the arts includes a large number of programs clearly directed to the benefit of the low-income population. That is the "bad news" about the distributional effects of arts subsidies. The "good news" is that unfavorable effects on the distribution of income would not weaken the general case for subsidies. As Musgrave has argued, the allocation and distribution functions should be handled separately in the public sector. If a public spending policy can be justified on efficiency grounds, it should be undertaken for that reason. If necessary, its distributional effects should be corrected by other policies that aim at achieving whatever the community believes to be the "correct" distribution of income.[23] Moreover, subsidy programs that effectively con-

---

[21] Throsby and Withers, *Economics of the Performing Arts,* pp. 188–89.

[22] Dick Netzer, "Arts and Culture" in Charles T. Clotfelter, ed., *Who Benefits from the Nonprofit Sector?* (Chicago: University of Chicago Press, 1992), pp. 174–206.

[23] Musgrave, *Theory of Public Finance,* chap. 1.

centrate their benefits on the low-income population would not, in any case, have perverse effects on income distribution.

Merit goods

Economic theory tells us that if society wishes to redistribute income from rich to poor it is better to make the transfers in cash rather than by providing specific goods or services to the poor at subsidized prices. Redistribution in kind – for example, subsidized low-income housing – can at best be as good as cash, but can never be better and may well be worse. The reason is that it may provide beneficiaries with goods or services that would not be their first choice if they were given cash to spend as they pleased.[24] Nevertheless, we find that governments frequently do assist the poor by offering them specific goods at subsidized or even zero prices. Low-income public housing and medical care are important examples in the United States. A possible explanation for subsidies in such cases is that the objects in question are what economists call "merit goods." This term was introduced by Musgrave to describe those goods that society has decided it would be desirable to provide in quantities greater than consumers would wish to purchase at market prices.[25] Instead of accepting consumer preferences as binding, the public or its legislative representatives decide to impose their own: a subsidy is paid to reduce the price of the merit good and thereby increase the quantity consumed.

Throsby and Withers believe it can be inferred from the public pronouncements of politicians in the countries they studied that "merit good considerations have probably been the most significant single explanation of government involvement in the arts."[26] Art is regarded as a good thing or, more precisely, as an *especially* good thing. Politicians are therefore willing "to support the arts even though they acknowledge that the resulting activity exceeds that which consumers would demand if left to their own devices."[27]

What exactly are merit goods? The concept has been much debated by economists. Some would say that merit goods are simply those things that a majority of the public or its representatives have agreed are so

---

[24] This point is demonstrated rigorously in almost every intermediate microeconomics text. See, e.g., Ross D. Eckert and Richard H. Leftwich, *The Price System and Resource Allocation,* 10th ed. (New York: Dryden Press, 1988), pp. 133–36.

[25] Musgrave, *Theory of Public Finance,* pp. 13–14.

[26] Throsby and Withers, p. 192. They quote supporting statements of politicians in Australia, New Zealand, Canada, Great Britain, and the United States.

[27] Ibid., p. 193.

worthy of consumption that they deserve to be subsidized. According to this explanation, good housing, health care, and the arts are merit goods because there is a political consensus favoring public support. This is not very satisfactory, however, because it does not tell us *why* a majority believe these objects of expenditure deserve special treatment.

If we ask *why* merit goods are special, a possible explanation is that they are a class of goods and services with the unique quality of being better for people than they realize. For example, consumers may be ignorant of the importance of adequate health care. Left to their own devices they would consume too little of it for their own good. By subsidizing it we lower its price and encourage them to consume more. With respect to the arts we would probably want to word that a little differently. The point would not be that the arts are "better" for people than they realize in some therapeutic sense, but rather that ignorance of the arts is keeping many people from experiences that they would greatly enjoy, if only they knew about them. This, however, is a justification for subsidies that we have already offered under the category of market failure due to lack of information. (Merit goods arguments have an annoying tendency to overlap with arguments made for public subsidy on other grounds.)[28]

Another possible explanation of the term "merit goods" would be that it describes a class of goods and services that have some sort of "inherent worth" or "intrinsic merit" that distinguishes them from ordinary consumer goods. Netzer appears to take that position when he writes of the NEA's policy of subsidizing wider distribution of modern dance throughout the United States: "Underlying that decision is the general merit-goods assumption that more exposure to modern dance is a good thing." In the same vein, he argues that a decision to subsidize the Metropolitan Opera, "must be based on a straightforward 'merit-goods' argument: the Met is a good thing that can be perpetuated only with fairly large amounts of public subsidy."[29] This is not so much an explanation in economic terms as it is a value judgment ("the Met is a good thing") that lies outside the realm of economic discourse.

Summary

We have presented a wide range of arguments favoring the use of government subsidies for art and culture. The strongest ones can be summarized as follows.

---

[28] See the discussion of housing as a merit good in James Heilbrun, *Urban Economics and Public Policy*, 3d ed. (New York: St. Martin's, 1987), pp. 323–26.

[29] Netzer, *The Subsidized Muse*, pp. 27, 123.

Over and above direct benefits to participants, the arts produce external benefits for society as a whole. The most important of these, we believe, are the cultural legacy preserved for future generations, the contribution made to a liberal education, and the collective benefits produced by artistic innovation. Survey evidence from Australia and Canada indicates that the general public *does* believe the arts produce external benefits and is willing to make substantial tax payments to support them.

The decreasing cost nature of museum output is an additional justification for subsidy, as is the fact that enjoyment of the arts is an acquired taste about which many consumers lack the information and experience to make informed choices.

Equity considerations provide an additional justification for subsidy. The egalitarian ethic suggests that all citizens should have at least some access to the nation's heritage of art and culture. To that end, subsidies are required to overcome the barriers of high prices and low incomes and the somewhat different problem of geographic inaccessibility.

The case against public subsidies

Among the most spirited attempts to make a case *against* public subsidy for the arts are those of the social philosopher Ernest van den Haag and the political scientist Edward Banfield.[30] Both write as conservatives opposing what they regard as the unwarranted proliferation of public spending programs.

Van den Haag summarizes his own position in three statements: "a) There is no good sociopolitical reason for the government to compel taxpayers to subsidize government selected art; b) to do so compels all classes to subsidize the middle class; c) to do so is more apt to harm than to help in the creation of actual, valuable art."[31]

No relevant external benefits

In supporting the first of these points, van den Haag appears to acknowledge the theoretical possibility that collective benefits from the arts could justify public subsidy, but rejects the argument that there are any such benefits in the case of the United States. He does not, however, run systematically through the list of collective benefits that

---

[30] Ernest van den Haag, "Should the Government Subsidize the Arts?" *Policy Review,* 10 (Fall 1979): 63–73; and Edward C. Banfield, *The Democratic Muse* (New York: Basic, 1984). Also see William D. Grampp, *Pricing the Priceless* (New York: Basic, 1989), chaps. 6, 7; and Harold Horowitz et al., "Public Support for Art: Viewpoints Presented at the Ottawa Meetings," *Journal of Cultural Economics,* 13, no. 2 (December 1989): 1–19.

[31] Van den Haag, "Should the Government Subsidize the Arts," p. 71.

others have alleged. Instead, he concentrates on denying that in the United States the high arts have made any contribution to establishing or maintaining our national identity. He leans heavily on the example of opera: "Whatever the value of opera ... it cannot be said, as it may be said in Italy or Austria, that opera has contributed to our national cohesion, history, culture, or consciousness – or that it has any chance of doing so now."[32] Since U.S. composers and producers have not established much of a native tradition in opera, this is not implausible, although it seems to dismiss out-of-hand the possibility that one purpose of subsidies might be precisely to foster such a native tradition. Unfortunately, van den Haag then applies the same argument to other arts:

> What is true for opera is as true for classical music, for dance, including ballet, and, by and large, for the great works of art in our museums. They did not play an important role in our history or in forging or celebrating our national bonds. . . . The contents of our museums have nothing to do with our national life, and they have not contributed to our national cohesion or identity.[33]

He thus completely overlooks strong U.S. traditions in several branches of the arts, including theater, modern dance, neoclassical ballet, and painting and sculpture. Indeed, there are entire museums devoted exclusively to U.S. painting and sculpture.

Moreover, van den Haag's line of argument clearly implies that European traditions cannot play a significant part in the development of U.S. culture. Historians of the arts are unlikely to accept that view. To cite only two contrary examples, the U.S. school of abstract expressionist painting, which achieved extraordinary influence in Europe as well as the United States in the 1940s and 1950s, certainly had its roots in early-twentieth-century European work, and the neoclassical style, which now dominates ballet in the United States and in a good many other countries, was developed in New York by George Balanchine, a Russian choreographer, using U.S. dancers and for a specifically U.S. audience. What these examples, in fact, suggest is how truly international all the great movements in high art have become.

In short, van den Haag not only ignores most of the cases of collective benefit that economists have suggested, but also constructs a very narrow argument in the one case he chooses to discuss. So far as collective benefits are concerned, he concludes that the activities that *do* contribute

---

[32] Ibid., p. 66.
[33] Ibid.

to the development of shared values and social cohesion in the United States – he mentions sports, TV, and rock concerts – get along very well without subsidy.

Subsidies and the distribution of income

Turning to van den Haag's second point, it is not clear whether he objects to the effects of arts subsidies on the distribution of income or to the fact that any taxes levied to pay for subsidies necessarily interfere with somebody's freedom to spend. Again relying heavily on the case of opera, he argues that subsidies benefit a middle- and upper-class audience by taking dollars from the general taxpayer who presumably would prefer to spend them on "unsubsidized movies or Broadway shows."[34] Assuming that van den Haag is here concerned with distributional effects, this statement is factually wrong: Netzer, in the very careful study cited earlier in this chapter, estimates that the net redistributional effect of arts subsidies and taxes in the United States is to take (moderately) from the well to do and give to the relatively poor. Those in the middle of the income distribution more or less break even. In addition, van den Haag appears to overlook two considerations. First, as we have argued, if a subsidy program is desirable to correct a misallocation of resources resulting from market failure, it should not be rejected on grounds of its distributional effects. Instead, the latter should be corrected by another set of policies dealing with the distribution of income. Second, if one insists nevertheless on looking at the distributional effects of allocation policies, it is certainly possible to conceive of arts subsidies that would not have an undesirable impact on the distribution of income. Thus, perverse effects in any one instance (such as opera) do not establish a general case against arts subsidies.

Subsidies actually harm the arts

Van den Haag's third point is that government subsidies will actually do more harm that good in the creation of genuine art. He believes that the government cannot tell good art from bad and must therefore hand out subsidies indiscriminately. But if funds are given indiscriminately, pseudoartists will be attracted to the field, and much of the government budget will be wasted in the production of "fool's gold." Worse yet, true artists may actually find it harder to succeed when subsidies have built a world of false art.[35] (Why these calamities have not occurred in Europe where arts subsidies have a long history,

[34] Ibid.
[35] Ibid., pp. 68–70.

is never discussed.) In speaking of "the government" as a judge of art, van den Haag seems to suggest the ludicrous picture of some committee of the Congress trying to decide which individual painters or composers or playwrights deserve support. In fact, as we shall see in Chapters 12 and 13, most public agencies assisting the arts rely on elaborate systems of professional review in an attempt to spend their money fruitfully. No one would suggest that they always succeed or that political considerations are never a factor. But it seems merely fanciful of van den Haag, by building supposition upon supposition, to argue that government funding has actually done more harm than good.

Banfield's argument

Banfield's objections to public subsidies for the arts are developed in *The Democratic Muse,* a book that ranges widely over aesthetics, political history, political theory, and economics, but only in relation to policy toward the visual arts. His views are in some respects similar to van den Haag's. He stresses the capacity of perfectly competitive markets to produce an optimum allocation of resources, recognizes the theoretical possibility that externalities could cause market failure, but then dismisses externalities as a justification for subsidy because he thinks economists have not shown them to have sufficient value.[36]

Banfield also discusses the possibility that imperfect information might be a justification for subsidy. He rejects it on the ground that if consumers think information will be useful to them, they will be willing to pay for it, and in that case the private market would automatically supply the information, subject to the usual constraint of cost.[37] This line of reasoning correctly describes how information is supplied to interested parties within the business sector but seems to miss the entire point of the argument with respect to the arts, which is that most consumers do not *know* that they will gain utility through familiarity with the arts and, therefore, will *not* pay for the introductory information or experience.

Like van den Haag, Banfield wonders *why* museums do not charge much higher prices for admission and, again like van den Haag, overlooks the "decreasing cost" argument for keeping entrance charges low and using subsidies to cover the resulting deficit. He recognizes that higher prices would make it more difficult for the poor to attend, but concludes that this "should be dealt with by redistributing income rather

[36] Banfield, *The Democratic Muse,* pp. 187–90.
[37] Ibid., pp. 192–93.

than by underpricing certain goods."[38] Although he does not discuss the concept, this reasoning certainly implies that he does *not* regard art as a merit good.

A constitutional argument

Banfield makes it clear that his opposition to government involvement with the arts does not depend solely on his doubts about the specific justifications that arts advocates have proposed. Rather, it rests on his conviction that the principles of what he calls "the American regime," as set forth in the Declaration of Independence and the Constitution, preclude such involvement. He is unsympathetic with the broader interpretation of the Constitution, which, since the 1930s, has held that Congress "had indisputable power to provide for whatever . . . would serve the general welfare."[39] On the contrary, writes Banfield:

> If it were clear that art significantly affects the quality of society, as opposed to the welfare of individuals, it would not follow that government might properly subsidize it or otherwise intervene in art matters. There are many things that affect society in ways that ennoble or debase men, ways that by common agreement are not the concern of government, either because it is incapable of managing them (e.g., enforcing rules of good manners) or because it is understood that government exists for other purposes.[40]

Interestingly, Banfield is silent about state or local government involvement with the arts, perhaps because in those cases he would be deprived of arguments based on his reading of the federal Constitution.

Sydney Smith and a friend were walking in Edinburgh one day when they overheard a heated argument between two people who leaned from upper windows on opposite sides of a narrow street. Smith remarked that they would never agree because they were arguing from different premises.[41] So it is in this debate. Those who are suspicious of any extension of government power will not easily be persuaded that a case

---

[38] Ibid., p. 189; and see van den Haag, "Should the Government Subsidize the Arts," pp. 72–73.

[39] Banfield, *The Democratic Muse*, p. 196.

[40] Ibid., p. 205.

[41] Smith's remark is reported in W. H. Auden's introduction to *Selected Writings of Sydney Smith* (New York: Farrar, Straus & Cudahy, 1956), p. xiv.

exists for subsidizing the arts. On the other hand, those who believe the government can play a constructive role even in what is fundamentally a "free-enterprise economy," will have relatively little difficulty justifying arts subsidies as a way of advancing "the general welfare."

12

Public and/or private support for the arts

Artistic institutions earn income by selling tickets to performances or, in the case of museums, by charging for admission. But in every economically advanced country, they also receive substantial additional support (the unearned income referred to in Chapter 8) either from the government in the form of grants or from private individuals and businesses in the form of charitable donations. In Western Europe, Canada, and Australia, most of the additional funding comes from the government, whereas the private sector contributes very little. The situation in the United States is quite different: additional support comes about equally from the public and private sectors. There is a lot of history behind this last statement, and it is worthwhile sketching it briefly to explain how we got to where we are now.

Traditional opposition to public support in the United States
Until the early 1960s, the federal and state governments in the United States offered virtually no continuous, direct financial support either to artists or to arts institutions, not to the performing arts, not to the fine arts.[1] Although government support for the arts was commonplace in Europe, opinion in the United States was quite hostile to the idea. First of all, until the period of the New Deal in the 1930s, a majority of Americans accepted the philosophy of laissez-faire, according to which government intervention in economic matters should be kept to a minimum. A government that did not subsidize agriculture or

---

[1] See Dick Netzer, *The Subsidized Muse* (Cambridge University Press, 1978), pp. 53–59, 79–80; and Milton C. Cummings, Jr., "Government and the Arts: An Overview," in Stephen Benedict, ed., *Public Money and the Muse* (New York: Norton, for the American Assembly of Columbia University, 1991), pp. 31–79.

housing, provide unemployment insurance to workers, or offer a sub-
sistence income to the poorest of its poor was not going to be asked to
subsidize operas, symphony concerts, or ballets. Second, the high arts
of the sort discussed here were thought to be "elitist" and therefore not
important to the masses, a further reason why the government need not
concern itself with them. Finally, the tradition in the United States was
that institutions like museums and symphony orchestras relied on
wealthy private individuals for gifts to supplement their earned income.
(In the case of museums, earned income was negligible, since admission
was usually free.) And the traditional system seemed to work well
enough, according to the standards of those times. Indeed, the institutions themselves generally opposed the idea of state or federal government support.[2] Probably, they were moved not only by strongly held
philosophic convictions, but also by fear that government aid would lead
inexorably to government meddling, if not to outright control.

Support from local government was another matter. When arts institutions like museums or symphony orchestras were first established
in the latter part of the nineteenth century, the local government often
helped out by donating land on which the museum or concert hall could
be built by its rich patrons. When the "City Beautiful" movement began
around 1900, many cities built so-called civic centers that typically included a large auditorium usable for concerts and perhaps operas. In
addition, local governments have always exempted religious, educational, and other nonprofit organizations from liability for the local
property tax. This amounts to a substantial benefit: in 1978, Dick Netzer
estimated its value to the arts sector as $150 million "at most."[3] At 1992
prices it would be worth somewhat more than twice that figure. Tax
exemption of any kind is usually referred to as a form of "indirect"
support.

A change of heart in the 1960s

Before World War II high art and culture in the United States
were dominated by European practitioners and traditions. (Theater and
modern dance were the principal exceptions.) During the interwar period, there was hardly an American to be found among the famous
pianists, violinists, or singers who toured the country in recital. Few if
any of the country's symphony orchestras had a U.S.-born conductor.

[2] See Milton C. Cummings, Jr., "To Change a Nation's Cultural Policy: The
Kennedy Administration and the Arts in the United States, 1961–1963," in
Kevin V. Mulcahy and C. Richard Swaim, eds., *Public Policy and the Arts*
(Boulder, Colo.: Westview, 1982), 141–68, cited at 157.
[3] Netzer, *The Subsidized Muse,* p. 44.

Opera in the United States was composed, produced, directed, and sung by Europeans. Art museums were dominated by European painting and sculpture. Ballet was seen principally when European companies came over on tour, for there were very few U.S. groups. This state of affairs was largely taken for granted.

After World War II, however, Americans became increasingly self-conscious about their country's cultural standing. No longer satisfied to boast that the United States was the home of Henry Ford, Thomas Edison, and Charles Lindbergh, they now wanted to be taken seriously as participants in the world of high art and culture as well. Before the end of the 1950s the Ford Foundation took up the banner of culture when it began a massive program of grants to support U.S. symphony orchestras.

Birth of the New York State Council on the Arts and the National Endowment for the Arts

Two charismatic political leaders took advantage of the new mood of the country at the beginning of the 1960s to introduce for the first time a policy of direct, ongoing state and federal support for the arts.[4] In 1960 under the leadership of Governor Nelson Rockefeller, who was an important patron of the arts in his own right, New York State established the New York State Council on the Arts (NYSCA). The first year appropriation was only $50,000, but by 1976 the council had an annual budget of $35 million and was a major source of funding for arts activity in the state. NYSCA's administrative structure became the model that the federal government and many of the other states later adopted in establishing their own programs in support of the arts.[5]

A year or two after NYSCA was established, President John F. Kennedy began to take an interest in the federal government's relationship to the arts. In 1962 he appointed the philanthropist August Heckscher to the position of special consultant on the arts. Among other things, Heckscher recommended the establishment of a national arts foundation with the power to offer grants to arts institutions and to state arts councils. Shortly afterward, President Kennedy was assassinated, and it fell to President Johnson (in this case as in so many others) to carry the Kennedy proposal to fruition.

At first there was a good deal of congressional opposition to the idea

---

[4] Accounts of these developments in much greater detail can be found in ibid., chap. 4; and in Cummings, "To Change a Nation's Cultural Policy."

[5] However, Arthur Svenson points out that Utah established the first state arts agency as early as 1899. See his "State and Local Arts Agencies," in Mulcahy and Swaim, *Public Policy,* pp. 195–211, cited at 196.

of federal financial support for art and culture. Netzer reports that southern Democrats and conservative Republicans (there were also liberal Republicans in those days) expressed the usual fear that government subsidies would lead to government control. Opponents also argued that government funding would reduce the incentive for the private support that was a justly cherished U.S. tradition.[6] Nevertheless, in 1965 Johnson obtained from Congress and signed legislation establishing not one foundation but two: the National Endowment for the Arts (NEA) and the National Endowment for the Humanities (NEH). The legislation authorized initial funding of $10 million to each of the endowments, but actual appropriations were well below that level in the first few years. By 1979, however, appropriations for the NEA had climbed to $149.6 million. As we shall see in a later chapter, when adjustment is made for inflation, that was to be the endowment's largest annual appropriation.

The manner in which NEA and the state councils operate to support the arts, the division of funding among the federal, state, and local governments, and the many issues of economic and political policy that arise in connection with public support will be taken up in Chapter 13. At this point we wish to pursue the question of how much donational support to the arts is given by the public sector as a whole and how much by the private sector in the United States and in other industrially advanced countries.

An international comparison of arts support

The most meticulous and comprehensive international comparison of the level of public and private donational support for the arts that has yet been carried out is Mark Schuster's study for the NEA.[7] At the outset Schuster realized that the data would have to be adjusted to take account of differences among countries in what arts policy comprehends. For example, in some European countries money spent caring for historical monuments is counted as an outlay for art and culture. In other places, assistance to libraries, to professional training for artists, or even to art education in grade schools is included in the arts budget. In the United States, however, the arts universe to which the NEA devotes itself is limited to the performing arts, the fine arts, and mu-

---

[6] Netzer, *The Subsidized Muse,* pp. 58–59.
[7] J. Mark Davidson Schuster, *Supporting the Arts: An International Comparative Study* (Washington, D.C.: U.S. Government Printing Office, 1985). Also see John Michael Montias, "Public Support for the Performing Arts in Europe and the United States," in Paul J. DiMaggio, ed., *Nonprofit Enterprise in the Arts* (New York: Oxford University Press, 1986), pp. 287–319.

seums. The U.S. definition is, in fact, the narrowest among the eight Schuster examined. For the sake of comparability, he therefore adjusted all other country's arts expenditures to eliminate funds spent on objects beyond the reach of the U.S. definition. His study therefore tells us how much financial support other countries give to the arts when that term has the scope implied by U.S. policy.

Schuster's study deals systematically with two other complications. First of all, in every country support for the arts is provided not only by the national government but also by states (or other regional governments) and by localities. Schuster tabulated funding at all three levels. Second, government assistance to the arts can take the form not only of "direct" support, for example, by means of a cash grant, but also of "indirect" support. The latter occurs when a government forgoes potential tax revenue through some provision favorable to arts institutions. Examples in the United States are the exemption of arts institutions from the local property tax and, even more important, provisions in the tax code that create an incentive for taxpayers to make charitable contributions to nonprofit arts organizations. In both cases, the forgone revenue is equivalent to an expenditure by government. Indeed, in the United States the sums lost through these provisions have sometimes been called "tax expenditures."

Too often in casual international comparisons of subsidies to the arts, the writer mentions only direct expenditures, and then only those of the central government, resulting in a very distorted picture. Schuster's study avoids these pitfalls. His results are summarized in Table 12.1, which shows expenditure per capita in the United States, Canada, and six Western European countries. It must be emphasized that while their orders of magnitude are probably correct, all the figures in Table 12.1 contain at least some elements that are estimated.[8]

Several things stand out in this table. First of all, at the time of the study the United States gave only $3.00 of direct aid to the arts per capita as compared with a range of $9.60 to $35 per capita in the other advanced industrial nations. But second, the United States provided $10.00 per capita of indirect aid in the form of tax benefits, whereas indirect aid was small or negligible elsewhere. Taking direct and indirect aid together puts the level of *total* U.S. assistance ($13 per capita) within the range for the other seven countries ($10 to $35 per capita), thus rebutting the crude charge that the U.S. grossly neglects the arts. However, these comparisons also show that the United States was 46 percent

---

[8] See Schuster, *Supporting the Arts,* for technical and methodological details and caveats.

Table 12.1. *Public support for the arts in selected countries*
(per capita expenditure)

Country	Year	Direct (dollars)	Indirect (dollars)	Total
United States	1983–84	3.00	10.00	13.00
Canada	1981–82	32.00	Small	32.00 +
Fed. Rep. of Germany	1982	27.00	Small	27.00 +
France	1983	32.00	Very small	32.00 +
Great Britain	1983–84	9.60	.40	10.00
Italy	1983–84	14.00	Very small	14.00 +
The Netherlands	1984	29.00	Very small	29.00 +
Sweden	1983–84	35.00	0	35.00

Source: J. Mark Davidson Schuster, *Supporting the Arts: An International Comparative Study* (Washington, D.C.: U.S. Government Printing Office, 1985), tables 3 and 4.

below the eight-country average. It ranked seventh among the eight countries – only Great Britain was lower – and lagged substantially behind Canada and most of the continental European countries.

The mathematics of indirect aid, or tax expenditures

Private donations to nonprofit institutions are encouraged in the United States by provisions in both the federal income tax code and the state codes in states that levy an income tax. Under the federal code, taxpayers who "itemize" their deductions are allowed to include as a deduction from their taxable income the amount of their cash contributions to such institutions, up to a limit that varies from 20 percent to 50 percent of adjusted gross income, depending on the circumstances. Although these provisions were orginally adopted as a matter of tax equity (if a taxpayer donates part of his or her income to charity, then that part is no longer available to be spent or saved at the individual's discretion, and it might be regarded as unfair to count it as "income"), they have been retained as a matter of deliberate policy to foster private support of charitable undertakings.

Contributions are tax deductible by the donor only if made to not-for-profit organizations that qualify under guidelines set by the Internal Revenue Service. Among these are the requirement that there be no distribution of net income or "profit" to any party and the rule that the organization may not engage in political activity or attempt to influence legislation. Obviously, nonprofit organizations in the fields of art and

Table 12.2. *Mathematics of charitable deductions*

	(A) Pre-1986	(B) Current
TI = taxable income (dollars)	100,000	100,000
t = marginal (or bracket) tax rate	.50	.31
G = deductible gift (dollars)	1,000	1,000
tG = tax saved by donor = revenue loss to government (dollars)	500	310
$(1 - t)G$ = cost of gift to donor (dollars)	500	690

culture take care to abide by the rules so that they can continue to receive contributions that are tax deductible by the donor. Individual artists, of course, are not eligible to receive such contributions, since for tax purposes they are treated as profit-making sole proprietors. But for that reason they *are* permitted to testify or lobby in legislative matters, just like other citizens, and in fact, they often provide important support for legislation favoring the arts.

Although the terminology of this subject may be complex, it is important to bear in mind that donations are deductible not from tax liability but from taxable income. Arithmetically, what happens under U.S. tax law is that the donor's tax liability is reduced by an amount equal to the donation multiplied by the tax rate in that person's marginal tax bracket. The higher the individual's marginal tax rate, the greater the tax reduction per dollar given away, hence the less the cost of the gift to the donor and the stronger the tax-based incentive to make donations.[9] The amount of tax saved by the individual is also the amount of revenue lost by the government on account of the charitable deduction. It is this lost revenue that constitutes the *indirect* support given by government to the nonprofit sector.

These relationships are clarified in Table 12.2. Algebraic definitions of terms are given at the left. The two columns at the right show the outcome for (A), a donor in the 50 percent bracket, which was the highest just before the Tax Reform Act of 1986, and for (B), a donor in the 31 percent bracket, the highest current rate. (Under the 1986 act, the top rate had been 33 percent, but modifications introduced by the

[9] Since 1990, aggregate itemized deductions have been reduced by 3 percent of the taxpayer's adjusted gross income above $100,000 for a married couple filing jointly. However, since this take back "comes off the bottom," it does not reduce the marginal incentive effect of the provision allowing charitable deductions.

Revenue Reconciliation Act of 1990 lowered the top rate on ordinary income to 31 percent and the rate on capital gains to 28 percent.)

The table allows us to examine the economics of charitable deductions from two different perspectives. Looked at chronologically, it shows that when marginal tax rates were reduced under the Tax Reform Act of 1986, the cost to donors of making gifts *rose*. In other words, the tax incentive to give money away was *weakened:* a gift of $1,000, which would have cost a donor only $500 under the old law, costs $690 under the new. This aspect of the matter raised some puzzling questions for the Reagan Administration. On the one hand, President Reagan tried (not very successfully, one must add) to *reduce* federal appropriations for the arts, relying on the justification that if the government withdrew support, private donors would respond by taking up the slack – an argument clearly implying that when government assistance to the arts *grows,* it displaces private donations. On the other hand, he also endorsed the 1986 act that cut marginal tax rates and therefore *weakened* the incentive to make private donations. (We will return to these issues later.)

The table can also be used to illustrate the effect a progressive tax rate structure has on incentives to donate. Assume now that in Column B the top row shows taxable income of $50,000 instead of $100,000. Then the table can be interpreted as showing that when an individual's income rises from $50,000 (Column B) to $100,000 (Column A), he or she rises into a higher marginal tax bracket (50 percent instead of 31 percent), and the tax saving achieved by making a charitable donation accordingly rises from 31 cents to 50 cents on the dollar. In other words, under a progressive income tax structure, the higher your income, the stronger your incentive to make charitable donations.

The rate structure of the U.S. federal income tax is not now very progressive, but that was not always the case. Before passage of the 1986 reform, rates ranged from 14 percent to a maximum of 50 percent. From 1965 until 1980, the top rate (not including occasional surtaxes) had been 70 percent.[10] That meant that a charitable gift cost the donor only 30 cents on the dollar, or even less if the donor lived in a state or city that also levied an income tax. Keeping in mind the fact that benefactors of museums, symphony orchestras, hospitals, and universities sometimes have the pleasure of seeing galleries, auditoriums, clinics, or

---

[10] For a chronology of U.S personal income tax rates from the inception of the tax in 1913 through the Tax Reform Act of 1986, see Joseph A. Pechman, *Federal Tax Policy,* 5th ed. (Washington, D.C.: Brookings Institution, 1987), table A.1, pp. 313–14.

dormitories named after them (and/or their spouses), it is easy to see why a strong tradition of giving away 30-cent dollars developed in the United States. It is also plausible that once the habit of charitable giving was in place, subsequent reductions in the progressivity of the income tax, which raised the donor's cost of giving, did not necessarily or immediately bring a cutback in donations.

Donating works of art

For museums in the United States, private support takes the form of donations not only of cash but also of works of art, and these, too, have been heavily influenced by tax considerations. For many years the donor was allowed to claim as a charitable deduction the market value of the work at the time the donation was made. That provided a powerful incentive to make donations-in-kind to museums, especially since the prices of high-quality works of art have risen sharply in recent years (see the discussion in Chapter 9). Consider the alternatives faced by a potential donor. Suppose that he or she had paid $10,000 for a painting in 1950 and that by 1980 its market value has risen to $200,000. If the owner then sells it and donates the proceeds to the museum, he or she is entitled to a charitable deduction of $200,000 but is also liable for tax on the $180,000 capital gain realized at the sale. In 1980 a donor in the top income tax bracket of 70 percent would have paid capital gains tax at the rate of 25 percent (since long-term capital gains were taxed at lower rates than ordinary income), amounting to $45,000 on the gain from the painting. On the other hand, if the owner simply gave the painting to the museum, he or she could still have claimed the $200,000 market value as a charitable deduction, while altogether avoiding payment of income tax on its gain in value. Thus, the incentive to donate works of art that had appreciated in value was even stronger than the incentive to make gifts of cash. By claiming a deduction at market value, a donor could often save in taxes far more than the work of art had actually cost.

Not surprisingly, both museum directors and potential donors of valuable art were delighted by these arrangements. However, the provision that allowed gains on appreciated works of art to escape taxation was widely regarded as inequitable and was effectively removed in the Tax Reform Act of 1986. But the story does not end there. In the 1980s, rapidly mounting prices for art had made it prohibitively expensive for museums to acquire worthwhile objects in the market. They became more than ever dependent on donated works to expand their collections. Soon after the 1986 act went into effect, museum officials complained that the flow of donated works was drying up. The Association of Art

Museum Directors in 1989 reported that for 119 major museums the value of donated works had risen from $76.1 million in 1985 to $143.0 million in 1986 (the last year before the new provisions took effect), then fallen to $94.6 million in 1987 and $67.2 million in 1988.[11] In 1990 Congress adopted a one-year restoration of the market-value tax deduction for appreciated works of art and manuscripts donated to museums, galleries, and libraries, later extended to June 30, 1992. Legislation containing a permanent extension was vetoed by President Bush the day after his defeat in November 1992, but might receive more favorable treatment at the hands of his successor.

Individual, corporate, and foundation support

Private donational support for the arts in the United States comes not only from individuals but also from private corporations and foundations. Corporate contributions are encouraged by tax provisions analogous to those for individual taxpayers: in calculating liability for the corporation income tax, the firm may deduct charitable contributions as an expense up to an amount equal to 10 percent of taxable income. The net cost of a donation is therefore $(1 - t) \times$ (amount of the gift), where t is the effective tax rate. The top-bracket income tax rate on corporations varied between 40 and 50 percent during the 1970s and early 1980s before being reduced to 34 percent by the Tax Reform Act of 1986. Thus, ironically, the tax incentive for corporate giving, like that for individual donations, was substantially weakened just at the time that a business-oriented Republican administration was calling for increased private-sector support for social, cultural, and educational endeavors.

How do the sources of private contributions rank in relative size? In his study for the NEA, Schuster found that, in 1982–83, individual contributions were by far the largest category, amounting to $3.650 billion out of a total of $4.365 billion. Corporations contributed $263 million and foundations the remaining $452 million.[12]

To put these numbers in perspective, bear in mind that total direct federal government support for the arts in fiscal 1983–84 came to only $266 million. (See Table 13.1.) Moreover, in addition to making charitable contributions, corporations also provide support for the arts through expenditures charged to their advertising and promotion budgets. For example, a corporation might sponsor in that way a series of summer "concerts in the park." Like any other increase in costs, such

---

[11] Survey results are reported in *A Sourcebook of Arts Statistics: 1989* (Washington, D.C.: National Endowment for the Arts, 1990), table 7.26.

[12] Schuster, *Supporting the Arts,* table 5.

Table 12.3. *Share of private donations in dance company budgets (percent)*

	Ford Foundation (1971)		Dance/USA (1984)	
	Share of contributed income	Share of total operating income	Share of contributed income	Share of total operating income
Operating income	—	100.0	—	100.0
Contributed income	100.0	38.2	100.0	37.6
Total private	71.3	27.2	76.9	28.8
Individuals	27.0	10.3	23.0	8.6
Foundations	32.2	12.3	20.0	7.5
Corporations	4.3	1.6	14.9	5.6
Other private	7.8	3.0	19.0	7.1
Total government	28.8	11.0	23.1	8.7
Federal	12.1	4.6	11.1	4.2
State and local	16.7	6.4	12.0	4.5

Note: The number of companies in the samples were 17 for 1971 and 31 for 1984.
Source: Dick Netzer, "Changing Economic Fortunes of Dance in the U.S.," in Grant, Hendon, and Owen, eds., *Economic Efficiency and the Performing Arts*, vol. 1 of the Proceedings of the Fourth International Conference on Cultural Economics (Akron, Ohio: Association for Cultural Economics). (The tables for this article were omitted in the published volume, but will be supplied.)

outlays also reduce profits and therefore cut corporate tax liability. Advertising and promotion outlays for the arts are *not* included in any of the contributions totals discussed in this section. In fact, the total value of such expenditures is simply unknown.

These comparisons probably understate the corporate share in private giving, since the individual and foundation totals include donations to a range of activity that comprises culture and the humanities as well as the arts, while the figure for corporations includes only the latter. Moreover, some corporate giving occurs through the corporations' own foundations and was therefore counted in the foundation total by Schuster.

Another perspective on private giving can be obtained by asking what percentage of recipients' income is accounted for by gifts from each category of sources. In this instance we have only sporadic data from disparate samples of performing arts firms. However, the numbers themselves are probably accurate for the samples and time periods covered. Table 12.3 presents data on dance companies assembled by Netzer from information collected by the Ford Foundation for 1971 and the service

Table 12.4. *Total corporate donations and donations to the arts*

Year	Total contributions ($ billions)	Percent to the arts	Estimated amount to the arts ($ millions)
1975	1.20	7.5	90
1980	2.36	10.9	257
1985	4.40	11.1	488
Percent change, 1975–85	+267		+442

Percent allocation of funds among beneficiaries, 1984

Museums	19.6	Employee matching gifts	5.8
Music	12.7	Arts funds and councils	5.4
Public TV and radio	12.1	Dance	2.3
Cultural centers	9.5	Libraries	1.6
Theaters	6.0	Other	25.0

Source: Michael Useem, "Trends and Preferences in Corporate Support for the Arts," in Robert A. Porter, ed., *Corporate Giving in the Arts 4* (New York: American Council for the Arts, 1987), tables 1 and 5.

organization Dance/USA for 1984. The table shows that the share accounted for by private contributions was relatively stable – 27 percent of operating income in 1971 and 29 percent in 1984. (The dollar amount, not shown, of course increased sharply.) The makeup of private donations, however, did change: the share of foundations fell markedly, but that decline was offset by a sharp increase in corporate giving. The latter, in turn, was the product of two factors: an increase in corporate donations to the arts and, within the arts category, a rise in the proportion going to dance companies.

Table 12.4 presents a profile of corporate donational activity from 1975 to 1985. Contributions to all sectors, including health, education, and other areas in addition to the arts, rose by 267 percent, but the proportion going to the arts rose as well, so that total contributions to the arts increased by a very hefty 442 percent. Michael Useem, from whose study these data have been selected, cautioned that the sharp growth of corporate donations might not continue. He pointed out that corporate profits are the single most important determinant of the level of contributions. Donations rose when profits were increasing early in the 1980s. But profits leveled off later in the decade. In addition, the wave of mergers and takeovers that swept through the business world in the late 1980s was probably unfavorable to corporate giving.[13] The consolidated firm was likely to donate less than had been given previously by its separate parts. That is even more likely to be the case when strenuous "belt tightening" is required after the spending binge of a takeover, which typically leaves the taken-over firm heavily in debt. Nevertheless, corporate charitable donations in current dollars rose an additional 32 percent from 1985 to 1990 (corrected for inflation, the increase was 4.2 percent), and the proportion going to art and culture held steady at 11.1 percent.[14]

The table also shows the allocation of corporate support for the arts in 1984 among categories of beneficiaries. The three leading categories by a considerable margin were museums (19.6 percent), music (12.7 percent), and public television and radio (12.1 percent). We shall have more to say about this in the next section.

Motives for charitable giving

It seems entirely reasonable that those who are actively interested in the arts and can afford to give a little something to charity should make donations to one or more arts enterprises. And just as churchgoers will probably give to the church they attend and college graduates to their alma mater, so devotees of the arts are most likely to make donations to the museums or performing arts companies they regularly attend. Clearly, such support is not entirely disinterested. Donors hope to contribute, in however small a way, to the maintenance or improvement of enterprises that are a source of personal pleasure. In addition, most nonprofit arts organizations nowadays actively encourage donations by offering potential supporters a range of benefits that increases in scope with the size of the donation. In the case of a ballet company such as the New York City Ballet, a minimum $60 donation may bring in return complimentary tickets to working rehearsals and demonstration programs, and a subscription to the company newsletter. At the other end of the scale, large donors will have priority in reserving choice seats and will be invited to an annual party, with the opportunity of meeting star members of the company. A museum will typically seek support through "memberships" that carry with them, for the lowest ranks, such privileges as free admission to ordinary events, a discount at the museum store, and a subscription to the ubiquitous

---

[13] Michael Useem, "Trends and Preferences in Corporate Support for the Arts," in Robert A. Porter, ed., *Corporate Giving in the Arts 4* (New York: American Council for the Arts, 1987), pp. ix–xv, cited at ix–x.

[14] Data are from *Giving USA,* 1991 edition (New York: American Association of Fund Raising Counsel, 1991), tables 3, 4, and 17.

newsletter. More expensive memberships will entitle donors to free lectures, preopening guided tours of special exhibitions, and so on. The benefits thus conferred on supporters are designed not only to give pleasure (which for the initiate they undoubtedly do), but also (consider the newsletter) to cultivate in donors a sense of "belonging to the family" or of being in the inner circle, which helps to perpetuate the charitable tie.

All of this costs a lot of money to carry out (mailing lists, direct mail solicitations, record keeping, paying for special events), but the motto is "You have to spend money to make money." In 1983 the Metropolitan Opera is reported to have employed a staff of 50 and spent $3.5 million on fund-raising. By so doing, they raised about $25 million from individuals, corporations, foundations, and government agencies.[15] It is now taken for granted in the United States that fund-raising from the private sector is an important function within any nonprofit arts institution. Indeed, public agencies would probably be reluctant to make grants to a nonprofit that did not appear to be "pulling its weight" in private fund-raising.

It is not surprising that corporate motives for giving are somewhat different from those of individuals. Some corporate managers may, indeed, believe that it is morally important for their firms to *be* good corporate citizens, but one suspects that they believe it is even more important that they be *seen* in that light. Thus, corporations are attracted to forms of giving that are visible or even attention grabbing. That explains, for example, the prominence of corporate support for public television programming, as indicated in Table 12.4. (So great was the generosity of the major oil companies toward public TV during the profitable early 1980s that the joke went around that PBS really stood for Petroleum Broadcasting System.) "Special events" to which the company name can be attached, such as a blockbuster art exhibition or a series of summer concerts in the park, also attract generous corporate support. Hence, the large share of corporate donations going, respectively, to museums and to musical performances.

But one should not be too cynical in interpreting motives. Corporations claim that their single most important criterion in making gifts is "impact on the local community," and many of their donations are no doubt intended to make the local community a better place to live in by strengthening its artistic or other cultural institutions.[16] Consider the

---

[15] Simon Jenkins, "Paying for the Arts," *Economist,* 293, no. 7368 (November 17, 1984): 1–4, 13–16, cited at 13, 15.

[16] Useem, "Trends and Preferences," table 6, p. xiii.

following example. The Pillsbury Company is a large food processing firm with headquarters in Minneapolis. In 1986 its total contributions came to $7.1 million, of which $931,000 were for art and culture. Recent recipients of major grants include the Minnesota Orchestra, the Minnesota Opera, the Guthrie Theater (in Minneapolis), and Twin Cities Public Television. Apparently there can be a coincidence of interests so that what is good for the community is also good for the company, and the company knows that. Of course, Pillsbury also makes grants in other localities, including one to the Dallas Symphony Orchestra.[17]

Corporations whose interests are more widespread than Pillsbury's will be less inclined to concentrate their donations locally. For example, United Technologies Corporation is a large aerospace manufacturer, with its head office in Hartford, Connecticut. In 1985 it contributed $2.3 million in support of art and culture. Although major grants were given to the Connecticut Opera and the Hartford Ballet, even larger sums went to the National Museum of Women in the Arts (Washington, D.C.), to the Metropolitan Museum of Art to support a major exhibit of Degas's art in the United States, Canada, and France, and to the Denver Art Museum in support of a tour of Native American Art in France and Germany.[18] One can infer from this list that United Technologies (a large exporter) is concerned with its image in many parts of the world.

Some observers worry that corporate support may eventually corrupt our culture by bending artistic production too much in the direction of whatever it is that corporations are willing to pay for and away from the more provocative and controversial forms of art that they admittedly try to avoid. It is well to be on guard against that threat, but the danger seems insufficient to justify shunning corporate support. Most arts institutions (and most of their audiences) probably would endorse a policy of "take the money and run."

Why so little private support for the arts in Europe?

As Mark Schuster's study (cited in Table 12.1) shows, private donational support for the arts is negligible in most European countries. Americans may find this puzzling, since European devotion to art in all its forms is well known. For many years U.S. economists believed that the explanation must lie in a difference in tax law. It was assumed that, in Europe, charitable contributions either were not deductible or were deductible only under severe restrictions. But Schuster's study included

---

[17] *Corporate Giving in the Arts 4*, p. 306.
[18] Ibid., pp. 391–92.

an examination of income tax law in Europe and Canada, and he found, on the whole, that their tax codes were *not* unfriendly to charitable giving.[19] Instead, he attributes the low level of private support in Europe to historical tradition. In the distant past, major European cultural institutions such as the Comédie Française or the Vienna State Opera owed their origins and subsequently their support to royal, or at least noble, patronage. In the nineteenth and twentieth centuries, these burdens were assumed by republican governments and municipalities. Private citizens, aware that "the government" was subsidizing arts institutions and that they as taxpayers were footing the bill, felt no obligation to make voluntary contributions. That is not to say that wealthy collectors might not sometimes donate valuable works of art to national or municipal museums, but a broad-based tradition of private charitable support for the institutions of art and culture never developed.

In the 1980s the climate of opinion began to change. After a long period of budgetary expansion, most European governments were trying to restrain public spending. Subsidies for the arts were either reduced or prevented from growing at their accustomed pace. For the first time both governments and the arts institutions themselves became seriously interested in what Schuster calls "the American model . . . with its heavy reliance on and encouragement of private sources of funding."[20] In 1990 the Policy Studies Institute published a detailed survey of arts funding in the United States, Canada, and five Western European countries.[21] Although the data on private support in the European countries were very sketchy, the institute did find some evidence that donations there, especially by corporations, were increasing. But the Europeans are starting from a very low level: in the typical case, private support in the late 1980s accounted for no more than 1 or 2 percent of the income of performing arts companies and museums. By contrast, the authors found that U.S. private contributions ranged from 26 percent of income for theater companies up to 37 percent for companies producing opera, while in Canada the proportion varied from about 10 percent for theaters and museums to 20 or 25 percent for orchestras and opera companies. We take up next the advantages and disadvantages of both the U.S. model of support and the European.

[19] Schuster, *Supporting the Arts,* pp. 48–54.

[20] Ibid., p. 48.

[21] *Cultural Trends 1990: Funding the Arts in Seven Western Countries,* no. 5 (March 1990), Andrew Feist and Robert Hutchison, eds. (London: Policy Studies Institute, 1990). The study contains copious data on attendance and performances, as well as on income, expenditures, and government support.

Advantages and disadvantages of private and/or public support

In debating the merits of the European as compared with the U.S. system of arts support, we are not suggesting that the nations in either camp should entirely abandon their own approach in favor of the other. Each system (and its local variations) is the expression of a long-standing cultural and political tradition that has to be understood in its own terms.[22] Nevertheless, it is instructive to examine the claims made for each.

Philosophically, those who favor the European system in which arts institutions are supported primarily by government subsidies start from the premise that art and culture are a national heritage and therefore logically deserve to be supported by the nation acting collectively. At the practical level, an alleged advantage is that the government can provide whatever funds are needed and in so doing relieve the institutions of unremitting and distracting pressure to raise money from private sources. Government funding, it is also argued, would be relatively stable, providing a more reliable basis for long-run planning than does private support. Perhaps more fundamental, support from the public budget is seen as a way of insulating the arts from the potential threat to their artistic freedom associated with dependence on the marketplace. As Schuster puts it, "The Swedish National Council for Cultural Affairs is struck by the paradox of encouraging greater corporate funding when one of the important goals of their national cultural policy is to 'combat the negative effects of commercialism in the cultural sector.' "[23]

Those who defend the "U.S. system" do not, of course, disparage government support. Rather, they argue that a combination of public and private funding, with heavy reliance on the latter, has some advantages over an almost exclusive reliance on the public budget. First of all, it diversifies the sources of income, which could make for greater stability than the European system under which arts budgets can be squeezed very hard during a period of public austerity. Second, diversity in funding sources also reduces the concentration of power over arts policy, which, in the European system, rests with government agencies. A secure base in private support gives institutions a freedom of action they lack when largely dependent on the government. Third, U.S. arts

[22] See Milton C. Cummings, Jr., and Richard S. Katz, eds., *The Patron State: Government and the Arts in Europe, North America, and Japan* (New York: Oxford University Press, 1987).

[23] Schuster, *Supporting the Arts,* p. 56.

institutions, because of their reliance on the individual donor, cultivate the donor's attention, understanding, and goodwill. In the long run, that probably helps to broaden the constituency for the arts, which should, in turn, ultimately provide benefits in the political realm.

There is plenty of ammunition with which to criticize the arguments on both sides. As to the alleged sufficiency of government funding, Simon Jenkins in the *Economist* argued that government support during the austere Thatcher years, while "secure," did not give Britain's arts institutions an adequate rate of growth. They have been falling behind those in other Western nations because "they have not won the spectacular [government] resources which their European colleagues have gained," while also failing to press for policy changes "that might have unlocked private resources."[24]

The question of stability

The alleged stability of government support must also be questioned in the light of sharp cutbacks by state and local governments in the United States in the early 1990s. Note also that the federal commitment to NEA, while stable in nominal dollars, was steadily eroded in real terms during the 1980s by rising prices. (See the discussion in Chapter 13.)

As for the stability of private giving, while individual donations appear to be a secure form of support in the United States, it remains to be seen whether corporate giving will be as reliable. We have pointed out that it is sensitive to changes in the level of profits (which can be quite volatile over the course of a typical business cycle) and also to changes in corporate structure resulting from mergers and takeovers. The record up to now is that corporate giving is much more variable year to year than are individual donations. We studied the variability in the four major categories of private giving – corporate, foundation, bequest, and individual – over the 30-year period from 1961 through 1990 by calculating the coefficient of variation (V) for the year-to-year growth rates in each category.[25] Individual giving displayed by far the most stable growth rate ($V = 0.44$) and bequests the least stable ($V = 1.83$), while corporate ($V = 1.27$) and foundation ($V = 1.17$) giving fell about midway between the extremes. *Total* donations ($V = 0.42$) were, of course, more stable than any of the components, clearly supporting the desirability of having diversified sources of support.

---

[24] Jenkins, "Paying for the Arts," p. 16.

[25] The coefficient of variation is defined as the standard deviation of a series divided by its mean: Data are from *Giving USA*, 1991 edition, table 3.

Interference with artistic freedom

Whether government agencies or powerful private donors are more likely to interfere with the artistic independence of arts institutions is an open question. Perhaps the word "interfere" is too dramatic (although we shall cite such a case). More often the donor's influence on artistic policy makes itself felt without direct interference: the recipient institution bends its policy to conform with the agency's or the donor's known preferences. Such effects are subtle and not easily demonstrated. However, no less an institution than the Metropolitan Opera offers a well-documented example. In 1983 as part of its centennial celebration, the Met commissioned new operas from two U.S. composers. One of these, "The Ghosts of Versailles" by John Corigliano and William Hoffman, was produced with considerable popular success in 1991–92. (It was the first *new* opera to have its premiere at the Met in 25 years.) However, it was reported in 1987 that the Met had cancelled the other commission from Jacob Druckman and also indefinitely postponed plans to produce Arnold Schoenberg's twentieth-century masterpiece "Moses und Aron." The Opera's general manager explained to the *New York Times* that it was impractical to try to fill the 3,800-seat auditorium by putting on contemporary works, and that influential members of the board of trustees are also opposed to new operas. As he put it, "The people who make contributions to opera are not too excited about contemporary work."[26] Thus do the tastes of private donors influence the artistic policies of their beneficiaries.

What about the influence of government donors? In Great Britain, Canada, Australia, New Zealand, and the United States, government grants for the arts are filtered through a semiindependent arts council (the Arts Council of Great Britain, founded in 1945, was the first and became the model) under arrangements that are intended to insulate arts policy from the tastes (or whims) of the politicians who vote the funds. Harry Hillman-Chartrand and Claire McCaughey explain the system as follows:

> The government determines how much aggregate support to provide, but not which organizations or artists should receive support. The council is composed of a board of trustees appointed by the government.... Trustees are expected to fulfill their grant-giving duties independent of the day-to-day interests of the party in power. Granting decisions are generally made by the council on the advice of professional artists working through a system of evaluation. The policy dy-

[26] *New York Times* (John Rockwell), May 27, 1987.

namic . . . tends to be evolutionary, responding to changing forms and styles of art as expressed by the community.[27]

Political controversy over controversial art

That this application of the "arm's length" principle does not always succeed in shielding the grant givers from political pressure was demonstrated in the United States in 1989 and 1990 by the widely publicized case of Senator Helms versus the NEA. In that famous battle, the senator took offense at two photography exhibitions that had received NEA support, arguing that one was pornographic and the other blasphemous.[28] Once he had pointed this out, with characteristic emphasis, on the Senate floor, it became difficult for other members to defend the NEA even if they disagreed with Senator Helms's judgment (and many of them clearly did not), since they were reluctant to stand accused of spending the taxpayers' money on indecent or blasphemous projects. The Senate voted to bar the NEA from supporting "obscene or indecent" work and also to cut off funds for the offending exhibitions. It was the first time since the endowment was founded in 1965 that Congress had violated the spirit of the legislation establishing it by attempting to intervene directly in its grant-determination process.[29] Later in the year, acting under the new guidelines, the chairman of the endowment first canceled and then restored a grant in support of an art exhibition entitled "Witnesses: Against Our Vanishing" that focused on the AIDS crisis.

Report of the independent commission

The position of the NEA was especially precarious at that time because its legislative authorization was due to expire in 1990, when its opponents would still be in full cry. In an attempt to obtain guidance on the issues of censorship, creative freedom, artistic merit, and public accountability in advance of reauthorization, Congress in 1989 approved the creation of the bipartisan, twelve-member Independent Commission to review the endowment's grant-making standards and procedures. The

---

[27] Harry Hillman-Chartrand and Claire McCaughey, "The Arm's Length Principle and the Arts: An International Perspective: Past, Present and Future," in Milton C. Cummings, Jr., and J. Mark Davidson Schuster, eds., *Who's to Pay for the Arts? The International Search for Models of Arts Support* (New York: American Council for the Arts, 1989), pp. 43–80, cited at 49–50.

[28] For a careful review of the entire episode, see Cummings, "Government and the Arts," *Public Money and the Muse*, pp. 63–79. In the same volume, see Kathleen M. Sullivan, "Artistic Freedom, Public Funding, and the Constitution," for a discussion of First Amendment implications of the controversy.

[29] *New York Times* (Michael Oreskes), July 27, 1989.

commission presented its report in September 1990.[30] Its most important recommendations were made under three broad headings.

First, in response to a specific charge from Congress, the commission decided that publicly funded art should, indeed, meet a higher standard than would apply to privately supported art. The commission agreed that as in the case of private support, artistic excellence should be the sole *aesthetic* standard, but it also suggested that since the endowment depends on public funds, it "must take into account the nature of public sponsorship" (p. 59). It recommended that language be added to the reauthorization act emphasizing that the arts belong to *all* the people of the United States and are expected by them to foster mutual respect for diverse values and beliefs. This was a none too subtle way of urging that the NEA not subsidize works of art that might strongly offend some part of the public.

Second, the commission called for major reforms in the NEA's grant-making procedures. These were intended to assure the president, Congress, and the people that the NEA would, in the future, carry out its mandate in a responsible and sensitive manner. These reforms will be discussed in detail in Chapter 13.

Third, the commission recommended that the NEA be reauthorized without *any* specific legislative restrictions on the content of art that it may fund and that it should rescind the requirement, adopted during the controversy with Senator Helms, that grantees certify that the works of art they propose will not be obscene. Determinations of obscenity, the commission argued, should be made by the courts under now well-established standards, rather than by the NEA, which is not equipped for such a task, and whose findings would, in any case, ultimately be challenged in court.

Thus, in the end the commission came down on what might be described as the side of "artistic freedom," and in opposition to "government censorship." From a political perspective, its findings and recommendations under the first two headings can be seen as the price it thought would have to be paid to gain acceptance for that final determination.

On the last day of the 1990 session of Congress, the NEA was reauthorized for three years in legislation that incorporated most of the

---

[30] The Independent Commission, *A Report to Congress on the National Endowment for the Arts* (Washington, D.C.: The Independent Commission, September 1990). Members of the commission were broadly representative of the lay public that has been actively involved with the arts. Four were appointed by President Bush and four each by the Democratic and Republican leadership in Congress. The cochairpersons were John Brademas and Leonard Garment.

Independent Commission's recommendations. There was one major exception: the commission had specifically rejected suggestions that the proportion of NEA funds passed through to state arts agencies be increased from the then mandated level of 20 percent. Congress turned down that advice and raised the state share substantially. We shall examine the logic, or otherwise, of that move in the next chapter.

In addition, the final legislation required the chairperson to ensure not only that artistic excellence and merit be the criteria on which applications are judged, but also that "general standards of decency" be taken into consideration. It has been suggested that this may conflict with the requirement elsewhere in the act that the final determination of obscenity rests with the courts. And the courts, it must be remembered, have *not* held that works of art must meet general standards of decency in order to avoid the charge of obscenity.

Nor did the controversy end with the 1990 reauthorization. In the spring of 1992, NEA Chairman John E. Frohnmayer, whose sometimes wavering defense of the endowment had pleased neither its friends nor its foes, was forced from office by an administration that was apparently fearful of the commotion the NEA's critics were likely to stir up during a presidential election year.

However one may evaluate the specific terms of the legislation reauthorizing the NEA, the whole controversy has undoubtedly had a chilling effect on the agency: it will be much more reluctant than in the past to back potentially controversial art projects. Some legislators will be pleased with that outcome, but most members of the arts community are alarmed. They point out that it is often the purpose of art to disturb our comfortable preconceptions, to be controversial, even outrageous. The *New York Times* reported that "Alexander Melamid, a Soviet artist now living in New Jersey, whose satirical anti-government work" was suppressed in Moscow in 1974, said: "The government is always the guardian of tradition, and art is the guardian of innovation. If there's no friction between the government and artists, it's abnormal."[31]

As one congressman who is very sympathetic to the cause of the arts explained: "There may be two irreconcilable forces here. One is the right of taxpayers to determine how their money is spent. The other is the absolute necessity to protect freedom of expression, particularly in the arts."[32] How can this impasse be resolved? Members of the arts community do not deny that taxpayers have their rights. Rather, the art world asks the political world, in the interest of free art, not to insist

---

[31] *New York Times* (Grace Glueck), November 19, 1989.
[32] Ibid., quoting Representative Pat Williams, Democrat from Montana.

on those rights. If that sounds like an elitist claim, so be it. In a prescient passage written in 1978, Lincoln Kirstein declared:

> It is time for the inventive, lyric, poetic, creative elite to come out of their closets and declare themselves – their worth, their difference in kind, their capacity, their energy, and their strength. Most of all – their necessity. . . . Elitism should be a rallying cry for that band of brothers and sisters who bear the culture of their country, for it is this cultivation of the only memorable residue that marks and outlives their epoch which justifies their permission to perform and produce as free agents, whatever the risk or cost to their countrymen.[33]

Conclusion

Building on the somewhat more theoretical foundation of Chapter 11, this chapter has explored the practice of arts support in the United States. A historical review and an international comparison provided useful perspectives for a description and evaluation of both public and private support. The next chapter takes a closer look at governmental policy toward the arts in the United States.

[33] Lincoln Kirstein, "The Performing Arts and Our Egregious Elite," in W. McNeil Lowry, ed., *The Performing Arts and American Society* (Englewood Cliffs, N.J.: Prentice-Hall, 1978), pp. 181–97, cited at 197.

13

Direct public support for the arts

At the beginning of Chapter 12 we described the relatively recent origin of ongoing, direct support for the arts in the United States by the state and federal governments, and attempted to explain why that kind of aid was so long in coming. We also pointed out the importance in the United States of private donations to the arts and of "indirect" governmental aid in the form of tax forgiveness for private donors. In Table 12.1 we cited Schuster's estimate of $3.00 per capita in 1983–84 for the combined amount of direct support for the arts by all levels of government in the United States, with an additional $10.00 per capita coming in the form of indirect support. The economics of indirect support and the advantages and disadvantages of a system that relies heavily on private contributions were analyzed at length in the remainder of Chapter 12. Public subsidies for art museums were described in Chapter 10. In this chapter we will look at direct government support for art and culture in greater detail.

The components of direct public support
Discussion of public funding for the arts in the United States often focuses on the amount provided by the National Endowment for the Arts. This is an understandable emphasis since the NEA's budget is the single largest source of contributed support and also symbolizes our national commitment to promoting and preserving the arts. For many years aggregate state support lagged far behind the level provided by the NEA. Although the New York State Council on the Arts was established in 1960, several years before the NEA was founded, other states were slow to follow suit or, when they did, began with very small appropriations. Writing in the mid-1970s, Netzer found that most state arts agencies were little more than vehicles created to receive funds

250

made available by the NEA, which, under its federal–state partnership program, had been channeling between 15 and 20 percent of its funds to the states in the form of direct grants to such entities.[1] Among the 50 states in 1974, only New York more than matched the federal agency's contribution to the state program. That soon changed, however. State funding began to increase rapidly in the late 1970s. By 1985 aggregate state appropriations drew even with funding for the NEA and by 1990 had far surpassed it. As we shall see, however, the rising trend of state aid reversed abruptly after that date.

The composition of direct government support for the arts in the United States is shown in Table 13.1. The first column reproduces data from Schuster's study for fiscal 1984. In that year the total came to $702 million (from which Schuster calculated the amount of $3.00 per capita). The federal government provided $266 million, the states $136 million, and local governments an estimated $300 million. In 1983–84 the NEA accounted for $162 million, or 61 percent of the federal total. Other major components were: the Smithsonian Institution, for which the History and Art programs, plus prorated administrative expenses, came to $41 million; the National Gallery of Art, which received almost $35 million; and the Institute of Museum Services (a federal entity already described in Chapter 10), which disbursed more than $20 million.

The second column of the table presents a similar tabulation (by the authors of this volume) for fiscal 1991. Total direct governmental support rose to an estimated $906 million, an increase of $204 million in seven years. Appropriations for the NEA rose only $12 million. The surge in state support accounted for the bulk of the increase. (The figures for local assistance are estimates that are not necessarily comparable in scope for the two years and may well underrepresent the growth in that component.)

Although total government funding for the arts increased in almost every year up until 1990, the main source of growth varied from period to period in a way that reflects changing voter attitudes and changing budget priorities at various levels of government. Table 13.2 shows appropriations for the NEA and for the aggregate of state arts agencies at roughly five-year intervals since the 1960s. The two left-hand columns show amounts in nominal dollars, that is to say, dollars of the dates given. The columns at the right are adjusted for inflation by converting to constant 1969 dollars.

In nominal dollars, appropriations for the NEA increased rapidly

---

[1] Dick Netzer, *The Subsidized Muse* (Cambridge University Press, 1978), table 4.4 and pp. 90–93.

Table 13.1. *Direct governmental assistance to the arts in the United States*

Source	Appropriations, fiscal year ($ millions)	
	1984	1991
Federal government, total	265.62	319.7
National Endowment for the Arts	162.00	174.1
Smithsonian Institution[a]	41.40	42.8
National Gallery of Art	34.64	49.8
Institute of Museum Services	20.15	25.7
John F. Kennedy Center for the Performing Arts	4.54	21.2[b]
Other D.C.-area institutions	2.90	6.3
State arts agencies[c]	136.46	258.1
Local governments (estimated)	300	328[d]
Total		
All levels	702	905.8
Per capita	3.00	3.58

[a]In 1984, art and history museums, plus allocated overhead; in 1991, art museums only, plus overhead. Figures for 1991 are estimated, in part from 1990 data.
[b]Includes $14.5 million to repair center's parking garage.
[c]The 50 states plus District of Columbia.
[d]Estimated by the authors. Not necessarily comparable in scope with Schuster's 1984 estimates.
Sources: For 1984, J. Mark Davidson Schuster, *Supporting the Arts: An International Comparative Study* (Washington, D.C.: U.S. Government Printing Office, 1985), tables 3, 4, A.1. For 1991, *Budget of the U.S. Government, 1992*; *Smithsonian Year 1990*; National Assembly of State Arts Agencies, *State Arts Agencies Legislative Appropriations, Annual Survey*, fiscal years 1991 and 1992, and *Update*, April 1992.

during the 1970s. Even when adjusted for inflation, NEA funding multiplied more than eight times over between 1970 and 1980. Matters changed abruptly with the election of President Reagan in the latter year. He came into office committed to a radical reduction in the role of government in the economy and to a corresponding cut in the level of federal spending. Some of his advisors favored the complete elimination of the arts and humanities endowments. In the end the president did not try to go that far. His initial budget for 1981–82 requested $88 million for the NEA, as compared with $158.8 million appropriated in the previous year. To the surprise of many observers, Congress came to the defense of the arts agency and insisted on appropriating $143.5

Table 13.2. *Growth of federal and state funding for the arts (thousands of dollars)*

Fiscal year ending	Spending in current dollars		Spending in constant dollars[a]	
	NEA	States[b]	NEA	States[b]
1966	2,534	1,271	2,863	1,436
1970	8,250	5,993	7,789	5,694
1975	74,750	54,290	50,916	37,034
1980	154,610	95,829	68,786	42,681
1985	163,660	155,128	55,773	52,911
1990	171,255	277,951	48,092	78,054
1991	174,083	258,127	46,910	69,557
1992	176,000	201,088	46,340	52,946

[a]Dollars of 1969, using Consumer Price Index as deflator.
[b]The 50 states plus District of Columbia.
Sources: National Endowment for the Arts, *1990 Annual Report; Budget of the United States Government*, Fiscal year 1993; National Assembly of State Arts Agencies, *Legislative Appropriations for State Arts Agencies: A Twenty-Year Perspective* (June 1989); and *State Arts Agencies Legislative Appropriations, Annual Surveys*, various years.

million.[2] Apparently, the strategy of spreading the money around among the 50 states had paid off: many members of Congress now saw that NEA funds were useful in their districts and, since the agency's total cost was so small relative to the size of the federal budget, decided it was an inappropriate place in which to seek savings. It has also been argued that behind-the-scenes pressure from influential leaders in business and philanthropy who were "appalled" at the budget cuts initially proposed for the arts, helped to move the White House away from what might have appeared to be a "Philistine" position.[3]

In subsequent years under President Reagan, much the same scenario was reenacted. The administration's budget would call for a reduction in funds for the NEA, albeit a much less drastic cut than in the first year. Congress, after a series of skirmishes, would vote to authorize at

[2] Kevin V. Mulcahy, "The Politics of Cultural Oversight: The Reauthorization Process and the National Endowment for the Arts," in Margaret Jane Wyszomirski, ed., *Congress and the Arts* (New York: American Council for the Arts, 1988), pp. 63–92, cited at app. B, p. 91.
[3] See Fraser Barron, "A Mission Renewed: The Survival of the National Endowment for the Arts, 1981–1983," *Journal of Cultural Economics*, 11, no. 1 (June 1987): 22–75, cited at 42–43.

least the level of the year before, and occasionally a little more. In this way, appropriations in nominal dollars increased very gradually during the 1980s. Inflation, however, ate away at the purchasing power of these moneys. By 1992 the real value of NEA funding had fallen 33 percent below its 1980 level and 39 percent below its 1979 peak.

State government support

Although state spending on the arts increased rapidly in the 1970s, it remained well below the level of NEA funding, which was also rising sharply. In the 1980s, however, when NEA appropriations leveled off, state spending continued to climb and, by 1985, was approximately equal to funding by the arts endowment. Moreover, state appropriations were rising substantially faster than the rate of inflation, so there was an increase in the "real" as well as the nominal level of support. Evidently, the states were in the process of discovering that the arts were "a good thing," and as their agencies acquired more experience in this new field, state governments became increasingly confident that funds for the arts would be well spent. Hence, the brisk increase in appropriations.

At the end of the 1980s, however, the boom in state spending for the arts came to an abrupt halt. Hurt by regional recessions that were reinforced by a downturn in the national economy, many states found tax revenue growth decelerating. Since the early 1980s, aid from Washington had increased very little, while the demand for services at the state level rose steadily. Faced with prospective budget deficits, unwilling to increase tax rates, and under great pressure not to reduce spending for such major social programs as education, health, and the suppression of crime, many states now became less accommodating to the arts. Aggregate state appropriations reached their peak in fiscal year 1990, then fell 7.1 percent in 1991 and 22.1 percent in 1992.[4] From 1992 to 1993, however, the state total declined only an additional 1.3 percent.

To those who regarded the states as a reliable source of assistance to the arts, the cutbacks in some of the large states came as a genuine shock. Appropriations in Massachusetts fell from $21 million in 1988 to $18 million in 1990 and $3.6 million in 1992. In New Jersey they fell from $23 million in 1989 to $12 million in 1991, in Michigan from $13 million in 1988 to $6 million in 1992, and in Virginia from $5 million in 1990 to $1.5 million in 1992. Perhaps most shocking of all, in New York, where state assistance began and where it had reached the most generous

---

[4] Data on state arts appropriations in this and the following paragraphs are from reports of the National Assembly of State Arts Agencies, Washington, D.C.

level, it was cut back from $59 million in 1990 to $31 million in 1992. These events raised questions about the future of government support for the arts in the United States even more serious than those occasioned by President Reagan's ill-fated 1981 assault on the NEA.

To keep the problem in perspective, however, it is important to note that there has always been a good deal of year-to-year variability in arts funding by individual states, reflecting the volatility of regional economies and the vagaries of state politics. For example, between 1969 and 1989, when, as we have seen, the trend in aggregate state support was strongly upward, arts appropriations in the state of Illinois rose 14 times, fell 4, and were unchanged twice; in California they rose 13 times, fell 6, and were unchanged once; in New York they rose 11 times, fell 3, and were unchanged 6. From 1981 through 1990, according to Netzer's calculations, dollar appropriations for arts agencies declined in an average of 10 states per year.[5] The implications of instability in state spending will be discussed later in this chapter. We next examine differences among the states in the level of public support given to art and culture.

Interstate variation in appropriations for the arts

To make meaningful comparisons of the level of support for the arts among states, one must look at state government spending per capita. For state governments in the aggregate, arts spending in 1990, the peak year for state support, amounted to $1.13 per capita. (Keep in mind that federal spending via the NEA came to only about 75 cents per capita in that year.) The aggregate state figure, however, concealed enormous differences among the states. Hawaii had by far the highest level at $7.84 per capita, followed by the District of Columbia ($5.74) and New York ($3.33). At the other end of the scale were Mississippi (18.6 cents), Texas (19.5 cents) and Louisiana (20.0 cents). Thus, the most supportive state spent 42 times as much per capita as the least generous did.[6]

What could possibly account for differences of that magnitude? Schus-

[5] See Dick Netzer, "Cultural Policy in an Era of Budgetary Stringency and Fiscal Decentralization: The U.S. Experience," in Ruth Towse and Abdul Khakee, eds., *Cultural Economics, 1990* (Berlin: Springer, 1992), pp. 237–45, cited at table 3; and Sharon Goff, *Legislative Appropriations for State Arts Agencies: A Twenty-Year Perspective* (Washington, D.C.: National Assembly of State Arts Agencies, 1989), app. A.

[6] *State Arts Agencies Legislative Appropriations – Annual Survey – Fiscal Years 1989 and 1990* (Washington, D.C.: National Assembly of State Arts Agencies, 1989), table 1.

ter employed multiple regression techniques in an attempt to find the answer.[7] He tested the hypothesis that state arts support per capita responds positively to the demand for funding, which can be measured within each state by the size of the audience (indicated by arts participation rates), the number of nonprofit arts organizations, and the number of resident artists. Since participation rates were published only for the 14 most populous states, his initial estimates were limited to that group. He found that these three variables, plus median level of education per state, could explain 76 percent of the interstate variation in state arts agency funding.[8] Participation rates, however, did not have a statistically significant effect. Dropping that variable, he was able to include all 50 states in the tests. Surprisingly, the best equation now explained only 10 percent of interstate variation, and none of the explanatory variables now had a statistically significant effect.[9] For the full array of states, then, interstate variation in arts funding per capita remained basically unexplained. In a subsequent analysis, Netzer tested the effect of other variables and found that state tax effort (defined as tax revenue as a percentage of personal income) was a significant positive factor. His results suggest that high-spending states, such as those in the Northeast, also tend to spend more liberally on the arts. But he also found considerable variability *within* regions and concluded that "interstate variation is highly idiosyncratic."[10]

Another perspective on state funding is obtained by looking at the percentage of its general fund expenditures that each state allocates to its arts agency. In no case can the percentage be described as more than minuscule, but in some cases it might well be described as less than that. In 1990 Hawaii again ranked as the highest, with a .31 percent budget share for the arts, followed by Florida with .23 percent and New York with .20 percent. At the low end again came Louisiana, Texas, and Mississippi with only .02 to .03 percent devoted to the arts.[11]

Despite year-to-year instability and vast interjurisdictional differences in level, state funding remains a large and critical source of support for the arts. We therefore take a careful look at this later in the section entitled "Patterns of State Aid."

---

[7] J. Mark Davidson Schuster, "Determinants and Correlates of Arts Support by States," in Douglas V. Shaw et al., eds., *Cultural Economics, '88: An American Perspective* (Akron, Ohio: Association for Cultural Economics, 1989), pp. 211–24.

[8] Ibid., table 3.

[9] Ibid., table 5.

[10] Netzer, "Cultural Policy in an Era of Budgetary Stringency," p. 242.

[11] *State Arts Agencies Legislative Appropriations*, table 1.

The division of functions between levels of government

Does it make sense to have all three levels of government – federal, state, and local – involved in subsidizing the arts, or could it be done more effectively by one or perhaps two of the three? This is a special case of a more general question that economists ask: in a multilevel system of government, which level can best provide which services?[12] Or as theorists in the field of public finance would put it, is there a rule that will give us the optimum assignment of functions among the various levels of government? The optimum assignment is the arrangement that will most effectively satisfy citizen preferences for public services; the principle of "fiscal equivalence" has been proposed as the rule to accomplish that.[13] This rule says that each function should be carried out by the level of government whose geographic area most nearly coincides with the area over which the benefits of the service extend. In a democratic society, the amount of a governmental service to be provided, and the taxes to pay for the service, are determined by the decision of voters. A basic requirement for rational decision making would seem to be that the citizens who vote on how much of the service to provide and how to pay for it be the same group who stand to benefit from the service. The principle of fiscal equivalence brings about precisely that congruence.

A few examples will illustrate the logic of the rule. National defense is a service whose benefits extend to all citizens. Its benefit area is thus nationwide. Hence, national defense should be voted on and provided at the federal (i.e., national) level. At the other end of the scale, consider services like fire fighting and garbage collection. These provide benefits over a strictly local area. Therefore, they should be voted on and financed by local government.

Some cases, such as primary and secondary education, are more complex. The direct benefits go to the students who attend each school and to their families. Thus, the direct benefit area is strictly local, which argues for provision by local government. But as we explained in Chapter 11, each student's primary or secondary education is also thought to produce an external benefit that accrues to the student's fellow citizens. Since the benefit area for the externality may be as wide as the state, or even the nation, it is appropriate that both the state and federal

---

[12] For discussion of the more general case, see James Heilbrun, *Urban Economics and Public Policy,* 3d ed. (New York: St. Martin's, 1987), pp. 381–88.

[13] See Mancur Olson, "The Principle of 'Fiscal Equivalence': The Division of Responsibilities among Different Levels of Government," *American Economic Review,* 59, no. 2 (May 1969): 479–87.

governments become involved, as indeed they do in the United States, in subsidizing local public education.

The case of the arts strongly resembles that of education. The existence of societywide external benefits from the arts, such as the legacy to future generations or the stimulation of innovation (both discussed in Chapter 11), justify subsidies from the federal government. A national commitment to "outreach" – the policy of making art more readily available to the poor and the geographically remote – likewise justifies federal involvement.

But why should local or state governments wish to subsidize the arts? Most of the alleged externalities of art accrue nationwide and so would not justify (and are unlikely to motivate) local or state funding. On the other hand, one external effect of arts activity that does *not* justify *federal* involvement, that is, its power of attracting tourist visits and of influencing business location decisions in favor of a particular city, *is* a possible justification for local government support. New York City is very much aware that the funds it provides to local arts institutions help maintain the city's worldwide cultural reputation, with attendant benefits for the local economy. Other cities, starting with less, are eager to make themselves attractive to business and tourism by encouraging the expansion of local arts institutions. (The local economic impact of arts activity will be taken up in detail in Chapter 15.)

State and local spending on the arts may also be justified by a desire to promote "outreach" within the state or locality itself, over and above the redistributional efforts paid for by the federal government. Certainly it is a major objective of most state arts councils to pay for within-state tours of art exhibits and performance companies in order to broaden the distribution of art and culture within state borders. For the same reason, cities may decide to pay local arts companies to perform in the public schools or to give free concerts in local parks. Thus, the involvement of all three levels of government in supporting art and culture may be quite rational, after all.

We turn next to an examination of the structure and grant-making procedures of the principal federal agency supporting the arts: the National Endowment for the Arts.

Structure and grant-making procedures of the NEA

The NEA is headed by a chairperson appointed by the president, with the advice and consent of the Senate. The term of office is four years, and the appointment may be renewed. Within the endowment the authorizing legislation also establishes a National Council on the Arts. The chairperson of the endowment is also chairperson of the council. Twenty-six additional council members are appointed by the president for six-year terms, once again with the advice and consent of the Senate. Members of the council are to be chosen from among private citizens who are recognized for their knowledge of or expertise in the arts and who have records of distinguished service or have achieved eminence in the arts. They may be practicing artists, civic cultural leaders, members of the museum profession, or others professionally associated with the arts, and are expected to provide a distribution across the major art fields. The chairperson, with the advice of the National Council, is authorized to carry out a program of grants-in-aid to nonprofit arts organizations, to public agencies, and to individual artists for a wide variety of purposes that can be interpreted as supporting the production and distribution of the arts. To carry out its functions the endowment has its own full-time staff who are responsible to the chairperson. It is also authorized, at its own discretion, to utilize outside experts.

Indeed, panels of outside experts play a crucial role in determining who actually gets a grant. Program areas in which the NEA proposes to offer support are determined by the chairperson with the advice of staff and the National Council and are sometimes mandated by Congress. But in sorting through the hundreds of applications to find those most worthy of support in each area, the NEA relies on the advice of its outside experts, or "peer panels." The purpose of this system is to prevent the development of a permanent bureaucracy that could control the flow of funds to the arts and ultimately impose an "official culture" on the nation. There is a panel for every subcategory in each program area. The panels pass their recommendations on to the National Council, which reviews them and presents its recommendations to the chairperson, who makes the final determination. However, during the first 25 years of the NEA's life the tradition had been established that panel decisions about grants were rarely set aside by the chairperson or council.

In Chapter 12 we reviewed the controversy that began in 1989 over NEA support for works that were allegedly pornographic or blasphemous. (It should be noted that support was indirect: NEA grants went not to the artists in question, but to arts organizations, which, in turn, elected to display the offending works.) During that time of troubles, the NEA's peer review process inevitably came in for a good deal of criticism. The Independent Commission, established by Congress in 1989, was specifically directed to examine the endowment's grant-making procedures and its panel system. In its report, the commission did call for substantial reforms. These were intended to strengthen the role of the chairperson, make the National Council more active, broaden the diversity of views represented on panels, and reduce the possibility of conflicts of interest by panel members.

The panel system had been a particular target of the NEA's critics. They asserted that the panels had, in effect, been captured by aesthetic sophisticates who promoted avant-garde art that was both offensive to ordinary Americans and a waste of the taxpayer's money. When Congress adopted legislation in 1990 reauthorizing the NEA for three years, it included provisions intended to ensure that the rate of turnover in panel membership be increased, that panels include knowledgeable laypersons, and that their membership be broadened to reflect a wider range of geographic and ethnic diversity, as well as artistic and cultural points of view. To meet the argument that panels had become self-serving, the reauthorization statute declared that no person who has an application pending before the NEA, or who is employed by an organization with such an application, may serve on the panel before which the application is pending.

The legislation also emphasized that the role of the peer review panels is limited to artistic matters. Recommendations concerning the amount of support to be awarded to each successful applicant are to be made by the National Council and forwarded to the chairperson, who makes all final determinations.

An outline of NEA programs

What do government agencies charged with supporting the arts actually do? To begin answering that question, consider Table 13.3, which summarizes the spending programs of the NEA in 1990. The first 12 programs, dealing basically with the separate artistic "disciplines," are listed alphabetically, from Dance through Visual Arts. The largest single program is Music, which absorbed almost 12 percent of 1990 obligations, followed closely by Media Arts, Museums, Theater, and Dance, to name only the larger categories.

Some of the upper 12 titles may not be self-explanatory.[14] Media Arts includes both film and TV. Under this heading the NEA is able to support independent filmmakers and independent producers of television material, as well as a number of ongoing arts programs on public television, such as "American Playhouse," "Dance in America," and "Live from Lincoln Center." Expansion Arts comprises grants to support the cultural activity of minorities, whether rooted in urban, rural,

---

[14] Program details in the following sections are from National Endowment for the Arts, *1990 Annual Report.*

Table 13.3. *Programs of the National Endowment for the Arts*

Program	Fiscal 1990 obligations (dollars)	Challenge grant commitments/ obligations (dollars)
Dance	9,614,738	1,775,725
Design Arts	4,240,000	869,057
Expansion Arts	6,648,000	476,479
Folk Arts	3,429,100	—
Inter-Arts	4,632,904	2,430,000
Literature	5,007,552	150,000
Media Arts	13,930,780	5,100,000
Museum	12,148,891	5,687,638
Music	16,485,500	4,238,705
Opera-Musical Theater	6,883,915	2,450,000
Theater	10,602,788	3,090,000
Visual Arts	5,899,695	1,050,000
Arts in Education	5,577,496	1,150,000
Local programs	2,812,988	1,925,000
State programs	26,090,100	585,538
Advancement	3,004,483	—
Challenge	268,854	—
Policy, planning, and research	909,966	—
Total funds obligated	138,187,850	30,978,142

Source: National Endowment for the Arts, *1990 Annual Report*, p. 334.

or tribal communities. The Inter-Arts category, as one might guess, includes grants to support interdisciplinary activities, but also supports artists' colonies, presenting organizations (described in Chapter 8), and service organizations that provide services to more than one art form, such as Texas Accountants and Lawyers for the Arts.

The NEA and the states
Larger than any of the "discipline" programs just discussed is the category of NEA aid to the states. As we pointed out at the beginning of this chapter, the endowment has long made grants to the states. Originally they were intended to encourage the development of state arts agencies, but they have continued long after that goal was achieved. In its 1975 reauthorization, Congress specified that the NEA must award not less than 20 percent of its program moneys directly to state arts agencies. Funds are distributed under several headings, of which Basic State Grants are by far the most important. These "no-strings-attached" grants are allotted annually according to a complex formula that is

strongly biased in favor of the least populous states. In 1990 the largest grant ($669,000) went to California, the smallest ($349,000) each to Vermont and Alaska. Although none of these amounts is very large, Alaskans were getting about 28 times as much per capita as Californians. Of course, it might be argued that the public interest in broadening the geographic distribution of the arts justifies this sort of differential. More important, perhaps, is the political motive (to which we have already alluded) of spreading the money around in order to sustain legislative support for the whole enterprise.

We pointed out in Chapter 12 that when the NEA was finally reauthorized in 1990, following a bruising battle with its critics, Congress (against the advice of the Independent Commission) mandated a further increase in the share of funds going to the states: Basic State Grants are to rise to 27.5 percent of NEA program funds by 1993. An additional 7.5 percent is to be allocated competitively to state and local programs to expand access to the arts in rural areas and inner-city neighborhoods. Thus, the mandated share going to the states and localities now rises to 35 percent. This substantial policy change came about not as a result of careful planning or lengthy deliberation, but rather because it was part of the price that congressional supporters of the NEA had to pay for the votes needed to rescue the endowment in its moment of peril. The outcome may well be a reduction in total government support for the arts, since many hard-pressed states will be tempted to substitute the newly available NEA funds for moneys they would otherwise have raised on their own.

An NEA program in detail: support for theater

To convey a better sense of the scope and organization of the major NEA programs, we look at one of the less complicated ones in detail. Table 13.4 breaks down the theater program into its components. Like every other grant-making institution (whether public or private), the NEA avoids giving its money away at random by setting up more or less well-defined categories under which it will entertain requests for support. The theater program is organized into four major categories containing a total of 11 grant headings. For each of the four categories, or their subdivisions, there is an advisory panel, made up of private citizens with professional expertise in the relevant fields. These peer review panels screen all grant applications and make recommendations for funding, in a process described earlier in this chapter.

In 1990, under its Theater program, the NEA made a total of 306 grants with an aggregate value of $10.6 million. Grants to Professional Theater Companies were by far the largest category, amounting to $7.8

Table 13.4. *Theater program of the National Endowment for the Arts, 1990*

	Number of grants	Program funds (dollars)
Professional theater companies	214	7,838,000
National resources		
Professional theater training	9	225,000
Professional theater presenters	10	450,000
Services to the field	20	662,345
Artistic advancement		
Ongoing ensembles	3	309,000
Special projects	12	314,443
Fellowships to individuals		
Playwrights	18	300,000
Directors	1[a]	150,000
Distinguished theater artists	4	100,000
Stage designers	1[a]	150,000
Mimes and solo performance artists	14	104,000
Total	306	10,602,788

[a]Grant to Theatre Communications Group to distribute individual fellowships of $15,000 each.
Source: National Endowment for the Arts, *1990 Annual Report*, pp. 249–67.

million, or 74 percent of the total. Most of these were either for general support of production expenses or to support the compensation of artists during that season. Although the total may sound large, it covered 214 awards, so the amount per grantee was typically small, never more than a minor fraction of a company's expenses. Far less imposing in magnitude was the program of grants to individuals. Fellowships to individual artists, including the program categories of Playwrights, Directors, Mimes and Solo Performing Artists, Distinguished Theater Artists, and Stage Designers, totaled only $804,000, of which the playwrights themselves, the artists without whom there would *be* no contemporary theater, received only $300,000, or 2.8 percent of the Theater program total. However, the NEA does make additional funds available for creative purposes. Under the heading of Artistic Advancement, the Special Projects program includes grants to theatrical companies for specific new plays or productions. (We return to the question of grants to institutions versus those to individual artists later in this chapter.) Another program under Artistic Advancement supports efforts by existing theater companies to develop or strengthen resident ensembles of actors and directors. Its rationale is the belief that ongoing ensembles produce better work than can be achieved when staffing has to start over from scratch with each new production. Finally, three programs are grouped under the heading of National Resources: Professional Theater Training supports salaries paid to master teachers at top-flight schools of theater arts; Professional Theater Presenters provides funds to presenting organizations to carry performances to areas that are underserved or to provide aesthetic diversity in areas where performance opportunities already exist; and Services to the Field makes grants to support publications in the field of nonprofit theater and to help organizations, such as the Theatre Communications Group, that provide technical assistance and information services to the field on a national scale.

What are matching grants?

So-called matching grants play an important role in government support for the arts. These are grants given with the stipulation that the beneficiary must match the grant amount out of other resources at some specific ratio. For example, except in the case of grants to individual artists, the NEA is forbidden by its enabling legislation to pay more than 50 percent of the cost of any project that it supports. Since the recipient institution must put up at least one dollar of its own money for each dollar received, the NEA can say that its program grants to institutions are "matched at least dollar-for-dollar."[15] Mark Schuster, however, argues that this form of government aid should be called "cofinancing" rather than matching grants, since the ratio of beneficiary's funds to grant funds is left open: it can be one to one or any higher ratio.[16]

Schuster explains that cofinancing was built into the NEA's rules from the beginning, primarily for political reasons. First, there was the fear that government funding might lead to government control. Since cofinancing would promote diversity in funding sources, it would allay that fear. Second, there was concern that government aid would supplant private funding. Cofinancing would help to prevent such substitution. Finally, some feared that federal support programs could become pro-

---

[15] *1990 Annual Report,* p. 29.
[16] J. Mark Davidson Schuster, "Government Leverage of Private Support: Matching Grants and the Problem with 'New Money,' " in Margaret Jane Wyszomirski and Pat Clubb, eds., *The Cost of Culture* (New York: American Council for the Arts, 1989), pp. 63–97, cited at 64.

hibitively costly unless a strict limit was placed on the government's share. Most states have adopted cofinancing for the same reasons.[17]

The right-hand column of Table 13.3 lists the commitments and obligations of the NEA in 1990 in their Challenge Grant program. These, in Schuster's lexicon, are true matching grants. For each dollar received from a challenge grant, the beneficiary must put up at least three dollars in *new* nonfederal contributions. Like other NEA grants, each challenge grant is made for a specific project, but the time period for the project is ordinarily several years rather than a single year, since the grants are intended to encourage the recipient institutions to do some long-run financial planning. The program was introduced in the hope of stimulating, or "leveraging," private support for the arts. Whether it succeeds in doing that depends on how successfully the government can enforce the requirement that "new" money be truly new. We return to that difficult question later. But whether or not challenge grants are economically successful, the program became politically popular during the Reagan years because it was consistent with that administration's emphasis on public–private partnerships. Great Britain, too, is experimenting with a type of challenge grant in the hope of attracting more private support to the arts.[18] (See the earlier discussion of European arts funding policies in Chapter 12.)

A third form of grant identified by Schuster is the "reverse matching grant."[19] Under this arrangement, the government offers to match any *increase* in donations to the arts by the private sector. It is a *reverse* match because instead of the government putting up the money and challenging the private donor to respond, the government offers in advance to match any new donation from the private sector. Also reversed is control over selection of the beneficiary. In the case of a challenge grant, the *government* selects the beneficiary and the beneficiary then finds donors. With a reverse matching grant, the *donor* chooses the beneficiary, thus automatically triggering a grant to that institution. The government agency gives up its right of selection.

The NEA has not employed reverse matching grants. They were tried, however, in the Commonwealth of Massachusetts, where Schuster studied their impact. He found that there were serious difficulties in defining and enforcing the requirement that the funds to be matched must be *new* money. Unfortunately, a reverse matching program creates a strong

---

[17] Ibid.
[18] For a description of the British initiatives, see Schuster, "Government Leverage of Private Support," p. 66.
[19] Ibid., pp. 66–67.

incentive for beneficiaries to contrive with donors to find ways of making "old" money appear to be "new." For example, suppose Corporation A had been giving $10,000 per year to the local symphony and Corporation B the same amount to the local opera. Both annual contributions were old money and would not qualify for a reverse match. But simply by exchanging beneficiaries, the two corporations could make their donations grant eligible, thus greatly increasing the benefits to both arts companies at no cost to the donors. The possible forms of such practices are too numerous to be listed here. The point is that to verify the validity of new money (and this is true for challenge grants as well as for reverse matching grants), would require much more detailed financial reporting by beneficiaries and oversight by granting agencies than is currently the practice in the United States.[20]

A standard economic rationale for matching grants in the field of art and culture is that they stimulate support for the arts from *non*governmental sources. But as the preceding discussion indicates, unless we can verify that new money is truly new, we really cannot be sure such grants do that. However, an unspoken political rationale may also be important. Government arts agencies find that matching grant programs appeal strongly to legislators when appropriations are under discussion. Schuster speculates that perhaps "the important leverage provided by matching grants lies less in the degree to which it leverages new *private* support than in its ability to leverage new *government* support for the arts."[21]

Should subsidies go to the buyer instead of the seller?

In the preceding discussion it was taken for granted that arts subsidies are paid to the *supplier* of the art, whether that be an orchestra supplying concerts, a theater producing plays, a museum displaying the fine arts, or an artist making a painting or a sculpture. In theory there is an alternative way of providing support for the arts: one could pay subsidies not to suppliers but to their potential audience. For example, instead of giving direct assistance to local performing arts enterprises, a city could issue vouchers to citizens, good for one admission to an arts performance of their own choice. Institutions accepting such vouchers in payment would be reimbursed by the city.

Such demand-side subsidies would seem to be an appropriate instrument to fulfill several of the purposes for which arts subsidies are intended and might be superior in some respects to the equivalent supply-

[20] Ibid., pp. 74–75.
[21] Ibid., p. 81.

side payments. For example, if the object is to encourage participation by those for whom lack of income is a barrier to attendance, vouchers could be distributed exclusively to those with low income. The supply-side equivalent would be a subsidy to performing arts companies conditioned on their willingness to offer some tickets at very low prices. But under that arrangement there can be no assurance that the subsidized tickets are going only to persons with low income. In fact, since box office personnel cannot be asked to apply an income test, it is probable that many of them would be purchased by regular attenders in search of a bargain. An additional advantage of the voucher scheme is that it would allow more consumer choice, because the vouchers would probably be acceptable at more venues than could be reached by equivalent supply-side subsidies. For that reason, economists generally argue that, in theory, vouchers produce more consumer utility per dollar of expenditure than do subsidies designed to lower the price of a particular good.

If we can assume (as seems reasonable) that vouchers would pay for tickets that would not otherwise be sold, then they can also be seen as a way of increasing the flow of unrestricted funds to arts organizations, in much the same way as would a no-strings-attached, supply-side grant for general operating support. In that role they would have the advantage (if one so regards it) of allowing consumer choice instead of bureaucratic decision to determine who gets the subsidy.

With so much to be said in their favor, why haven't vouchers been used more widely? Part of the answer may be that vouchers are an idea without a constituency. Arts company fund-raisers no doubt prefer to work for grants earmarked for their own institution rather than for a voucher program whose benefits might go elsewhere, while public officials dispensing funds for the arts may prefer to have a handle on the money they give away, such as supply-side subsidies provide them. Artists may be uncomfortable with what could be perceived as the need to "pander" to the tastes of voucher recipients in order to secure revenues. Better, perhaps, to seek to persuade peer review panels of the worthiness of one's art.

In addition, vouchers for the arts suffer from several practical flaws. First, if one had to conduct a means test for each potential recipient of an arts voucher, administrative costs would be very high in relation to the value of the thing to be distributed. (That would not be true in most other proposed voucher schemes, for example, using them to subsidize housing for those with low incomes.) An even more serious drawback is the difficulty of targeting the benefits. How could the authorities prevent the recipient of a voucher from selling it to a third party whom they had no desire to assist? A partial solution to these difficulties would be to distribute vouchers to some easily identifiable group, such as students, many of whom fit the type arts subsidies are intended to help and who could be required to identify themselves in order to use the voucher at the box office. Indeed, half-price tickets for students are a fairly common practice in the performing arts and for admission to museums. But these are not subsidized by the public sector.

An experimental voucher program operated in Minneapolis/St. Paul from the mid 1970s to the early 1980s. The Twin Cities Metropolitan Arts Alliance, with funding from several local foundations, offered a voucher program to arts organizations. Voucher recipients included individuals on welfare, union members, and school teachers, representing, respectively, low-income families, a group with relatively low exposure to the arts, and a group influential in shaping tastes. The overall goal was to build audiences, with some expectation that small and medium-size organizations would reap disproportionately larger benefits. From September 1, 1975, to August 31, 1980, some 100 arts organizations redeemed 198,179 vouchers for a total of $525,127. However, 5 relatively large organizations – including the Guthrie Theater, Minnesota Orchestra, and Children's Theater Company – accounted for $347,498, or about two-thirds of this total. Each of the other 95 groups received, on average, slightly more than $300 per year from the program, so it is not surprising that cessation of foundation funding did not result in a widespread outcry for continuation.[22]

Patterns of state aid

In many respects, state arts agencies operate in the same way as the NEA does. Almost all employ peer review panels in determining who shall receive grants, and most require, as the NEA does, that their grants to institutions be matched at least one-for-one by funds from other sources. The distribution of support among disciplines is not greatly different from that of the NEA (which was shown in Table 13.3). In 1986, Music topped the list, receiving 17.3 percent of state grant dollars, followed by Visual Arts (13.6 percent), Theater (12.6 percent), Dance (8.6 percent), and Opera-Musical Theater (3.9 percent).[23] Like the NEA, the states give relatively little money *directly* to artists. Indeed,

[22] This information is gleaned from numerous unpublished sources, including funding proposals, unbound program descriptions, and related materials constituting the archives of the Twin Cities Metropolitan Arts Alliance and currently held by the Center for Nonprofit Management of the University of Saint Thomas.

[23] *The Arts in America: A Report to the President and to the Congress* (Washington, D.C.: National Endowment for the Arts, 1988), p. 451.

some states are specifically forbidden to make such awards. In 1987 only 1 percent of state art funds were so allocated.[24] (Of course, individual artists may receive state aid *indirectly* via supported institutions.) Again like the NEA, the state arts agencies increasingly emphasize what has come to be called "multiculturalism," in other words, support for the cultural activity of diverse minority groups. Data are not yet available, however, on the dollar amount of such support.

In a careful comparison of state and federal funding for the arts, Paul DiMaggio confirmed the basic similarity in their spending patterns among disciplines. The one marked difference he found was that state arts agencies allocated a much smaller share to the media arts – only 4.7 percent, as compared with 10.9 percent for the NEA.[25] This difference is logical enough, when one recognizes that a large proportion of mass media productions are intended for a nationwide rather than a statewide audience.

Unlike the NEA, which is limited by law to making grants for specific "projects and productions," state agencies can, and do, offer general operating support to arts institutions. Indeed, such grants, which accounted for 39 percent of all funds awarded in 1986, are by far the largest single category of state aid.[26] The justification for such spending is usually that the state wants to underwrite artistic excellence when that is demonstrably present within its borders. To that end, operating support grants are often specifically limited to a defined group of "major" institutions, which can be assumed already to have achieved excellence. But this form of aid persists not only because of the excellence of its beneficiaries, but also because major museums, symphony orchestras, and ballet and opera companies have political and financial heavy hitters on their boards of directors who can put their influence behind institutional pleas for state support. As we shall see in the next section, local arts agencies, too, are important providers of general operating support to resident arts institutions.

It is ironic that although the states have been *willing* to provide general operating support, the year-to-year instability in the level of individual state appropriations, described earlier in this chapter, makes the states unreliable as financial partners. Writing in 1990, even before some of

[24] *The State of the State Arts Agencies, 1989* (Washington, D.C.: National Assembly of State Arts Agencies, 1989), p. 22.
[25] Paul J. DiMaggio, "Decentralization of Arts Funding from the Federal Government to the States," in Stephen Benedict, ed., *Public Money and the Muse* (New York: Norton, for The American Assembly of Columbia University, pp. 216–52, 1991), cited at 237.
[26] *The Arts in America*, p. 447.

the sharpest cuts in state funding, Netzer concluded that "this record of instability greatly limits the potential role of the state government as a supplier of baseline operating funds."[27]

Local arts agencies

In a country as large and decentralized as the United States, containing more than 19,000 municipalities, the number of local arts agencies can only be estimated, and the estimates vary from 1,500 to more than 2,500.[28] Unlike their counterparts at the state level, local arts councils are not necessarily public entities. In many cities they are independent, private, not-for-profit organizations. Surveys indicate that private agencies outnumber public ones by almost three to one but that larger cities are more likely to have the public type.[29] In recent years, local arts agencies may well have been the fastest growing source of public support for the arts.

Unfortunately, the large number of local arts agencies (LAAs) and the fact that many of them are small and understaffed has made it impossible even for their own service organization to collect data on the aggregate level of support they offer to the arts.[30] Thus, in Table 13.1 the figure for local government assistance to the arts is clearly flagged as an estimate. LAAs grew up largely as a result of local initiative. Either the city government itself or else private citizens already involved in the affairs of the city's arts institutions saw a need for joint action to support and expand local cultural activity. Americans have always been great civic "boosters." From the 1960s onward, boosterism took up the cause of culture. Not only was art a good thing in itself, but it was also said to be good for the local economy, a strong argument in the minds of local boosters. (See further discussion of this point in Chapter 15.)

What local arts agencies do

The next thing to be said about LAAs is that they are *not* simply small-scale replicas of either the NEA or the state arts agencies. The NEA and the state agencies can be described as grant-making entities, pure and simple. LAAs are much less easily characterized. They perform

---

[27] Netzer, "Cultural Policy in an Era of Budgetary Stringency," p. 11.
[28] *The Arts in America,* p. 391.
[29] Ibid., p. 396.
[30] In 1990, the National Assembly of Local Arts Agencies (Washington, D.C.) published the *State of the Field Report,* containing the results of surveys conducted in 1987 and 1989. Although the surveys provided much useful information, coverage was not sufficient to support an estimate of the aggregate level of LAA activity.

Table 13.5. *Revenue sources of local arts agencies, 1991*

	Private local agencies (percent)	Public local agencies (percent)
Public funding	38	87
Earned income	38	8
Private contributions, total	24	5
Corporations	10	N.A.
Foundations	6	N.A.
Individuals	5	N.A.
Other	3	N.A.

Source: National Assembly of Local Arts Agencies, from a statistical survey of local arts agency finances in fiscal year 1991.

many and diverse functions and not the same functions in every place. Grant making, though reportedly on the rise, is not their only job.

In *The Arts in America,* the NEA summarizes the activities of local arts agencies in these words:

> LAAs are primarily concerned with creating opportunities for artistry to occur. . . . Their activities often involve organizing and sponsoring festivals which celebrate and showcase the art and artists of the community; providing exhibition spaces and distribution outlets for art; commissioning works of art; presenting attractions from outside the community not otherwise available; providing housing for creative events, whether in the concert hall or studio; and working to ensure that the full spectrum of the community's cultural diversity is reflected in the artistic opportunities available to its residents.[31]

Not surprisingly, the revenue sources of private LAAs differ systematically from those of the legally "public" group. The data in Table 13.5, based on a sample survey of 205 local agencies, show that the latter obtain 87 percent of their revenue from public sources, compared with only 38 percent for the former. Private contributions and earned income make up the other 62 percent of private agency revenue. That they obtain 10 percent of their total funding from corporations suggests that they have been reasonably successful in appealing to the local business sector.

[31] *The Arts in America,* p. 394.

Supporting major cultural institutions

The financial arrangements under which localities support the construction or operation of major cultural facilities are so various that they defy easy generalizations. In the larger cities, the city or the county government sometimes owns the major performing arts facilities. Los Angeles County, for example, owns the Hollywood Bowl, which it leases to the Los Angeles Philharmonic. The county's Parks and Recreation Department pays maintenance costs. Los Angeles County also provides direct operating support to the County Museum of Art and the Music Center, which received $11.3 million and $7.8 million, respectively, in 1988.[32] Under a recently adopted master plan, the city of Dallas has established a downtown Arts District. For institutions building new facilities there, the city will pay 75 percent of land costs and 60 percent of the cost of construction, as well as providing maintenance and a degree of ongoing operational support. Ownership of facilities so constructed rests with the city. The Dallas Museum of Art and the much acclaimed new Morton H. Meyerson Symphony Center have already been completed under this plan.[33]

In Chicago major institutions built on parkland receive general operating support from the Chicago Park District, an agency with independent taxing powers. Such support amounted to $24.9 million in 1987.[34] In the same year New York City's Department of Cultural Affairs had an operating budget of $72 million, larger than that of any state art agency and second in size only to the NEA's. Most of that fund was spent on operating support for 32 cultural institutions that occupy city-owned land. In addition, the city provided $51.8 million under its capital budget to support construction by cultural institutions.[35]

On a per capita basis, the direct expenditures by these cities to support art and culture are far greater than those of either the states or the federal government. The highest state expenditure in 1990 was Hawaii's $7.84 per capita, followed by New York State at $3.33. As Table 13.1 shows, the federal government's direct outlays in 1991 were only about $1.25 per person. Yet New York City's Department of Cultural Affairs spends approximately $10.00 per capita, without including capital ex-

---

[32] Mary Berryman Agard and June Spencer, *50 Cities, Local Government and the Arts* (Madison, Wis.: Opinion Research Associates, 1987), p. 79.

[33] Ibid., pp. 43–44.

[34] Ibid., p. 66.

[35] Ibid., p. 85. The most complete description of New York City's extensive programs in support of art and culture can be found in *Funding for Culture: The Cultural Policy of the City of New York,* a report to the mayor by the Mayor's Advisory Commission for Cultural Affairs, June 1983.

penditures, and Chicago, Philadelphia, and Los Angeles, when support from all city sources is counted, may spend that much, as well.

In many cities, United Arts Funds have sprung up, independent of, but acting in parallel with, the local arts agencies. These are private-sector fund-raising groups, similar to the charitable-sector funds known as the United Way, but focusing exclusively on art and culture. The American Council for the Arts reported that in 1986, 49 United Arts Funds raised a total of $56 million, of which 52 percent came from business and 30 percent from individual contributions. Eighty percent of the money was distributed in the form of general operating support to local arts institutions, such as symphonies, theaters, opera and dance companies, and museums.[36]

Issues in public policy

Government support for the arts obviously raises numerous issues of public policy. Many of them have already been taken up in this chapter, or in Chapters 11 and 12, but three of the most persistent remain to be discussed. They can be described as aid to established companies versus geographic spread, elitism versus populism, and aid to institutions versus aid to individual artists. As we shall see, these issues are interrelated.

Aid to established companies versus geographic spread

Since the NEA and the state arts agencies were first established, there has been a degree of competition for funds among potential benefi-ciaries. One manifestation of this was the fact that in the early years the large, "established" institutions – a group that would include the major museums, symphony orchestras, and opera, ballet, and theater companies – did not want to see arts appropriations spread among "new-comers" to the arts scene. The major institutions and their supporters believed that they were entitled to the lion's share of government aid both because they were artistically more worthy than the "Johnny-come-latelies" and because it was they who had organized the lobbying cam-paigns that produced federal and state funding in the first place.

Netzer has shown that this contest was played out dramatically in New York State during the 1970s.[37] In fiscal year 1970, the New York State Council on the Arts received an appropriation of $2.3 million. A quan-tum leap to $20.1 million occurred in the next year. The state's major cultural institutions had argued for the increase as essential to help them

---

[36] *The Arts in America*, p. 407.
[37] Netzer, *The Subsidized Muse*, pp. 81–85.

cover widening financial deficits. The new legislation for the first time specifically authorized NYSCA to provide general operating support to its beneficiaries, and most of the additional money was spent for that purpose.

A second quantum leap occurred between fiscal 1974 and 1975, when the council's appropriation was increased from $16.4 million to $35.6 million. Again, the state's major cultural institutions argued strongly for the increase on the basis of their large "earnings gap." In an attempt to ensure that the "majors" would continue to get their share, the state legislature included a requirement that at least 50 percent of NYSCA support go to "primary" organizations. But those who favored greater geographic dispersion of funds also came away with something: the legislation required that NYSCA spend at least 75 cents per capita in each of the state's counties.

And in the next year, the council, which had initially drawn up a list of 72 primary organizations, expanded the number to 117. Netzer reports that this brought "vigorous protests from the arts establishment," which "felt betrayed by their own creature."[38] Perhaps they have subsequently learned to accept the geographic dispersion of arts funds as the political price paid for maintaining legislative support; for experience tells us that under the U.S. political system, it is very difficult to focus subsidies narrowly on the most deserving. To get votes for appropriations one has to spread the benefits around to some who may be less worthy. NYSCA has stronger support in the New York state legislature because every one of the state's 62 counties gets its little share. Similarly, the NEA benefits politically from spreading its largesse to every state and to most congressional districts. Indeed, DiMaggio argues that state and federal arts funding patterns are similar (as was shown earlier in this chapter), precisely *because* the political demands and constraints faced by funding agencies are similar at both levels of government.[39]

Elitism versus populism

The opposition of established arts companies to the spread of arts funding among relative newcomers is an aspect of the larger debate of elitism versus populism, always latent in U.S. cultural discourse. As Margaret Wyszomirski points out, the issue rose to the surface in 1977, at the beginning of the Carter administration.[40] Major arts institutions, especially in New York City, became convinced that the NEA, under

[38] Ibid., p. 87.

[39] DiMaggio, "Decentralization," pp. 228–29, 251.

[40] Margaret Wyszomirski, "Controversies in Arts Policymaking," in Kevin V. Mulcahy and C. Richard Swaim, eds., *Public Policy and the Arts* (Boulder, Colo.: Westview Press, 1982), pp. 12–15.

its newly appointed Chairman Livingston Biddle, was moving toward a more populist position, and that consequently their share of NEA funding was threatened. In this debate, to put it in its simplest terms, the elitists are the devotees of the so-called high arts – theater, opera, dance, "serious" or "classical" music, the fine arts, and museums – while populists are more interested in, or at least *also* interested in, folk art, crafts, ethnic and minority art, and nontraditional art. The elitists think of themselves as the defenders of "excellence" and "quality." The populists are advocates for artistic "pluralism" and "democratic" access to the arts. When the debate grows heated, the language becomes more colorful: elitists call populists "basket weavers" (a dismissive reference to their fondness for crafts and folk art), while populists accuse elitists of "snobbism" (because of their dismissive attitude toward the demonstrably more popular forms of culture). The content of the debate is summarized (and somewhat oversimplified) in the following list of opposing values, tendencies, or positions.

Elitists	*versus*	Populists
Aristocratic		Democratic
High art		Popular art
Artistic excellence		Equality of access
Established companies		Artistic pluralism
"Snobbism"		"Basket weaving"

In the background lies an enduring theme of U.S. history: the political contest between rural interests (originally, nineteenth-century farmers) and the interests of the economically dominant "big cities" of the Northeast (originally, nineteenth-century railroad magnates, financiers, monopolists). In that tradition, big cities were seen as centers of sophistication, sin, and corruption, while the rural United States was the "heartland," the home of democratic simplicity and virtue. Even today these perceptions, which were first voiced almost two hundred years ago, retain their power to shape our attitudes. Elitists in the arts must carry the burden of sin and corruption associated with the big city, while populists continue to bathe in the pure light of virtue emanating from our mythical rural origins.

When Ronald Reagan became president in 1981, observers of the official arts scene wondered whether an avowedly conservative administration would reassert elitist values at NEA after what was thought to have been a modest shift toward populism during the Carter years.[41] President Reagan did appoint several conservatives from the art world

---

[41] See, e.g., Robert Pear, "Reagan's Arts Chairman Brings Subtle Changes to the Endowment," *New York Times* (April 10, 1983).

to the National Council on the Arts, which advises the NEA, and they did express what might be called elitist views. But the NEA steered more or less the same course as before. If anything, the new emphasis on "multiculturalism" meant spending even more money on what were essentially "populist" undertakings.

In fact, as Robert Pear argued in the *New York Times,* the elitist–populist debate poses a particular problem for political conservatives in the United States. Most of that group see the free market as the ideal mechanism for governing the economy because they believe it faithfully records the preferences of consumers, and consumers ought to be sovereign. But the free market makes it clear that the vast majority of consumers want popular art, not high art. To subsidize high art therefore is to reject the conservative presumption in favor of market outcomes.[42]

Perhaps this philosophical dilemma made it difficult for conservatives under Reagan to set the NEA on a more elitist course. As Wyszomirski points out, in the debate between elitists and populists, the NEA takes an officially neutral stance.[43] It could hardly do otherwise, since it is committed both to supporting excellence (the principal demand of the elitists) and to striving for democratic pluralism and access (in accordance with populist values). Neither of those competing ends is going to be given up. The practical decision as to how much money is allotted for each of them is ultimately determined by the politics of funding.

Grants to institutions versus grants to individual artists

Another persistent policy issue in the arts is the question of aid to institutions versus aid to individual artists. It was shown earlier in this chapter that an overwhelmingly large share of funds in the NEA's theater program goes to arts organizations rather than to individual creators. That pattern is typical of government support for the arts in the United States and can probably be explained by a combination of the following factors. First, it is less expensive administratively to give money away in large lots than in small, and one cannot give a really large sum to an individual artist. Second, donors have confidence in the ability of established arts organizations to spend money productively; they are less confident of individual artists. Third, they consider grants to individual artists to be politically risky. One can never be sure that the artist will not produce something that is politically embarrassing. It might seem that all three of these objections could be overcome by making a substantial grant to an intermediary institution, such as an

---

[42] Ibid.
[43] Wyszomirski, "Controversies in Arts Policymaking," p. 14.

established art gallery, which in turn, would make subgrants to individual artists of its own choosing. But that was the route by which NEA funds went to allegedly offensive photography exhibits in the late 1980s, and we have seen that the strategy of indirect support provided no effective political cover in that famous controversy.

So the preference for organizations over individuals is largely explained by the principle of "safety first." That is unfortunate, since shaking people up, and even disturbing the peace, is one of the acknowledged functions of art. But especially in the aftermath of Senator Helms's attack on the NEA for having supported art that was allegedly blasphemous or pornographic (see the discussion in Chapter 12), an increase in the share of NEA funds going to individual artists seems extremely unlikely.

Indeed, the NEA–Helms controversy raised a fourth policy issue that is likely to persist in coming years: should the NEA or state/local arts agencies explicitly limit their awards to projects that pass some official test of decency? This question, too, can be related to the elitist–populist debate. Supporters of the Helms position argued that the works they found pornographic were the products of an oversophisticated, decadent, elitist, big-city art world that had rejected the wholesome values of ordinary U.S. citizens. The theme of rural innocence and virtue in contest with urban sin and corruption is unfortunately alive and well in U.S. politics.

PART V

Art, economy, and society

14

The arts as a profession:
education, training, and employment

The "starving artist" is one of the enduring stereotypes of our culture. Are artists really in such dire straits? If so, why would anyone choose to become an artist? In this chapter, we will seek to determine whether and to what extent the stereotype has validity; we will try to understand what motivates artists to pursue their chosen professions; and we will gain some insights into how the arts labor market works. These will not be simple tasks. To offer just one example, it is not always clear exactly who is an artist and who is not.[1] We take up this matter in the next section, where we also examine some of the facts about artists. We will then develop some economic concepts to help in understanding these facts. Employing these concepts, we will next analyze specific "labor markets" in the arts. Finally, we will be able to use this framework and applications to consider merits and shortcomings of possible intervention strategies in arts labor markets.

A statistical description of artists

Those professions that the Bureau of the Census classifies as artists are listed in Table 14.1. It should be noted that these definitions do not distinguish between commercial artists and other artists, or between whether artists' employers are profit-making or not-for-profit. The dancer category may include both Las Vegas showgirls and members of the Zenon company in Minneapolis. Furthermore, this classification

---

[1] See, e.g., Gregory Wassall, Neil Alper, and Rebecca Davison, *Art Work: Artists in the New England Labor Market* (Cambridge, Mass.: New England Foundation for the Arts, 1983).

Table 14.1. *Census definitions of artists*

Actors and directors, including individuals associated with the production and
   performance of dramatic works for stage, motion pictures, and the
   broadcasting media
Architects, including those involved with building and landscape architecture
Authors, self explanatory
Dancers, self explanatory
Designers, including decorators and window dressers
Musicians and composers
Painters, sculptors, craft artists, and printmakers, intended to be broadly
   representative of creative visual artists
Photographers, including video camera operators
Radio and television announcers
Teachers of art, drama, and music in higher education
Other artists

---

scheme is broader than that typically used by scholars in the field.[2]
Individuals are placed in categories in accordance with their own reports
of income sources during the reporting period.[3] Hence, the actor who
is supporting herself by working as a bartender between performing
engagements will be classified in census and employment statistics as a
working bartender rather than an unemployed actor.

Two of the factors that should influence career choice – employment
prospects and earnings – are indicated in Tables 14.2 and 14.3. The first
of these shows what has happened to employment and unemployment
among artists over much of the decade of the 1980s. The total number
of artists expanded from about 1.3 million in 1983 to over 1.6 million
in 1989, an average annual increase of about 3.7 percent. Designers and
architects – two professions not included among the arts categories covered in this book – accounted for much of this growth. More relevant
to our interests is the growth among selected categories of performing
and visual artists. The average annual growth rate among actors and
directors was 7.1 percent, an expansion of some 36,000 people over the

---

[2] For example, Heilbrun selected only actors and directors, dancers, musicians
   and composers, and painters and sculptors. See James Heilbrun, "Growth and
   Geographic Distribution of the Arts in the U.S.," in D. V. Shaw et al., eds.,
   Artists and Cultural Consumers (Akron, Ohio: Association for Cultural Economics, 1987), pp. 24–35.
[3] The problems with this approach and an alternative technique have been discussed in Gregory Wassall and Neil Alper, "Occupational Characteristics of
   Artists: A Statistical Analysis," *Journal of Cultural Economics,* 9, no. 1 (June
   1985): 13–34.

Table 14.2. *Artist labor force and unemployment, 1983–89*

Occupation	1983	1984	1985	1986	1987	1988	1989
All artists							
(no. in thousands)	1,301	1,418	1,482	1,500	1,558	1,557	1,617
Unemployment rate							
(percent)	6.0	4.7	5.0	4.1	3.5	2.9	2.8
Actors/directors	71	78	91	93	98	112	107
Unemployment rate	15.7	13.3	15.4	7.7	9.8	10.6	10.4
Announcers	41	59	54	58	62	56	53
Unemployment rate	6.7	6.2	5.3	5.9	4.7	6.4	2.9
Architects	108	109	133	135	136	145	161
Unemployment rate	4.3	1.8	2.2	1.9	1.0	1.2	2.4
Authors	64	72	71	77	86	83	83
Unemployment rate	2.5	1.4	1.4	2.6	0.8	0.9	1.4
Dancers	12	14	17	18	16	17	17
Unemployment rate	—[a]	—	—	—	—	—	—
Designers	415	466	504	504	546	525	548
Unemployment rate	5.2	3.9	3.9	4.0	2.7	2.8	2.5
Musicians/composers	170	174	163	171	177	158	174
Unemployment rate	8.6	7.3	6.5	3.9	4.7	4.6	2.4
Painters/sculptors/etc.	192	220	207	194	198	219	232
Unemployment rate	3.3	3.5	3.2	2.7	3.4	2.0	1.3
Photographers	119	128	134	131	131	121	114
Unemployment rate	5.0	3.9	3.5	2.7	4.0	3.6	1.9
Teachers of art/etc.	43	41	42	43	41	49	45
Unemployment rate	2.2	2.4	2.4	1.9	1.6	2.7	0.7
Other artists	66	57	66	76	67	72	83
Unemployment rate	7.1	5.8	5.6	7.8	4.5	2.1	2.3

[a]Data base is too small for reliable estimates.
Source: National Endowment for the Arts, Research Division Note 33, September 24, 1990.

period covered, while the number of dancers and choreographers grew by 6 percent annually. Despite the relatively high growth rate, this latter group contributed an increase of only 5,000 artists. The musician category rose by 4,000 over the period, but this amounted to less than a 1 percent average annual increase. It is interesting to note that the highest unemployment rates over the period were found in the actor and musician categories, two occupations with relatively high rates of union membership. We will return to this issue later.

Table 14.3 presents median earnings for artists by sex in 1979. A comparison of the last two rows shows that median earnings of all artists were only about 64 percent of the earnings of all professional workers.

Table 14.3. *Artist median earnings by sex, 1979 (dollars)*

Occupation	Total	Men	Women
Actors/directors	12,564	14,397	9,396
Announcers	8,144	8,639	6,377
Architects	19,220	20,123	10,859
Authors	6,956	10,337	4,625
Dancers/choreographers	5,404	7,576	4,976
Designers	10,656	16,979	6,232
Musicians/composers	5,561	7,074	3,186
Painters/sculptors/etc.	8,576	12,091	5,773
Photographers	10,085	12,116	5,217
Teachers	11,787	16,901	6,906
Other artists	7,218	9,521	4,745
All artists	9,803	13,455	5,713
Professional/technical workers	15,206	19,189	10,581

Source: National Endowment for the Arts, "Artists Real Earnings Decline 37 Percent in the 1970s," Research Division Note 10, March 5, 1985.

Some performing artists – dancers and musicians – fared even less well, earning about a third as much as all professional workers. Only architects' earnings exceeded those of all professional workers. Perhaps not surprisingly, female artists earn less than their male counterparts; the earnings of female artists as a whole were approximately 42 percent of the earnings of male artists. In comparison among all professional and technical workers, women earned about 55 percent as much as men. We would offer the conjecture that the nature of the arts is consistent with part-time work, and to the extent that women are more likely to engage in part-time work than men, their annual earnings will be lower.

Within any group of workers, including artists, we would normally expect that more highly educated individuals would earn higher incomes. A recent study by Randall Filer indicates that while this is generally true for the arts, some exceptions exist. Some of Filer's findings are displayed in Table 14.4. Each cell in the table includes two figures. The upper number is total median earnings for *all* artists in the category, including those working part-time and less than year-round; the lower one is median earnings for only full-time, year-round workers. For artists working full-time all year, college graduates earned a median of $15,005, which was about 20 percent higher than the $12,505 earned by high school graduates. Of course, this largely reflects the impact of the architect and designer categories, where a college degree may be regarded as a vital credential for acceptance in the field. However, in those in-

Table 14.4. *Median earnings of artists by education, 1979 (dollars)*

Top number: Total median earnings
Bottom number: Median earnings, full-time, full-year workers

Occupation	Less than high school	High school graduate	Some college	College graduate	Postcollege
Actors/directors	4,045	8,845	10,005	12,505	15,005
	16,005	14,005	15,455	17,820	19,805
Announcers	2,505	7,065	7,105	10,585	13,005
	9,745	10,405	11,160	13,005	18,010
Architects	6,125	12,005	16,005	18,005	20,005
	10,255	17,360	20,005	21,008	22,005
Authors	5,255	6,005	5,115	7,005	8,005
	10,625	11,215	12,255	13,005	14,103
Dancers/	3,345	5,455	4,005	6,005	4,005
choreographers	7,905	10,005	9,525	10,005	—
Designers	5,005	7,505	10,690	12,005	14,005
	9,830	12,770	16,005	16,005	18,005
Musicians/com-	3,505	5,010	4,005	5,145	6,705
posers	9,005	10,005	10,405	11,945	15,005
Painters/sculptors	5,270	8,065	8,005	8,005	7,255
	12,005	12,008	12,170	12,005	12,005
Photographers	5,005	9,885	8,910	10,215	9,740
	12,005	14,005	12,705	13,225	12,010
Teachers	9,303	3,955	2,005	6,505	14,195
	—	19,020	10,710	14,505	19,005
Other artists	4,005	6,330	6,005	8,875	7,598
	9,820	11,045	12,005	13,165	14,290
All artists	4,410	7,505	8,005	10,005	13,755
	10,005	12,505	14,465	15,005	18,505
Professional/	9,885	12,005	12,005	15,005	18,605
technical	13,120	15,005	16,005	19,005	22,905

Source: Randall K. Filer, "Arts and Academe: The Effect of Education on Earnings of Artists," *Journal of Cultural Economics*, 14, no. 2 (December 1990):18.

stances where credentials are relatively less important when compared with talent, education seems less valuable. For example, a college education generated little if any financial reward for painters and sculptors, or for dancers and choreographers. We can summarize the position of artists by noting that the median earnings of artists with a college degree

Table 14.5. *Comparative mean incomes of artists by selected countries*

Category	United States ($–1979)	Norway (NKr–1979)	Canada ($Can–1981)
Actor/director	19,283 (1) [1.00]	99,502 (1) [1.00]	20,299 (1) [1.00]
Author	13,941 (2) [0.72]	89,600 (3) [0.90]	19,269 (2) [0.95]
Photographer	11,575 (3) [0.60]	61,700 (4) [0.62]	16,083 n(3) [0.79]
Painter/sculptor	10,345 (4) [0.54]	45,200 (6) [0.45]	10,665 (5) [0.53]
Musician/composer	8,280 (5) [0.43]	90,139 (2) [0.91]	12,978 (4) [0.64]
Dancer/choreographer	7,167 (6) [0.37]	57,585 (5) [0.58]	10,159 (6) [0.50]
Coefficient of variation (std. dev./mean)	.37	.30	.29

Notes: Numbers in parentheses indicate income rank among artists in nation. Numbers in brackets indicate ratio of income within category to income of highest paid category in a nation.
Sources: National Endowment for the Arts, "Artists Real Earnings Decline 37 Percent in the 1970s," Research Division note 10, March 5, 1985, p. 3. Statistisk Sentralbyrå, *Kulturstatistikk 1982* (Oslo: Kongsvinger, 1982), table 70, p. 101; Canada Council, *Profile of Arts Employment 1981*, Working Document 525, January 15, 1984, table 24, pp. 65–67.

are no higher than the earnings of all professional workers who have only a high school diploma.

International comparisons

We can gain additional understanding by comparing data for U.S. artists and selected counterparts elsewhere. For this purpose Table 14.5 uses the census job definitions and includes data for Canada and Norway. Although the Canadian and Norwegian data have been adjusted to correspond more closely to the U.S. categories, differences in definitions dictate that the reader use caution in interpreting the comparative statistics. However, some items are worth noting.

In each instance, the actor and director category represents the highest paid group of artists. This very likely reflects the popularity of movies, television, and theater, the high salaries of "superstars" in this category, and the relative strength of unions representing this group.[4] Authors rank second in both Canada and the United States and are in a near tie for second in Norway. It should be noted that unsuccessful authors – those with low incomes from writing – very likely settle into another occupational category for data collection purposes. Photographers are third in both Canada and the United States, and fourth in Norway. Painters and sculptors rank fourth in the United States, sixth in Norway, and fifth in Canada. Musicians and composers are fifth in the United States, second in Norway, and fourth in Canada, despite their relatively strong unions. And last in the United States and Canada are the dancers and choreographers, who also hold the next to last spot in Norway.

Of considerable interest is the finding that the salary spread among artists is much greater in the United States than in the other two nations. Dancers earn only 37 percent as much as actors and directors in the United States, compared with at least 50 percent as much in the other two nations. The coefficient of variation – a measure of relative dispersion in incomes, calculated as the standard deviation divided by the mean – is .37 for U.S. artists' income, while its values for Norway and Canada are somewhat lower at .30 and .29, respectively. The higher U.S. variation might reflect greater reliance on a market mechanism and the impersonal forces of supply and demand to finance the arts, while both Norway and Canada, with a stronger tradition of government support, can ensure smaller income disparities among artists.

Labor markets in the arts

In Chapter 4 we introduced the principles of supply and demand and demonstrated their application in the markets for a variety of goods and services. Precisely the same principles can be applied to a "labor market" where the supply of and demand for the services of human resources interact. In the case of a typical product, supply and demand together determine the product price and the quantity of the product sold during some time period. In a labor market for artists, the price is the wage paid to the artist, and the quantity can be thought of as the number of artists employed. Thus, the labor market determines both

---

[4] The superstar phenomenon and the role of unions are discussed later in this chapter.

the earnings of artists and the number of artists who will find work. In this section we will consider in somewhat greater detail the operation of the demand and supply elements in the labor market for artists. We may speak, for example, of the market for new college graduates, the market for computer programmers, or the market for dancers. These markets serve to determine wage levels and other terms of employment for each category of workers, and they allocate labor among its many competing uses.

Despite what many observers might regard as anomalies, the market for artists bears similarities to other labor markets. Arts labor markets generally are not mentioned in standard texts of labor economics. Perhaps this is because the market is so small – artists constituted less than 1 percent of all civilian workers in 1989 – or perhaps it is because the operations of this market are so poorly understood or are perceived as so divergent from more typical markets. However, we will begin with the assumption that artists display the same motivations and behaviors as everyone else: they are rational utility maximizers who seek the highest combination of monetary and nonmonetary reward for their efforts.[5]

Labor market theory and the arts

In this section we will develop the theory underlying operation of arts labor markets. As already indicated, the fundamental analytical tool is the interaction of the demand for artists, as expressed by a variety of employers, and the supply of the artists themselves. In a competitive market, with no market imperfections, the prices of productive factors and the level of their employment are determined by these forces of supply and demand. The basic principles are no different from those that apply in product markets or in other resource markets: the greater the demand or the less the supply of a service, the higher will be its price. Conversely, the less the demand or the greater the supply, the lower will be the price.

The assumptions that underlie the demand side of a "perfect" market are: (1) employers have complete and accurate knowledge of wages, labor availability, labor productivity, and related matters; (2) employers are rational profit maximizers, which means that they employ workers and other factors of production in a fashion consistent with the highest

---

[5] This is consistent with the conclusions of Gregory Wassall and Neil Alper, who surveyed a number of arts labor market studies. See their "Toward a Unified Theory of the Determinants of the Earnings of Artists," Northeastern University, unpublished paper presented to the International Conference on Cultural Economics, Umeå, Sweden, 1990.

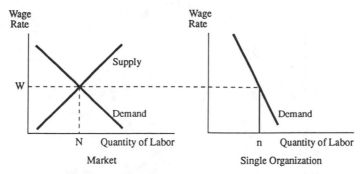

Figure 14.1. Market and organization labor supply and demand.

possible profit; (3) no single employer is sufficiently large to influence wages; (4) employers do not collude to influence the market; (5) artists in a given market are homogenous, that is, they are perfect substitutes for each other.

Corresponding assumptions pertaining to the supply side of the artist labor market are: (1) artists have perfect knowledge of market conditions, including employment opportunities and wages; (2) artists respond rationally to differences in wages and other benefits; (3) artists are perfectly mobile between jobs and among geographic regions; and (4) there are no unions or other artificial restrictions on supply. In the next section we will discuss the failure of some of these assumptions to coincide with the reality in some arts labor markets, but at this point they will help us to develop an understanding of "ideal" market outcomes.

The supply and demand forces in the artist labor market are illustrated in Figure 14.1. The left-hand panel represents the market for, say, actors. The downward-sloping demand curve suggests that should actors ever become less expensive, theaters and other employers will have an incentive to increase the number employed. Conversely, a higher prevailing wage creates an incentive to economize on the employment of actors.[6]

The supply curve slopes upward to the right, indicating a tendency for additional actors to offer their services in the market as wages rise. The point where the two lines cross is, of course, the market clearing wage, such that the number of actors offering their services equals the number desired by employers, and that number is N.

[6] The astute reader will note here that theaters cannot easily reduce the number of actors employed. For example, the typical play has a fixed number of cast members, and a reduction in actors employed might mean deleting a character. We will return to this difficulty later.

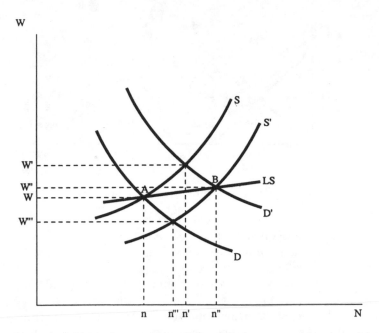

Figure 14.2. Market supply and demand changes and long-run labor supply.

The right-hand panel represents the situation facing the individual employer. In a more competitive situation, such as might exist in the New York City market for actors and in a few other very large markets, a typical employer is likely to be quite small relative to the overall market and hence unable to influence the market wage. We refer to such an employer as a "price taker." In this case the individual theater must pay the market-determined wage of W and is able to hire n actors at that wage. As drawn, the demand curve for the individual organization is relatively inelastic in the short run.

We can use the diagram in Figure 14.2 to explain more fully the distinction between short- and long-run demand and supply curves. The curves labeled D and D' are short-run demand curves; each is observed at some point in time where the conditions underlying demand are unchanged. In moving from D to D', from one short-run demand curve to a second, we have allowed at least one of the underlying conditions – for example, income or consumer tastes – to change. Similarly, S and S' represent two short-run supply curves, and a movement from one to the other indicates that the conditions underlying the supply of artists have altered. Circumstances entailing such changes will be explained and illustrated more fully in the next section.

The intersections of D and S at point A and of D' and S' at point B constitute two short-run equilibria, and a line such as LS drawn through these points may be said to represent a long-run relationship. In this case, it is a long-run supply curve, and the transition from point A to point B can be an interesting process, as we will develop below.

The demand for artists: Artists are able to command a salary or wage to the extent that some audience or clientele exists for their work. For example, if no one ever wanted to attend a dance performance and no tickets were sold, there would be no need for dancers and no need to entice anyone to become a dancer. The market demand for dancers would be nonexistent. But if dance is a popular art form, and if people are willing to pay to view a performance, then some dancers will be hired at a salary in return for performing. The demand for dancers is *derived* from the demand for dance performances. Similarly, if no one ever purchased a painting, there would be no need for painters and no incentive to enter the profession. But if people are both willing and able to acquire paintings, there will be a demand for painters to produce them, and the potential earnings will entice some persons to enter the profession.

The value of the artist to the employer has two components. The first is the artist's marginal productivity, that is, what the artist adds to the "quantity" of the employer's output. The second component is the unit price of that output, since the additional product multiplied by the unit price yields the additional revenue to the employer.[7] If this additional revenue, called the "marginal revenue product" of the artist, exceeds the wage rate, employing the artist adds to the employer's "profit" (or reduces losses).

It follows that the demand for artists depends on those factors that influence demand for their final product. These factors include consumer incomes and consumer tastes and preferences. For example, if consumer incomes rise, this would be reflected in a shift of the product demand curve, and hence of the artist demand curve, to the right, as depicted in Figure 14.2 by the shift from D to D'. If the conditions underlying supply do not change, so that S remains the supply curve, the result

---

[7] In an imperfectly competitive product market, the demand curve is downward-sloping, and any increase in output fostered by the additional employee will cause a fall in the market price. Accordingly, the value of the employee is determined by multiplying the additional output by the *marginal revenue*, not the price. For a review of the concept of marginal revenue, see Chapter 5.

would be a higher wage earned by the individual artist ($W' > W$) and more artists employed ($n' > n$).

The same effect might be generated by changes in consumer tastes. For example, many corporations and government units now make a concerted effort to incorporate the visual arts into their working spaces, many going so far as to hire curators to ensure the quality of art acquisitions. This increased desire to acquire works of art is an example of what we mean by a change in consumer taste. In this case, it would cause a rightward shift in the demand curve, just as an increase in consumer income would do. Likewise, arts outreach programs, often supported by public funds, are intended to develop a greater appreciation for the arts – in other words, increasing the taste for art – again shifting the demand curve to the right, for example, from D to D'.[8]

The supply of artists: The typical upward-sloping artist supply curve, as portrayed in Figure 14.1, can be interpreted to mean that higher expected earnings can entice additional arts labor into the market. In the short run, higher earnings for, say, dancers, brought about by a change in consumer tastes, may entice those who are sufficiently skilled to abandon their temporary positions as waitpersons and typists and to return to the stage. This is represented by a movement up the short-run curve, S, in Figure 14.2. Due to the higher wage W', $n' - n$ additional dancers have entered the market immediately. In addition, more attractive earnings should enhance the long-run appeal of an arts career, so that younger aspirants will enter education and training programs to hone their skills in preparation for eventual employment. With the passage of time, very likely a few years, the supply curve will have shifted to S', meaning that at any given wage level, more artists are offering their services than did previously.

If demand conditions have not altered further, so that D' remains the demand curve, the new equilibrium is point B, and the wage associated with this is W''. It is as if demand shifted along a long-run labor supply curve, LS, with the wage rising from W to W'' while the number of artists employed increases from n to n''. The new, young artists who entered the education and training pipeline in anticipation of the relatively rich reward of W' may be a bit disappointed to discover the somewhat less enticing reward of W''.

Conversely, a reversal of artistic fortunes, such as a decline in public

---

[8] Other factors can influence consumer tastes for the arts. For example, the "dance boom" of the mid-1970s is alleged by some to have been influenced by the popular movie *Turning Point*.

support, may lead to a decline in demand and a movement down a supply curve. The resulting wage decline and unemployment may send performers scurrying into alternative jobs in the short run. This is illustrated in Figure 14.2 by a movement *down* the short-run supply curve S'. As demand falls from D' to D, wages fall to W''' from W'', and employment levels decline to n''' from n''. But the point n''', W''' does not lie on the long-run supply curve for artists, and so cannot be a long-run equilibrium position. In the long run, the dismal pecuniary reward will discourage many aspirants from setting out on the difficult path to artistic employment, so the short-run supply curve shifts from S' back to S. The final outcome, given full adjustment on the part of those preparing themselves for artistic careers, would be wage and employment levels of W and n, respectively, which *does* lie on the long-run supply curve LS.

Some realities of the market for artists

The arts represent – for us, at least – an unusually interesting application of labor market theory. In the foregoing sections we relied on some simplifying assumptions to develop a better understanding of how arts labor markets might ideally work. Many of the assumptions of a perfectly competitive market are violated in actual labor markets, and especially so among artists. For example, painters and sculptors are not homogenous or perfect substitutes; they differ in talent, style, and media. Neither are dancers, musicians, or actors, whose talent, voice, and practice habits will vary. Members of a corps de ballet may appear virtually identical from the back of the balcony, but they are in fact distinct individuals with different levels of performing ability.

There is little agreement on the value of works of art, that is, the market price, much less perfect knowledge of artist wages.[9] Arts employers frequently are incorporated as not-for-profit organizations, which raises the question of whether they can be regarded as profit maximizers in the conventional sense. Like workers in other professions, artists may not be able to move freely from place to place in search of fame and fortune. And many performing artists, especially actors and musicians, are members of unions that effectively support their wages and stipulate work rules.

In addition, the marginal productivity of artists, especially of performing artists, is difficult or impossible to measure. It is not at all clear how much "output" an additional second violin contributes to a sym-

---

[9] The reader will remember the importance of trial and error in setting the prices of art works, as discussed in Chapter 9.

phony orchestra. The conductor, the musicians, and the cognoscenti may recognize a "fuller sound," but those with a less discriminating ear – most of the audience, perhaps – are less likely to notice any change. This makes the worth of an individual performer very difficult to ascertain.

In the sections that follow, we consider a few examples of these complications in some detail. In the next section we explore the impact of unions, and we make special reference to the performing arts. Then we seek to develop an understanding of the so-called superstar. Finally, we examine the visual artist.

Unions and the performing arts: Among the best-known unions in the arts field are Actors' Equity and the American Federation of Musicians, and we will confine our inquiry to the markets for the performing artists represented by these unions. In our earlier discussion we treated the supply of and demand for labor, including artistic labor, as behaving much like supply and demand in any other market. The demand curve has a negative slope and the supply curve a positive one. The intersection of the two is the market wage rate. When we discussed the theory of the arts labor market, we presented a theater's demand curve for actors as a rather typical, downward-sloping relationship between wage and number employed. The short-run demand curve – that which exists *during* a single season, when the theater has committed itself to the fixed costs associated with the season – may in fact be perfectly inelastic, as depicted by line D in Figure 14.3.[10] Given an actor supply curve of S, the theater will hire n actors at a wage of W and a total actor wage expense represented by the area of the rectangle $0nAW$. We will suppose that this wage is an outcome of negotiations between an Actors' Equity local affiliate and the theater management. Since the wage of W is a minimum, the portion of S below W is not attainable and is represented by a dashed line.

If the union successfully negotiates a higher wage such as W' for the ensuing season and if the theater is unable to pass the higher costs on to ticket buyers, then the theater may choose to offer productions with smaller casts. This would be reflected in a shift of the demand curve from D to D' and of actors employed from n to n'. The total actor wage costs would in this instance change to $0n'BW'$.

Consequently, a line drawn through points A and B can be taken to represent a long-run demand curve, where a theater's decision making is no longer confined to a single season. A shift up in the effective supply

[10] This is consistent with our treatment in Chapters 6 and 7.

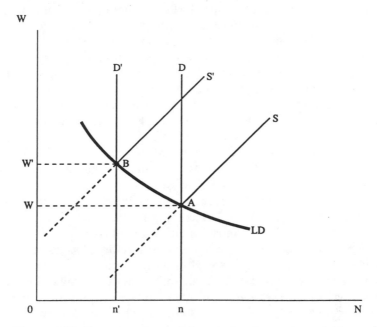

Figure 14.3. Long-run demand for performing artists: single organization.

curve will, after a period of adjustment, lead to a movement up the long-run demand curve. A clear outcome of actor demands for higher wages is that some actors – equivalent in this case to $n - n'$ – will no longer be employed. And this outcome – a rise in unemployment due to union activity – is widely recognized among economists.

It is not uncommon nowadays for actors to double up, playing multiple roles in a given production, provided their characters are not on stage simultaneously. Many new plays are written, and old plays often are restaged, with fewer parts, so that the expense of actors can be borne more easily. These are consistent with higher rates of unemployment that result from nonmarket wage increases such as those secured by union activity.

A musical organization such as a symphony orchestra in an analogous situation also has an inelastic short-run demand curve for musicians. An employment level such as n in Figure 14.3 may represent both the orchestra's traditional "sound" and a minimum number of musicians as negotiated by the orchestra and the American Federation of Musicians. For example, contracts with the very best U.S. symphony orchestras typically stipulate a minimum number of musicians, often in excess of a hundred. These contracts also include a guaranteed annual wage. For the Chicago Symphony and the Philadelphia Orchestra, the guaranteed minimum annual wage at the entry level in 1990–91 was $59,280.[11] These large and renowned organizations may, through sophisticated fund-raising and marketing activities, be able to cover such higher expenses. Smaller organizations, however, may be discouraged from developing full-size orchestras. For example, musical talent aside, the Alabama Symphony, with 72 musicians, and the Rochester Philharmonic, with 59 full-time and 23 part-time musicians, will never achieve the sound of the larger organizations. One might conjecture that, in those examples, more musicians would be employed if salaries – guaranteed minimums of $24,100 in Alabama, $32,928 in Rochester – were lower.[12]

These union-negotiated wages, especially of the major orchestras, seem to be quite attractive. According to one source, in the 1980–81 season over 1,100 musicians applied for 47 full-time positions in the major orchestras. One second violin position in Chicago attracted 240 applicants.[13] Interestingly, some attribute this apparent oversupply *not* to the attractiveness of union scale, but rather to the near unscrupulous behavior of music schools, academies, and conservatories, which persist in attracting and graduating students when so few positions are available.[14]

The superstar: Most of the second violins in an orchestra may be regarded as close substitutes for one another.[15] But none of them likely has the drawing power of Isaac Stern or Itzhak Perlman. Stern, Perlman, and a number of other especially talented performers are among the "superstars" of the live performing arts. While most of the public might associate stardom with the movies – the box office draws who command salaries of $1 million or more per movie – here we focus on the live performing arts.

---

[11] Those orchestras with stipulated minimum number of musicians include the Boston, Chicago, and San Francisco symphonies; the New York and Los Angeles philharmonics; and the Cleveland and Philadelphia orchestras. See "Wage Scales and Conditions in the Symphony Orchestra, 1990–1991 Season," American Federation of Musicians.

[12] The sliding scale represented by the lower minimums in Alabama and Rochester, as compared to, say, Chicago, is intended to make allowance for the differing circumstances in smaller cities. Nonetheless, the scale probably exceeds purely market-determined salaries. Data are from ibid.

[13] George Seltzer, *Music Matters* (Metuchen, N.J.: Scarecrow Press, 1989), p. 222.

[14] Ibid.

[15] Some contracts specify that the seating of musicians within a section will be rotated from one performance to another, reinforcing a perception of homogeneity or substitutability.

Performing companies differ in how they utilize the superstar. For example, orchestras rarely have a resident superstar other than, perhaps, the conductor. (Pinchas Zukerman, formerly with the St. Paul Chamber Orchestra, comes to mind.) They rely on itinerant superstars, lining up a number of prominent soloists for each season. Some ballet companies – for example, American Ballet Theater in the not too distant past – feature resident superstars as principal dancers, while others – for example, the Joffrey – are less reliant on big names. Broadway productions and major opera companies customarily secure the services of superstars.

We would reasonably expect the more talented performers to command a higher return, but the rewards to superstars seem disproportionately skewed. Sherwin Rosen has attributed this to the interaction of restricted supply of the best talent with expanded demand due to market exposure.[16] According to one observer:

> [The superstars'] fees are high, over $40,000 per concert for some soloists, and they are worth it. The presence on an orchestral program of a great soloist will sell out the concert (and the series of concerts) in many cities. The star system works – audiences will come to see and hear the soloist despite the program or the quality of the orchestra or conductor.[17]

We can construct an example in the classical music field. Aficionados are likely to acquire a collection of recorded music as one substitute for the more expensive live performance. But since the number of possible soloists available for recording, say, a Beethoven piano concerto, far exceeds the current annual output of new recordings, only a relatively few pianists gain exposure in this fashion. Hence, they become the recognized names – the "riskless commodity" – sought by impresarios and music directors. Although, in point of fact, most listeners would not be able to detect differences in the quality of play among a large number of performers, they seem to prefer the sure thing to the unknown.[18]

---

[16] Sherwin Rosen, "The Economics of Superstars," *American Economic Review,* 71, no. 5 (December 1981): 845–58.

[17] Seltzer, *Music Matters,* p. 179.

[18] We are intrigued by both the efficiency and fairness aspects of the superstar phenomenon: is there simply not enough work to go around, given the large number of concert-class pianists, or do young performers encounter discrimination? This may constitute a basis for further research.

The visual arts: Visual artists – painters, sculptors, and so on – are especially distinct as many are self-employed and, as indicated in Chapter 9, often create speculative works.[19] In this case, the artist engages in "inventory investment," and the inventory is disposed of through some combination of promotional and pricing techniques. The "wage" is the selling price minus the cost of materials, studio expenses, and other related outlays. As an artist becomes more popular, his or her works may command a higher price, which can be interpreted as a greater demand for his or her "labor services" and a higher "wage." An artist will continue to be self-employed, pursuing a livelihood in this manner, so long as the combination of fees for services and expected return on investment (including such nonpecuniary returns as fame) justify the resources expended.

Becoming an artist: investment in human capital

The choice of a career is one of the most important, and perhaps most difficult, faced by an individual. Among the factors influencing such a choice are expected earnings, working conditions, training and education requirements, discrimination, and personal preferences. Most people, given a choice between two opportunities that are otherwise similar, will select the one that entails the higher wage or salary. It seems fair and safe to say also that most people will prefer to work fewer hours per day, not to have to undergo lengthy and sometimes expensive training, and to select the job that suits them best. Why, then, would anyone select a career that entails notoriously low wages, long and uncertain hours, the possibility of injury, arduous preparation and training, and innate talent, to boot? As we have suggested earlier in this chapter, the conventional wisdom holds that careers in the arts have just such characteristics.

As a first step in considering this matter, we must introduce the concept of "human capital." Ordinarily we think of a firm's investment in its physical plant, or productive capability, as the creation of capital. A firm undertakes such investment, or creates capital, if the expected return justifies the investment. In an analogous situation, an individual will "invest" in education or training, or an employer will invest in an employee, if justified by the expected return. Such investment in a person enhances that person's "human capital." For example, a dancer will incur the costs of classes – investment in his performing ability, or

---

[19] Commercial artists, who may work for an employer or who may act as independent contractors, participate in a reasonably well organized market and very likely have good information about their value in that market.

human capital – if he thinks his return (most likely in the form of higher earnings) will be sufficiently enhanced.

To make this concept more precise, we will retrieve a concept introduced as Equation 9.6:

$$P_t = \frac{C + P_{t+1} + S}{1 + r} \qquad (14.1)$$

where P_t is the amount someone would be willing to pay for an asset, the quantity $C + P_{t+1} + S$ represents the dollar value of the return to acquiring the asset, and r is a market interest rate. With slight modification, we can write

$$F_t = \frac{\Delta W_{t+1}}{1 + r} \qquad (14.2)$$

where F_t is the fee that the student would be willing to pay for the class if ΔW_{t+1} is the increment in the wage that the dancer will realize as a result of the class. We can make this a bit more concrete with a hypothetical example. Suppose a dancer estimates that a class with a famed teacher will increase her earnings next year by $2,000.[20] The market interest rate is 10 percent, expressed for our purposes in decimal form, .10. Then the amount the dancer would be willing to pay for the class is

$$F_t = \frac{\$2,000}{1 + .10} = \$1,818$$

If the class is priced at, say, $1,750, which is less than the maximum amount she would be willing to pay, she will invest in herself by taking the class. If, on the other hand, the class is priced at $1,850, she will pass up the opportunity.

More generally, if the perceived return to preparing for and entering an artistic profession is sufficiently high, relative to the cost of investing in human capital, individuals with the appropriate skills will be enticed into that profession. The return, including pecuniary and nonpecuniary components, must compensate the worker for resources expended in training and education and for the risk inherent in artistic endeavors.

---

[20] Presumably, such a class would enhance earnings potential over several years, but the treatment of a multiyear period is a bit more complex, although the basic idea is the same. Hence, we stick with just two time periods. The reader wishing to pursue the matter may consult any finance or managerial economics text. See, e.g., Mark Hirschey and James L. Pappas, *Fundamentals of Managerial Economics,* 4th ed. (Orlando, Fla.: Dryden, 1992), esp. chap. 15.

In addition, the return must at least equal that offered by the best alternative occupation for a given artist. If becoming an artist becomes cheaper, relative to the return, more individuals will become artists at each wage rate, ultimately shifting the supply curve to the right, as we depicted in Figure 14.2. This would occur, for example, if the costs of artistic training were subsidized via public support of a high school of the arts, as is the case in New York City and the state of North Carolina. From the individual artist's perspective, this is a reduction of F_t in Equation 14.2, and it makes artistic education seem more worthwhile. The eventual rightward shift of the supply curve results in an increase in employment ($n'' > n'$) but a *decrease* in the market wage ($W'' < W'$), an outcome not usually anticipated by those advocating subsidized training. If the performer herself fails to take this into account, she could be sadly disappointed in a level of compensation that does not in fact justify her human capital investment.

A summation

The factors that influence the supply of and the demand for artists interact to determine artists' incomes, and several economists have sought to identify those that are most relevant.[21] We will draw on their work to answer some of the question posed at the outset of this chapter.

Are artists in danger of imminent starvation? Filer contended that the "starving artist" is largely a myth. He analyzed 1980 U.S. Census data to support his conclusion that "when personal characteristics and productive attributes are standardized, the average artist earned about 10 percent less in 1979 than he or she would have earned in nonartistic employment." On the other hand, the studies make it clear that *sole* reliance on artistic earnings would have been insufficient for a large number of artists. Second jobs are a doubled-edged sword: they enable artists to attain a higher standard of living, but they inhibit investment in artistic human capital by reducing practice, class, and rehearsal time.

---

[21] Randall K. Filer, "The 'Starving Artist' – Myth or Reality? Earnings of Artists in the United States," *Journal of Political Economy,* 94, no. 1 (February 1986): 56–75; Gregory Wassall, Neil Alper, and Rebecca Davison *Art Work;* Gregory Wassall and Neil Alper, "Determinants of Artists' Earnings," in William S. Hendon et al., *The Economics of Cultural Industries* (Akron, Ohio: Association for Cultural Economics, 1984), pp. 213–30; and Gregory Wassall and Neil Alper, "Occupation Characteristics of Artists: A Statistical Analysis," *Journal of Cultural Economics,* 9 (1985): 13–34; Charles M. Gray, "The Smell of the Greasepaint, the Roar of the Crowd: What Are They Worth?" presented at the annual meeting of the Midwest Economics Association, Chicago, April 1984.

Artists also earn less than workers with similar educational levels, but we can offer the conjecture that the nonmonetary benefits of an artistic career offer some additional compensation.[22] So, rest assured: although many artists will not be well paid, few are likely to starve; and so long as artistic careers retain some inherent appeal, we will continue to have artists.

[22] This conjecture is at least partially supported by the results of Gray's study previously cited.

15

The role of the arts in a local economy

Art and culture of the kind analyzed in this volume – the live performing arts and galleries and museums – are preeminently urban activities. Painters, composers, and playwrights may live anywhere they like, but the economics of live performance as well as gallery and museum display dictate that their output will be seen for the most part in cities. The explanation is quite simple. Like beauty parlors, health clubs, and hospitals, the live performing arts and museums share the characteristic that whatever it is they offer must be consumed where it is produced. Some restaurants may be willing to deliver a meal to your home, but no theater company, so far as we know, will put on its production in your living room. Although an art exhibition may travel from the museum that organizes it to other museums and galleries, and some performing arts companies regularly go on tour, the net income from such endeavors is held down by their high cost in relation to revenue earned. Thus, even after allowing for possible income from touring companies and traveling exhibitions, most arts institutions are economically viable only in places where the local arts audience is big enough to support them, and basically that means in cities or metropolitan areas that are sufficiently large.[1] How large is large enough depends on two factors: the cost characteristics of the service in question and the density of demand for it. The greater the per capita demand for a service, the smaller the minimum-size city needed to support it and the larger the

---

[1] The presence of summer music festivals or summer theater in small rural communities is not an exception to this principle, since the communities are places with a large summer or tourist population, and the performing organizations (other than summer theaters) usually have winter homes in large cities.

number of places that provide the service will be. On the other hand, the larger the production unit required for efficient operation, the larger a city must be to support that service and the smaller the number of places that will be served.

The geographic distribution of ordinary retail stores and service activities shows how these principles operate. Small towns provide a market large enough to support a drugstore, or barber shop, but not a department store or health club. Medium-size cities can support a department store or health club, but not a stock exchange, investment banking firm, or major league baseball club, for which a very large city is required. For each service there is a minimum market size, or threshold, below which that activity is not generally viable. That the famous Green Bay Packers professional football team make their home in metropolitan area of only 195,000 is clearly an anomaly since the other 27 teams in the National Football League are all located in metropolitan areas with a population of at least 1.2 million.[2]

As cities grow larger they pass successively higher size thresholds and consequently supply not only more of each good but also more *kinds* of goods. Thus, Chicago not only has more drugstores, supermarkets, and department stores than nearby South Bend, but also provides types of services not found in South Bend at all, for example, investment banking, a commodity exchange, and major league baseball.[3]

The concentration of art and culture in urban centers

Similar considerations govern the location of professional performing arts institutions and art museums. A small city might have only a professional theater. A medium-size city might have several theaters and, in addition, an art museum and a symphony orchestra. A large city will probably have additional museums and also an opera company and a ballet. This line of reasoning suggests that arts activity not only increases with city size, but, more interesting, that it increases *faster* than city size. That being the case, it will also be true that the larger the city, the larger its art and culture industry will be in relation to its economy. Likewise, it would follow that a disproportionately large share of a nation's arts activity would be found in its large cities.

[2] Except for Green Bay, the Indianapolis Metropolitan area is the smallest, with a 1990 population of 1,249,822. See U.S. Department of Commerce, Bureau of the Census, *State and Metropolitan Area Data Book, 1991,* table 2.

[3] This line of reasoning is developed in a branch of urban study known as "central place theory." For an introductory analysis, see James Heilbrun, *Urban Economics and Public Policy,* 3d ed. (New York: St. Martin's, 1987), chap. 5.

The role of economies of agglomeration

Abetting the concentration of arts activity in large cities is the force of what students of urban development have identified as "economies of agglomeration." These are the savings in unit cost that accrue to certain kinds of firms when a large enough number of them locate in the same city. The savings usually occur because the firms are able to share a common pool of highly specialized inputs, the very existence of which depends on there being a concentration of local buyers. The art and culture industry clearly displays economies of agglomeration. New York City, for example, became a center for producing radio and television programming from the 1920s onward because it already had a vast pool of acting, directing, and writing talent, centered around the Broadway theater, on which radio and later television producers could draw. In the same way, radio and television production was eventually drawn to Hollywood by the pool of talent working in the motion picture industry. And in a reversal of that relationship, a substantial number of motion pictures are now filmed in New York because the city already has the skilled personnel and equipment used to shoot TV programs.

These examples of economies of agglomeration are cases in which one industry is attracted to a given location because it can make use of inputs already drawn to that place by another industry. But economies of agglomeration also operate within single industries. For example, Hollywood became the center for motion picture production because the presence of some firms soon attracted others that could use the same specialized inputs that were unavailable, or at least less abundant, elsewhere. Or look at economies of agglomeration from the perspective of an individual performer: a novice interested in learning modern dance might come to New York City because that is where the concentration of teachers and job opportunities is greatest. A few years later that dancer might put together a new company and would base it in New York, because that is where the largest pool of first-rate dance talent can be found. As these cases illustrate, when economies of agglomeration operate the result can be stated very simply: activity attracts more activity.[4]

In Table 15.1 we attempt to substantiate these assertions about the geographic concentration of art and culture. Direct verification is difficult because we lack good data on the extent of arts activity at the local level. The calculations reported in Table 15.1 use the number of artists residing in a given locality as a proxy for arts activity. The data

[4] Ibid., pp. 15–18, 75–77.

Table 15.1. *Geographic distribution of performing artists and painters/sculptors*

Geographic area	Performing artists		Painters/sculptors	
	1970	1980	1970	1980
U.S. (total number)	103,512	220,930	100,893	153,162
	Percent distribution			
Metropolitan areas				
Largest 10	35.2	40.3	43.1	33.6
New York	11.4	14.1	15.2	10.2
Los Angeles	8.6	12.7	6.6	5.9
Second 10	10.4	9.7	11.9	12.5
Third 10	7.2	6.6	7.1	7.5
Fourth 10	4.7	4.9	4.6	5.1
Fifth 10	3.3	2.8	2.9	2.6
Fifty largest	60.8	64.3	69.5	61.4
Remainder of United States	39.2	35.7	30.5	38.7
	Artists per 10,000 of population			
U.S. total	5.09	9.75	4.96	6.76
Metropolitan areas				
Largest 10	7.57	18.13	9.04	10.48
New York	10.22	26.45	13.29	13.34
Los Angeles	12.73	37.52	9.46	12.08
Second 10	6.06	10.19	6.78	9.13
Third 10	6.12	10.26	5.84	8.08
Fourth 10	5.39	9.82	5.08	7.04
Fifth 10	5.03	7.95	4.27	5.24
Fifty largest	6.70	13.77	7.47	9.11
Remainder of United States	3.71	6.40	2.81	4.79

Source: Published and unpublished tabulations of U.S. Census data on artists in the labor force, from the Research Division, National Endowment for the Arts.

are from the U.S. Census tabulation of persons by occupation and place of residence. "Performing artists" include three occupations: actors and directors, dancers, and musicians and composers. The single occupation of "painters and sculptors" is taken to represent the visual arts.[5] The

[5] For a discussion of possible drawbacks in using these data as a proxy for local arts activity, see James Heilbrun, "Growth and Geographic Distribution of the Arts in the U.S.," in Douglas V. Shaw et al., eds., *Artists and Cultural Consumers* (Akron, Ohio: Association for Cultural Economics, 1987), pp. 24–35, cited at 26.

visual arts and performing arts are shown separately because, as it turns out, they exhibit quite different locational characteristics.

The upper panel of the table displays the total number of performing artists and of painters and sculptors in the United States in 1970 and 1980 and its percent breakdown among the 50 largest metropolitan areas, when these are arranged into five groups of 10 each, ranked by size. A careful look at the figures reveals the extent to which arts activity is concentrated into the largest metropolitan areas. For example, in 1980 there were almost 221,000 U.S. performing artists, of which 40 percent were found in the 10 largest metropolitan areas. But since those areas contained only 21.7 percent of the nation's population, they had almost twice their proportionate share of artistic activity. At the other end of the list, the smallest 10 among the 50 metropolitan areas had 2.8 percent of all performing artists, but since they contained 3.4 percent of the total U.S. population, that was less than their proportionate share.

The special cases of New York and Los Angeles

The upper panel of Table 15.1 shows how heavily performing arts activity is concentrated in New York and Los Angeles, the nation's two leading arts centers. In 1980 the New York metropolitan area had 14.1 percent and the Los Angeles metropolitan area nearly 13 percent of all performing artists, although their shares of U.S. population were only 5.2 percent and 3.3 percent, respectively. Thus, they had three or four times their proportionate share of arts activity. We have already described how economies of agglomeration operate in the arts. Undoubtedly, the dominant positions of New York and Los Angeles reflect the fact that as a result of economies of agglomeration, they became centers not just for the live performing arts, but also for mass media productions that require dancers, musicians, composers, actors, and directors.

How much of the concentration of the performing arts in New York and Los Angeles is accounted for by the pull of the mass media and how much by traditional live performance? The labor force data employed in Table 15.1 do not allow us to distinguish those sectors. Some inferences can be drawn, however, from information obtained from the Theatre Communications Group, a service organization for nonprofit theater companies in the United States. In 1989 TCG had 333 member and associate member companies, including almost all the major "regional" theaters. Table 15.2 shows the distribution of those theaters among the same metropolitan areas grouped in Table 15.1. For comparison, it also shows the distribution among those areas of actors and directors (the theatrical component of "performing artists" as displayed

Table 15.2. *Number of theater companies versus number of actors/directors*

Geographic area	Actors/ directors (1980)		Professional theater companies (1989)	
	Number	Percent	Number	Percent
U.S. total	67,180	100	333	100
Metropolitan areas				
Largest 10	38,664	57.6	134	40.2
New York	14,510	21.6	57	17.1
Los Angeles	16,081	23.9	12	3.6
Second 10	5,274	7.9	52	15.6
Third 10	3,062	4.6	16	4.8
Fourth 10	2,206	3.3	11	3.3
Fifth 10	1,219	1.9	9	2.7
Fifty largest	50,497	75.2	222	66.7
Remainder of United States	16,683	24.8	111	33.3

Sources: For theater companies, unpublished tabulations of membership in Theatre Communications Group (membership is limited to well-established professional companies); for actors and directors, sources cited in Table 15.1.

in Table 15.1). In 1980 Los Angeles had 23.9 percent and New York 21.6 percent of all the actors and directors in the United States, figures that were reflected in the high levels of concentration shown for those metropolitan areas in Table 15.1. But New York in 1989 had 17.1 percent of all TCG theaters, while Los Angeles was the location of only 3.6 percent.

A comparison between the distribution of actors and directors and the distribution of theaters suggests that most of New York's actors and directors were employed in the live theater, while an overwhelming proportion of those in Los Angeles must have been working not in the theater but in motion pictures and TV. We lack data to make such comparisons for musical or dance activity. However, it seems likely that they would display a similar pattern, indicating that Los Angeles is largely a center for the media arts, while New York, though it does some production for the mass media, remains primarily a center for live performance.

An apparent anomaly in Table 15.2 is the sharp decline in the number of theaters from 52 in the second quintile of metropolitan areas to only 16 in the third quintile. This is probably the effect of TCG's membership qualifications, which exclude very small theaters. Metropolitan areas that are too small to support TCG-size theaters may be served by smaller organizations. That would explain why the number of actors and directors does not fall off nearly as fast as the number of TCG theaters over the midrange of the table.

Locational patterns in the visual arts

What can we say about the locational pattern of painters and sculptors? The upper panel of Table 15.1 shows that in 1970 visual artists were more heavily concentrated in the 10 largest metropolitan areas than were performing artists. But by 1980, these positions had reversed. The percentage of painters and sculptors to be found there fell from 43.1 to 33.6 percent, while the percentage of performing artists rose from 35.2 to 40.3. Thus, the table makes it clear that while performing arts activity became slightly *more* centralized between 1970 and 1980, visual artists were becoming systematically more *de*centralized.[6] The New York metropolitan area's share fell sharply from 15 to 10 percent. The share of the 50 largest metropolitan areas in the aggregate declined from nearly 70 to just over 61 percent. That, in turn, means that the proportion of visual artists living in smaller metropolitan areas and in nonmetropolitan parts of the United States rose from 30.5 to nearly 39 percent.

It should not surprise us that visual artists are less concentrated into large cities than are performing artists, and are becoming even less so over time. We have already explained why performing arts companies tend to locate in cities and especially in large cities. Since the performers themselves must live close to their place of work, they too live in cities. Painters and sculptors, in the language of location theory, are much more "footloose." They need not live close to the particular gallery that handles their work. A few visits per year are probably enough to maintain the relationship. Georgia O'Keeffe lived in New Mexico, while exhibiting regularly in New York. As transportation improved and living costs in urban areas increased, some visual artists who formerly lived in cities have moved to less expensive locations. Of course, many continue to live in large cities, where, presumably, they find the company of fellow artists stimulating, enjoy the ease of browsing in museums and galleries, or find the social environment, with its tradition of involvement in the arts, to be especially congenial. New York and Los Angeles remain

---

[6] For further analysis of these trends, see James Heilbrun, "The Distribution of Arts Activity among U.S. Metropolitan Areas," in Douglas V. Shaw et al., eds., *Cultural Economics, 88: An American Perspective* (Akron, Ohio: Association for Cultural Economics, 1989), pp. 33–40.

the dominant centers, but San Francisco, Seattle, and Washington, D.C., also have relatively large populations of painters and sculptors.

Measuring the relative size of the local arts sector

The lower panel of Table 15.1 uses the number of artists per ten thousand of population as a measure of the relative size of the arts sector in a given area. The total number of U.S. performing artists more than doubled between 1970 and 1980, while population increased only 11 percent.[7] Consequently, for the nation as a whole the number of performing artists per ten thousand of population almost doubled from 5.09 in 1970 to 9.75 in 1980, indicating that the performing arts industry was growing rapidly in size relative to the national economy. Relative growth occurred in all metropolitan areas but was especially pronounced in New York and Los Angeles, where, by 1980, there were respectively 26.45 and 37.52 performing artists per ten thousand of population. In addition, New York and Los Angeles had respectively 13.34 and 12.08 painters and sculptors per ten thousand. For the two categories combined, those were by far the highest figures among all U.S. metropolitan areas, confirming what our previous analysis led us to expect, namely, that the largest cities would have the largest arts sectors relative to the size of their economies. Indeed, New York and Los Angeles are probably the only U.S. cities in which the business of art and culture is truly important to the local economy.

We turn next to studies of how the arts sector interacts with and influences economic activity in the city as a whole.

Economic impact studies

In the 1970s, advocates for the arts discovered that assertions about the positive economic impact of the art and culture industry made an effective case for greater state and local government support. The argument worked because it took advantage of two U.S. traditions: first, the long-established interest of state and local governments in promoting economic growth within their borders; second, the hard-headed, show me in dollars and cents attitude of locally influential business people whose support was crucial to local arts subsidies. The result was a series of "economic impact studies" that attempted to measure the significance of the local arts industry in actual dollar terms. The word "attempted"

---

[7] Some of the growth resulted from revisions in the occupational classification system between the two census dates. See Thomas F. Bradshaw, "An Examination of the Comparability of 1970 and 1980 Census Statistics on Artists," in William S. Hendon et al., eds., *The Economics of Cultural Industries* (Akron, Ohio: Association for Cultural Economics, 1984), pp. 256–66.

is used advisedly because of the conceptual and practical difficulties of carrying out such studies and the questions raised in some quarters about lack of objectivity.[8]

Studies of the economic impact of the arts try to measure the proportion of economic activity in a city that is attributable to its arts industry. The principles involved are perfectly general and could be used to measure the impact of any identifiable local industry. The usual approach is to estimate the size of three flows of spending that originate in the arts sector and that, in combination, measure its impact. The three flows are commonly referred to as direct, indirect, and induced spending and are described in the next sections. Ideally, these flows should be estimated from an *input–output model* of the local economy. Such a model systematically traces out the dollar value of purchases by each industry from every other industry that are required to produce one year's total output in the economy being studied. Originally developed by Wassily Leontiev in the 1930s and 1940s for the U.S. economy as a whole, input–output models have also been devised for local, state, and regional economies.[9] When studies of the economic impact of the arts have been done in metropolitan areas for which such a model does not exist, the researchers have nevertheless usually made use of input–output concepts and borrowed essential parameter values from input–output studies of other localities.

Direct spending

Direct spending is the easiest category to measure. It consists of the expenditures for goods and services by all institutions defined as being in the local arts sector. The list would presumably include all museums, galleries, and performing arts companies located within the city or metropolitan area. In theory, spending by individual local artists such as painters and sculptors should also be counted, since they are producing art locally, but up to this time lack of data has precluded doing so. The amount of direct spending by the arts sector is usually ascertained by conducting a questionnaire survey of the relevant institutions.

---

[8] For a discussion of the uses and abuses of arts impact studies and an extensive bibliography of the subject, see Anthony J. Radich and Sharon Schwoch, eds. *Economic Impact of the Arts: A Sourcebook* (Denver, Colo.: National Conference of State Legislatures, May 1987).

[9] See Walter Isard, *Methods of Regional Analysis: An Introduction to Regional Science* (New York: Wiley; Cambridge, Mass.: MIT Press, 1960), chap. 8, or William H. Miernyk, *Elements of Input–Output Analysis* (New York: Random House, 1965).

Since the purpose of these studies is to measure the *local* impact of spending, it is necessary to exclude moneys spent to buy goods or services *outside* the local area. Thus, if a theater has its costumes made in another city, their cost would not be included as part of direct local spending but would be a "leakage" of spending into the outside world. As we shall see, the higher the rate of leakage, the smaller the total impact of the arts sector will turn out to be.

Indirect and induced spending

The economic impact of the arts sector does not end with its direct spending, for the goods that are directly purchased by arts institutions also have to be produced, and to the extent that they are produced locally that effort gives rise to further rounds of local spending. For example, suppose that a theater company has its programs printed locally. Its payment to the printer is a direct local expenditure, as previously defined. But that is only the first round of local effects. To produce the program the printer buys paper, ink, and electric power, and pays rent in a commercial building. Perhaps the paper and ink are imported from outside the area, so payments for those items are leakages rather than contributions to local activity. But commercial building space and electricity are local products, so the printer's payments for those items constitute a second round of local spending, and to the extent that the commercial landlord and the electric company buy inputs locally, there ensues a third round. Indeed, a series of ever-diminishing rounds continues until the accumulated leakages finally exhaust the initial direct spending impulse. The sum of all rounds of business spending subsequent to the first "direct" round is the "indirect" spending that results from the theater's activity.

In tracing out the secondary effects of direct spending, wages and salaries are treated separately from expenditures on goods and services, but the principle is the same: wage and salary payments made by the theater to its staff are part of its direct expenditures and give rise to a series of further rounds of activity as the stores in which employees shop purchase local goods to replenish their stocks or the landlords to whom they pay rent spend money on local goods and services to operate and maintain buildings. The sum of these diminishing further rounds is the "induced" local spending attributable to operation of the theater.

Multiplier effects

The total economic impact of the arts sector on the local economy is the sum of the direct, indirect, and induced spending attributable to it. An input–output model produces these numbers directly. If such a model is not available, the first step is to measure direct local spending of the arts sector by means of a local survey. The amount of *total* spending attributable to the arts can then be estimated by applying a "multiplier" to the observed level of direct spending, that is, total spending = direct spending × multiplier. The value of the appropriate multiplier can be borrowed from an input–output study carried out for some other city.

It can be shown that the value of the multiplier varies inversely with the rate at which spending "leaks out" of the local economy. One can see intuitively that the smaller the leakage at each round of spending, the higher will be the proportion of each round that is respent locally, and therefore the larger will be the ratio of indirect and induced effects to direct effects. Algebraically, the multiplier is most easily represented as follows: We denote the multiplier as K and the marginal propensity to respend dollar receipts locally as *mprl*.[10] Although a full derivation will not be given here, it can be shown that

$$K = \frac{1}{1 - mprl}$$

In the algebraic statement one can see that the higher the marginal propensity to respend locally, the smaller the value of the denominator and the higher the value of K. To illustrate with plausible values, if *mprl* = .5, K = 2, while if *mprl* = .6, K = 2.5. We would expect that the larger the population of the metropolitan area being studied, the larger the value of the multiplier. The analysis of threshold effects at the beginning of this chapter indicated that the larger the metropolitan area, the greater the variety of goods and services it would produce. That being so, it follows that the larger the area, the less the need to import, the higher the marginal propensity to respend locally, and therefore the larger the multiplier.

The arts industry in the New York metropolitan area

In 1983 the Port Authority of New York and New Jersey published a report that measured the size of the arts industry in the New York–New Jersey metropolitan area, a region comprising 17 counties

---

[10] In "Keynesian" terms, the marginal propensity to respend locally equals the marginal propensity to consume minus the marginal propensity to import. The multiplier approach is generally traced to the work of John Maynard Keynes, who developed it in his *General Theory of Employment, Interest, and Money,* chap. 10.

Table 15.3. *The arts industry: New York–New Jersey metropolitan region, 1982 (millions of dollars)*

Type of activity	Direct expenditure	Total economic impact
Nonprofit cultural institutions	612	1,310
Art galleries and auction houses	175[a]	360
Commercial theater and road companies	323	650
Motion picture and TV production	1,000	2,000
Arts-motivated visitor spending	652	1,300
Total	2,762	5,620

[a]Includes only expenditures for goods and services other than the artwork itself. Thus the figure represents value added in the conduct of business rather than value of total sales.
Source: The Port Authority of New York and New Jersey and the Cultural Assistance Center, *The Arts as an Industry: Their Economic Importance to the New York-New Jersey Metropolitan Region*, May 1983, tables 35 and 42.

in the two states.[11] It is unusual among economic impact studies because the Port Authority had its own input–output model of the New York regional economy on which to base it and enough financing to avoid having to make research compromises. Consequently, it is probably the best such U.S. study that has been done. Table 15.3 summarizes the central findings of the study. Cultural organizations were divided into four groups: (1) nonprofit cultural institutions (comprising museums and not-for-profit performing arts companies); (2) art galleries and auction houses (a profit-making group); (3) commercial theater, including Broadway, Broadway road companies, and the commercial portion of Off-Broadway theater; and (4) motion picture and television production. Arts-motivated visitor spending (fifth row of table) makes up a final category of activity, which is logically distinct from the first four and will be explained below.

The first column of the table shows direct expenditures and the second column total economic impact for each of the five categories of activity in 1982. Indirect and induced expenditures, which are not shown separately, make up the difference between the two columns. For the arts industry as a whole, direct expenditures amounted to $2.762 billion.

[11] The Port Authority of New York and New Jersey and the Cultural Assistance Center, *The Arts as an Industry: Their Economic Importance to the New York–New Jersey Metropolitan Region*, May 1983.

Total economic impact came to $5.620 billion, indicating that the multiplier effect, which differed slightly among categories, averaged 2.03.

By themselves, of course, these numbers mean nothing. To put them in perspective, the Port Authority offers comparisons with some other New York industries. They find that in terms of direct revenues, the arts come somewhat ahead of management consulting and public relations, engineering and architectural services, computer and data processing services, hotels and motels, and advertising. The last-named comparison is perhaps the most compelling, since one thinks of New York as undoubtedly the advertising capital of the United States, if not of the world. In terms of direct and indirect impacts, the arts generate about two-thirds as many dollars as the region's entire port industry. Finally, the study estimates that the arts account for about 2 percent of total regional product (the regional analog of GDP). If that sounds unimpressive, the text adds that "against the scale of total regional product no industry looms very large."[12]

Arts-motivated visitor spending, the last line in Table 15.3, is the Port Authority's estimate of the financial contribution made by visitors from outside the region who come to New York to participate in one of its arts activities and, while there, spend money on local transportation, restaurants, hotels, and shopping. The amount of this ancillary spending was estimated from questionnaire surveys. The cost of tickets to events visited was, of course, excluded since it is already counted in the data from the arts organizations themselves. It is well known that arts attenders usually spend on dinner, transportation, and parking considerably more than they pay for their seats at the performance. But if those members of the audience live within the study region, one cannot credit such spending to the arts: they might have eaten dinner in a restaurant *without* going to the theater. Or if they did not do so, we can assume they would have spent their money on something else within the region. In order not to overstate visitor impact attributable to the arts, the Port Authority counted spending only by those who visited the region primarily to attend the arts or else extended for that reason a trip made for some other purpose.[13] Under that rule, the arts get no credit for the role they may play in attracting business conventions to New York, even though that role may be considerable. The figures in Table 15.3 can therefore be regarded as a lower-bound estimate of the net gain to the region from ancillary spending attributable to the arts.

[12] All comparisons are ibid., p. 135.
[13] Ibid., pp. 27–29 and 77–88.

The arts as an export industry

In the balance-of-payments accounts of any nation, receipts from foreign tourists are a credit item, a financial inflow that helps to pay for purchases from abroad and stimulates the domestic economy in the same way as an export of goods or services would. The same is true for a city or metropolitan area. Arts-motivated visitor spending in New York is the equivalent of an export and has the same stimulative effect on the local economy as would selling apparel or financial services to the outside world. The Port Authority found that in addition to $652 million of visitor spending, the arts in New York were responsible for three other categories of exports: Broadway road companies remitted $101 million in net payments; nonprofit touring arts companies that visited New York brought $15 million of net spending to the city; and in addition to their ancillary consumption, arts-motivated visitors spent $60 million buying theater tickets in New York. Thus, the arts could be credited with generating at least $828 million of exports from the New York area, making them one of the region's major export industries.[14] The figure would be even higher if lack of data had not prevented inclusion of export receipts from TV and film production.

It seems reasonable to assume that in London, Paris, and some other major European cities, the economic impact of the arts is at least as great as it is in New York. It has already been pointed out that, among U.S. cities, Los Angeles also has a very large arts industry, although quite different from New York's. As we shall show in the next section, however, in most U.S. cities the arts are economically far less important than the Port Authority found them to be in New York.

The art industry in six smaller U.S. cities

In the late 1970s, the National Endowment for the Arts sponsored research on the economic impact of art and cultural institutions in six small to medium-size U.S. metropolitan areas: Columbus, Ohio, Minneapolis/St. Paul, St. Louis, Salt Lake City, San Antonio, and Springfield, Illinois.[15] The project used a methodology developed for the NEA by David Cwi and Katherine Lyall in a pilot study in Baltimore. Table 15.4 shows some of the results for the six cities in the aggregate and for Minneapolis/St. Paul, the largest of the six and widely regarded

---

[14] For a discussion of this aspect that predated the Port Authority study, see Dick Netzer, "The Arts: New York's Best Export Industry," *New York Affairs*, 5, no. 2 (1978): 50–61.

[15] National Endowment for the Arts, Research Division Report no. 15, *Economic Impact of Arts and Cultural Institutions*, January 1981.

Table 15.4. *Comparison of economic impact studies of the arts industry*

	Six cities (NEA)[a]	Minn./ St. Paul (NEA)[a]	N.Y.–N.J. area (PA)
Per capita measures of size			
All arts			
1. Direct expenditure (dollars)	9.96	15.24	181.7
2. Attendance	.95	1.34	4.24
3. Exports (dollars)	1.52	2.21	54.47
Nonprofit arts			
4. Direct expenditure (dollars)	8.45	13.05	40.30
5. Attendance	.95	1.34	3.54
Audience structure and exports			
All arts			
6. Visitors as percentage of audience	20.0	13.6	19.6
7. Arts-motivated visitors as percentage of audience[b]	4.1	4.1	9.3
8. Exports as percentage of direct effects[b]	15.2	14.4	30.0

[a]NEA dollar figures have been adjusted as follows to improve comparability with Port Authority (PA) categories: all dollar figures were increased 48% to compensate for inflation between 1978 and 1982; in Rows 1 and 4 ancillary spending by the resident audience has been excluded, although the NEA counted it as direct expenditure; in Row 4 ancillary spending by visitors has also been excluded from the NEA figures, since it is not available for nonprofits in the Port Authority study.

[b]In the NEA studies, ancillary spending by visitors to each region was credited to the arts only if the visitor reported coming for the "sole" purpose of arts participation. The Port Authority credited ancillary spending to the arts for those whose "major" purpose in visiting was arts participation or who extended their visit for that purpose. The NEA rule would appear to be more restrictive, reducing the percentages in Row 7 of the first two columns. Since visitor spending is a major component of exports, that would also reduce values in Rows 3 and 8.

Sources: Six cities and Minneapolis/St. Paul: NEA study cited in note 15. New York–New Jersey: Port Authority study cited in note 11.

as the one with the most highly developed arts sector. The information has been arranged to facilitate comparison with the Port Authority's results for New York. The upper panel of the table presents several measures of the size of the arts sector in the three areas. In order to remove the effect of sheer population size, which differs radically across these areas, the measures are adjusted to a per capita basis. The table's lower panel presents several ratios that can be taken to measure aspects of arts industry structure.

Row 1 of Table 15.4 shows direct expenditure attributable to the arts, as that category was previously defined in discussion of the Port Authority study. The arts in New York annually generate $182 of direct expenditure per capita, compared with only $15.24 in Minneapolis/St. Paul and $9.96 in the six cities as a whole. The differences in magnitude are striking. A major explanation is the fact that New York has two large commercial sectors within its arts industry – namely, the Broadway theater and motion picture and TV production – whereas the six cities have only nonprofit institutions, such as museums and symphony orchestras. If we limit the comparison to the nonprofit sector (see Row 4), direct expenditure in New York falls to $40.30 per capita, only three times its level in Minneapolis/St. Paul and four or five times the level in the six cities together. (Note *a* in the table explains some adjustments made for this comparison.)

Table 15.4 shows that attendance per capita differs less dramatically among areas than does direct expenditure. When the commercial theater is included (Row 2), attendance per capita is 4.24 times per year in New York. In the six cities and in Minneapolis/St. Paul, where there is no commercial theater, per capita attendance is respectively only .95 and 1.34 times per year. Excluding commercial theater in New York (see Row 5) reduces attendance there to 3.54 times per year, still about three times its level in the other places. Why should the difference be less dramatic for attendance than for direct expenditure? Probably because unit costs are higher in New York than in the other cities, which would tend to inflate New York's direct expenditures. But also, New York has two arts segments that generate spending but do not produce "admissions," namely, art galleries and auction houses, and movie and TV production.

With respect to these size comparisons, however, a major caveat must be entered. Unfortunately, pressure of time prevented the NEA researchers from surveying all local arts institutions or even drawing representative samples in the six cities studied. Consequently, we know that the magnitudes reported in the upper panel of Table 15.4 represent something less than the whole, but we don't know how much less. In each case the surveys covered the major museums of art and science, the symphony orchestra, one or more theaters and dance companies, and the occasional opera or botanical garden, for a total of 49 institutions in the six cities. The authors of those studies made no attempt to estimate what proportion of the local arts sector they had measured. Let us assume that it was somewhere between half and three-quarters, not in terms of number of institutions but of volume of activity. In that case, we would have to increase the numbers for Minneapolis/St. Paul and the other cities in the upper panel of Table 15.4 by somewhere between 33 and 100 percent. On a per capita basis, they would still be well below New York's level.

Arts audiences and arts exports

The lower panel of the table presents some measures of audience structure and of the relative importance of arts exports. For these structural measures, no adjustment need be made for city size, since size does not directly affect their magnitude. Row 6 shows visitors, defined as those coming from outside the metropolitan area, as a percentage of the total audience at museums and the performing arts. The percentage is almost identical for the six-city aggregate and for New York, but is considerably lower in Minneapolis/St. Paul.

Row 7 shows arts-motivated visitors as a percentage of the total audience. Here we find a striking difference: the figure is 9.3 percent in New York, well over twice the level of 4.1 percent registered in the six cities and in Minneapolis/St. Paul individually. (However, see the caveat in Table 15.4, Note *b*.) This difference is economically important in two ways. First, as was previously explained, arts-motivated visitors are the only members of the audience whose ancillary spending – the money they pay for transportation, hotels, meals, and shopping while on their visit – can be legitimately counted as direct expenditure attributable to the arts. Consequently, differences in Row 7 generate differences in Row 1. Likewise, arts-motivated visitor spending is the principal component of arts "exports." So differences in the level of exports, as revealed in Rows 3 and 8, are affected by differences in the relative size of the arts-motivated visitor audience.

When museum audiences are compared with those for the performing arts, an interesting contrast emerges. In the six cities it studied, the NEA found that despite considerable variation among institutions of the same type, nonlocal visitors generally made up a considerably higher fraction of the audience at museums than at the performing arts. The explanation is straightforward. Most museums are open at least six days a week and have no limit on the number to be admitted. Therefore, the out-of-towner can attend with virtually no advance planning. Not so for the performing arts, as any visitor who has tried to attend on the spur of the moment can attest. Ballet, opera, and symphony performances take place only during limited "seasons." Tickets are required and may be sold out months ahead of time. Consequently, attending performing arts events, especially from out of town, requires a lot of advance planning. While that holds down the proportion of visitors to total audience for the performing arts as compared with museums, the NEA found that it also *raises* the proportion of those visitors who report that the arts are the sole reason for the trip.[16]

Something more must be said about exports. How can the 2- or 3-fold difference in the relative size of the arts-motivated visitor audience, as shown in Row 7, become the 25- to 35-fold difference in art industry exports revealed by Row 3? Part of the answer is that Broadway road companies, which contribute more than $6 per capita to New York's art exports, have no counterpart in the other cities. More important, however, is the fact that the average arts-motivated visitor to New York was responsible for $127 of ancillary spending per visit, while his or her counterpart in Minneapolis/St. Paul or in the six-city group reportedly spent only $26 or $14, respectively. Again, one may ask, how can that be? Apparently, the average visit to New York was longer in duration. Beyond that, we can only speculate: New York's prices are higher, but not that much higher; perhaps New York also offers visitors a larger or more tempting variety of things on which to spend their money. Whatever the explanation, Row 3 of the table does show that art industry exports are significant for the New York–New Jersey metropolitan area, but virtually negligible for average U.S. cities, if those in the NEA study are assumed to be representative.

Have economic impact studies been misused?

It was pointed out at the beginning of this section that studies of the local economic impact of the arts were developed in the 1970s primarily as an advocacy tool, a way of persuading state and local officials and local business people that art and culture were worthy of generous public and private support. In that role they proved very effective, probably, as Anthony Radich and Sonja Foss have suggested, because by relying on dollars-and-cents economic arguments and building on the premise that economic development is a good thing, "they bridge differences or reduce psychological distance between arts advocates and those they must persuade," namely, the business people and public officials who are influential in making funds available for the arts.[17]

In this chapter we have described two of the best of those studies.

---

[16] Ibid., pp. 18–19.

[17] Anthony J. Radich and Sonja K. Foss, "Economic Impact Studies of the Arts as Effective Advocacy," in Radich and Schwoch, eds., *Economic Impact of the Arts,* p. 90.

Anyone who carefully reads the originals will be impressed with the care their authors take to avoid overstating the size of the arts sector and to warn readers against misusing the estimates they provide. However, not all economic impact studies were as scrupulous as those cited, and even the best of them may have been misused in subtle ways. There can be no objection to a study that makes an honest and informed effort to measure the sheer size of the arts sector in a local economy. But as Bruce Seaman argues, economic impact studies can be faulted for the fact that those who use them (especially noneconomists), frequently draw incorrect or misleading inferences from them, and the form and content of the studies virtually invite such errors.[18]

How to misinterpret an economic impact study

Typical misinterpretations can be illustrated with a single hypothetical example. Suppose that in some medium-size city, an economic impact study shows the arts industry to account for $40 million of direct and $80 million of indirect spending per year. Advocates using the study emphasize that it proves the arts to be "big business," important to both employment and income in the city. The unstated implication is that if the arts sector were to falter, the city would lose $120 million per year of spending, together with the associated jobs. But this is unlikely to be true because, as Seaman emphasizes, it overlooks the pervasiveness of substitutability among objects of expenditure.[19]

Look first at consumer spending. Part of the direct expenditure of arts institutions included in the $40 million total is accounted for in ticket sales by the resident theater company, the local symphony orchestra, and the opera company. But if these institutions did not exist, local citizens would presumably spend their money on something else. Perhaps they would go to the movies more often or spend more on health clubs, restaurant meals, or birthday presents. The *pattern* of consumer spending would be different, but there is no reason to assume that the *total* would be smaller, and the same argument extends to the flows of indirect expenditure resulting from the initial spending impulse. However, one possible change in pattern does deserve mention: if the arts were no longer available locally, consumers might travel more frequently to other cities to visit a museum or attend a play, concert, opera, or ballet. That would reduce local spending, just as an increase in imports of other goods and services would. But the effect would probably be

---

[18] Bruce A. Seaman, "Economic Impact Studies: A Fashionable Excess," in ibid., pp. 43–75.
[19] Ibid., pp. 52–55, 57.

very small, since it is likely that only a minor fraction of former arts spending would be diverted to other places.

Substitutability also operates in connection with public support. In most cities a portion of the direct expenditure of nonprofit arts institutions, especially museums, is paid for by local government subsidies. Arts advocates might stress the importance of the jobs and income traceable to that financial support. But again, there is no reason to assume a unique connection. If the city did not subsidize the art museum, it might either spend more on other local services, with a presumably equivalent impact on jobs and income, or else reduce taxes, which would permit an offsetting increase in consumer spending.

One alleged advantage of the arts over some other local service activities is that they can attract visitors from outside the metropolitan area whose spending within the city is a net addition to local income and stimulates economic growth in the same way as an export of goods would do. We have shown, however, that in most cities the export component of arts activity is small, probably too insignificant to make or break the case for local government or business support.

At a deeper level, Seaman points out that many economists have also questioned the emphasis on particular export industries (sometimes identified as "basic" industries) as generators of local economic growth.[20] Very briefly, their argument is that if one local export industry falters, it will often be replaced by another, provided the locality's economic environment, which is largely shaped by its "service" sector, remains healthy and attractive. The experience of certain New England cities illustrates the point. In the decades down to 1950, many of them saw their exports dry up, as the textile industry moved from New England to the South. But in the 1960s and 1970s, electronics and other "high-tech" enterprises took their place, becoming important local exporters and engines of growth. Those industries were attracted to New England by its highly skilled labor force and the world-renowned engineering and scientific capability of its universities. Thus, particular export industries are replaceable if the local service sector is strong. It is therefore an attractive service sector, not the individual export industries, that is indispensable for long-run growth.

The arts and the local quality of life

A final economic argument said to favor promotion of the arts is that their presence can help to attract business firms into a metropolitan area, thus stimulating local economic growth. Unfortunately,

[20] See ibid., pp. 57–61; and Heilbrun, *Urban Economics,* pp. 163–65, 170–71.

studies of business location decisions have not shown that art and culture are significant determinants of locational choice.[21] The factors most commonly mentioned by firms that have relocated are such things as the cost and availability of land and labor, transportation connections, proximity to markets, commuting distances, and local tax rates. When "quality-of-life" variables are mentioned, the most prominent are likely to be features like good climate, accessibility of recreational facilities, low crime rate, and high-quality schools rather than the amenities of art and culture. In a nationwide sample survey that asked employers about factors affecting recruitment of new employees, local cultural facilities ranked a distant 12th among 14, and were said to be very important by only 7 percent of respondents.[22]

Nevertheless, a strong cultural sector does help to create a favorable image of a city. One study found that officials concerned with local economic development were apt to cite such amenities "as an important indicator of the general level of a community's civility and culture. The presence of these amenities is used to suggest that a community is progressive, resourceful, concerned about itself, and energetic."[23]

The business community, too, is aware of the importance of art and culture to the local environment. We showed in Chapter 12 that business firms often make substantial contributions to the support of the arts in their home town. While they may be motivated partly by a concern for public relations, it can hardly be doubted that they also believe their contributions are an effective way of making the local community a better place in which to live. Economists, on the whole, would agree with that way of looking at the matter: if the arts deserve local support, it is not because they are instruments of economic development, but because they make an indispensable contribution to the well-being of the women and men who make up the local community.

[21] See James L. Shanahan, "The Arts and Urban Development," in William S. Hendon, James L. Shanahan, and Alice J. MacDonald, eds., *Economic Policy for the Arts* (Cambridge, Mass.: Abt Books, 1980), pp. 295–305, cited at 303–04; and Seaman, "Economic Impact Studies," p. 60.

[22] John Landis, Cynthia A. Kroll, and Barbara J. Johnson, *Responses to High Housing Prices: Economies, Firms and Households,* vol. 1 (Berkeley: Center for Real Estate and Urban Economics of the University of California, August 1990), table V.8, p. 91.

[23] David Cwi and Katherine Lyall, *Economic Impacts of Arts and Cultural Institutions: A Model for Assessment and a Case Study in Baltimore,* National Endowment for the Arts, Research Division Report no. 6, November 1977, pp. 21–24.

16

The mass media, public broadcasting, and the cultivation of taste

Art is said to be an "acquired" or "cultivated" taste. That is in no way a disparaging statement. It certainly does not imply that a taste for art is somehow unnatural, artificial, or pretentious, as if all those people who claim to enjoy listening to Beethoven's string quartets or Bach's cantatas were just kidding. Rather, it means that one has to be familiar with art to find pleasure in it, and the more familiar with it you become, the more pleasure you find.

As pointed out in Chapter 4, taste is obviously one of the most important variables determining the level of consumer demand for art (or for any other consumer good). If the public's taste for art increases, the demand curve for art shifts to the right along the supply curve: unless the supply curve is perfectly vertical, more will be produced and more will be purchased (see Fig. 4.7). But if taste itself depends on exposure, we are in danger of being trapped in a suboptimal position, in the following sense. Some expenditure of time and/or money by consumers in making themselves more familiar with art would yield gains in future utility more than sufficient to cover the outlay. The optimal (and rational) decision would be to make the outlay, but since consumers are unaware of the possible future gain, they do not do so. To put it in less formal terms, consumers would greatly enjoy art if they were familiar with it; however, familiarity comes only with exposure, and the public will not expose themselves to it since they have not the taste. This vicious circle can only be broken by such policies as subsidizing the distribution of art (a possibility we discussed in Chapter 11) or providing an effective program of arts education to every student (a proposal we return to in the next chapter).

Impact of the mass media

From the point of view of high art the situation is aggravated by the collective impact of the mass media – television, radio, motion pictures, and the culture of advertising that uses and is used by them. The taste for popular art is also an acquired one, but in this case the public gets plenty of exposure and is almost guaranteed to acquire the taste because the mass media, by which all our lives are surrounded, or indeed invaded, provide little else. In the competition between popular culture and high art, the rise of the commercial mass media biases the outcome very sharply in favor of the former. This too can be viewed as a self-reinforcing process, or vicious circle. The mass media cater to the taste of the majority, in this case for popular culture such as the various forms of rock or country music; exposure through the mass media reinforces that taste; audience surveys then inform commercial producers that popular culture is, indeed, what audiences want, and the profit motive ensures that the media will continue giving it to them.

This is not to suggest, of course, that what we have called high art would predominate in the absence of the mass media. There is a spectrum of tastes in art, recreation, and entertainment reflecting a multitude of influences, among which exposure through the mass media is only one. But there is little doubt that the mass media do influence the outcome by catering to the taste of the majority and virtually ignoring everyone else. Economists have frequently pointed out that even when there are three television stations competing in a single market, none will adopt programming aimed at minority tastes (minority here referring not necessarily to an ethnic group, but simply to those whose tastes differ from the broad majority). Rather, each broadcaster will conclude that it is more profitable to go for a share of, say, the 90 percent majority than to try to please a possibly elusive 10 percent minority.[1]

Radio

Radio stations are much more numerous, less expensive to operate, and therefore satisfied with smaller market shares then are television broadcasters. In most communities, radio stations specializing in music try to develop a characteristic "sound" or musical profile. To do that they typically concentrate on one particular kind of rock, country, or other popular music, or sometimes confine themselves just to the

[1] See, e.g., Glenn A. Withers, "The Cultural Influence of Public Television," in James L. Shanahan et al., eds., *Markets for the Arts* (Akron, Ohio: Association for Cultural Economics, 1983), pp. 31–43, cited at 31; and Roger G. Noll et al., *Economic Aspects of Television Regulation* (Washington, D.C.: Brookings Institution, 1973), pp. 50–51.

"Top 40." Rarely do they offer anything but "popular" music. The principal sources for broadcasts of "classical" or "serious" music are the noncommercial, publicly operated stations affiliated with a public radio network such as National Public Radio (NPR), American Public Radio (APR), or student-operated stations at colleges and universities. In 1990 there were 9,447 commercial and 1,489 noncommercial radio stations in the United States. Only 79 of the stations in the commercial sector (or less than 1 percent) maintained a classical music format, whereas in the noncommercial sector 334 stations (or about 22 percent) did so.[2] Public stations with professional staffs and substantial size and output power made up a little more than 300 of the noncommercial total.[3] The proportion of this group with a classical music format was undoubtedly higher than 22 percent.

In some cases the local market is large enough so that one or two commercial, advertising-supported radio stations can make a go of it with serious music. In the New York metropolitan area, for example, serious music is provided by two commercial stations as well as by the major public station. But such cases are unusual because they are made possible only by exceptional market size. For the most part, the listening public is offered popular music, becomes familiar with it, likes it, and wants to hear more. And, of course, a very large industry has grown up devoted to producing more, so that listeners will not be disappointed. (In this way, the market also clearly influences the direction in which musical talent flows.)

Television

The cultural impact of commercial broadcast television is analogous to that of commercial radio. So little of what we would call high culture is shown today on commercial TV that the category (whatever one might call it) does not even turn up in statistical studies of what goes out over the airwaves. For example, in his very detailed review of programming on prime-time network television during six months of 1974, Harvey Levin lists only one cultural program, a single "musical drama," shown only once.[4] By contrast, a study of public television program content indicated that between 1974 and 1986 the proportion

---

[2] *The Broadcasting Yearbook, 1991*, pp. F.103, F.112. A radio format is defined as programming over 20 hours weekly. Thus, a single station can have more than one format.

[3] Corporation for Public Broadcasting, *Public Broadcasting and You* (Spring 1990), p. 6.

[4] Harvey J. Levin, *Fact and Fancy in Television Regulation* (New York: Russell Sage Foundation, 1980), table 3.2.

Table 16.1. *Growth of electronic media*

	1950	1960	1970	1980	1990
Percentage of households with television	9.0	87.1	95.3	97.9	98.2
Average viewing hours per day	4.6	5.1	5.9	6.6	6.9
Percentage of TV households					
With cable	N.A.	N.A.	6.7	19.9	56.4
With VCR	N.A.	N.A.	N.A.	1.1	68.6

Sources: *Statistical Abstract of the United States, 1979*, table 986; *1989*, table 900; *1991*, table 919; and Nielsen Media Research.

of programs classified as cultural varied from 17.9 to 22.8 percent of total broadcast hours. (The study's definition of cultural, however, is probably somewhat broader than the one employed in this book.)[5]

As pointed out in Chapter 2, commercial television broadcasting on a consequential scale began immediately after World War II and gained viewers rapidly. Table 16.1 shows that only 9 percent of U.S. households had a television set in 1950. By 1960 the proportion had risen to 87 percent, and average viewing per day was reported to be 5.1 hours. By 1990, 98 percent of households had sets (often more than one). Viewing per day reached a peak of 7.2 hours in 1987, then declined slightly to 6.9 hours in 1990. Obviously, television has become a major cultural force.

Broadcast television, like radio, is dominated by the advertising-supported commercial sector. In 1978, 516 of the available VHF channels were licensed to operate commercially, while only 111 were licensed to public (i.e., nonprofit) entities.[6] Why licenses are required in order to broadcast and how their number is limited will emerge in the next pages.

To argue, as we have done, that the mass media cultivate the taste for popular art by insistently reproducing it, is to imply that if they devoted more time to the high arts, they could also stimulate the taste for those forms. That may seem a doubtful proposition, given the weight of the forces supporting popular culture, and we know of no hard evidence to support it. In this chapter we will argue the need for a public broadcasting system to supplement private, commercial networks. But the argument does not stand or fall on the ability of broadcasting to

[5] National Endowment for the Arts, *A Sourcebook of Arts Statistics: 1989*, tables 8.59 and 8.60.
[6] *A Public Trust: The Report of the Carnegie Commission on the Future of Public Broadcasting* (New York: Bantam, 1979), table C.1.

influence taste. It would be sufficient grounds for some sort of public intervention that the private commercial system ignores the preferences of a sizable minority of potential listeners and viewers.

Some caveats

Before we go further, two caveats are in order. First, the radio, television, and cable industry is so complicated that a single chapter cannot possibly do it justice and is therefore in danger of oversimplifying complex issues. Indeed, it was explained in Chapter 1 that broadcasting, writing and publishing, and the motion picture industry would be omitted from the field to be studied because, among other reasons, each would require a book unto itself. The electronic media are discussed in this chapter only in respect to their special role in the development of taste and the dissemination of culture. No attempt is made at a full description of the economics of the broadcasting or cable industries. In the pages that follow, much is omitted, including the relationship between networks and stations, the role of independent producers, the content of cable programming, and the interaction between broadcasting and cable transmission. The discussion of television is largely confined to the earlier-established, very high-frequency (or VHF) sector, occupying Channels 2 through 13; little is said about ultrahigh-frequency television stations (or UHF), the poor sisters of the broadcasting industry, consigned to Channels 14 through 83.

Second, it must be kept in mind that the electronic media industry is subject to almost continuous transformation as wave after wave of technological innovation sweeps through it. Table 16.1 shows how rapidly the successive revolutions first of broadcast television, then of cable, and, most recently, of the videocassette recorder have taken hold. There is no reason to believe the industry will be less dynamic in the future. Thus, almost anything written about it today is in danger of sounding outdated tomorrow.

Federal regulation of broadcasting

Television, like the radio broadcasting out of which it grew, is a federally regulated industry. Regulation began with the Radio Act of 1927 as a way of sorting out the assignment of signal frequencies, so that broadcast signals would not interfere with one another. The act created a Federal Radio Commission. Noll, Peck, and McGowan summarize its powers as follows:

> The commission was given the power to assign wavelengths and determine the power and location of transmitters. Licenses were to be

granted for three years, but only if the commission determined that the award would serve the "public convenience, interest, or necessity." When more than one group applied for a given frequency assignment, the public interest was to guide the commission's decision among them; licenses could be transferred only with the commission's approval and could be revoked for misconduct, but censorship powers and control of program content were specifically denied the commission.[7]

Under the Communications Act of 1934 the Federal Radio Commission became the Federal Communications Commission (FCC) and was given the power to regulate telephone communications as well as broadcasting. In most respects, the regulatory framework established in 1927 was retained. Thus, when television became a reality, it was subject to regulation under the guidelines that had originally been laid down for radio.

Regulation justified by market failure
It should be recalled that in Chapter 11, market failure was cited as the principal justification for regulation, and "externalities" were listed among the important causes of market failure. Broadcast signal interference is quite obviously an external effect of one economic unit on another, so the regulation of broadcasting fits very well into the theory of externalities developed in Chapter 11. There is an additional argument at work, however. The electromagnetic spectrum usable for broadcasting belongs to the public at large, like the air we breathe or the water in our rivers. No original private claims on it are recognized. It is public property. Hence, the purpose of regulation is not just to keep private users from interfering with one another, but also to promote the public interest.

Noll, Peck, and McGowan tell us that the FCC, in attempting to regulate broadcasting in the public interest, has adhered to four objectives: first, to establish stations "in as many localities as possible"; second, to bring about an "acceptable level of diversity in program content"; third, to ensure that broadcasting fulfills its "role as public servant"; and fourth, "to maintain an acceptable level of competition."[8] They point out that these objectives are not necessarily compatible.

An initial complication is that the number of VHF signals that can be simultaneously broadcast over a given region without mutual interference is limited by the width of the electromagnetic spectrum. The VHF spectrum could theoretically accommodate up to seven simultaneous signals per locality. However, to ensure that signals from adjacent

[7] Noll et al., *Economic Aspects of Television Regulation*, p. 98.
[8] Ibid., p. 99.

markets do not interfere with one another through spatial overlap, the FCC has rarely made available more than three commercial and one public VHF license per locality.

The decentralization objective

The objective of maintaining stations in as many different localities as possible is rooted in the U.S. tradition of defending local autonomy against the threat of centralized economic or political power. No doubt political pressure from members of Congress and locally elected officials also weighed in on the side of localism. But in this instance a price was paid in terms of reduced competition in each market. If the FCC had assigned VHF licenses so as to develop regional rather than local markets by authorizing fewer stations with greater transmission range, much of the nation could have received up to seven VHF channels.[9] There would have been fewer cities with stations, but more competition in each market. An economist qua economist, however, cannot say whether the assumed political or social benefits of localism outweigh its economic costs in terms of reduced competition.

Scarcity value of broadcast licenses

From the preceding discussion it is clear that the authorized number of broadcasting licenses depends not only on the natural limitations of the electromagnetic spectrum, but also on the particular plan by which the FCC divides it up. There is also no question about the fact that limitations on their number, resulting in what economists call relative scarcity, have made TV broadcasting licenses exceedingly valuable. The extra income that accrues to a license owner on account of the relative scarcity of licenses is a form of "scarcity rent" or, as it is sometimes called by economic theorists, "economic rent."[10] Economic rent is defined as a payment to a factor of production in excess of what must be paid to bring it into use. Since the electromagnetic spectrum exists in the state of nature and is nonreproducible, the spectrum space handed over to a licensee has no cost of production. Therefore, the return attributable to the use of the licensed segment is an economic rent. In this case, since the factor of production is space on the broadcast spectrum, it can also be referred to as "spectrum rent." It has sometimes

---

[9] Ibid., p. 101.

[10] This should not be confused with the more popular usage of the term "rent," in the sense of a periodic payment, such as renting an apartment, a car, or a floor-sanding machine.

been proposed that such rent be taxed and the proceeds used to subsidize public broadcasting. We return to this question later.

The quality of commercial broadcast programming

Although two of the FCC's objectives – an acceptable level of program diversity and service to the public – relate directly to program content, many observers would argue that the commission has not been successful in achieving them. It is true that both networks and local stations devote a good deal of time and effort to news broadcasts and political events, which help them to fulfill the commission's public service objective. From 1986 to 1988, news and information programs on the commercial networks made up 17 to 19 percent of evening program hours. The percentage of total hours was probably at least as high. For the sake of comparison, in 1986 16.4 percent of public TV's total broadcast hours were devoted to news and public affairs.[11]

It is the content diversity objective that is farthest from realization. If by diversity we mean that the viewer is offered a choice among game shows in the early evening or between sitcoms or police dramas in prime time, or among movie reruns still later on, then there is a good deal of diversity in U.S. broadcasting. But if by diversity we mean that commercial TV might also with reasonable frequency offer documentaries, educational programs, or what we have referred to as high culture, then the verdict is likely to be negative.[12]

The effect of advertisers on programming

Commercial broadcasters are in the business of selling advertising time. Advertisers buy time and pay for it in proportion to the size of the audience delivered, as measured by the ratings services. "Entertainment programs" in their various forms attract the largest audiences. Hence, commercial broadcasters are under constant pressure to shun documentaries, educational programs, and high culture in favor of entertainment. The problem is *not* that commercial broadcasters, at least those in the larger markets, cannot afford to offer more diverse and less remunerative programming. As we shall see, the substantial spectrum rents that accrue to licensees would easily pay for more "merit pro-

---

[11] For public TV, see *Sourcebook: 1989,* table 8.59; for commercial networks, see Christopher A. Sterling and John M. Kittross, *Stay Tuned: A Concise History of American Broadcasting,* 2d ed. (Belmont, Calif.: Wadsworth, 1990), table 7.A (data copyrighted by L. W. Lichty).

[12] See Levin, *Fact and Fantasy,* chap. 3, on program diversity and chap. 13 on content regulation.

gramming." The problem, rather, is that the FCC has not found the will or the way to bring sufficient pressure on them to do so. The commission has almost never refused a license renewal in order to enforce some higher standard of program service on a licensee. More direct action, for example, the imposition of explicit quantitative program requirements (assuming the necessary rules could be spelled out), might violate the broadcasters' right of free speech, assertedly protected by the First Amendment to the U.S. Constitution. In any case, such an approach has not been tried.

In recent years two changes have altered the context in which the argument about television program quality is carried on. First, public broadcasting has developed into a going enterprise, potentially able to supply the serious, high-quality programs not found on commercial stations. Indeed, the more cultural programming became available on PBS, the less of it the commercial broadcasters were inclined to offer. Brian Rose noted that (in the early 1970s) "the development and growth of PBS seemed to free the commercial networks from maintaining their previous levels of prime-time cultural offerings. . . . By the 1980s they had virtually abandoned the field of cultural production to PBS."[13] One might therefore argue that instead of trying (unsuccessfully) to persuade commercial broadcasters to devote spectrum rents to producing (or buying) quality programs, we should in some fashion tax those rents and use the proceeds to help pay for enhanced programming and a wider reach for the public system. We will return to this question later.

The second change comes from numerous technological innovations, among them cable television and more recently the home videocassette recorder, laser videodisc, backyard dish antenna, and satellite master antenna television (SMATV). These new modes of communication compete directly with television broadcasting. Each offers an alternative to reliance on locally broadcast signals and thus increases the range of choice available to the consumer. Some analysts argue that this increase in competition makes it desirable to deregulate at least some aspects of commercial broadcasting.[14] That is a debate we need not enter here. Instead, we will look into the question of whether cable itself has increased the amount of art and culture available to television viewers.

---

[13] Brian G. Rose, *Television and the Performing Arts,* a handbook and reference guide to cultural programming (Westport, Conn.: Greenwood, 1986), pp. 10, 12.

[14] See the papers collected in Eli M. Noam, ed., *Video Media Competition* (New York: Columbia University Press, 1985).

Narrowcasting: the promise of culture on cable

What we now call "cable television" began in 1948 as a way of bringing broadcast TV signals to local markets where reception was blocked by uneven topography. The organizer of a network would build an antenna on high ground and then carry the signals along newly installed cables to the homes of subscribers.[15] The industry grew slowly through the 1950s and 1960s. The importation of programming other than what could be received from broadcasters was in various ways impeded by FCC regulation, and this had the effect of limiting the attractiveness of cable to areas where broadcast reception was poor.

Two changes produced a cable television boom in the 1970s. First, the FCC relaxed its regulations and, second, the invention of signal transmission via satellites fixed in space greatly improved the process of importing distant signals. Cable companies could now offer a far greater number of simultaneous programs than were available in any one market over the air. As shown in Table 16.1, by 1980, 20 percent of all U.S. television households were wired for cable, and by 1990 the proportion had reached 56 percent.

As the number of cable-connected homes increased in the late 1970s, media analysts began to talk about the revolutionary possibilities of what they called "narrowcasting."[16] We have already described the economic incentives that drive over-the-air broadcasters to try to maximize audience size by designing programs that will appeal to the tastes of the majority. In that process the tastes of smaller groups (say, less than 15 percent of the potential audience) are simply ignored. Narrowcasting seemed to offer a way out. It was suggested that since so many channels were available on the typical cable network, it might now actually be profitable to devote some of them to the satisfaction of minority tastes, such as the taste for high culture (or at least for higher culture than was available on commercially broadcast TV). Thus was born the notion of "art and culture on cable." Not only would lovers of the arts be pleased, but also performing arts companies would have a new and much needed source of revenue and employment. Television would not only offer high art, but would also contribute to its growth and prosperity. Unfortunately, it did not work out that way.

Between December 1980 and June 1982, four commercial cable channels were launched to offer nationwide viewers a richer combination of art, culture, and sophisticated entertainment than had ever before been

[15] This summary of cable TV's early history is based on Kirsten Beck, *Cultivating the Wasteland* (New York: American Council for the Arts, 1983), pp. 1–14.

[16] Ibid., pp. 16–20.

attempted in the commercial sector. The four are described briefly in the following paragraphs.

CBS Cable

CBS Cable began operation in October 1981. It was intended to be advertising supported. Moreover, instead of simply importing cultural programming from such highly regarded sources as Britain's BBC or ITV, CBS Cable was determined to produce at least some of its own shows. An advantage of doing that would be to earn revenue from subsequent resale of the material. Among the in-house productions for TV mounted by CBS Cable were dance works such as Twyla Tharp's *Baker's Dozen* and dramatic pieces such as Elizabeth Swados's *Songs of Innocence and Experience* and Athol Fugard's *Sizwe Banzie Is Dead*.[17] The quality of CBS Cable's productions received high critical praise, but advertising revenues fell disastrously short of expectations and re-sales never materialized. By December 1982 losses were said to have reached $50 million. CBS decided to shut the channel down.

The Entertainment Channel

In June 1982, RCA and Rockefeller Center, Inc., launched The Entertainment Channel (TEC) as a joint venture. It was intended to be subscriber supported and to be on the air 24 hours a day. Its programs were slightly more "popular" in orientation than those on CBS Cable. For example, TEC obtained exclusive U.S. rights to BBC material. (BBC programs such as "Upstairs, Downstairs" had already been re-broadcast with enormous success on U.S. public television.) TEC also intended to draw heavily on the Broadway theater for its programming, producing for TV such expensive hits as the composer Steven Sond-heim's *Sweeney Todd*.

TEC's executives denied that the channel intended to deliver what might be thought of as "high-brow culture," insisting that their aim was simply to provide entertainment, but better, less boring enter-tainment than was commonly found on network TV. Whatever the intended mixture, not enough viewers thought it worthwhile to pay the subscription premium. TEC closed down in March 1983, with losses reported to be $34 million. In a technical sense, one could say it did not "go out of business" since in a subsequent merger, it became part of the Arts and Entertainment Network.

[17] Ibid., pp. 63–64.

Arts and Entertainment Network

A&E began in April 1981 as the ARTS channel, a joint venture of the Hearst Corporation and the American Broadcasting Company. It started modestly, offering only three hours of programming a night. Though originally intended to be supported by unobtrusive corporate "underwriters," it eventually also attracted advertising. The initial programming consisted largely of what we have called high culture, but production costs were minimized by relying heavily on already existing material imported from Europe, rather than investing large sums in original productions. A&E is reported to have lost about $8 million a year through 1983, but its backers were willing to sustain it.[18] It has continued and now offers many more hours of service per week, but an examination of program listings shows that it has moved distinctly away from high culture toward a mixture that includes movies, comedy, nature shows, and documentaries on history and current affairs.

Bravo

Another culture channel that has survived, Bravo began operation in December 1980 as a joint venture of three cable system operators. It is a subscription service. Like A&E it began modestly but gradually expanded its offerings until it was on the air in the evening and nighttime hours, seven days a week. Programming is divided between the performing arts and movies, not the usual run of Hollywood products, but rather foreign and domestic films that have received serious critical approval. Over the years the proportion of time devoted to movies has increased at the expense of other performing arts material. The price of survival has apparently been to move away from high culture.

Lessons of the cable experience

As always when complex ventures fail, different observers will offer different explanations. One account of the failure of CBS Cable and TEC might be that their backers underestimated the start-up costs and were not prepared to wait long enough before breaking even. To support that view one might note that both Bravo and A&E started with less ambitious immediate goals but eventually made a go of it. On the other hand, both also moved away from high culture in the process of "finding a niche" in the entertainment spectrum. A possible conclusion, especially if one were suspicious of "special pleading" for the arts,

---

[18] *New York Times*, "Cable TV Notes," October 6, 1983.

would be that a market for art and culture broad enough to support an exclusively cultural channel just is not there.

A more complex answer is supplied by David Waterman's study of the launching of the channels.[19] His conclusions can be summed up as follows. First, the audience for culture is *not* "a cohesive group of avid (i.e., frequent) viewers" waiting to watch almost *any* cultural program that comes along. Rather, there are opera buffs, balletomanes, theater lovers, and so on. They will not necessarily watch every program in their own field of interest, much less in other fields. Thus, the audience for any *single* program is likely to be small. But second, the cost of producing original cultural programs for TV is very high and was probably underestimated by the cable groups that proposed to try it. Finally, the new culture channels faced competition from one well-established and, as it turned out, rather formidable competitor: public television.

Waterman reports that "in the 1982–3 season public television offered about 35 hours per month of original prime-time cultural programming, a little over 40 percent of its total prime-time schedule." Moreover, public stations at that time were assisted by the FCC's "must carry" rules, first propogated in 1965, which required cable systems to carry the signals of most television stations broadcasting within their local area. Since public television was by then a nationwide system, that meant the new culture channels were likely to be faced with a competing public channel in every home they reached in a major market. (The must carry rules were later invalidated by the federal court of appeals on First Amendment grounds.)

Not only did public television offer a good deal of culture, it also in Waterman's words had a "reputation for consistently first rate productions," which established "the industry standard for high quality cultural programming." PBS had to spend a lot of money to achieve that high quality. Waterman's calculations led him to estimate that "CBS Cable's total [cultural] programming investment per year was less than one-quarter that of PBS." He concluded that the very great cost of high-quality original programming in *any* category dims the prospect that narrowcasting ventures can eventually become financially "self-supporting," a position that is simply reinforced by our showing in Chapter 8 that television production costs are by their very nature subject to cost inflation on account of productivity lag.

Although Waterman does not say so, this line of thought leads to the

---

[19] David Waterman, "Arts and Cultural Programming on Cable Television: Economic Analysis of the U.S. Experience," in *Economic Efficiency and the Arts* (Akron, Ohio: Association for Cultural Economics, 1987), pp. 240–49.

conclusion that if we really want culture on television, we will have to rely on subsidized public TV to present it. And since the cost of program production seems to rise ineluctably, we had better be prepared to increase the public subsidy as we go along. In this way we arrive at the question, How should public television be paid for?

Paying for public broadcasting

The Public Broadcasting System (PBS), as it is known in the United States, came into being with the passage by Congress of the Public Broadcasting Act in 1967. The individual units that were brought together to form the system had previously been known as educational television or radio stations.[20] They were nonprofit enterprises, usually operated by universities or supported by state or local governments. During the 1960s educational broadcasting had received some funds from the federal government and substantial support from the Ford Foundation. Nevertheless, because of its decentralized origins, by far the greater part of its income came from state or local tax sources, and this continued to be the case for some years after the federally sponsored public system went into operation.

Public support of public broadcasting

The financial history of PBS is summarized in Table 16.2. Federal support comes principally through appropriations made to the Corporation for Public Broadcasting, which was set up under the 1967 act to oversee the development of a physically interconnected system for public television and public radio, to underwrite national programming (CPB was not itself permitted to produce programs), and to act as a conduit in the distribution of federal funds to individual stations. By 1973 the federal appropriation to CPB had grown to $35 million, while other federal agencies (chiefly the NEA and NEH) added grants of $20.6 million. Yet the combined federal contribution amounted to only 21.8 percent of public broadcasting's total income of $254.8 million. State and local support accounted for 50 percent, and private sources, including foundations, individuals, and corporations, 28.2 percent.

In the ensuing years, many of the friends of public broadcasting argued for more generous federal support on the ground that budgetary constraints were preventing the system from realizing its full potential. A

---

[20] On the origin of public broadcasting in the United States and its history through 1977, see Carnegie Commission on the Future of Public Broadcasting, *A Public Trust* (New York: Bantam, 1979), chap. 2. For the years 1977–89, see Sterling and Kittross, *Stay Tuned*, pp. 479–84.

Table 16.2. Sources of public broadcasting income

Source	1973 Amount ($ millions)	1973 Percent	1983 Amount ($ millions)	1983 Percent	1990 Amount ($ millions)	1990 Percent
Total income	254.8	100	899.2	100	1,581.4	100
Federal appropriation to CPB	35.0	13.7	137.0	15.2	229.4	14.5
Federal grants	20.6	8.1	26.7	3.0	38.0	2.4
State and local tax-based	127.3	50.0	318.3	35.4	473.8	30.0
Private, total	71.9	28.2	417.1	46.4	840.2	53.1
Individuals	25.4	10.0	196.4	21.8	363.7	23.0
Business	9.6	3.8	119.8	13.3	262.4	16.6
Foundations	20.2	7.9	24.9	2.8	71.1	4.5
Private colleges and universities	—[a]	—[a]	23.7	2.6	31.2	2.0
Other private	16.7	6.6	52.2	5.8	111.8	7.1

[a]Included in other private for 1973.
Sources: National Endowment for the Arts, A Sourcebook of Arts Statistics: 1989, table 8.61; Corporation for Public Broadcasting (CPB), Public Broadcasting Income Fiscal Year 1990, December 1991, table 2, and unpublished CPB tabulations.

1988 report, for example, argued that "the system and the public stations cannot do great programming unless there is a large increase in national funding, plus a guarantee that these funds will be available two years, five years, even ten or twenty years from now."[21] Such pleas were not notably successful. As Table 16.2 shows, the federal contribution did increase in absolute amount, but declined as a fraction of total system income to only 16.9 percent in 1990. The relative decline in state and local support was even sharper.

Private support of public broadcasting

What rescued the system from financial disaster was the rapid growth of private funding, which increased to 53.1 percent of total income. Public television stations, as anyone who watches regularly can verify, had turned to their individual listeners and to large corporations for tax-deductible contributions. (For a discussion of the economics of such contributions, see Chapter 12.) That might seem like a good thing, the virtues of voluntarism being what they are. Yet it does raise serious questions of policy. To gain individual contributions, stations are inevitably drawn to produce programming that will appeal to the moneyed middle or upper middle classes, to the exclusion of "demographically unattractive" audiences who are also underserved by commercial broadcasting.[22] Corporate support raises equally serious problems. Producers for public television who seek corporate sponsorship know that they must avoid subjects that might be in any way controversial. The result is an increasingly bland menu of programs.

How should public broadcasting be financed?

The manner in which public broadcasting should be paid for has been debated by economists, broadcasters, and public servants since the system's inception. The basic issues are, on the financial side, adequacy, stability, and predictability of funding, and on the political side, accountability, but with independence from political interference, and central versus local control.

Passage of the Public Broadcasting Act in 1967 was largely attributable to the influence of a report by the first Carnegie Commission entitled *Public Television: A Program for Action*, issued in January of that year

---

[21] Working Group for Public Broadcasting, *Public Broadcasting: A National Asset to be Preserved, Promoted and Protected* (Columbus: Ohio State University School of Journalism, December 1988), p. 1.

[22] Ibid., p. 3.

(and now referred to as "Carnegie I" to distinguish it from the report of a second commission in 1979).[23] Concerned about the danger of political interference with the content of public broadcasting, the commission recommended that programming funds for the system be derived from a special tax on the sale of television sets, the proceeds of which would be specifically dedicated to public broadcasting.[24] Such an arrangement would have insulated programming from the ordinary appropriation process, with its potential for putting political pressure on the system. (In the wake of the confrontation between Senator Jesse Helms and his supporters and the NEA, discussed in Chapter 12, no one is likely to underestimate that potential.) It was also suggested that the new tax would provide an adequate and reliable source of funds to encourage long-run planning. At the same time, the commission recommended that general operating support for stations be provided out of regular appropriations to the (then) Department of Health, Education, and Welfare. In the event, congress and the administration rejected the notion of a dedicated tax, so the federal contribution has always been financed by appropriations, although these have usually been approved for three years at a time, in recognition of the long planning period needed for successful program development.[25]

Opposition to a dedicated tax, as well as reluctance to increase federal support to the levels sought by public television's advocates, comes primarily from those who fear the development of a substantially centralized public system. The Nixon administration, for example, apparently believed that "the eastern liberal elite" was biasing CPB-sponsored public affairs programs against its policies during the Vietnam War. Many local television stations also reportedly feared central control over public affairs programming.[26] On the other hand, defenders of centralization argue that it is the best way to assemble the massive resources needed to finance superior programming, not only in public affairs but in science, education, and the arts, as well. As one observer put it, "The problem is that the technology cries out for centralization," but centralization conflicts with local autonomy.[27] Because local autonomy is a cherished value in the United States, it should not surprise us that the

[23] Carnegie Commission on Educational Television, *Public Television: A Program for Action* (New York: Harper & Row, 1967).
[24] Ibid., pp. 68–73.
[25] On the pros and cons of using dedicated taxes to support public broadcasting, see *A Public Trust*, pp. 140–43.
[26] See ibid., pp. 41–45.
[27] Comment of Professor James A. Capo to the authors.

tug-of-war between those favoring centralization and those supporting localism has been the source of constant political tension within the world of public broadcasting.

Commentators on the problem of financing public broadcasting in the United States do seem to agree that a balance among funding sources is desirable to prevent any *one* source from obtaining undue influence over programming. Just what proportions constitute a proper "balance" is not a question we will try to resolve, although we do believe that those arguing for a larger federal role have made a strong case. We turn next to the question of how broadcasting and cable systems can or should be financed.

Alternative systems compared

Each system of paying for and operating broadcasting or cable results in a different distribution of burdens and benefits among socioeconomic groups. For example, U.S. commercial broadcasting is supported by advertising revenues. Economists usually argue that in the long run the cost of advertising is passed on to the general consumer in the form of higher product prices. Thus, the burden of supporting commercial TV ultimately falls on the general consumer. On the benefit side, we must distinguish between direct benefits to viewers and indirect benefits or externalities that may accrue to the general public. Obviously, the direct benefits of commercial television go to the people who watch it, that is, to its audience. Although almost everyone watches *some* television, there can be no presumption that the direct benefits are spread across the population in the same way as the burdens. For example, families of equal income may pay about the same amount in higher prices as a result of advertising but may watch television in very unequal amounts. Advertising-supported TV is distinctly *not* a system under which each beneficiary pays for what he or she gets.

Indirect benefits are a more complicated story. Commercial television carries a considerable amount of news and information programming. Those who watch it presumably get direct benefits. But it might be argued that such programming also provides an external or indirect benefit to *all* citizens by raising the general level of the public's awareness and understanding of important issues. The FCC certainly takes the position that news and information programs serve the public interest. Licensees probably carry more such programming on account of FCC licensing than they would do if entirely unregulated. Thus, at least part of the indirect benefits of broadcast news and information must be attributed to FCC regulation. Broadcasters might argue that such pro-

Table 16.3. *Incidence of benefits and costs of commercial and public broadcasting*

Type of financial support	Financial burden is borne by	Direct benefits go to
Commercial systems		
(A) Advertising supported with FCC regulation (existing system)	General consumer	Viewers of commercial TV
(B) Pay or subscription TV	Viewers of pay channels	Viewers of pay channels
Public systems		
(C) Subsidized out of general government revenues (existing system)	General taxpayer	Viewers of public broadcasting
(D) Subsidized by tax on sale of TV sets (Carnegie I)	Purchasers and manufacturers of new sets	Viewers of public broadcasting
(E) Subsidized by fee on set owners (existing British system)	Set owners and manufacturers	Viewers of public broadcasting
(F) Subsidized by tax on TV advertising revenue	Commercial broadcasters, advertisers, consumers	Viewers of public broadcasting
(G) Subsidized by spectrum rent or fee (Carnegie II)	Spectrum users (licensees)	Viewers of public broadcasting

grams are being paid for out of their profits but recognize an obligation to absorb that cost in return for the privilege of using the airwaves free of charge. However, if some special tax (of the sort discussed later in this section) were levied on commercial broadcasting in order to support the public networks, commercial licensees would undoubtedly argue that paying the tax relieves them of any obligation also to serve the public interest by paying for unprofitable news and information programs. The merits of that argument, as we shall see, are debatable, but it would certainly be put forward.

Table 16.3 attempts to assign among various economic classes the burdens and benefits of the alternative ways of financing and operating television. It is unnecessary to show indirect benefits in the table, since no matter what the mode of finance, the indirect benefits of either news and information programming or programs of art and culture always go to the general public. In the interest of brevity, the analysis of financial burden is necessarily somewhat simplified. Row A summarizes the analysis we have just offered of advertising supported broadcast TV. Row B deals with pay or subscription TV distributed via cable. Under that system the viewer is both the recipient of the direct benefits and the one who bears the financial burden. In this case, you *do* get exactly what you pay for. The indirect benefits, if there are any, would flow to the general public, as in all other cases.

Pay or subscription TV appeals to some economists because it allows consumer choice, operating through a pricing mechanism, to guide program content.[28] It is not a satisfactory solution, however, if one takes distributional effects into account. If it is regarded as desirable that all families have access to programs of news, information, art, or culture, or to educational programming, then a pay system is unacceptable since it will tend to exclude the poor.

The remainder of the table deals with alternative ways of financing public broadcasting and can be thought of as applying equally to public television or public radio. There is a difference between public and commercial systems, however, that must be noted here: based on the program content data cited earlier in this chapter, it is probable that on a per viewer basis, the public system produces more indirect benefits or externalities per day (especially via art, cultural, and educational programming) than the commercial system does. Thus, although indirect benefits always go to the general public, they are probably more substantial relative to direct benefits for public than for commercial systems.

Row C summarizes the effects of the present system of financing public broadcasting. Government subsidies (whether from the federal, state, or local level) are paid out of general revenues rather than earmarked taxes. Thus, the financial burden is borne by the general taxpayer who may not also be a viewer or listener receiving *direct* benefits. That might be thought inequitable. On the other hand, the *indirect* benefits go to the general public. To that extent, laying the burden on the general taxpayer seems justified.

Row D covers the proposal of the first Carnegie Commission in 1967. Carnegie I favored the imposition of a tax on the sale of new TV sets,

---

[28] See the discussion in Noll et al., *Economic Aspects of Television Regulation*, chap. 5.

with the proceeds earmarked to pay part of the cost of public broadcasting. As we have already pointed out, the proposal was not adopted. The burden of such a tax would have been divided in uncertain proportions between purchasers of new sets, who would probably have paid a higher price including the tax, and manufacturers and distributors, who might have received a lower after-tax return. The political virtue of the proposal was that it would not have immediately burdened current set owners (a very large constituency). But from an equity standpoint, that was a weakness: current set owners would have been getting a "free ride": they would receive direct benefits (assuming they watched public TV), but at no cost.

More recently, the Working Group for Public Broadcasting proposed a dedicated 2 percent tax on factory sales of all consumer electronic products (whether imported or domestic) and on all electronic equipment used in broadcasting. They estimated that the proceeds in 1987 would have been about $600 million, sufficient to more than double the federal contribution to public broadcasting in that year.[29] This proposal in not shown separately in Table 16.3. As a sales tax, its effects would resemble those already shown in Row D, except that the burden would fall on purchasers and manufacturers of all electronic products, instead of only new TV sets.

In contrast to a sales tax, the British system (Row E) levies a yearly license fee on all owners of radios and TV sets, with the proceeds going to support public broadcasting (the BBC). The burden of the fee is presumably divided between set owners and manufacturers and distributors. The latter two may sell fewer sets as a consequence of the fee and/or have to sell them at a lower after-tax price. When the BBC was Great Britain's only broadcaster, one could assume that set owners were also viewers or listeners and therefore received the direct benefits of the public system. Under those circumstances, the license fee was a roughly equitable way to cover costs. That manufacturers and distributors of sets probably bore some of the burden could also be regarded as equitable, since the fee paid for a system of broadcasting without which there would have been no market for sets. Since 1954, however, Britain has had a parallel advertising-supported system under the Independent Broadcasting Authority. Consequently, the equity argument for the license fee on set owners is now a bit weaker. Owners who now watch or listen only to the commercial stations pay the fee without receiving direct benefits.

Row F summarizes the probable effects of a tax on television and

[29] *Public Broadcasting*, p. 9.

radio broadcast advertising revenue, another special charge that has sometimes been proposed to raise revenue for the support of public broadcasting. This proposal has some obvious political advantages. First of all, it would be a "hidden tax" in the sense of not being visible to the general public. Second, since the advertising revenues in question are large, a very low rate of tax could produce revenues that would be substantial in relation to the size of public broadcasting's budget. The proposal gets lower marks on equity grounds, however. If the burden were to rest entirely on commercial broadcasters, one might argue that it is a roughly equitable way of recapturing for the public benefit part of the income they obtain from using the broadcast spectrum free of charge. But broadcasters would attempt to shift some of the burden on to advertisers in the form of higher rates, and advertisers in turn would try to shift it forward to consumers through higher prices. The tax thus runs the risk of laying a burden on the general consumer, who may not be a direct beneficiary (i.e., viewer or listener) of public broadcasting. If the objective is to find a special tax that could be levied on broadcasters and not shifted by them to the general public, then the clear choice is a rent or fee charged to users of the broadcast spectrum, a proposal to which we now turn.

Charging for the commercial use of the spectrum

It was pointed out earlier in this chapter that the capacity of the electromagnetic spectrum to carry broadcast signals is limited, and that licenses to use it for TV broadcasting are therefore extremely valuable but have nevertheless been given away free of charge by the FCC. A special fee or tax on the spectrum rent appropriated by commercial users has therefore sometimes been proposed as a way of raising revenue to support public broadcasting. Row G in Table 16.3 summarizes its probable effects, if applied to commercial broadcasters. The crucial entry is in the second column: the burden of the fee or tax would remain with the licensees. Economic theory tells us that they could not shift it forward to viewers or listeners, advertisers or consumers. Thus, a fee or tax on the use of the spectrum would effectively take back some of the free gains made by license holders. An additional argument in its favor is that by putting a rational price on the spectrum, it would encourage users to treat spectrum space as the scarce resource that it is and, therefore, to use it more efficiently.[30]

The second Carnegie Commission, in its 1979 report on public broadcasting, was moved by this logic. The commission recommended that

[30] See Noll et al., *Economic Aspects of Television Regulation*, pp. 53–54.

federal appropriations to support public broadcasting be substantially increased and that fees charged to private users of the electromagnetic spectrum be introduced to offset part of the additional cost.[31] The commission recognized that such fees would have to be charged not just to broadcasters but to *all* private users of the airwaves. In today's terms that means it would also apply to CB radio operators, cellular telephone systems, radio-call taxis, and the like. Since the fee would be collected from so many nonbroadcasters, the commission did not suggest that the proceeds necessarily be earmarked for public broadcasting. They did suggest, however, that Congress might find it appropriate to earmark the amounts paid by commercial broadcasters.

Under present institutional arrangements, the economic value of the broadcast spectrum is not directly observable. When an existing radio or TV station is sold by its current license holder the price covers the value of not only the license, but also the building or studios, the equipment, and the goodwill that goes with the station. (Goodwill comprises intangible assets like name recognition, reputation, and business and professional connections.) We could observe the pure value of a license only if there were a free market in such rights and they could be bought and sold or rented independently of the other assets needed to operate a station. Although such a market does not exist for broadcast licenses, there are analogous markets for other rent-earning resources, and economic analysis can tell us a good deal about how they operate.

Spectrum rent as a form of "economic rent"

As pointed out earlier in this chapter, spectrum rent is a form of what economists define as "economic rent." The resource scarcity that gives rise to economic rent (hereafter referred to simply as rent) is most commonly illustrated by the case of urban land. In 1990, before a subsequent decline in land prices, some sites in midtown Manhattan sold for more that $2,000 per square foot.[32] Since the land itself had no cost of production apart from relatively minor expenses for draining and grading, almost the entire value can be regarded as pure rent. In the case of urban land, the scarce factor for which rent is being paid is the accessibility conferred by the given site.

Because developable land is traded in a relatively free market, land values like those just cited can be observed in actual sales. However, it is often more convenient to think of economic rent not as the sales value

---

[31] *A Public Trust*, pp. 143–45.
[32] Calculated from data in *1991 Austrian Roth Manhattan Land Price Index*, February 10, 1992.

of an asset, but rather as a payment per time period for using it. The relationship between the sales value (i.e., capital value) of an asset and its annual rental value is, fortunately, straightforward: the capital value of an urban site or of a broadcasting license is the present value of the stream of annual net returns a purchaser expects it to yield in the future. For example, if a prospective buyer believes a given TV license will yield a net return of $500,000 a year into the indefinite future and the rate of interest for purposes of capitalization is 10 percent, he or she will bid $5 million for the license.[33]

But what do we mean by "net return"? TV and radio stations generate *gross* revenue by selling advertising time to sponsors. From that gross revenue one must deduct the annual cost of equipping, operating, and maintaining the station to arrive at the residual that we call the annual *net* return from owning a license. Whether prospective buyers of a TV station would expect that annual net return to grow, shrink, or remain the same in future years is, of course, uncertain. If the population and/ or average income level in the market area served were to grow, we would expect the demand for advertising time to increase. If production costs remained constant while demand rose, the rent available to the license holder each year would obviously increase, and the value of the license would rise. On the other hand, the home entertainment business is highly sensitive to technological change. First cable transmission and then the home videocassette player entered the market to compete for audiences with broadcast TV. These and other innovations not even in sight might *reduce* advertisers' demand for broadcast time and hence cut down future net rents per licensee.

A closer look at spectrum fees or taxes

Although the amount of economic rent flowing to U.S. television broadcasters each year cannot be directly observed, it can be estimated by studying the financial performance of TV stations. Harvey J. Levin carried out such a study using data for 1975. He estimated that 352 of the 492 stations on the air that year earned economic rents and that these rents in the aggregate amounted to $416.9 million, or about 25 percent of the $1.644 billion in revenue they received.[34]

How much of the market value of television stations is accounted for by capitalization of these estimated annual net rents? Levin does not answer that question directly, but it can be inferred from his results that

---

[33] This is very much like the argument developed in Chapter 9, in which the price of art is determined in part by the expected return.

[34] Levin, *Fact and Fantasy*, pp. 111–20.

on average something over half of their sales price is a payment for the value of the broadcasting license per se. These are not trivial sums by any reckoning.

From the fact that rent is a payment to a factor of production that is nonreproducible and therefore fixed in supply, two important conclusions about a tax on rent follow. The first concerns economic efficiency, while the second has to do with equity. The efficiency conclusion is that a tax on economic rent will not interfere with the efficient operation of the price system in allocating resources. Since the resource in question is fixed in supply, taxing it will not reduce the amount supplied. Consequently, owners will not raise their prices as a result of the tax, and prices throughout the economic system will remain unchanged. In the technical jargon of economics, such a tax is labeled "neutral" because it has no effect on the way the economy allocates its resources. It should be noted that none of the other taxes summarized in Table 16.1 (Rows C, D, E, and F) can be called neutral. Each would affect relative prices in some way, thus reducing the efficiency with which the price system does its job of resource allocation.[35]

The second conclusion follows from the first. Since owners do not raise their prices in response to the tax, they are unable to shift its burden forward to advertisers or consumers. Instead, their net rent will fall by the amount of the tax. This conclusion is entered in Row G of Table 16.1. The fact that the burden of a spectrum tax or fee would remain with license holders can be regarded as equitable because licensees were originally given exclusive rights to use the electromagnetic spectrum free of charge, even though, properly speaking, the spectrum belongs to all of us. Thus, the spectrum tax or fee merely reclaims for the public its rightful property. It must be added, however, that this brief discussion makes the matter sound simpler than it is. In practice, a host of conceptual and administrative complications would have to be sorted out before a spectrum tax could be adopted.[36]

Objections to spectrum fees

We must also consider outright objections to the spectrum fee itself. First, there is a possible defect in the equity argument, although not necessarily a fatal one. The defect lies in the fact that the free gift of licenses often occurred years ago. Present holders may have purchased

---

[35] On the "excess burden" imposed by taxes that are nonneutral, see any text on public finance, e.g., Richard A. Musgrave and Peggy B. Musgrave, *Public Finance in Theory and Practice,* 5th ed. (New York: McGraw-Hill, 1989), chap. 16.

[36] See Levin, *Fact and Fantasy,* chap. 14, for an extended discussion.

them from the original licensees only the day before yesterday. In that case, they would have paid a price that fully reflects (i.e., capitalizes) the expected future economic rent to be garnered from the license. The original holders would have escaped with "the booty." It might well seem inequitable to attempt to recapture it from current licensees, who would certainly protest in loud, clear tones. This objection would lose force, however, to the extent that the tax, as seems likely, was designed to recover only a minor fraction of the present value of licenses.

Broadcast licensees can also be expected to object to a spectrum fee on several other grounds. First, they will point out that broadcast TV is already under great competitive pressure from the newer technologies of cable and the home videocassette player. To impose an additional tax on them at this point, they would argue, is rather like hitting a person who is already down. Second, they will say that the FCC already burdens them with the requirement that they provide a certain minimum of public service programming, which they now pay for out of income from their commercially profitable broadcasts. They can be expected to argue that if a special tax is levied on commercial license holders in order to fund public broadcasting, the commercial sector would no longer have an obligation also to provide public-interest broadcasts. Strictly speaking, this last argument is a nonsequitur. If the economic rent being earned by commercial licensees is sufficiently large, there is no reason why some of it should not be recaptured by a spectrum fee and an additional part via public-interest programming. But the first two arguments, one a matter of equity, the other of actual and prospective competitive pressure, cannot be dismissed lightly.

Since a spectrum fee would have to be charged to *all* private users, not just to commercial broadcasters, opposition to it would come from many powerful business interests. Under present circumstances there is almost no prospect that such a fee would be adopted. If it were proposed, the argument would probably be made that "we could have done it 20 years ago, but not today." And very likely, as has been the case with proposals for a special tax on urban site rent, the same argument was made 20 years ago. So far as increased federal support is concerned, public broadcasting appears to suffer under the rule propounded to Alice by the Red Queen: "Jam tomorrow and jam yesterday – but never jam *to-day*."

Conclusion

Although this chapter on the mass media is much less comprehensive than a full-length study of the subject would be, it may offer more detail than one would expect to find in a book on the high arts.

This treatment is warranted, we believe, by two factors that were discussed: the role of the electronic media in shaping the public's cultural tastes, and the media's as yet unrealized potential for financing and presenting the arts.

17

Conclusion: innovation, arts education, and the future of art and culture in the United States

It has been a theme of this book that the arts with which it deals – and especially the live performing arts – must compete for the consumer's attention with a popular culture that is powerfully propagated by the mass media of radio, television, the movies, and the culture of advertising and promotion in which they are enmeshed. In the face of that competition, the arts have not fared badly.

We demonstrated in Chapter 2 that there was a measurable arts boom in the 1970s and that growth continued into the 1980s, but with increasing signs of weakness in some sectors, especially after the middle of that decade. In Chapter 13 we showed that the early 1990s brought sharp reductions by some states and localities in the level of government support for the arts. These cutbacks, coupled with the apparent slowdown in the growth of arts audiences, put many arts institutions in financial jeopardy. Were these merely troubles of the moment, or was the long-run trend now running against the arts? Understandably, there was a great deal of anxiety in the art world about the answer to that question.

It is always risky simply to extrapolate into the future from recent experience. It may be worthwhile, nevertheless, to consider the situation of the arts sector by sector in order to reason out what we think the future may bring.

Competition, sector by sector
Competition between popular culture and the high arts can be analyzed at two different levels of aggregation. At the macro level, involvement with popular culture, especially through the medium of television, claims so much of most Americans' leisure time, that many have not developed the familiarity with the high arts that might lead them to become participants. For the national average household, time

350

spent watching television increased steadily from 40:02 hours per week in 1960 to 49:14 hours per week in 1980.[1] That is stiff competition, indeed. When asked in 1982 to indicate barriers to increased attendance at the arts, only 30 percent of metropolitan-area respondents checked "too expensive," but 43 percent selected "not enough time," making it by far the leading answer among 22 possibilities.[2] (Of course, TV watching is not the only reason time may be lacking. For example, the rise in women's labor force participation is also an important factor.) The weak position of the high arts in competition with popular culture is the result of very powerful cultural trends that will be difficult to alter, but a major effort to promote arts education might modify them. We examine that possibility later.

At the micro level, the ability of the individual live performing arts to compete with popular culture varies across art forms. We propose to look at two factors that help to explain that variation. The first is *technological* innovation. Here the question is, How powerful is the competition of nonlive modes of production with the particular live art form? The second factor is *artistic* innovation. In this case the question becomes, How effectively do artistic innovations in the particular art form build and hold an audience?

Symphony concerts

Among the four live performing arts we have considered – theater, symphony concerts, opera, and dance – symphony concerts have clearly suffered the most from the competition of nonlive performance. (See the decline in the number of concerts and in attendance shown in Table 2.2.) In Chapter 3 we pointed out that, in theory, the availability of art through the mass media could either stimulate demand and thereby *increase* the rate of live participation, or satisfy demand and therefore *reduce* the rate of live attendance. In the case of music, recordings and sound systems have been developed through wave after wave of technological innovation to the point that they compete very strongly, indeed, with live sound. It is difficult not to believe that this remarkable technology has, in fact, reduced the demand for attendance at symphony concerts. You can sit at home with your shoes off and your feet up, as the advertising copywriter might put it, and hear a concert of your own choice in greater comfort and at much less expense of time and money than would be required to hear it live. No doubt, live performance is

---

[1] *A Sourcebook of Arts Statistics: 1989* (Washington, D.C.: National Endowment for the Arts, 1990), table 8.54.
[2] Ibid., table 9.29.

better (unless the recorded artists are notably superior to those in the concert hall), but is it enough better to justify the expense and bother? Evidently, a great many music lovers think not.

At the same time, artistic innovation in the composition of "serious" music has not in recent decades been sufficiently attractive and exciting to build and hold audiences. In the eighteenth and nineteenth centuries, audiences listened to the music of their own time and were, for the most part, charmed by the innovations of contemporary composers. But in the twentieth century, at least in the realm of concert music, contemporary work has largely failed to capture the public's allegiance. If we assign Mahler, Sibelius, and Strauss to the nineteenth century, as might be justified on artistic grounds, Stravinsky is probably the only twentieth-century composer whom the public would rank as high as the major figures of earlier times. A few other twentieth-century composers, including Bartok, Shostakovitch, Prokofiev, and Copland, have entered the standard repertory. Nevertheless, symphony orchestra programs are largely made up of compositions from the distant past. Indeed, our concert halls have often been called musical museums. One study showed that, in 1965–70, works by just 14 composers of the eighteenth and nineteenth centuries accounted for 50 percent of the symphonic repertory in the United States.[3] The total share of those centuries' music in the repertory must have been considerably larger. Unfortunately, the musical museum has apparently lost its charm, especially for those who have yet to attain middle age.

The sociologist Richard Peterson points out that classical music has had difficulty building its audience in recent years primarily because of its failure to attract devotees among young adults. The baby-boom generation, born between 1945 and 1965, grew up listening to rock, soul, and folk music, forms that, he writes, "spoke directly to them about their felt needs and experiences." When this vast cohort matured in the 1970s and 1980s, they did not give up the music of their youth, as many earlier generations had done, to move on to classical music. The explanation, Peterson argues, is that the music they grew up with accustomed them to a "new aesthetic" (of political and social relevance, among other things) that "challenges the foundation of the classical Western art music aesthetic." He speculates that a new "world music," comprising elements of jazz, rock, folk, and traditional classical music, and duly incorporating the new aesthetic, could become the dominant "art

---

[3] Calculated from data presented in Philip Hart's massive study, *Orpheus in the New World: The Symphony Orchestra as an American Cultural Institution* (New York: Norton, 1973), table 17.B.

music" of the twenty-first century.[4] In that case, the "serious music" industry and the concert scene would be transformed in ways we can hardly imagine; audience growth might be one very interesting consequence.

Dance

For dance as a live art – including both ballet and modern dance – the situation is exactly opposite to that of symphony concerts. The competition from recorded performance is negligible, not because one cannot film dance performances to distribute via television or videotape, but because dance is a three-dimensional art, and serious dance fans do not find the two-dimensional versions more than minimally satisfying. Without a technological breakthrough into three-dimensional reproduction, recorded dance cannot compete with the live thing. Furthermore, dance benefits from artistic innovation to a far greater extent than does concert music. The field of modern dance is made up of a multitude of mostly rather small companies, each under the guidance of its own chief artist-choreographer – Martha Graham, until her death, and Paul Taylor are famous examples – a presiding genius who usually presents only her or his own works and can be relied on to devise at least one or two new offerings each season. Innovation keeps the level of audience excitement high. Dance fans *expect* to see something new each year, perhaps even at each performance, and return again and again *because* of innovation, not in spite of it.

The situation is not very different for ballet. Although old chestnuts (or, depending on one's point of view, classics) from the nineteenth century, such as *The Nutcracker, Sleeping Beauty,* and *Giselle,* are still with us, the reputation of twentieth-century choreography from masters like George Balanchine and Sir Frederick Ashton is at least as high. Despite practical difficulties in trying to combine the old and the new, a tradition of presenting both is well established in almost every company and helps to bring the audience back, year after year.[5] Moreover, old

---

[4] Richard A. Peterson, "Audience and Industry Origins of the Crisis in Classical Music Programming: Toward World Music," in David B. Pankratz and Valerie B. Morris, eds., *The Future of the Arts* (New York: Praeger, 1990), pp. 207–27. Also see the discussion of "a growing cultural eclecticism" in the United States in Lawrence W. Levine, *Highbrow/Lowbrow* (Cambridge, Mass.: Harvard University Press, 1988), pp. 243–56.

[5] On the difficulties encountered by American Ballet Theater, see Margaret Jane Wyszomirski and Judith H. Balfe, "Coalition Theory and American Ballet," in Balfe and Wyszomirski, eds., *Art, Ideology and Politics* (New York: Praeger, 1985), pp. 210–41.

works may actually be new for a given audience: because recorded dance is relatively unsatisfactory, few recordings exist, and for that reason works that actually are not brand-new, when mounted for the first time in a given city, can create the same excitement as a newly made work would do. With that built-in advantage, it will be a long time before the ballet world runs out of innovation.

Theater

The competitive situation of the theater is only slightly different from that of dance. It is perfectly possible to record a theatrical production on tape to be shown on television or on a VCR. (Indeed, how can we distinguish between a "play" shown on television and a "drama" written specifically for that medium?) In fact, however, very few plays made for the stage are transferred to television or videotape, and only a few are made into movies. If you want to see nonlive drama, you can go to the movies or turn on the television set, but what you see will not be the same sort of thing that is put on in live theater. Although the growth of movie audiences after the invention of talking pictures came partly at the expense of live theater, the theater survived and ultimately expanded through the new system of permanent regional theaters. (See the discussion in Chapter 2.) It seems clear that the competition of nonlive performance is not as strong for the theater as it is in the case of music.

Artistic innovation, which is taken for granted in the theater, helps to maintain audience interest. On Broadway, most of each season's output consists of new plays or new musicals. It is the excitement of seeing new works that brings the habitual theatergoer back, again and again. (Indeed, before the development of Off-Broadway, when the Broadway theater was the only game in town, some theater lovers complained that the classics were not staged often enough.) The nonprofit, regional theater that has proliferated since the end of World War II cannot subsist entirely on brand-new plays. Most regional theaters try to present a mixture of the classics and the contemporary, but relatively new works do make up a large proportion of their yearly programs.[6] And as in the case of dance, a work written 30 – or 130 – years ago may

---

[6] In its biannual reference guide to the nonprofit, professional theater entitled *Theatre Profiles,* Theatre Communications Group lists the productions staged by each member company over a two-year period. For a study of trends in the repertory of those companies, see Paul DiMaggio and Kristen Stenberg, "Conformity and Diversity in American Resident Theaters," in Balfe and Wyszomirski, eds., *Art, Ideology and Politics,* pp. 116–39.

still be new to the audience in a given town. So the theater certainly has the advantage of artistic novelty to build and hold its audience.

Opera

It is plausible to argue that the ability of opera to withstand the competition of nonlive performance falls somewhere between that of the theater and that of symphonic music. Operatic music can be recorded and played back at the listener's convenience just as successfully as symphonic music can. However, the "production values" that apparently make up a significant part of opera's appeal for many of its devotees, are entirely lost on recordings and not very successfully captured on film, TV, or tape. So the live performance of an opera is a good deal more exciting than the nonlive. Moreover, the introduction of "supertitles" is a technological innovation that further enhances the attraction of live performance for many attendees.

What about artistic innovation? The answer is best divided into two parts. On the one hand, opera programming (probably because of the higher cost per production) is even more conservative than the programming of symphony concerts; very little is heard that was written later than the beginning of the twentieth century.[7] The contrast with the eighteenth and nineteenth centuries could not be starker: in those days audiences listened to operas written in their own time. But because opera involves dramatic as well as musical elements (the production values just mentioned), other kinds of innovation are possible: one can mount a new production, set the action in a different period, or alter the dramatic interpretation. Old wine in new bottles, perhaps, yet the combination may be quite attractive. Still, one cannot be very optimistic about the long-run prospects for opera, unless new works can be developed that will excite new audiences.

Art museums

Interestingly, the ability of art museums to attract and hold audiences can be examined under the same headings that we have applied to the live performing arts. There is the same problem of com-

---

[7] See *Profiles,* the annual publication of Opera America, which lists the productions of each U.S. and Canadian company, tabulates the most frequently staged works, and indicates the U.S. and world premieres that member companies presented during the year. For analysis of the forces that make programming in the major U.S. opera houses so conservative, see Rosanne Martorella, "The Relationship Between Box Office and Repertoire," in Arnold W. Foster and Judith R. Blau, eds., *Art and Society: Readings in the Sociology of the Arts* (Albany: State University of New York Press, 1989), pp. 307–24.

petition between the object itself (the original work of art) and a reproduction of it, usually in full color, made possible by modern technology. Or to speak more realistically, the actual object on display in
a given museum competes for the art lover's attention not so much with
its own reproduction, as with the thousands of reproductions of great
art from all over the world that the interested viewer can find in handsomely printed books at home or in the public library. If the museum
is small, or its collection not very distinguished, that competition may
be very strong, indeed. Most of us would say that a reproduction is
never the same as the real thing: it is usually much smaller and is bound
to lack the texture or three-dimensionality of the original, to say no
more. Yet Edward C. Banfield, the political scientist and art collector
whose definition of art was quoted in Chapter 9, has argued that high-
quality reproductions deserve to be given a serious role in the art life
of the nation. He specifically points out the advantages they offer to the
millions of people who do not live close to a major museum.[8]

As for artistic innovation, whatever one may think of them, one
cannot accuse contemporary painters and sculptors of failing to provide
that. And innovation does appear to fire up the interest of collectors in
buying contemporary work. So far as museums are concerned, however,
innovation has a different meaning. With the exception of a few that
specialize in contemporary art, most museums are devoted to assembling
and preserving the great works of the past. New acquisitions in any one
year, unless from a major bequest, are rarely sufficiently exciting to
affect attendance. How then can museums overcome the public's feeling
of being already thoroughly familiar with its collection? The answer is
through special exhibitions and the occasional blockbuster. These are
the "innovations" that stir up public attention and increase attendance.
Moreover, they can be defended as artistically worthy events rather than
mere promotional stunts when, as is often the case, they have genuine
aesthetic power. (See discussion in Chapter 10.)

Our discussion of artistic and technological innovation has focused on
the latter as a source of *non*live art that eventually offers serious competition to the *live* forms. There is another side to the story, however.
Technological innovation can also stimulate, or become the means to,
artistic innovation within the traditional fields.[9] For example, electronic
synthesizers are now employed by some composers, dance can be extended into what are called "multimedia" performances, and in the

---

[8] Edward C. Banfield, *The Democratic Muse* (New York: Basic, for the Twentieth
Century Fund, 1984), chap. 6.
[9] We are indebted to David Pankratz for pointing this out.

visual arts, sculptors have taken up welding, or made designs out of neon lights, while painters develop ways of using new materials like acrylic paints. Without question, theatrical writing and production has been influenced by motion picture and television technique. A notable instance of technology stimulating design was cited in Chapter 8: the modern movement in architecture had its origin in the desire of architects to adapt their art to the industrial age by using machine-made materials and new methods of construction in place of designs based on the ancient handicrafts. It is not for the authors of this volume to judge the success or failure of these technologically inspired innovations. We must recognize, however, that technological change is often the root of artistic innovation. Thus, it provides an aesthetic opportunity, as well as a source of competition for traditional forms.

The question of audience age

There may well be a connection between artistic innovation, audience age, and potential audience development. Anyone who has attended the lively arts may have noticed that dance and theater audiences are younger, on average, than the audiences at symphony concerts or the opera. An NEA research report that reviewed the results of more than a hundred audience studies confirms the observation. The measure chosen as a summary indicator of the age of the audience for each art form was the median of the median ages reported in the relevant studies. The median age for ballet and modern dance was found to be 33 and for theater 34, as compared with 40 and 41 for symphony and opera audiences, respectively. The median for art museums was 31.[10] (Only science museum audiences, with a median age of 29, were younger.) However, it is probably the greater ease (because hours are flexible and no reservation is required) and the much lower cost of visiting an art museum as compared with attending the live performing arts, rather than anything attributable to innovation, that attracts a significantly younger audience to museums.

It was suggested in the previous section that theater and dance companies present the public with new and innovative works far more frequently than do symphony orchestras and opera companies. The age data just cited are consistent with that argument. The young are more open than their elders to exploring and appreciating new works of art. Hence, the more innovative art forms attract younger audiences. But

[10] Paul DiMaggio, Michael Useem, and Paula Brown, *Audience Studies of the Performing Arts and Museums: A Critical Review,* National Endowment for the Arts, Research Division Report no. 9, November 1978, table 2.

whether having a younger audience is, in itself, favorable for future audience development is unclear. It *is* favorable if the institution can hold onto its young members as they grow older, while continuing to attract young entrants to the audience, as well. But if people grow more resistant to innovation as they age, then the more innovative art forms will lose older audience members for the same reason they are gaining younger ones. Perhaps there is a lifetime taste cycle typified by the playgoer who was attracted by the innovative works of Tennessee Williams in the 1950s but does not go to the theater in the 1990s because "they don't make plays like that anymore." In that case, having a younger audience today need *not* augur well for the future.

It should be recalled, however, that artistic innovation may be favorable to audience growth in the live performing arts not only through its efficacy in attracting the young, but also because it can keep live performance one step ahead of the nonlive versions that compete with it for attention. But to speak at a deeper level, innovation is part of the creative process in art. We demean art itself if we imply that artistic innovation is no more than a promotional strategy.

Multiculturalism and the future of the high arts

Very little has been said in this book on the subject of multiculturalism, a topic that might be thought to lie outside the economics with which we have been dealing. Yet in speculating about the future of art and culture in the United States, one cannot ignore it. What the dominant U.S. majority usually think of as non-European ethnic minorities – African, Hispanic, and Asian-Americans – now make up a substantial proportion of the U.S. population and, sometime in the next century, may well constitute a majority. On the other hand, the modes of art discussed in this book developed largely out of European cultures. Prospects for their continued growth in the United States might be thought to depend in part on how well they can adapt in an increasingly multicultural society.

In the fields of theater and dance, perhaps there is no serious problem. Those forms have a natural audience in all ethnic groups. The works of black playwrights are frequently produced, black filmmakers are becoming successful, and black actors and actresses have begun to make their way in the theater and in motion pictures. In the field of modern dance, there have long been black companies, choreographers, and performers, and there is a well-established black ballet company, the Dance Theater of Harlem. Much the same thing can be said for Hispanic-American dance.

Symphony and opera present a different picture. Music, like dance, is a pancultural art, but *symphonic* music and opera, as they have developed in Europe and the United States, may not be, and their future U.S. growth will be limited to the extent that they do not appeal to non-European segments of the population. No doubt the managers and boards of directors of opera companies and symphony orchestras are aware of the problem and would like to build up the minority component of their audiences.[11] That is particularly the case since their institutions are necessarily based in large cities, where ethnic minorities are most highly concentrated. It would be pointless, however, to speculate on the likelihood of their success.

Arts education and educational reform

We have been pondering the future of art and culture in the United States. What role can or should arts education play in shaping that future? Those who speak for the arts have long argued that U.S. elementary and secondary schools unpardonably neglect arts education. Critics have therefore advocated a radical expansion and, in some cases, an equally radical restructuring of in-school arts education. Calls have been made, as well, for expansion of adult education in the arts.[12]

Advocates for arts education undoubtedly share a deep conviction that understanding art is as necessary to our well-being as is the command of those other great objects of our schooling: languages, mathematics, science, history, and social studies. But for those involved with the arts, there is also a more practical motive for advocacy: the hope that more and better arts education will help to protect and enlarge the domain of art in U.S. life. Before examining that possibility, however, we take a brief look at the recent history and current status of school-based arts education.

In the late 1980s, two very different reports suggested that despite more than a decade of advocacy, little or no progress had been made in either extending or improving arts education in U.S. schools.[13] Although there is now wide popular support for school reform, some

---

[11] See, for example, the speech by Dr. Thomas Wolf to the 1992 Conférence of the American Symphony Orchestra League in *The Financial Condition of Symphony Orchestras* (Washington, D.C.: American Symphony Orchestra League, June 1992), pt. 1, app. A.

[12] See Judith H. Balfe and Joni Cherbo Heine, eds., *Arts Education Beyond the Classroom* (New York: American Council for the Arts, 1988).

[13] See National Endowment for the Arts, *Toward Civilization: A Report on Arts Education*, May 1988, pp. 22–25, 33; and Charles Fowler, *Can We Rescue the Arts for America's Children?* (New York: American Council for the Arts, 1988), pp. 13–19.

versions favor change in a direction not likely to be helpful to the arts. The recent demand for educational reform has been motivated largely by a concern that schooling deficiencies are a threat to the nation's well-being because they undermine its economic competitiveness. The highly influential 1983 report of the National Commission on Excellence in Education sounded the alarm in its opening paragraph:

> Our Nation is at risk. Our once unchallenged preeminence in commerce, industry, science, and technological innovation is being overtaken by competitors throughout the world. . . . What was unimaginable a generation ago has begun to occur – others are matching and surpassing our educational attainments.[14]

Accordingly, the commission emphasized the need to ensure that every student be well prepared in subjects that could be seen to have a direct, practical impact: English, mathematics, science, social studies, and computer science. These were the "Five New Basics." The arts were paid lip service, but no more, as they were relegated to the category of things that schools "should also provide."[15] Charles Fowler has pointed out that many educational reformers continue to advocate a larger place for the arts in the curriculum.[16] But unless they can overcome the powerful "back-to-basics" advocates, it seems likely that the arts will continue to be treated as a frill, nice to have in the curriculum if time and money permit, but never accorded the priority that would make those resources available.

Unresolved issues

It must also be said that the cause of arts education has probably been held back by the persistence of important unresolved questions within the field itself. Among the "perennial" issues listed by Fowler (who must be ranked as a very *friendly* critic), one finds the following.[17] First, there is no agreement as to *which* arts should be taught. Visual art and music are the two that have been traditionally included in the curriculum. What ought to be added? The possibilities include dance, drama, design, film, creative writing, poetry, and assorted crafts. Can or should these be offered, as well?

Second, there is the question of who ought to do the teaching. Should

---

[14] National Commission on Excellence in Education, *A Nation at Risk* (Washington, D.C.: U.S. Department of Education, April 1983), p. 5.

[15] Ibid., pp. 24–27.

[16] Fowler, *Can We Rescue the Arts?* pp. 25–28.

[17] Ibid., chap. 3.

the arts be taught by the classroom teacher or by a specialist? If a specialist, what expertise is wanted – training in the art form or in pedagogy, or both?

Third, whose culture is to be taught? Ethnic minorities in the United States increasingly insist that their own cultural traditions not be neglected when art and culture are made part of the public school curriculum. Multiculturalism is now accepted by politicians, government agencies, and educators as a desirable policy, but it is not easily translated into curriculum and course content in a way that will satisfy all parties. How, for example, does one achieve a balance between teaching the dominant culture and giving weight to the cultures of ethnic minorities?

Fourth, should arts courses emphasize creating art or appreciating it? Historically in the United States, most precollege courses have tried to teach creativity. Students were given a hands-on opportunity to paint, to model in clay, or to perform music. Some critics argue that the relatively low status of the arts in the educational hierarchy is a direct result. The whole enterprise could be dismissed by an unsympathetic observer as just fooling around in the studio. An alternative curriculum, now endorsed by the Getty Center for Education in the Arts, has been called "discipline-based arts education" and would try to give students an understanding not only of art production, but also of the more "academic" approaches to art through art history, criticism, and aesthetics.[18] Its supporters argue that, among other things, the discipline-based approach would be more rigorous, and would therefore attract support for arts programs from those who are sympathetic with the demands of the excellence-in-education movement, now so influential in the United States.

Finally, there is the question of evaluation. Very little is known about the effectiveness of alternative approaches to arts education.[19] Should students who have taken such courses be regularly tested to see what they learned? Supporters of discipline-based arts education obviously

---

[18] See *Beyond Creating: The Place for Art in America's Schools* (Los Angeles: Getty Center for Education in the Arts, 1985), pp. 3–7, 12–21; and the discussion in David B. Pankratz, "Arts Education Research: Issues, Constraints and Opportunities," in David B. Pankratz and Kevin V. Mulcahy, eds., *The Challenge to Reform Arts Education: What Role Can Research Play?* (New York: American Council for the Arts, 1989), pp. 1–4.

[19] The only nationwide assessments of student achievement in the arts occurred in the 1970s. See *Toward Civilization*, pp. 25 and 93–94; and Laura H. Chapman, *Instant Art, Instant Culture* (New York: Teachers College Press, 1982), pp. 63–68 and 81–85.

think that they should, and that such tests would enhance the "academic respectability" of the field. Adherents of the older "creativity" approach argue that one cannot readily test for its results and that courses devised to have testable outcomes are likely to be incompatible with that approach.

Predictably, recognition of these questions gives rise within the field to a demand for more research. But as David B. Pankratz has pointed out, there are also important, unsettled issues within the field of arts education research itself. Their resolution is inhibited by many factors including the lack of reliable, ongoing funding.[20]

Can arts education stimulate the demand for art?

As we explained in Chapter 4, economists think of taste, or consumer preferences, as one of the principal determinants of demand. We also argued that the taste for art can be described as a "cultivated" taste, meaning that one has to be familiar with a given form of art to develop a taste for it, and the more familiar one becomes, the stronger the taste grows. The economist Tibor Scitovsky has been a notable advocate of investing in "consumption skills," so that we will better know how to enjoy the use of our increasing wealth and leisure. He points to a liberal arts education as one source of training in those skills.[21] Advocates for the arts might well hope that arts education, by helping to cultivate the appropriate tastes, will directly stimulate the public's demand for the "higher" forms of art and protect them against the powerful competition of "popular" culture.

We do not know much about the effectiveness of arts education. In the nature of the case, it is difficult to evaluate a student's understanding of art, but in any event, few evaluative studies of arts education have been carried out. Some insights have been gained, however, from research into factors associated with adult participation in the arts. Several such studies have found that early childhood socialization in the arts is positively correlated with adult attendance. Socialization comprises such experiences as childhood lessons, youthful participation or attendance, or growing up with parents who were interested in the arts.

In a project for the NEA, Alan R. Andreasen and Russell W. Belk

---

[20] See David B. Pankratz, "Arts Education Research: Issues, Constraints, and Opportunities," in Pankratz and Mulcahy, eds., *The Challenge to Reform Arts Education*, pp. 1–28.

[21] See "Arts in the Affluent Society: What's Wrong with the Arts in What's Wrong with Society," reprinted in Tibor Scitovsky, *Human Desire and Economic Satisfaction* (New York: New York University Press, 1986), pp. 37–45, esp. 39–42.

surveyed 1,491 respondents in four southern cities on a wide range of questions to uncover attitudes, experiences, and demographic factors associated with past or prospective future attendance at symphony and theater performance.[22] For both symphony and theater, they found that interest in the art form when growing up was an important predictor of likely attendance as an adult. However, they do not tell us why some children develop an early interest, while others do not. Further light on that question was provided by William G. Morrison and Edwin G. West's study of answers provided by 340 Canadian survey respondents.[23] The authors were particularly interested in finding out what sort of "childhood exposure" was associated with adult attendance. Accordingly, they used an equation to explain attendance that contained variables for education, income, and two forms of "exposure": whether or not the respondent (1) was "taken to the arts as a child," and (2) had "participated in the arts as a child." Participation was defined as taking part "in activities such as school drama, dancing or learning a musical instrument." Education and income, of course, proved to be highly significant explanatory factors. Participation as a child was also significant, but interestingly, the experience of being taken to the arts as a child was not found to have a statistically significant effect.

Findings from the survey of public participation in the arts

The fullest picture of educational factors associated with participation in the arts emerged from the 1982 Survey of Public Participation in the Arts that John Robinson and his associates carried out for the NEA. Using 2,678 individual responses from that survey, Richard J. Orend examined the association between participation as an adult and various forms of training or other experiences with the arts prior to age 24.[24] Like the authors previously cited, he avoids calling the relationship between early experiences and later participation a causal one, since the correlations revealed in his analysis do not in themselves prove causality.

The socialization experiences reported in the 1982 survey were classified into three groups:

[22] *Audience Development: An Examination of Selected Analysis and Prediction Techniques Applied to Symphony and Theatre Attendance in Four Southern Cities.* Research Division Report no. 14 (Washington, D.C.: 1981).

[23] William G. Morrison and Edwin G. West, "Child Exposure to the Performing Arts: The Implications for Adult Demand," *Journal of Cultural Economics,* 10, no. 1 (June 1986): 17–24.

[24] Richard J. Orend, *Socialization and Participation in the Arts* (Washington, D.C.: National Endowment for the Arts, 1989).

1. Lessons taken in music, visual arts, acting, ballet, creative writing, and crafts
2. Appreciation classes in music and in art
3. Home exposure and attendance at art events

Unfortunately, the original survey questionnaire did not distinguish between lessons and classes given privately, and those taken in school or at some other place, such as a community center. Thus, the results that Orend reports do not necessarily apply to *school-based* arts education. It might be a reasonable conjecture, however, that appreciation courses are very likely to have been taken in school or college, while lessons might occur either in or out of school, and especially in the case of music, are at least as likely to have been taken privately as publicly.

The category of home exposure and attendance captures what we usually mean by a home environment favorable to the arts. It includes the experiences of being taken to art museums or galleries, or to live performances of plays, classical music, or dance, or living in a home where adults listened to classical music or opera.

The most general conclusion emerging from the survey data is that any kind of socialization in the arts "is likely to be reflected in higher rates of adult participation in related activities."[25] The strongest relationships reported were between childhood music or art lessons and adult participation as players of music or makers of art. In this book we have not dealt with participation in that sense, so we will not be examining those results. Table 17.1 shows, however, that the relationship between socialization experiences and participation as a member of the audience at a live performance or as a visitor to a museum or gallery are also quite robust. For example, the first row under music appreciation classes shows that only 7.2 percent of individuals who never took such classes attended at least one classical music performance in the year prior to the survey. By contrast, 37.7 percent of those who took such classes in more than one age period attended a concert. Thus, the highest figure is a more than fivefold multiple of the lowest. Elsewhere in the table, the multiples range from threefold to almost sevenfold.

Scanning down the six panels of the table reveals that the connection between socialization experiences and participation in the related art form is always positive, is usually stronger if the experience occurred closer to adulthood, and is always stronger if it was continued over a longer period. Comparing the maximum participation rates across so-

---

[25] Ibid., p. 39.

Table 17.1. *Early experience and later participation in the arts*

Type of socialization experience	Percent who participated during previous year	
	Visited art museum or gallery	Attended classical music performance
Music lessons		
None		6
Before 12 years of age		14
12 to 17		11
18 to 24		16
All three time periods		41
Music appreciation classes		
None		7.2
Before 12 years of age		9.7
12 to 17		20.2
18 to 24		30.6
More than one period		37.7
Art appreciation classes		
None	15.8	
Before age 18	30.4	
18 to 24	53.2	
More than one period	71.1	
Heard classical music at home		
Never		6.6
Occasionally		21.0
Often		22.5
Visited museums or galleries during childhood		
Never	14.4	
Occasionally	35.0	
Often	45.9	
Attended classical music concerts during childhood		
Never		6.4
Occasionally		18.6
Often		30.5

Sources: First panel: Richard J. Orend, *Socialization and Participation in the Arts* (Washington, D.C.: National Endowment for the Arts, 1989), fig. 3. Remaining panels: Richard J. Orend, *Socialization in the Arts*, a report to the NEA under contract no. NEA-C86-179, April 22, 1987, app. tables 15–19.

cialization experiences, it appears that lessons and appreciation classes have stronger effects than do the three socialization measures associated with the home environment (the last three panels of the table). However, the higher rates of participation associated with art appreciation classes, versus those in music, do *not* indicate that the former are necessarily more effective. Rather, they reflect the fact that the public's overall participation rate is much higher for museums and galleries than for symphony concerts. (See Table 3.1, or compare the entries under "none" in Table 17.1).

The role of socioeconomic status

One question that might be asked about these results concerns the possible effect of socioeconomic differences among respondents. We showed in Chapter 3 that individual participation rates in the arts increase sharply with higher income, occupational status, and educational attainment. Suppose that those who reported taking lessons and appreciation classes or enjoyed other arts socialization experiences in childhood also rank higher on the socioeconomic scale than respondents who did none of those things. Perhaps it is their higher current status rather than their childhood socialization experiences that accounts for their higher current rate of participation. To put it very simply, the rich can afford concerts more easily than the poor. Orend did, indeed, look into the effect of socioeconomic differences on his findings. He reports that results obtained when social and demographic variables were employed together with socialization predictors "demonstrate the continued strength of the socialization predictors, even when controlling for other factors. Socialization predicts current behavior even when the significant effects of education have been removed."[26]

In another study undertaken for the NEA, Mark Schuster used data from the 1985 survey to analyze the effects of both demographic and socialization variables on attendance at art museums. He found that socialization experiences had significant power to explain attendance even when the effects of education, income, age, race, and gender were statistically controlled. Thus, Schuster's results for 1985 are consistent with Orend's, which had been based on the earlier 1982 survey.[27]

---

[26] The quotation is from Richard J. Orend, *Socialization in the Arts,* a report to the NEA under contract no. NEA-C86-179, dated April 22, 1987 (ERIC no. ED 283 768), p. 73. This is the report on which the published version already cited is based.

[27] J. Mark Davidson Schuster, *Perspectives on the American Audience for Art Museums,* a research monograph based on the 1985 Survey of Public Participation in the Arts, Cambridge, Mass., July 1987 (mimeo), pp. 69–77.

Certainly, one would feel more confident in reaching conclusions if *direct* studies of the effectiveness of arts education could be undertaken to see if they confirm findings derived indirectly from the Survey of Public Participation in the Arts. Since school-based arts education is the instrument at the command of public policymakers, we particularly need studies of that approach. (See note 19.) In the meantime, however, after all the caveats have been entered, we are entitled to believe that art education *does* stimulate public participation in the arts.[28]

Yet we are left in an unhappy position. It was shown in this chapter that the direction now being taken by educational reform in the United States may not be favorable to the cause of making more room in the public school curriculum for courses devoted to the arts. And given the budgetary constraints that appear to rule public policy decisions at all levels of government just now, it is unlikely that the money to fund new initiatives in arts education would be made available, even if educational opinion were unanimous in demanding it. The implications are unpleasant: If we fail to fund arts education in the public schools, we risk allowing the arts to remain essentially an activity of the well to do, serving to reinforce boundaries of class and status instead of helping to transcend them.[29]

Lincoln Kirstein, that venerable and eloquent prophet, has described art and culture as "the only memorable residue that marks and outlives [one's] epoch." In the same essay, he said of the arts that "in the United States, our prime complaint is not what we do, or how it is done, but how little we have for what we might do."[30]

[28] It is interesting to note that C.D. Throsby and G.A. Withers, while mentioning the caveats, also concluded their study of the arts with a plea for more attention to arts education. See *The Economics of the Performing Arts* (New York: St Martin's, 1979), pp. 301–2.

[29] We are indebted to Judy Balfe for this last point.

[30] Lincoln Kirstein, "The Performing Arts and Our Egregious Elite," in W. McNeil Lowry, ed., *The Performing Arts and American Society* (Englewood Cliffs, N.J.: Prentice-Hall, 1978), pp. 197 and 194.

INDEX